THE
WORKING
WRITER

Fifth Edition

THE
WORKING
WRITER

Toby Fulwiler

University of Vermont

PEARSON

Prentice
Hall

Upper Saddle River, New Jersey 07458

Library of Congress Cataloging-in-Publication Data

Fulwiler, Toby
   The working writer/Toby Fulwiler—5th ed.
      p. cm.
   ISBN 0–13–227896–0
   1. English language—Rhetoric.   2. Report writing.   I. Title.
   PE1408.F82 2007
   808'.042—dc22

                                    2006004342

Editorial Director: Leah Jewell
Senior Acquisitions Editor: Brad Potthoff
Editorial Assistant: Tara Culliney
Production Liaison: Joanne Hakim
Director of Marketing: Brandy Dawson
Senior Marketing Manager: Windley Morley
Marketing Assistant: Kara Pottle
Assistant Manufacturing Manager: Mary Ann Gloriande
Cover Art Director: Jayne Conte
Cover Design: Bruce Kenselaar
Director, Image Resource Center: Melinda Patelli
Manager, Rights and Permissions: Zina Arabia
Manager, Visual Research: Beth Brenzel
Manager, Cover Visual Research & Permissions: Karen Sanatar
Image Permission Coordinator: Richard Rodrigues
Photo Researcher: Francelle Carapetyan
Full-Service Project Management: Bruce Hobart/Pine Tree Composition, Inc.
Composition: Pine Tree Composition, Inc.
Printer/Binder: Hamilton Printing Company
Cover Printer: Phoenix Color Corp.

Credits and acknowledgments borrowed from other sources and reproduced, with permission, in this textbook
appear on page 375.

Pearson Education LTD., London
Pearson Education Singapore, Pte. Ltd
Pearson Education, Canada, Ltd
Pearson Education—Japan
Pearson Education Australia PTY, Limited

Pearson Education North Asia Ltd
Pearson Educación de Mexico, S.A. de C.V.
Pearson Education Malaysia, Pte. Ltd
Pearson Education, Upper Saddle River,
   New Jersey

10 9 8 7 6 5 4 3 2 1
ISBN 0-13-227896-0

FOR **LAURA**
My Partner in Life, Love, and Work

Contents

Part Four
Research Across the Disciplines   231

Preface

The basic approach of *The Working Writer* remains the same from edition to edition: to address the needs of working undergraduate writers in a friendly, writer-to-writer manner, and to present the process of writing as both rigorous and delightful. *The Working Writer* presents a process approach to the teaching of writing, examining the different but overlapping stages of writing we call planning, drafting, researching, revising, and editing. The book stresses the rhetorical issues of audience, purpose, and voice throughout, as well as the details of field, library, and Internet research—with particular attention to evaluating sources. All chapters emphasize that writing well is a matter of making wise choices rather than following formulas or rules.

NEW TO THIS EDITION

The fifth edition of *The Working Writer* includes up-to-date strategies for conducting Internet research and for documenting Internet sources correctly according to newly revised MLA and APA conventions. The research chapters guide writers through the many stages of the process, which is viewed here as yet another matter of making choices: from keeping a project log and learning how to find sources (including the proliferation of electronic choices), to conducting field research, to using and documenting sources. These chapters offer strategies for planning, organizing, and writing major research papers.

New to this edition: Chapter 3, "Reading Images Critically," emphasizing the many uses visual rhetoric plays in twenty-first century communication; Chapter 22, "Writing Across and Within the Disciplines," pointing out similarities and differences in academic writing as form, style, and conventions vary from discipline to discipline; and Chapter 28, "Writing on the Job," emphasizing writing tasks commonly encountered in the workplace, including newsletters, brochures, business letters, and memos. In addition, Chapter 25, "Conducting Online Research," is radically rewritten while Chapter 27, "Working with Sources," includes a comprehensive new discussion of "plagiarism" and ways to avoid it.

SUPPLEMENTARY MATERIAL FOR INSTRUCTORS AND STUDENTS

For more details on these supplements, available for college adoptions, please contact your Prentice Hall representative.

Instructor's Manual

Adopters of *The Working Writer* may visit the catalog page for this text at www.prenhall.com to request access to the Online Instructor's Manual. This valuable resource contains teaching tips for each chapter and facilitates teaching composition in a workshop style.

Prentice Hall Pocket Readers

Enhance this writing guide with a Prentice Hall Pocket Reader! Each reading in our pocket readers has been carefully selected for quality and teachability, making each the perfect companion for any writing course.

To order this text packaged with . . .

ARGUMENT: A Prentice Hall Pocket Reader, by Christy Desmet, Deborah Miller and Kathy Houff, specify package ISBN 0-13-222809-2

LITERATURE: A Prentice Hall Pocket Reader, by Mary Balkun, specify package ISBN 0-13-222808-4

PATTERNS: A Prentice Hall Pocket Reader, by Dorothy Minor, specify package ISBN 0-13-222807-6

THEMES: A Prentice Hall Pocket Reader, by Clyde Moneyhun, specify package ISBN 0-13-222806-9

PURPOSES: A Prentice Hall Pocket Reader, by Stephen Reid, specify package ISBN 0-13-222804-1

WRITING ACROSS THE CURRICULUM: A Prentice Hall Pocket Reader, by Stephen Brown and *PAPERS ACROSS THE CURRICULUM,* by Judith Ferster, specify package ISBN 0-13-175293-6.

The New American Webster Handy College Dictionary
To order this text with a dictionary, specify package ISBN 0-13-229086-3.
The New American Roget's College Thesaurus
To order this text with a thesaurus, specify package ISBN 0-13-229085-5.

ACKNOWLEDGMENTS

I'd like to acknowledge the continued stimulation and ideas I receive from students at the University of Vermont. I would also like to thank my thoughtful editor at Prentice Hall, Brad Potthoff and his oh-so-smart assistant Tara Culliney. Thanks also to Brandy Dawson, our shrewd and thoughtful Director of Marketing and, of course, my skillful copyeditor, Tally Morgan, and production manager, Bruce Hobart at Pine Tree Composition. Finally, thanks to the following reviewers who reviewed this book and offered suggestions for improving it: Kathleen De Grave, Pittsburgh State University; Edward Huffstetler, Bridgewater College; Gary D. Christenson, Elgin Community College; John Marlin, The College of St. Elizabeth; and Paula Eschliman, Richland College.

THE
WORKING
WRITER

PART ONE

THE ELEMENTS
OF COMPOSITION

CHAPTER ONE

Why Writing Matters

I am the absolute worst writer. I will never forget when I had to write my college essay. I thought it was good and then I brought it downstairs to have my parents read it and they tore it apart. By the time they were finished with it, I had to rewrite it five times. I was so mad, but the weird part was, the final copy was exactly what I wanted to say. They had to tear it out of me.

JESSICA

I like to write. Writers are nothing more than observant, perceptive, descriptive people.

PAT

You can count on one thing, attending college means writing papers—personal and critical essays in English, book reviews and reports in history, research reports in psychology and sociology, position papers in political science, lab reports in biology, and so on. Some of these assignments will be similar to those you've done in high school, some will be new, and all will be demanding.

When I asked a recent class of first-year college students to talk about themselves as writers, several began by describing their habits and attitudes: John, for example, said he wrote best "under pressure," while Kevin wanted to write at his own pace, on his own time, and "hated deadlines." Becky preferred writing when she "felt strongly or was angry about something," Doug when the assignment "asked for something personal," but Lisa enjoyed writing any paper so long as the "assignment was clear and fair."

Other students talked about where and when they wrote. Amy, for example, said she did most of her writing "listening to classical music and, if it is a nice day, under trees." Jennifer felt "most comfortable writing on her bed and being alone." Dan said he could write anywhere, so long as he had "a good computer," and José, "as long as it was after midnight." In fact, there proved to be as many different perspectives on being a writer as there were students in the class.

WHY IS WRITING HARD?

Even professional authors admit that writing is not easy. In writing this book, I encountered numerous problems, from organizing material to writing clearly to finding time and meeting publication deadlines. What, I wondered, did first-year college writers find difficult about writing? Were their problems similar to or different from mine? Here is what they told me:

Jennifer: "I don't like being told what to write about."

Amy: "I never could fulfill the page requirements. My essays were always several pages shorter than they were supposed to be."

Jill: "I always have trouble starting off a paper . . . and I hate it when I think I've written a great paper and I get a bad grade. It's so discouraging and I don't understand what I wrote wrong."

Omar: "Teachers are always nitpicking about little things, but I think writing is for communication, not nitpicking. I mean, if you can read it and it makes sense, what else do you want?"

Cara: "I hate revising. I had this teacher in high school who insisted we rewrite every paper over and over again, and that got really boring. Once I've said what I have to say, I don't have anything else to say."

Mike: "If I'm in a bad mood or don't have the right beginning, I find myself stumbling and not giving a hoot about whether it's right or not."

Kennon: "Putting thoughts down on paper as they are in your mind is the hardest thing to do. It is like in music—to make the guitar make the sound you imagine in your head, to make the words on the page paint the picture in your head."

I wasn't surprised by these answers, since I, too, remember wondering: What did teachers want? How long was enough? How do you get thoughts into words? Why all the nitpicking?

◆ WRITING 1

What do you find difficult about writing? Do you have a problem finding subjects to write about? Or do you have trouble getting motivated? Or does something about the act of writing itself cause problems for you? Explain in your own words by writing quickly for five minutes without stopping.

WHAT DO YOU LIKE ABOUT WRITING?

Though any writer will tell you writing isn't easy, most writers will also describe it as interesting and exciting. So I asked our first-year students what it was about writing that gave them pleasure.

> *Jolene:* "If I have a strong opinion on a topic, it makes it so much easier to write a paper."
>
> *Rebecca:* "On occasion I'm inspired by a wonderful idea. Once I get going, I actually enjoy writing a lot."
>
> *Casey:* "I enjoy most to write about my experiences, both good and bad. I like to write about things when I'm upset—it makes me feel better."
>
> *Darren:* "I guess my favorite kind of writing is letters. I get to be myself and just talk in them."

Like my students, I prefer to write about topics that inspire or interest me, and I find personal writing such as letters especially easy, interesting, and enjoyable.

◆ WRITING 2: EXPLORATION

What kind of writing do you most enjoy doing? What do you like about it: Communicating? Exploring a subject? Playing with words? Something else?

WHAT SURPRISES ARE IN STORE?

At the same time I was teaching these first-year students, I was also teaching an advanced writing seminar to seniors. Curious about their attitudes toward writing, I asked them: "What has surprised you the most about writing in college?"

> *Scott:* "Papers aren't as hellish as I was told they'd be. In fact, I've actually enjoyed writing a lot of them—especially after they were done."
>
> *Aaron:* "My style has changed a lot. Rather than becoming more complex, it's become simpler."
>
> *Kerry:* "The most surprising and frustrating thing has been the different reactions I've received from different professors."
>
> *Rob:* "I'm always being told that my writing is superficial. That I come up with good ideas but don't develop them."

John: "The tutor at our writing lab took out a pair of scissors and said I would have to work on organization. Then she cut up my paper and taped it back together a different way. This really made a difference, and I've been using this method ever since."

Chrissie: "Sharing papers with other students is very awkward for me. But it's extremely beneficial when I trust and like my group, when we all relax enough to talk honestly about one another's papers."

As you can see, most advanced students found ways to cope with and enjoy college writing. Several reported satisfying experiences sharing writing with each other. I'm sorry that some students, even in their last year, could not figure out what their instructors wanted—there *are* ways to do that.

◆ WRITING 3: EXPLORATION

Think about your experience with writing in the last school you attended. What surprised you—pleasantly or not—about the experience? What did you learn or not learn?

WHY IS WRITING SO IMPORTANT?

I also asked these advanced students why, in their last year, they had enrolled in an elective writing class: "What made the subject so important to you?"

Kim: "I have an easier time expressing myself through writing. When I'm speaking, my words get jumbled—writing gives me more time, and my voice doesn't quiver and I don't blush."

Rick: "Writing allows me to hold up a mirror to my life and see what clear or distorted images stare back at me."

Glenn: "The more I write, the better I become. In terms of finding a job after I graduate, strong writing skills will give me an edge over those who are just mediocre writers."

Amy: "I'm still searching for meaning. When I write I feel I can do anything, go anywhere, search and explore."

Angel: "I feel I have something to say."

Carmen: "It's simple, I love words."

I agree, easily, with virtually all of these reasons. At times writing is therapeutic, at other times it helps us clarify our ideas, and at still other times it helps us get and keep jobs.

◆ WRITING 4: EXPLORATION

Look over the various answers given by the college seniors and select one. Do you agree or disagree with the student? Explain.

WHAT THE SENIORS ADVISE

Since my advanced students had a lot to say about writing, I asked them to be consultants: "What is your advice to first-year college writers?" Here are their suggestions:

> *Aaron:* "Get something down! The hardest part of writing is starting. Forget the introduction, skip the outline, don't worry about a thesis—just blast your ideas down, see what you've got, then go back and work on them."

> *Christa:* "Plan ahead. It sounds dry, but planning makes writing easier than doing laundry."

> *Victor:* "Follow the requirements of the assignment to the T. Hand in a draft for the professor to mark up, then rewrite it."

> *Allyson:* "Don't think every piece you write has to be a masterpiece. And sometimes the worst assignment turns into the best writing. Don't worry about what the professor wants—write what you believe."

> *Carmen:* "Imagine and create, never be content with just retelling a story."

> *Rick:* "When someone trashes your writing, thank them and listen to their criticism. It stings, but it helps you become a better writer."

> *Jason:* "Say what you are going to say as clearly and as straightforwardly as possible. Don't try to pad it with big words and fancy phrasing."

> *Angel:* "Read for pleasure from time to time. The more you read, the better you write—it just happens."

> *Kim:* "When choosing topics, choose something that has a place in your heart."

These are good suggestions to any writers: Start fast, think ahead, plan to revise and edit, listen to critical advice, consider your audience, be clear, read a lot. I hope, however, that instructors respond to your writing in critically helpful ways and don't "trash" it or put it down. Whether or not you take some of the advice will depend on what you want from your writing: good grades? self-knowledge? personal satisfaction? clear communication? a response by your audience? When I shared these suggestions with first-year students, they nodded their heads, took some notes, and laughed—often with relief.

♦ WRITING 5: EXPLORATION

What else would you like to ask advanced college students about writing? Find a student and ask, report back.

WHAT ELSE DO YOU WANT TO KNOW?

I knew that my first-year students had already received twelve years' worth of "good advice" about learning to write, so I asked them one more question: "What do you want to learn about writing that you don't already know?" In parentheses, I've provided references to chapters of this text that answer these questions.

Emma: "Should I write to please the professor or to please myself?" *(See Chapter 4, "The Elements of Composition.")*

José: "I'm always being told to state my thesis clearly. What exactly is a thesis and why is it so important?" *(See Chapters 10, "Explaining Things"; 11, "Arguing For and Against"; and 12, "Interpreting Texts.")*

Jolene: "How do I develop a faster way of writing?" *(See Chapter 6, "Strategies for Starting.")*

Amy: "Is there a trick to making a paper longer without adding useless information?" *(See Chapters 15–16, which address revising.)*

Sam: "How do I learn to express my ideas so they make sense to common intelligent readers and not just to myself?" *(See Chapters 18–20, which address editing.)*

Scott: "How can I make my writing flow better and make smooth transitions from one idea to the next?" *(See Chapter 18, "Working Paragraphs.")*

Terry: "I want to learn to like to write. Then I won't put off assignments until the last minute." *(See Chapters 5–7 which demystify writing.*

Jennifer: "I have problems making sentences sound good. How can I learn to do that?" *(See Chapter 19, "Working Sentences.")*

John P.: "I would like to develop some sort of personal style so when I write people know it's me." *(See Chapter 4, "The Elements of Composition.")*

Jeff: "I want to become more confident about writing research papers. I don't want to have to worry about whether my documentation is correct or if I've plagiarized or not." *(See Part Four, "Conducting Research.")*

Woody: "Now that I'm in college, I would like to be challenged when I read and write, to think, and ask good questions, and find good answers." *(See Chapter 2, "College Reading.")*

Pat: "I don't want to learn nose-to-the-grindstone, straight-from-the-textbook rules. I want to learn to get my mind into motion and pencil in gear." *(See Chapter 6, "Strategies for Starting.")*

Heidi: "I would love to increase my vocabulary. If I had a wider range of vocabulary, I would be able to express my thoughts more clearly." *(I'm not sure this book addresses that directly, but the more reading and writing you do, the more words you'll learn!)*

Jess: "I'm always afraid that people will laugh at my writing. Can I ever learn to get over that and get more confident about my writing?" *(See Chapter 7, "Sharing and Responding.")*

I can't, of course, guarantee that if you read *The Working Writer* your writing will get easier, faster, longer, clearer, or more correct. Or, for that matter, that your style will become more personal and varied, or that you will become a more confident and comfortable writer—no handbook can do that for you. Becoming a better writer depends on your own interest and hard work. It will also depend on your college experience, the classes you take, and the teachers with whom you study. However, whether in class or on your own, if you read this text carefully and practice its suggestions, you should find possible answers to all these questions and many more.

I admit that there was at least one student's concern for which I really had no good response. Jessica wrote, "My biggest fear is that I'll end up one semester with four or five courses that all involve writing and I'll die." Or maybe I do have a response: If you become comfortable and competent as a writer, you'll be able to handle all the writing assignments thrown your way. Even if you can't, Jessica, you won't die. It's just college.

◆ SUGGESTIONS FOR WRITING AND RESEARCH

Individual

1. Interview a classmate about his or her writing experiences, habits, beliefs, and practices. Include questions such as those asked in this chapter as well as others you think may be important. Write a brief essay profiling your classmate as a writer. Share your profile with a classmate.
2. Over a two-week period, keep a record of every use you make of written language. Record your entries daily in a journal or class notebook. At the end of two weeks, enumerate all the specific uses as well as how often you did each. What activities dominate your list? Write an essay based on this personal research in which you argue for or against the centrality of writing in everyday life.

Collaborative

As a class or in small groups, design a questionnaire to elicit information about people's writing habits and attitudes. Distribute the questionnaire to both students and instructors in introductory and advanced writing classes. Compile the results. Compare and contrast the ideas of students at different levels and disciplines and write a report to share with the class. Consider writing a feature article for your student newspaper or faculty newsletter reporting what you found.

CHAPTER TWO

Reading Texts Critically

Now that I'm in college, I would like to be challenged when I read and write, to think, and ask good questions, and find good answers.

WOODY

To read and write well in college means to read and write critically. In fact, a major goal of most college curricula is to train students to be critical readers, writers, and thinkers so they can carry those habits of mind into the larger culture beyond college. What, you may ask, does it mean to be critical? How does being a critical reader, writer, and thinker differ from being a plain, ordinary, everyday reader, writer, and thinker?

Being critical in writing means making distinctions, developing interpretations, and drawing conclusions that stand up to thoughtful scrutiny by others. Being critical in reading means knowing how to analyze these distinctions, interpretations, and conclusions. Becoming a critical thinker, then, means learning to exercise reason and judgment whenever you encounter the language of others or generate language yourself.

Most of *The Working Writer* explores strategies for helping you become an accomplished critical writer. This chapter, however, explores strategies for helping you become a more accomplished critical reader and emphasizes as well the close relationship between critical reading and critical writing.

◆ WRITING 1

Describe yourself as a reader, answering some of these questions along the way: How often do you read on your own? What kinds of reading do you do when the choice of reading material is up to you? Where and when do you most commonly do your reading? What is the last book you read on your own? Who is your favorite author? Why?

UNDERSTANDING WRITTEN TEXTS

To understand a text, you need some context for the new ideas you encounter, some knowledge of the text's terms and ideas, and knowledge of the rules that govern the kind of writing you're reading. It would be difficult to read Mark Twain's novel *The Adventures of Huckleberry Finn* with no knowledge of American geography, the Mississippi River, or the institution of slavery. It would also be difficult to read a biology textbook chapter about photosynthesis but know nothing of plants, cell structure, or chemical reactions. The more you know, the more you learn; the more you learn, the more careful and critical your reading, writing, and thinking will be.

Many college instructors will ask you to read about subjects that are new to you; you won't be able to spend much time reading about what you already know. To graduate, you've got to keep studying new subjects that require, first, that you understand what you read and, second, that you can critically assess and write about this new understanding. As you move through the college curriculum, you will find yourself an expert reader in some disciplines, a novice reader in others, and somewhere in between in the rest—often during the same semester.

If getting a college degree requires that you read one unfamiliar text after another, how can you ever learn to read successfully? How do you create a context, learn a background, and find the rules to help you read unfamiliar texts in unfamiliar subject areas? What strategies or shortcuts can speed up the learning process? Let's consider some strategies for doing this.

As an experiment, read the following short opening paragraph from an eight-paragraph *New York Times* story titled "Nagasaki, August 9, 1945." When you have finished, pause for a few moments, and think about (1) what you learned from it, (2) how you learned what you learned, and (3) what the rest of the story will be about.

> In August 1945, I was a freshman at Nagasaki Medical College. The ninth of August was a clear, hot, beautiful summer day. I left my lodging house, which was one-and-one-half miles from the hypocenter, at eight in the morning, as usual, to catch a tram car. When I got to the tram stop, I found that it had been derailed in an accident. I decided to return home. I was lucky. I never made it to school that day.
>
> MICHAITO ICHIMARU

How did you do? It is possible that your reasoning went something like mine, which I reconstruct here. Note, however, that although the following sequence presents ideas one after the other, that's not how it seemed to happen when I read the passage for the first time. Instead, meaning seemed to occur in flashes, simultaneously and unmeasurably. Even as I read a sentence for the first time, I found myself reading backward as much as forward to check my understanding. Here are the experiences that seemed to be happening.

1. I read the first sentence carefully, noticing the year 1945 and the name of the medical college, "Nagasaki." My prior historical knowledge kicked in as I *identified* Nagasaki, Japan, as one of the cities on which the United States dropped an atomic bomb at the end of World War II—though I did not remember the precise date.

2. I noticed the city and the date, August 9, and wondered if that was when the bomb was dropped. I *asked* (silently), "Is this a story about the bomb?"

3. Still looking at the first sentence, a reference to the writer's younger self ("I was a freshman"), I guessed that the author was present at the dropping of this bomb. I *predicted* that this would be a survivor's account of the bombing of Nagasaki.

4. The word *hypocenter* in the third sentence made me pause again; the language seemed oddly out of place next to the "beautiful summer day" described in the second sentence. I *questioned* what the word meant. Though I didn't know exactly, it sounded like a technical term for the place where the bomb went off. Evidence was mounting that the narrator may have lived a mile and a half from the exact place where the atomic bomb detonated.

5. In the next-to-last sentence of the paragraph, the author says that he was "lucky" to miss the tram. Why, unless something unfortunate happened to the tram, would he consider missing it "lucky"? I *predicted* that had the author gone to school "as usual" he would have been closer to the hypocenter, which I now surmise was at Nagasaki Medical College.

6. I then *tested* my several predictions by reading the rest of the story, which you, of course, could not do. My predictions proved correct: Michaito Ichimaru's story is a firsthand account of witnessing and surviving the dropping of the bomb, which in fact killed all who attended the medical college, a quarter of a mile from the hypocenter.

7. Finally, out of curiosity, I looked up Nagasaki in the *Columbia Desk Encyclopedia* and *confirmed* that 75,000 people were killed by this second dropping of an atomic bomb, on August 9, 1945; the first bomb had been exploded just three days earlier, on August 6, at Hiroshima.

You'll notice that in my seven-step example some parts of the pattern of identifying/ questioning/predicting/testing/confirming occur more than once, perhaps simultaneously, and not in a predictable order. This is a slow-motion description—not a prescription or formula—of the activities that occur in split seconds in the minds of active, curious readers. No two readers would—or could—read this passage in exactly the same way, because no two readers are ever situated identically in time and space, with identical training, knowledge, and experience to enable them to do so. However, my reading process may be similar enough to yours that the comparison will hold up: reading is a messy, trial-and-error process that depends as much on prior knowledge as on new information to lead to understanding.

Whether you read new stories or watch unfamiliar events, you commonly make meaning by following a procedure something like mine, trying to identify what you see, question what you don't understand, make and test predictions about meaning, and consult authorities for confirmation or information. Once you know how to read successfully for basic comprehension, you are ready to read critically. Learn the following reading strategies to improve your reading comprehension:

1. *Identify.*   Read first for what you recognize, know, and understand. Identify what you are reading about. Read carefully—slowly at first—and let meaning take hold where it can.
2. *Question.*   Pause, and look hard at words and phrases you don't know or understand. See if they make sense when you reread them, compare them to what you do know, or place them in a context you understand.
3. *Predict.*   Make predictions about what you will learn next: How will the essay, story, or report advance? What will happen? What theme or thesis will emerge? What might be the point of it all?
4. *Test.*   Follow up on your predictions by reading further to see if they are correct or nearly correct. If they are, read on with more confidence; if they are not, read further, make more predictions, and test them. Trial and error are good teachers.
5. *Confirm.*   Check your reading of the text with others who have also read it and see if your interpretations are similar or different. If you have questions, ask them. Share answers.

♦ WRITING 2

Select a book you have been assigned to read for one of your courses and find a chapter that has not yet been covered in class. Read the first page of the chapter and then stop. Write out any predictions you have about where the rest of the chapter is going. (Ask yourself, for example, "What is its main theme or argument? How will it conclude?") Finish reading the chapter and check its conclusion against your predictions. If your predictions were close, you are reading for understanding.

READING CRITICALLY

How people read depends on what they're reading; people read different materials in different ways. When they read popular stories and magazine articles for pleasure, they usually read not to be critical but to understand and enjoy. In fact, while pleasure readers commonly go through a process similar to the one described in the last section—identifying, questioning, predicting, and testing—they usually do so rapidly and unconsciously. Since such reading is seldom assigned in college courses, whether they go further to confirm and expand their knowledge depends solely on their time, energy, and interest.

When people read college textbooks, professional articles, technical reports, and serious literature, they read more slowly and carefully to assess the worth or validity of an author's ideas, information, argument, or evidence. The rest of this chapter describes the strategies that lead readers from *understanding* texts to *interpreting* and *evaluating* them *critically,* paying special attention to the strategies of *previewing, responding,* and *reviewing.*

Although critical reading is described here as a three-stage process, it should be clear that these activities seldom happen in a simple one-two-three order. For example, one of the best ways to preview a text is to respond to it briefly as you read it the first time; as you respond, you may find yourself previewing and reviewing, and so on. But if you're not engaging in all three activities at some time, you're not getting as much from your reading as you could.

Previewing Texts

To be a critical reader, you need to be more than a good predictor. In addition to following the thread of an argument, you need to evaluate its logic, weigh its evidence, and accept or reject its conclusion. You read actively, searching for information and ideas that you both understand and can make use of—to further your own thinking, speaking, or writing. To move from understanding to critical awareness, you plan to read a text more than once and more than one way, which is why critical readers *preview* texts before reading them from start to finish.

To understand a text critically, plan to preview before you read, and make previewing the first of several steps needed to appraise the value of the text fully.

First Questions

Ask questions of a text (a book, an article, a Web page) from the moment you look at it. Ask first questions to find general, quickly gleaned information, such as that provided by skimming the title, subtitle, subheads, table of contents, or preface.

- What does the title suggest?
- What is the subject?
- What does the table of contents promise?
- What is emphasized in chapter titles or subheads?
- Who is the author? (Have I heard of him or her?)
- What makes the author an expert or authority?
- How current is the information in this text?
- How might this information help me?

You may not ask these first questions methodically, in this order, or write down all your answers, but if you're a critical reader you'll ask these types of questions before you commit too much time to reading the whole text. If your answers to these first questions suggest that the text is worth further study, you can continue with the preview process.

Second Questions

Once you've determined that a book or article warrants further critical attention, it's very helpful to skim selected parts of it to see what they promise. Skim reading leads to still more questions, the answers to which you will want to capture on note cards or in a journal.

- Read the prefatory material: What can I learn from the book jacket, foreword, or preface?
- Read the introduction, abstract, or first page: What theme or thesis is promised?
- Read a sample chapter or subsection: Is the material about what I expect?

- Scan the index or chapter notes: What sources have informed this text? What names do I recognize?
- Note unfamiliar words or ideas: Do I have the background to understand this text?
- Consider: Will I have to consult other sources to obtain a critical understanding of this one?

Previewing *Iron John*

One of my students gave me a book called *Iron John*. To find out more about the book, I previewed it by asking first questions and second questions, the answers to which I've reproduced here for illustration.

ANSWERS TO FIRST QUESTIONS

- The title *Iron John* is intriguing and suggests something strong and unbreakable.
- I already know and admire the author, Robert Bly, for his insightful poetry, but I've never read his prose.
- The table of contents raises interesting questions but doesn't tell me much about where the book is going:
  1. The Pillow and the Key
  2. When One Hair Turns Gold
  3. The Road of Ashes, Descent, and Grief
  4. The Hunger for the King in Time with No Father
  5. The Meeting with the God-Woman in the Garden

ANSWERS TO SECOND QUESTIONS

- The jacket says, "*Iron John* is Robert Bly's long-awaited book on male initiation and the role of the mentor, the result of ten years' work with men to discover truths about masculinity that get beyond the stereotypes of our popular culture."
- There is no introduction or index, but the chapter notes in the back of the book (260–267) contain the names of people Bly used as sources in writing the book. I recognize novelist D. H. Lawrence, anthropologist Mircea Eliade, poet William Blake, historian/critic Joseph Campbell, and a whole bunch of psychologists, but many others I've never heard of. An intriguing mix.

This preview, which took maybe ten minutes, confirmed that *Iron John* is a book about men and male myths in modern American culture by a well-known poet writing a serious prose book in friendly style. Apparently, Bly not only will examine current male mythology but will make some recommendations about which myths are destructive and which are constructive.

Previewing is only a first step in a process that now slows down and becomes more time-consuming and critical. As readers begin to preview a text seriously, they often make notes in the text's margin or in a journal or notebook to mark places for later review. In other words, before the preview stage of critical reading has ended, the *responding* stage has probably begun.

♦ WRITING 3

Select any unfamiliar book about which you are curious and preview it, using the strategy of first and second questions discussed in this section. Stop after ten minutes, and write what you know about the text.

Responding to Texts

Once you understand, through a quick critical preview, what a text promises, you need to examine it more slowly, evaluating its assumptions, arguments, evidence, logic, and conclusion. The best way to do this is to *respond,* or "talk back," to the text in writing.

Talking back can take many forms, from making margin notes to composing extensive notebook entries. Respond to passages that cause you to pause for a moment to reflect, to question, and to read again, or to say "Ah!" or "Aha!" At points of high interest, take notes.

If the text is informational, try to capture the statements that pull together or summarize ideas or are repeated. If the text is argumentative (and many of the texts you'll be reading in college will be), examine the claims the text makes about the topic and each piece of supporting evidence. If the text is literary (a novel, play, or poem), pay extra attention to language features such as images, metaphors, and crisp dialogue. In any text, notice words the author puts in **boldface** or *italic* type: They have been marked for special attention.

Note what's happening to you as you read. Ask about the effect of the text on you: How am I reacting? What am I thinking and feeling? What do I like? What do I distrust? Do I know why yet? But don't worry too much now about answering all your questions. (That's where reviewing comes in.)

Responding can take many forms, from **annotating** in the text margins to extensive **freewriting** in a **journal** or notebook, to **cross referencing** ideas, but it should involve writing. The more you write about something, the more you will understand it.

Annotating

To read any text critically, begin with pen or pencil in hand. If you own the book, mark places to be examined further, but be aware that mere underlining, checking, or highlighting does not yet involve you in a conversation with the text. If you don't own the text, write on sticky paper pasted in the margins or keep a running conversation in a notebook. To annotate look for:

- Points of agreement and disagreement with claims or assertions
- Convincing examples that support claims or assertions
- Implications or consequences of believing the author
- Personal associations with text material
- Connections to other texts you've read
- Recurring images, symbols, phrases, ideas

Freewriting

A second powerful way of responding to texts is to write freely about your reactions to the reading. All you do is write fast about an idea and see where your thoughts go, a process that often helps you clarify your own thoughts about the ideas in the text. When you freewrite, write to yourself in your own natural style, not worrying about sentence structure, spelling, or punctuation. Nobody else need ever read this; its purpose is to help you tie together ideas from your reading with the thoughts and experiences in your own mind. In thinking about a main theme, the value of wildness in *Iron John,* I wrote the following:

> 9/30 Bly praises the "Wild Man" in us, clearly separating "wildness" from barbarism and savagery—hurting others. Also suggests that modern men are wounded in some way—literally?—but only those who examine their wounds gain higher knowledge. In an interview I once heard him talk about warriors—men who seek action (mountain climbing? skiing? Habitat for Humanity?) to feel whole and fulfilled. So men (why not women too?) test themselves—not necessarily against other men—against nature or even themselves. Harvey says sailing is his warrior activity. Is backpacking mine?

My freewriting reacted to one idea in the text (*wildness*), moving to another (*being wounded*), digressing by remembering a TV interview, raising a question (*why not women too?*), and concluding by raising a question about himself (*Is backpacking mine?*). Freewriting generates questions at random, catches them, and leaves the answering for later.

Cross-Referencing

To move beyond annotating (commenting on single passages) and freewriting, try cross-referencing (finding relationships among passages) in which you use a coding system to show that one annotation, passage, or idea is related to another. Some students write comments on different features of the text in different colors, such as reserving green for nature images, blue for key terms, red for interesting episodes, and so on. Other students write their notes first and then go back and number them, perhaps 1 for plot, 2 for key terms, and so on.

◆ WRITING 4

Keep a reading journal for one article, chapter, or book that you are assigned to read this semester. Be sure to write something in the journal after every reading session. In addition, annotate and cross-reference the text as you go along to see what patterns you can discover. Finally, make a paragraph outline of the text. Write about the result of these response methods in your journal. Did they help? Which ones worked best?

Reviewing Texts

To *review* you need both to reread and to "re-see" a text, reconsidering its meaning and the ideas you have about it. You need to be sure that you grasp the important points within the text, but you also need to move beyond that to a critical understanding of the text as a whole. In responding, you started a conversation with the text so you could put yourself into its framework and context; in reviewing, you should consider how the book can fit into your own framework and context. Review any text you have previewed and responded to as well as anything you've written in response: journal entries, freewriting, annotations, outlines. Keep responding, talking back to the text even as you review, writing new journal entries to capture your latest insights.

Reviewing can take different forms depending on how you intend to use the text—whether or not you are using it to write a paper, for example. In general, when reviewing a text you have to understand what it means, to interpret its meaning, to evaluate its soundness or significance, and to determine how to use it in your own writing.

Reviewing to Understand

Reviewing to understand means identifying and explaining in your own words the text's main ideas. This task can be simplified if you have outlined the text while responding or have cross-referenced your annotations to highlight relationships among ideas. In reviewing to understand, you can reread portions of articles that you previewed, considering especially abstracts, if there are any; first and last paragraphs; and sections titled "Summary," "Observations," or "Conclusions." In a book, you can reconsider the table of contents, the introductory and concluding chapters, and central chapters that you recognize as important to the author's argument or theme.

Reviewing to Interpret

Reviewing to interpret means moving beyond an appreciation of what the text says and building your own theory of what the text *means*. An interpretation is an assertion of what you as a reader think the text is about.

In reviewing to interpret, look over any of your journal entries that articulate overall reactions to the text's main ideas. What did you see in the text? Do you still have the same interpretation? Also reread key passages in the text, making sure that your interpretation is reasonable and is based on the text and is not a product of your imagination.

If you plan to write a critical paper about a text, it's a good idea to confirm your interpretation by consulting what others have said about that text. The interpretations of other critics will help put your own view in perspective as well as raise questions that may not have occurred to you. Try to read more than one perspective on a text. It is better to consult such sources in this reviewing stage after you have established some views of your own, so that you do not simply adopt the view of the first expert you read.

Reviewing to Evaluate

Reviewing to evaluate means deciding whether you think the text accomplishes its own goals. In other words, is the text any good? Different types of texts should be judged on different grounds.

ARGUMENTS.   Many texts you read in college make arguments about ideas, advancing certain *claims* and supporting those claims with *evidence*. A claim is a statement that something is true or should be done. Every claim in an argument should be supported by reliable and sufficient evidence.

At the responding stage, you probably started to identify and comment on the text's claims and evidence. In reviewing, you can ask the following questions to examine and evaluate each part of the argument to see whether it is sound:

- Is the claim based on facts? A *fact* is something that can be verified and that most readers will accept without question. (Fact: The title of the book is *Iron John;* the author is Robert Bly; it was published in 1990; the myth of Iron John is found in several ancient folktales that have been written down and can be found in libraries; and so on.)
- Is the claim based on a credible inference? An *inference* is a conclusion drawn from an accumulation of facts. (Bly's inferences in *Iron John* about the warrior in modern man are based on his extensive study of ancient mythology. His inferences have a basis in the facts, but other readers might draw other inferences.)
- Is the claim based on opinion? An *opinion* reflects an author's personal beliefs and may be based on faith, emotion, or myth. Claims based on opinion are considered weak in academic writing. (Bly's "dark side of men" is metaphorical and not factual. Some readers would consider it a fair inference based on the savage history of humankind; others would dismiss it as Bly's opinion, based on emotion rather than on facts and careful reasoning.)

All three types of evidence—facts, inference, and opinions—have their place in argumentative writing, but the strongest arguments are those that are based on accurate facts and reasonably drawn inferences. Look out for opinions that are masquerading as facts and for inferences that are based on insufficient facts.

INFORMATIONAL TEXTS.   In reviewing informational texts, like reviewing argumentative texts, you need to make sure that the facts are true, that inferences rely on facts, and that opinions presented as evidence are based on expertise, not emotion. Informational texts don't make arguments, but they do draw conclusions from the facts they present. You must decide whether there are enough reliable facts to justify these conclusions. Consider also whether you think the author is reliable and reasonable: Is the tone objective? Has all the relevant information been presented? Is this person an expert?

LITERARY TEXTS.   Short stories, poems, and plays don't generally make arguments, but they do strive to be believable, to be enjoyable, and to be effective in conveying their themes. One way to evaluate literature is to reread journal entries in which you responded to the author's images, themes, or overall approach. Then look through the text again, guided by any annotations you've made, and ask whether you think the author's choices were good ones. Look in particular for repeated terms, ideas, or images that will help you see the pattern of the text as a whole. Evaluating literature is often very personal, relying on individual associations and responses, but the strongest critical evaluations are based on textual evidence.

Reviewing to Write

Reviewing a text to use in writing your own paper means locating specific passages to quote, paraphrase, or summarize in support of your own assertions about the text. When you quote, you use the exact language of the text; when you paraphrase, you restate the text in your own words; when you summarize, you reduce the text to a brief statement in your own words. When you identify a note card that contains a passage to quote, paraphrase, or summarize, make sure that you have recorded the page on which the passage occurs in the text so you can find it again and so you can prepare correct documentation.

READING AND WRITING

Reading and writing, like producing and consuming, are two sides of the same coin. When you study one, you inevitably learn more about the other at the same time. The more you attend to the language of published writers, the more you will learn about your own language. The more you attend to your own written language, the more you will learn about the texts you read.

In fact, many of the reading strategies you use to understand and evaluate published texts work equally well when reading your own writing. You can preview, respond to, and review your own or your classmates' writing to gain a critical understanding of your writing and to discover strategies for effective revision.

◆ SUGGESTIONS FOR WRITING AND RESEARCH

Individual
Select a short text. First, read it quickly for understanding. Second, read it critically as described in this chapter. Finally, write a short (two-page) critical review of the text, recommending or not recommending it to other readers. (For more detailed information about writing critically about texts, see Chapter 12, "Interpreting Texts.")

Collaborative
As a class or in small groups, agree on a short text to read and write about according to the preceding directions. Share your reviews in small groups, paying particular attention to the claims and evidence each writer uses in his or her review. Rewrite the reviews based on the responses in the groups. (For more information about responding to others' texts, see Chapter 7, "Sharing and Responding.")

CHAPTER THREE

Reading Images Critically

I especially enjoy reading magazine articles illustrated by photographs, drawings, and maps. Is it OK to add illustrations to college papers as well? And if it is, what are the rules for doing that?

KEVIN

Of all five senses, the one most people trust first is their eyes. They believe what they see firsthand, and they believe the photographs, films, videos of others. Well-known examples of the power of visual images to shape public opinion and national policy include the photographs of Depression-era poverty, Vietnam war casualties, and Iraqi prisoner-of-war abuse; films of the Nazi Holocaust victims and JFK assassination; and videos of the Rodney King beatings, space shuttle disasters, and the 9/11 terrorist attacks.

Many Americans spend a substantial portion of their time watching visual images via television and computers as well as photographs, illustrations, charts, and advertisements in every possible media, including books, newspapers, magazines, pamphlets, posters, and billboards. Even the college curriculum is as much visual as verbal, including Internet research, computer graphics, and Power Point presentations. It is as important to read both visual and verbal texts with a critical eye in order to understand, discuss, and assess their worth.

This chapter examines those elements of visual literacy most likely to complement the verbal literacy emphasized in most first-year writing classes. We believe a critical understanding of visual texts helps students as both a consumers of the frequent images they encounter in reading and viewing as well as producers who now so easily incorporate images into their own writing as well (see Chapters 17 and 18, as well as sample student essays in Chapters 9 and 10).

To illustrate the critical reading of visual images, the first part of this chapter draws on the collection of 77,000 black and white photographs compiled by the Farm Security Administration (FSA) under the Department of Agriculture from 1937 to 1945, now housed in the Library of Congress. As part of the New Deal programs to put Americans back to work during the Great Depression, the FSA commissioned out-of-work artists, historians, writers, folklorists, musicologists, and photographers to capture in text, tape, and celluloid as many elements as possible of American culture. The latter half of the chapter draws on contemporary visual images culled primarily from the colorful world of commercial advertising.

THE ELEMENTS OF VISUAL COMPOSITION

To compose either an effective essay or a strong picture, the "composer" works with a number of elements which turn out to be remarkably similar from one medium to the other. Both pictures and stories contain **information** presented by a composer who has a particular **point of view** and **arranges** them in two-dimensional space. Likewise, stories are ordered sequentially so that they illustrate certain **themes** or meanings, some emphasized more than others. In addition, images can serve focused rhetorical purposes in a manner similar to verbal texts, such as **describing, narrating, explaining,** and **persuading.**

Information

Both words and pictures convey information, but each does so in importantly different ways. In English, words are written sequentially, left to right, and so the reader's attention is directed toward meaning according to where the text begins, where it goes next, and how it ends. A look at a daily newspaper or Web page reveals textual information further augmented by headlines, titles, subtitles, bold face, italics, and white space. By the time readers get to college, they have internalized many predictive strategies to help them critically understand a great variety of written texts (see Chapter 2).

Visual images present a different set of problems for critical readers. For example, in looking at a photograph or drawing, information is presented simultaneously, so viewers can, start or stop anywhere they like—at least theoretically. Since visual information is presented simultaneously, its general meaning may be apparent at a glance, while more nuanced or complicated meaning may take a long time to figure out and, even then, odds are it will vary from one viewer to another.

Look at the accompanying photograph, "Roadside Stand" taken by Walker Evans in 1936, near Birmingham, Alabama. It presents a lot of information at at glance, but what does the photograph say or mean? Why did Evans shoot it? What did he find of special interest there? What did he intend for viewers to take away?

What, among all those vegetables and words, do we focus on? Are you struck by the informality of the roadside market in contrast with today's modern supermarkets? Do you notice the careful order in what is otherwise a low-rent store? Or are you left wondering why the two boys are holding the watermelons? In this image, the visual information is augmented by the addition of verbal signs, but does that make the meaning any more clear? For instance, what is the relationship between the "*house-mover*" sign and the fish and farm market? What do we think of a merchant who advertises, "*honest weights and square deals*"? Is the

How many words are needed to convey this information?

sign reassuring or suspicious? While this photo supports the cliché, *"a picture is worth a thousand words,"* as it would take at least that many words to capture the details portrayed here, what, exactly, does that *"worth"* mean? Would a writer who used a thousand words to describe this scene point readers more specifically to one meaning rather than another?

In contrast to the multiple meanings in the Evans photograph, would be a billboard, or poster designed with one specific meaning in mind—to sell you a product or idea. For example, look at the accompanying War Gardens for Victory poster in common circulation during World War II: What is this poster selling? If you have any doubts, look closely at the visual image: Why is that woman carrying a basket of vegetables? Why does she wear overalls and carry a hoe? And who is the intended audience?

Different from both the open roadside photograph and the deliberately persuasive Victory Garden poster, are visual images that provide useful information faster than print alone, such as a weather forecasting chart from a daily newspaper.

Who will tend the victory gardens?

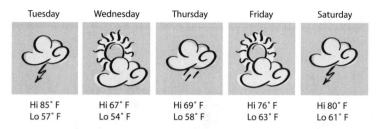

How long does it take to "read" this weather forecast?

To think critically about visual *information,* first identify what objects, facts, processes, or symbols are portrayed in the image. Taking all the information together, ask if there is a main or unifying idea: Is the meaning open to multiple interpretations, such as the Evans photograph? Is it suggested but not stated, as in the film poster? Or is it clear and unambiguous, as in the weather forecast? As a viewer, pausing to answer such questions will likely sharpen your critical faculties and increase your understanding of the visual information you encounter and help you use images more wisely in texts that you create.

Point of View

In written texts, *point of view* refers to the "person" from whose vantage point the information is delivered. Writing from the first person (I), the writer tells the story so you expect his personal perspective. Writing from the second person (you), the writer addresses readers directly and presumes to know something about them. Writing from the third person (he, she), the writer focuses on an external subject, without personal reference, so that her viewpoint is never directly stated. In photographs, drawings, or paintings, *point of view* refers to the place from which the image-maker looks at the subject—where the photographer places his camera, the artist her easel. For illustrative purposes, we'll continue to use photographic images to examine critical decisions that affect perspective.

Photographs that haven't been manipulated in a darkroom or digitally by a computer don't lie. Nor do they tell the whole truth, either. Yes, they reproduce the subject in front of the camera, as it exists the moment the shutter is clicked, but they don't show anything to the left or right, above or below, or what went before or after. A camera aimed to the east omits information north, west, and south, and so on. In other words, any photograph is the result of placing a camera in a certain place, at a certain height and distance, at a specific time of day, using a particular lens, film, and, possibly, filter. And all these decisions, about where, when, and how to place the camera create the visual point of view. A good example of the limited truth revealed by photographs can be found in the real-estate advertisements where the photograph of the house that's for sale doesn't reveal the landfill next door or the factory across the street—though you might infer such limitations from a low selling price or confirm them by driving past the house itself.

Look at the photograph of the Filipino lettuce pickers by Dorthea Lange. What information does it convey? What first catches your attention—the dirt gullies, the big cabbages, the open sky, or the working pickers? If you are drawn first to the people, as most of us are, what is noteworthy about the people in this picture—size? posture? clothing? arrangement? Where has Lange placed her camera? How can you tell? And how does her camera placement affect the meaning you attach to the photo?

What is the photographer's point of view?

By way of contrast, look at Walker Evans' photograph, below, of the tenant-farmer family of Bud Fields set in rural Alabama. What do you notice first—the setting? the group? a specific face? What is your impression of either the whole group or of a specific individual? What words would you use to describe these people? Does the place from where the photo was taken influence how you judge these people? If so, in what way? If Evans placed the camera at eye level deliberately—which I suspect he did—what do you think he wanted viewers to think when looking at the photo?

How does the camera judge these people?

To think critically about *point of view*, identify the place or stance from which the image maker viewed the subject. Ask about the effect this particular point of view has on how viewers think or feel about the subject. What would happen if the vantage point were somewhere else—above or below, left or right of what it is now? In other words, what would change in the image if the *point of view* were changed?

Arrangement

The term *arrangement* in visual texts might be compared to terms such as *order, organization,* or *structure* in verbal texts, though the differences are substantial. While writers arrange or put together a story, essay, or poem to take place over time—that is, the time it takes a reader to follow the text, line by line, through a number of pages—visual image makers arrange pictures in the two-dimensional space of their viewfinder, paper, or canvas so as to invite viewers to read in space rather than time. In visual texts, then, *arrangement* refers to the ways the various parts of a picture come together to present a single coherent experience to the viewer. As far as this book is concerned, all texts, whether verbal or visual, fact or fiction, are open to critical analysis by viewers who know what to look for.

One thing to look for is **pattern**—predictable, repeated elements within the visual field that the eye notices and seems attracted to. Just as sonnets, sestinas, and haiku follow patterns of line, so too do visual compositions, only lines here are created by light rather than words. Both documentary and commercial photographers often use visual patterns to lead viewers to an intended meaning. Look, for example, at Dorthea Lange's photo and ask about pattern: What does the curving pattern of the furrowed field lines have to do with the meaning of this photograph? What do the patterns of light and dark also contribute to meaning? And what is the role of the single human dwelling in this carefully plowed plain? What do all the elements taken together make us think or feel?

How does pattern affect meaning?

Lange took this photograph in 1938, so if we add historical hindsight to photographic pattern, our interpretation grows: We know that such power plowing of thousands of acres of the Great Plains was a precursor to the Depression era dust bowl. If the visual imagery alone suggested loneliness, poverty, and abandonment, the historical knowledge only confirms it.

Another visual element at work in the Lange photograph is **balance**—the proportional weight of each visual component and how it does or does not hold the eye's attention. In Lange's photo, the larger dark shading of the left side is balanced by the smaller but lighter field on the right as the larger and darker land mass balances the smaller but lighter sky—balance is achieved because the light, which attracts more attention, is offset by a darker but larger mass. In addition to balancing light and dark as Lange does or as Jack Delano does in the photograph of school dancers, what other visual elements might work in the same way? In the Delano photograph, try dividing the image vertically in two with an imaginary line separating the right from the left half of the photo. On the left side you see a dozen or so small figures, while on the right you see only part of one. What's the visual effect? Where does your eye travel? And what is the net effect? What's interesting to me is that each side seems to hold its own, allowing the eye to comfortably take in the activity in the whole gymnasium (we noticed the basketball hoop at building's end and remembered such rehearsals ourselves). The many smaller and darker dancers on the left seem offset by the larger and lighter dancer on the right. What difference, you might ask, does it make that the halves of the picture balance each other? How does this balance by numbers, size, and light contribute to a photo's meaning? As we see it, the visual balance adds a strong dimension of order and stability to the image, suggesting, perhaps, a world that is comfortable, safe, and secure. While the photograph portrays action on a small scale, it hints at peacefulness at large.

How do size, number, and light make meaning?

To think critically about *arrangement,* identify repeated elements within the visual image. Can you locate the center of gravity or weight in a given picture? Do you think the center was found or fabricated? Where do patterns of light/dark, large/small, and number lead the eye? How do pattern and balance contribute to meaning in a two-dimensional frame? What does the arrangement suggest about the meaning of the image?

Theme

Both verbal and visual texts may be said to have themes—statements that identify the larger meaning of the text being read or viewed. In a verbal texts, this theme, thesis, or controlling idea (it's called lots of things) may be stated early (informational reports), late (feature stories), or accumulate by inference over the length of the whole text (personal essays and creative nonfiction). Though a visual text is usually perceived all at once in a single viewing, its theme may or may not be either strongly stated or quickly apparent. The themes of some of the photos we've looked at seem more obvious than others: For instance, Lange's photo of the Filipino lettuce pickers is a strong statement about the difficulty and dignity of work, while the specific meaning in the more information-packed roadside vegetable stand by Walker Evans seems more difficult to pin down.

What determines whether a theme is obvious or even present in a photograph? Sometimes theme seems to be more in the eye of the beholder than the mind of the photographer—or so such a case could be made for Jack Delano's dancers; the viewers' associations with school gymnasiums and after-school dance classes may be responsible for our particular interpretation.

What does the fine print tell you?

However, would you say the same thing of Marian Post Wolcott's photo of the movie theater? What visual elements catch your attention? The man ascending the angled staircase? The graphic and stark light and dark patterns? And what do the verbal elements such as the large advertisement for Dr. Pepper or the cowboy movie poster help? In this photo, you

What is this woman's story?

may have to look at the fine print to decide this is not a nostalgic picture of times past in small-town America, but a chilling reminder of the dark side of the American past. Looking more closely, the eye is drawn to the center of the photo where the small print below the staircase, "*COLORED ADM. 10 C*," combines with the silhouetted figure ascending the staircase, to remind us that discrimination was once public policy.

Documentary photographers incorporate a number of strategies to shape the themes of material found in both the natural and the developed world. That is, such photographers work within the same limits as nonfiction writers who are not supposed to invent material that doesn't exist. In fact, the elements we've looked at so far—subject, point of view, arrangement—all contribute to the thematic content of a photograph. By shooting from far away rather than close up or by cropping images in the darkroom, photographers focus viewer attention on the point they want to make.

What caption would you give this photograph?

Look, for instance, at two versions of Dorthea Lange photographs of a rural family that appears down and out on their luck. The close-up is well known and goes by the name "Migrant Mother" (previous page). The longer view before the photographer moved in close, reveals the whole family, the tent, and the setting. It is neither titled nor well known. In fact, I was surprised to find it when looking through the Dorthea Lange collection in the Library of Congress. What, we might ask, makes the closeup famous and the long shot run-of-the-mill? Is it only the fact that the camera is closer in one than the other? Is there something about the figures or facial expressions? Or is it a question of information, one having more, the other less?

To think critically about *theme,* notice your first reactions to an image: What caught your attention first? Second? What emotions did you feel, and why? What ideas came to mind and where do you think they came from? How do the elements of *information, point of view,* and *arrangement* combine to support make a thematic statement?

Words

Adding words to images brings us full circle, back to the specificity of verbal texts. In magazine ads, words point to or add details about an automobile, toothpaste, or food product. In television commercials, oral voice-overs tell us what meaning to attach to the image we are watching. And in political campaign posters, words enhance and embellish the image of a man or woman who seeks our vote. Text is often added to images to make sure the image is interpreted in a particular way. For example, in the accompanying photograph, can you identify the man addressing a crowd near the Washington monument? In case at first glance you didn't, the title of the poster tells you it is Martin Luther King giving his famous speech, "I have a dream" (1963). Without words, the King poster is still very powerful, since the image pattern and balance keep your eyes fixed on King; and it is likely that many viewers would recognize King from television documentaries or history lessons. Here is a case where the words are only necessary to viewers unfamiliar with the man.

However, words may be added to images to create specific messages neither alone would convey. Look at the "Abusing" poster (next page) and notice the interplay of words and image: What surprises you about this poster? Who do you think it is aimed at? What audience attitude or values did the poster makers count on? Where would you imagine it being displayed? Where would you not display it? Regardless of your answers to

I HAVE A DREAM
Martin Luther King Jr.

Does this poster need a title?

these questions, it seems apparent that neither words nor image alone convey the same message as the two together.

Each week, *The New Yorker* magazine runs a cartoon caption contest on its back page, showing a cartoon drawing without words. Readers are invited to make up captions that would turn the drawing into a cartoon that makes a particular point. I found the drawing by Mike Twohy (below) in the April 25, 2005 issue of the magazine and began making up captions, which I found far more difficult than I imagined. Where do you begin? First I asked, what was possibly funny or surprising about this drawing? Of course, it's the researcher who's wearing a rat costume instead of a lab coat. OK. But while the costume is out of the ordinary, especially in a laboratory setting, a man in a rat costume, in and of itself, doesn't mean anything in particular and is not all that funny. So, how do you find words that, together with the drawing, create not only meaning, but humor? I now invite you to do the same. Add words to this drawing so

Which is more important, word or image?

that it makes a point and is funny. After you've given it a good college try, read further to see what captions *The New Yorker* judges most interesting.

Can you compose a caption for this cartoon?

Reproduced here are the most interesting three captions to the "researcher in the rat-costume" cartoon selected by *The New Yorker* and published in the May 9 issue. I noticed right away that each begins with the rat costume, as I tried to, but then directs our attention to a different part of the cartoon to make what turn out to be very different points. Larson focuses on the mice ("their trust"), Futterman on the researcher ("myself"), and Baerkircher on the costume itself ("a thousand tiny lab coats").

This image-first exercise is a simple illustration of the malleability of images, suggesting that images without words seldom have definitive meanings.

While a single image may be worth many words, it takes only a few words to change what that meaning might be—a principle of reader/viewer manipulation exploited by commercial advertisers, political campaigners, advocacy groups alike.

To think critically about the mixing of words with images, look at any poster, campaign ad, or commercial. What would be lost if either words or image were subtracted? Imagine how other words or images might change the meaning. *(If you have good ideas here, have you considered a career in advertising?)*

> # THE FINALISTS
>
> *"First, you must gain their trust."*
> Russell Larson, Wallingford, Conn.
>
> *"More important, however, is what I learned about myself."*
> Roy Futterman, New York City.
>
> *"Well, it was just easier than making a thousand tiny lab coats."*
> Fred Baerkircher, Kent, Ohio.

Which caption do you prefer?

Color

The images we've looked at so far have been in black and white since the visual elements stand out more clearly without the distraction of color. I also believe that black and white images have their own substantial place in the world of images, as the lack of color allows greater weight to be place on compositional elements. I don't think, for instance, that any of the black and white photos looked at so far would be improved in any way by the addition of color—colored versions of "Filipino lettuce workers" or "Migrant Mother" would simply be different, not better, photographs.

That said, I realize that most of the commercial and aesthetic images you'll encounter today in magazines and films as well as on television and computer monitors will be in color, so it pays to ask additional critical question of color as well. In visual texts, color adds powerful dimensions in detail and enrichment that the more abstract black and white cannot. Because I am unable to include color images in *The Working Writer,* you might want to look at a copy of any glossy magazine with lots of color images as you continue reading.

Particular colors suggest specific moods. Think about your own personal reactions to different colors—what color do you select to paint your room? What is your favorite color for, say, clothing or cars? While these may differ greatly according to personal preferences, aren't there actually traditional symbolic values attached to different colors in literature and art? Why, for instance, does red often symbolize, on the one hand, anger or war, and on the other, romance or passion? Why does black suggest danger or death? And why does white stand for innocence or purity? Are the reasons for these associations arbitrary or logical?

Particular colors also suggest or reinforce social and political ideas. What, for example, is suggested by adding a red, white, and blue American flag to a magazine advertisement for an American automobile, political poster, or bumper sticker? What does it mean when somebody adds a yellow ribbon to the tree in front of a house or image of a yellow ribbon sticker to the tailgate of a pick-up truck? In and of themselves, colors don't specify political positions, arguments, or ideas, but used in conjunction with specific words or forms—a flag or ribbon, for example—the emotional power of color can be influential.

To think critically about color, notice whether it enhances or distorts the reality of the image. Imagine the image in shades of black, white, and gray: Ask what would be lost, what gained if color were subtracted. Does the color work with or against the other compositional elements we've been looking at?

Images of Persuasion

With the notable exception of radio, nearly every spoken or written message Americans encounter is accompanied by a visual component to strengthen its appeal. Institutions of every kind—commercial, governmental, educational—advertise their goods and services visually, in carefully designed booklets, brochures, posters, billboards, bumper stickers, lawn signs, refrigerator magnets, commercials, and advertisements to catch viewer attention. No doubt you've grown up with magazine ads and television commercials in which visual information adds an emotional appeal to the product. So prevalent, for instance, are the following ads, that all I need do is mention them to let your visual memory kick in: Ford, Chevy, and Dodge trucks slogging through mud and conquering mountainous terrain to haul huge loads to difficult destinations—*Wow! Gotta get me one of them tough trucks!* Burger King cheeseburgers, Taco Bell tacos, and Subway submarine sandwiches portrayed in large, colorful, and juicy images—*Hey, that makes me hungry!*

Visual images sell ideas as well as products, and the emotional appeal of images can be just as strong in black and white as color. The accompanying photographic image shows the graffiti covered walls of a narrow and shadowy hallway, a "FOR RENT" sign signifying a low-rent apartment building. Analyze this image: Why does the hallway so dominate the space on this poster in contrast to the small printed message at the bottom? What is the emotional effect created by the glaring and reflected light? While bright, is this a hallway in which you'd feel comfortable, a building in which you'd want to live? If the hallway image catches your attention,

What's the exit strategy?

The best way out is by coming in.

The Hernandez family found a way out of poverty – it started by coming in to a family literacy program. No surprise, given that a majority of adults who learn with their kids improve in everything from language skills to getting their GED. Together, they learn "literacy" isn't just about reading and writing, it's about developing skills – skills they use for a better life. Know a family we can help? Or would you like to help? Call **1-877-FAMLIT-1**, or visit us at **www.famlit.org**.

National Center for Family Literacy

maybe you'll look closer look at the white print on the hallway floor that serves to title the image: *"The best way out is coming in."* Now what does that mean—a hallway to exit rather than enter? (A definite yes here!) If so, what does it mean to "come in"? Where do your eyes go next in search of an exit strategy? To the next largest print on the poster, at the bottom, where the sponsoring agency is identified as the *National Center for Family Literacy?* If so, does the way out have something to do with reading, writing, and communication skills? But who is the audience this poster is aimed at? In which magazines or on what bulletin boards would you expect to see it? Any that you regularly read?

In contrast to the realistic, gritty image of an apartment hallway, is the equally interesting but more simple and abstract public service advertisement sponsored by Project Safe. What are the persuasive elements in this message? The image or the print? Why so much blank space in the center? Why the white vertical lines? To lead our eyes to the bold horizontal print at the top of the bars? To be addressed directly as an ex-con, "you"? But is the ex (or existing) con the only or really intended audience? Who else might Project Safe have in mind? And what is the reason we're being warned? The answer seems found in the last and lowest lines in the ad, with the title, *"Gun Crimes Hit Home."* Gun crimes lead to jail time and a lot more hardship—avoid guns! And where would this ad be posted—A school? Community center bulletin board? Pool hall window? Telephone pole?

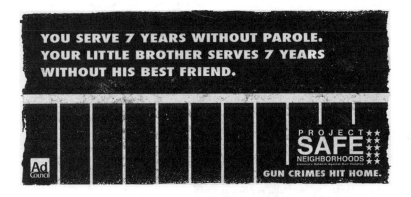

In contrast to the persuasively serious is what might be called the persuasively comic, where the viewer is sold a product or idea through humor rather than dire warning. You've only to think about the television commercials that make you laugh aloud—and many are very, very funny, but quickly dated, so we won't refer to specific ones here. However, consider the advertisement on the next page: Our eyes are drawn first to the dominant photograph that takes up most of the space on the page, showing what appears to be a teacher and her class of elementary school students sitting for a school photo. Ok. But something seems out of order, not quite right. What on earth are they sitting in front of? A parking garage! Not at all the classic school building we've come to expect with such class photos. What gives? We laugh, of course it's sort of a joke—this would never happen—would it? And that, of course, is what the sponsor, the National Trust Historic Preservation, wants to ensure. We laugh. We get the message. Preserve good buildings.

We'll end this chapter with one final persuasive image, actress Brooke Shields dressed in white with cigarettes sticking out of her ears. We laugh, but again we ask, what gives?

- How is our attention caught?
- Who is the intended audience? Why do we think so?
- What dominant visual elements are at work here?
- What to do you believe about the ad?
- What do you question about the ad?
- What are the ad's unspoken assumptions?
- How necessary is the verbal text in the background?

As you know well, both words and pictures in the hands of skilled writers, artists, and photographers can be powerfully persuasive. Consequently we believe both verbal language and visual images need to be viewed critically so that readers and viewers understand, first, the meaning of the message and, second, the intent behind the meaning. And we be-

No one looks back fondly
on the time they spent in a parking garage.

lieve that, as writers and creators of images, the same critical understanding will advance your own writing and art.

ADDING IMAGES TO YOUR WRITING

It is easy to incorporate visual images into papers, portfolios, and Web pages to inform, entertain, and engage readers in ways text alone does not. Images are often included in verbal texts to break up dense textual space or signal a shift in content. While readers appreciate such images, they seldom pay close attention to them. Whenever possible, use images to expand understanding rather than merely to decorate the paper you're writing. Here are some possibilities:

- Use images that save you a thousand words. For example, many of the images that illus-

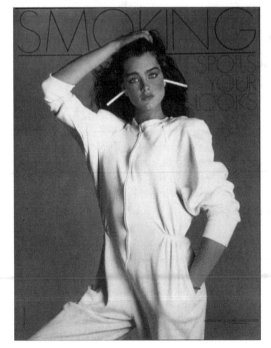

What's for sale here?

trate this chapter are especially rich in visual information.

- Use images that convey useful information quickly in the shorthand way of charts and graphs, as does this *Regional Sales Distribution* chart.
- Use images that make abstract ideas concrete. It would take a lot of words and a long time to describe a cartoon character such as a Smurf to somebody who had never seen the television show (see student paper, Chapter 10).

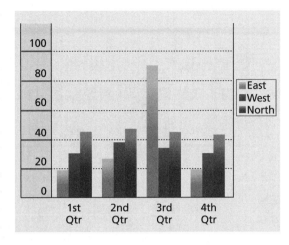

- Control the size and layout of images using a computer program such as *MS Paint* or *Adobe Photoshop* or by judicious cutting and pasting with scissors and tape.
- Position images where they belong—or as close as possible—in your text.
- Refer to the image in the text to explain its reason for being there.
- Label each image appropriately, following conventions such as MLA style in formal papers (*Figure 1: Roadside Stand Near Birmingham, AL, by Walker Evans*) or more casually, as we did in this chapter.
- If publishing on a Web site, make sure the image is in the public domain (as is the Walker Evans photograph above) or secure permission from copyright holder.

◆ SUGGESTIONS FOR WRITING AND RESEARCH

Individual

Choose any image from the Depression series of photographs in this chapter, and make up a story to go along with the situation depicted. What clues in the picture did you choose to focus on? Why? Did these clues appeal to your emotional or rational sense?

Write one paragraph each on this same picture as evidence for a historical interpretation, as an editorial making a cultural criticism, as a piece of forensic evidence in a court case, as a work of art, and as an advertisement. What visual elements within the photograph have greater or lesser importance depending on what kind of object you assume the photo to be?

Collaborative

As a class, complete the individual exercise above. Then compare your answers to these questions to those of other students, and discuss the similarities and differences.

CHAPTER FOUR

The Elements of Composition

I find it very confusing moving from one professor to another.
They all expect different things. I still haven't learned yet
what makes a "good" paper as opposed to a "bad" paper.

JENNIFER

Why do teachers always make you write about what they want you to and never
what you want to? What is the writing for anyway?

ERIC

I would like to develop some sort of personal style so when I write people know it's me.

JOHN

The focus, structure, and style of every paper you write are determined by your situation—why you are writing (purpose) and to whom (audience). Taken together, purpose and audience largely determine the voice in which you write. While this chapter asks you to consider each of these fundamental elements of composition in isolation, in truth, most writers usually think about them subconsciously and simultaneously. In any case, the following discussion may be useful when you are assigned to write an academic paper.

WRITING FOR A PURPOSE

People write to discover what's on their minds, figure things out, vent frustrations, keep records, remember things, communicate information, shape ideas, express feelings, recount experiences, raise questions, imagine the future, create new forms—and simply for pleasure. They also write when they're required to in school, to demonstrate knowledge and solve problems. But no matter what the task, writers write better when they do so purposefully—when they know what they want to accomplish. This section examines three broad and overlapping stages of writing: discovering, communicating, and creating. It discusses strategies to accomplish each one effectively.

Writing to Discover

Writing helps people discover ideas, relationships, connections, and patterns in their lives and in the world. In college, students write to discover paper topics, develop those topics, expand and explain ideas, and connect seemingly unrelated material in coherent patterns. In this sense, writing is one of the most powerful learning tools available.

Writing is especially powerful because it makes language and therefore thoughts stand still, allowing thoughts to be examined slowly and deliberately, allowing ideas to be elaborated, critiqued, rearranged, and corrected. Playwright Christopher Fry once said, "My trouble is that I'm the sort of writer who only finds out what he is getting at by the time he's got to the end of it." In other words, his purpose and plan become clear only after he has written a whole draft; he knows that the act of writing will help him find his way. But rather than considering this inventive power of writing "troublesome," to use Fry's words, you can consider it a solution to many other problems. Once you know that writing can generate ideas, advance concepts, and forge connections, then you can use it deliberately and strategically to help you write college papers.

Discovery can happen in all writing. Any time you write, you may find new or lost ideas, implications, and directions. However, sometimes it pays to write with the specific intention of discovering. Discovery writing is often used before actual drafting to explore the subject and purpose of a paper or to solve writing problems once drafting and revising have begun.

◆ WRITING 1

Describe a time when you used writing for discovery purposes. Did you set out to use writing this way, or did it happen accidentally? Have you used it deliberately since then? With what results?

Writing to Communicate

The most common reason for writing in college is to transmit ideas or information to an audience. College students write essays, exams, and reports to instructors, as well as letters, applications, and résumés to potential employers. The general guidelines for such writing are well known: Communicative writing needs to be obviously purposeful so both writer and reader know where it's going. It needs to be clear in order to be understood. It needs to include assertions supported by evidence in order to be believable. And it needs to be conventionally correct in terms of spelling, mechanics, and grammar in order to be taken seriously. While there are interesting exceptions to these guidelines (see Chapter 13), they are the rule in most academic writing situations.

Thesis-Based Writing

Many academic assignments ask you to write *thesis-based* papers, that is, papers that assert, explain, support, or defend a position or idea. Your assertion about the idea or position is called the paper's *thesis*. Since most academic papers are assigned so that instructors can witness and assess student knowledge, stating a thesis makes clear what, exactly, the paper's claim or position is. The thesis, broadly speaking, is the place to summarize the main idea to make it explicit to readers. For example, the thesis of this chapter is stated in the first paragraph: that *the focus, structure, and style of papers are determined by purpose and audience.* This claim is then supported throughout the rest of the chapter.

Some thesis-based papers present the thesis first, usually in the opening paragraph to tell readers what's coming. Such *thesis-first* papers are common in academic as well as technical and scientific writing because they emphasize the transmission of an idea or information clearly, directly, and economically, thus helping readers get rapidly to the point. In contrast, *delayed-thesis* papers do not state conclusions up front but examine a variety of conditions or circumstances to be considered before a decision is made. Such papers emphasize the process by which the writer discovered knowledge as much as the knowledge itself. Whether first or delayed, a thesis-driven paper explicitly answers the critical reader's question "So what?" Why does this paper exist? What's it about? Common thesis-based assignments in college include the following, which are examined in more detail in subsequent chapters:

- *Explaining ideas.*   The purpose of explaining something is to make it clear to somebody who knows less about the subject than you do. You explain best by following a logical order, using simple language, and providing illustration and examples of what you mean. (See Chapter 10.)
- *Arguing positions.*   The purpose of arguing is to persuade readers to agree with your position. College assignments frequently ask you to explore opposing sides of an issue or several different interpretations of a text and then to take a stand advocating one point of view. (See Chapter 11.)
- *Interpreting texts.*   The purpose of interpreting a text is to explain to others what the text means, to tell why you believe it means this, and to support your reading with reasons based on evidence from the text. (See Chapter 12.)

Question-Based Writing

Still other papers assigned in college may have, as their larger purpose, more personal or reflective dimensions, and never directly state a thesis at all. Such exploratory papers might pose questions to which specific answers are illusive or examine dimensions of the writer's self in relation to the larger world. These *question-based* papers might be said to emphasize the play of the writer's mind more than the direct transmission of knowledge. However, these papers, too, answer—though less directly—the critical reader's questions "So what? Why does this paper exist? What's it about?" Common question-based assignments include the following, which are examined in more detail in subsequent chapters:

- *Recounting experience.*   People narrate personal stories to share common experiences with others and to learn, in the telling, the meaning of those experiences for themselves. (See Chapter 8.)
- *Exploring identity.*   People examine their own lives to find out important things about who they are, how they got that way, or where they're going next. (See Chapter 9.)
- *Profiling people.*   Writers profile other people to find out how other lives are lived, valued, and expressed, and, in the process, to learn about our shared culture. (See Chapter 9.)

- *Experimenting with nonfiction.* Writers speculate, muse, and ponder about an infinite number of ideas and issues in our world, and share them with others, to find out what these ideas mean and what, along the way, the world means. (See Chapter 13.)

◆ WRITING 2

When is the last time you wrote to communicate something? Describe your purpose and audience. How successful were these acts of communication? How do you know?

Writing to Create

When you write to imagine or create, you often pay special attention to the way your language looks and sounds, its form, shape, rhythm, images, and texture. Though the term *creative writing* is most often associated with poetry, fiction, and drama, it's important to see any act of writing, from personal narratives to research essays, as potentially creative.

When you write to create, you pay less immediate attention to your audience and subject and more to the act of expression itself. Your goal is not so much to change the world or to transmit information about it as to transform an experience or idea into something that will make your readers pause, see the world from a different angle and perhaps reflect upon what it means. You want your writing itself, not just the information it contains, to affect your readers emotionally or esthetically as well as intellectually.

In most college papers, your primary purpose will be to communicate, not to create. However, nearly every writing assignment has room for a creative dimension. When writing for emotional or esthetic effect in an otherwise communicative paper, be especially careful that your creativity serves a purpose and that the communicative part is strong on its own. You want your creative use of language to enhance, not camouflage, your ideas. (See Chapter 13.)

INTENSIFYING EXPERIENCE.   When Amanda recounted her experience picking potatoes on board a mechanical potato harvester on her father's farm, she made her readers feel the experience as she did by crafting her language to duplicate the sense of hard, monotonous work:

> Potatoes, mud, potatoes, mud, potatoes, that was all I saw in front of me. They moved from my right side to my left, at hip level. A conveyor belt never stopping. On and on and on. The potatoes passed fast, a constant stream. My hands worked deftly, pulling out clods of dirt, rotten potatoes, old shaws, and anything else I found that wasn't a potato. It was October, the ground was nearly frozen, the mud was hard and solid. Cold. Dirt had gotten into my yellow rubber gloves, had wedged under my nails, increasing my discomfort.

This is a creative approach to essay writing because the writer uses a graphic, descriptive style to put readers at the scene of her experience rather than summarizing it or explaining explicitly what it meant to her.

EXPERIMENTING WITH FORM.   Keith created a special language effect in an otherwise traditional and straightforward academic assignment by writing a poetic prologue for a research essay about homeless people in New York City. The full essay contains factual information derived from social workers, agency documents, and library research.

> The cold cement
> no pillow
> The steel grate
> no mattress
> But the hot air
> of the midnight subway
> Lets me sleep.

Using the poetic form creates a brief emotional involvement with the research subject, allowing readers to fill in missing information with their imaginations. Note, however, that the details of the poem (*cold cement, steel grate, subway*) spring not from the writer's imagination but from his research notes and observations.

◆ WRITING 3

Describe a time when your primary purpose in writing was to create rather than to discover or communicate. Were you pleased with the result? Why or why not?

ADDRESSING AUDIENCES

The better you know your audience, the better you're likely to write. Whether your writing is judged "good" or not depends largely on how well it's received by the readers for whom it's intended. Just as you change the way you speak depending on the audience you're addressing—your boss, mother, instructor, friend, younger brother—so you change the way you write depending on the audience to whom you're writing. You don't want to overexplain and perhaps bore the audience or underexplain and leave it wanting.

Speakers have an advantage over writers in that they see the effect of their words on their listeners and can adjust accordingly. A puzzled look tells the speaker to slow down, a smile and nod says keep going full speed ahead, and so on. However, writers can only imagine the reactions of the people to whom they're trying to communicate.

I believe all college papers need to be written to at least two audiences, maybe more: first, to yourself, so you understand it; second, to your instructor who has asked you to write it in the first place. In addition, you may also be writing to other students or for publication to more public audiences. This chapter examines how expectations differ from one audience to the next.

Understanding College Audiences

It might help to think of the different audiences you will address in college as existing along a continuum, with those closest and best known to you (yourself, friends) at one end and those farthest from and least known to you (the general public) at the other end:

Self—Family—Friends—Instructor—Public

While the items on your continuum will always differ in particulars from somebody else's, the principle that you know some audiences better than others will always be the same and will influence how you write. The audience of most concern to most college students is the instructor who will evaluate their learning on the basis of their writing.

◆ WRITING 4

Think back over the past several weeks and list all the different audiences to whom you have written. To whom did you write most often? Which audiences were easy for you to address? Which were difficult? Why?

Shaping Writing for Different Audiences

To shape your writing for a particular audience, you first need to understand the qualities of your writing that can change according to audience. The context you need to provide; the structure, tone, and style you use; and your purpose for writing can all be affected by your audience. (Structure, tone, and style are important elements of voice.)

CONTEXT.   Different audiences need different contexts—different amounts or kinds of background information—in order to understand your ideas. Find out whether your readers already know about the topic or whether it's completely new to them. Consider whether any terms or ideas need explaining. For example, other students in your writing group might know exactly whom you mean if you refer to a favorite singer, but your instructor might not. Also consider what sort of explanation would work best with your audience.

STRUCTURE.   Every piece of writing is put together in a certain way: some ideas are discussed early, others late; transitions between ideas are marked in a certain way; similar ideas are either grouped together or treated separately. How you structure a paper depends in large part on what you think will work best with your particular audience. For example, if you were writing an argument for someone who disagrees with your position, you might begin with the evidence with which you both agree and then later introduce more controversial evidence.

TONE.   The tone of a piece of writing conveys the writer's attitude toward the subject matter and audience. How do you want to sound to your readers? You may, of course, have a different attitude toward each audience you address. In addition, you may want different audiences to hear in different ways. For example, when writing to yourself, you won't mind sounding confused. When writing to instructors, though, you will want to sound confident and authoritative.

STYLE.   Style is largely determined by the formality and complexity of your language. You need to determine what style your readers expect and what style will be most effective in a given paper. Fellow students might be offended if you write in anything other than a friendly style, but some instructors might interpret the same style as disrespectful.

PURPOSE.   The explicit purpose of your writing depends more on you and your assignment than on your audience. However, certain purposes are more likely to apply to particular audiences than others. Also, there are unstated purposes embedded in any piece of writing, and these will vary depending on whom you're addressing. For example, is it important that your readers like you? Or that they respect you? Or that they give you good grades? Always ask yourself what you want a piece of writing to do for or to your audience and what you want your audience to do in response to your writing.

Let's follow the way writing generally needs to change as you move along the scale away from the audience you know best, yourself.

WRITING TO YOURSELF.   Every paper you write is addressed in part to yourself, and some writing, such as journals, is addressed primarily to yourself. However, most reports, essays, papers, and exams are also addressed to other people: instructors, peers, parents, or employers. Journal writing is your opportunity to write to yourself and yourself alone. When you write to yourself alone, you don't need to worry about context, structure, tone, or style; only purpose matters if you are the sole reader. However, if you make a journal entry that you might want to refer to later, it's a good idea to provide sufficient background and explanation to help you remember the event or the idea described if you do return to it. When you are the reader of your own writing, choose words, sentences, rhythms, images, and punctuation that come easiest and most naturally to you.

WRITING TO PEERS.   Your peers are your equals, your friends and classmates, people of similar age, background, or situation. Some of your assignments will ask you to consider the other students in the class to be your audience, for example, when you read papers to each other in writing groups or exchange papers to edit each other's work.

The primary difference between writing to yourself and writing to peers is the amount of context and structure you need to provide to make sure your readers understand you. If your paper is about a personal experience, you need to provide the explanations and details that will allow readers who did not have your experience to fully understand the events and ideas you describe.

If your paper is about a subject that requires research, be sure to provide background information to make the topic comprehensible and interesting in a structure (for example, chronological order, logical order, cause-effect sequence) that makes sense. Be direct, honest, and friendly; peers will see right through any pretentious or stuffy language.

You usually write to peers to share a response to their writing, to recount an experience, to explain an idea, or to argue a position. In a writing class, the most important implicit purpose is probably to establish a good working rapport with your classmates by being honest, straightforward, and supportive.

WRITING TO INSTRUCTORS.   Instructors are among the most difficult audiences for whom to write. First, they usually make the assignments, so they know what they want, and it's your job to figure out what that is. Second, they often know more about your subject than you do. Third, different instructors may have quite different criteria for what constitutes good writing. And fourth, each instructor may simultaneously play several different roles: a helpful resource, a critic, an editor, a coach, and, finally, a judge.

It is often difficult to know how much context to provide in a paper written for an instructor unless the assignment specifically tells you. For example, in writing about a Shakespearean play to an English professor, should you provide a summary of the play when you know that he or she already knows it? Or should you skip the summary information and write only about ideas original with you? The safest approach is to provide brief background information but to explain all ideas, support all assertions, and cite authorities in the field. Write as if your instructor needed all this information and it were your job to educate him or her.

When writing papers to instructors, be sure to use a structure that suits the type of paper you are writing. For example, personal experience papers are often chronological, reports may be more thematic, and so on. (The chapters in Part Two describe conventional structures for each type of paper discussed there.)

One of your instructor's roles is to help you learn to write effective papers. But another role is to evaluate whether you have done so and, from a broader perspective, whether you are becoming a literate member of the college community. Therefore, your implicit purpose when you write to instructors is to demonstrate your understanding of conventions, knowledge, reasoning ability, and originality.

WRITING TO PUBLIC AUDIENCES.   Writing to a public audience is difficult for all writers because the audience is usually both diverse and unknown. The public audience can include both people who know more and those who know less than you; it can contain experts who will correct the slightest mistake and novices who need even simple terms explained; it can contain opponents looking for reasons to argue and supporters looking for reasons to continue support. And you are unlikely to know many of these people personally.

You usually have some idea of who these anonymous readers are or you wouldn't be writing to them in the first place. Still, it is important to learn as much as you can about any of their beliefs and characteristics that may be relevant to the point you intend to make. What is their educational level? What are their political, philosophical, or religious beliefs? What are their interests?

When you don't know who your audience is, provide context for everything you say. If you are referring to even well-known groups such as the NCAA or ACLU, write out the full names the first time you refer to them (National Collegiate Athletic Association or American Civil Liberties Union). If you refer to an idea as postmodern, define or illustrate what the term means. (Good luck!) Your writing should be able to stand by itself and make complete sense to people you do not know.

Your purpose and structure should be as clear as possible, with your opening paragraph letting this audience know what's to come. Your tone will depend on your purpose, but generally it should be fair and reasonable. Your style will depend on the publication for which you are writing.

◆ WRITING 5

How accurate do you find the preceding discussion about different college audiences? Describe circumstances that confirm or contradict the description here. If instructors are not your most difficult audience, explain who is.

FINDING A VOICE

Each individual speaks with distinctive voice. Some people speak loudly, some softly, others with quiet authority. Some sound assertive or aggressive while others sound cautious, tentative, or insecure. Some voices are clear and easy to follow while others are garbled, convoluted, and meandering. Some create belief and inspire trust while others do not.

An individual's voice can also be recognized in the writing he or she produces. A writer's voice, like one's personality, is determined by factors such as ethnic identity, social class, family, or religion. In addition, some elements of voice evolve as a writer matures, such as how one thinks (logically or intuitively) and what one thinks (a political or philosophical stance). And each writer's voice may change depending upon the occasion or situation. Writers can exert a great deal of control over their language. They create the style (simple or complex), the tone (serious or sarcastic), and many other elements. Writers try to be in control of as many elements of their writing voice as they can.

Defining Voice

The word *voice* means at least two distinctly different things. First, it is the audible sound of a person speaking (*He has a high-pitched voice*). Speaking voices distinguish themselves by auditory qualities such as pitch (high, low, nasal), pace (fast, slow), tone (angry, assertive, tentative), rhythm (regular, smooth, erratic), volume (soft, loud), and accent (Southern, British, Boston). Applied to writing, this meaning cannot be taken literally; unless writers read their work aloud, readers don't actually hear writers' voices. However, the language on the page can re-create the sound of the writer talking. Careful writers control, as much as they can, the sound of their words in their readers' heads.

Second, *voice,* especially when applied to writing, suggests who a person is and what he or she stands for. Written voices convey something of the writers behind the words, including their personal, political, philosophical, and social beliefs. In addition, writers' beliefs and values may be revealed in the way they reason about things, whether they do so in an orderly, scientific manner, or more intuitively and emotionally.

◆ WRITING 6

In your own words, describe the concept of voice. Do you think writers have one voice or many? Explain what you mean.

ANALYZING VOICE

Readers experience a writer's voice as a whole expression, not a set of component parts. However, to help you understand and gain control of your own voice, let's examine the individual elements that combine to make the whole.

TONE.   Tone is your attitude toward the subject and audience: angry, anxious, joyous, sarcastic, puzzled, contemptuous, respectful, friendly, and so on. Writers control their tone, just as speakers do, by adopting a particular perspective or point of view, selecting words carefully, emphasizing some words and ideas over others, choosing certain patterns of inflection, and controlling the pace with pauses and other punctuation. For example, note how your tone might change as you speak or write the following sentences:

- The English Department was unable to offer enough writing courses to satisfy the demand this semester.
- Why doesn't English offer more writing courses?
- It's outrageous that so many students were closed out of first-year writing courses!

To gain control of the tone of your writing, read drafts of your paper aloud and listen carefully to the attitudes you express. Try to hear your own words as if you were the audience: Decide whether the overall tone is the one you intended, and reread carefully to make sure every sentence contributes to this tone.

STYLE.   Style is the way writers express themselves according to whom they are addressing and why. Style is found in the formality or informality, simplicity or complexity, clarity or muddiness of a writer's language. For example, in writing to a friend, you may adopt an informal, conversational style, characterized by contractions and simple, colloquial language:

John. Can't make it tonight. Spent the day cutting wood and am totally bushed.

In writing to instructors, however, you may be more formal, careful, and precise:

Dear Professor James,

I am sorry, but my critical essay will be late. Over the weekend, I overextended myself cutting, splitting, and stacking two cords of wood for my father and ended up with a sprained back. Would you be willing to extend the paper deadline for one more day?

In other words, the style you adopt depends on your audience, purpose, and situation. To gain control of your style, think about how you wish to present yourself, and shape your words, sentences, and paragraphs to suit the occasion.

STRUCTURE.   The structure of a text is how it's put together: where it starts, where it goes next, where the thesis occurs, what evidence fits where, how it concludes. Structure is the pattern or logic that holds together thoughtful writing, revealing something of the thought process that created it. For example, a linear, logical structure may characterize the writer as a linear, logical thinker, while a circular, digressive structure may suggest more intuitive, less orderly habits of mind. Skillful writers, of course, can present themselves one way or the other depending on whom they're addressing and why.

The easiest way to gain control of an essay's structure is to make an outline that reveals visually and briefly the organization and direction you intend. Some writers outline before they start writing and stick to the outline all the way through the writing. Others outline only after writing a draft or two to help control their final draft. And still others start with a rough outline they continue to modify as the writing modifies thought and direction.

VALUES AND BELIEFS.   Your values include your political, social, religious, and philosophical beliefs. Your background, opinions, and beliefs will be part of everything you write,
but you must learn when to express them directly and when not to. For example, including your values would enhance a personal essay or other autobiographical writing, but it may
detract attention from the subject of a research essay.

To gain control of the values in your writing, consider whether the purpose of the assignment calls for an implicit or explicit statement of your values. Examine your drafts for
words that reveal your personal biases, beliefs, and values; keep them or take them out as
appropriate for the assignment.

AUTHORITY.   Your authority comes from confidence in your knowledge and is projected through the way you handle the material about which you are writing. An authoritative voice is often clear, direct, factual, and specific, leaving the impression that the writer
is confident about what he or she is saying. You can exert and project real authority only over
material you know well, whether it's the facts of your personal life or carefully researched
information. The more you know about your subject, the more clearly you will explain it,
and the more confident you will sound.

To gain control over the authority in your writing, do your homework, conduct thorough research, and read your sources of information carefully and critically.

◆ WRITING 7

Describe your own writing voice in terms of each of the elements outlined in this section (tone, style, structure, values, authority). Then compare your description with a recent paper you have written. In what ways does the paper substantiate your description?
In what ways does it differ from your description? How do you account for any differences?

THE WRITING PROCESS

The rest of this chapter identifies five discrete but overlapping and often nonsequen-
tial phases of the writing process as practiced by most serious writers—planning, composing, revising, researching, and editing—and explains how this handbook reflects this
process.

Planning consists of creating, discovering, locating, developing, organizing, and trying out ideas. Writers are doing deliberate planning when they make notes, turn casual lists
into organized outlines, write journal entries, compose rough drafts, and consult with others. They also are doing less deliberate planning while they walk, jog, eat, read, browse in
libraries, converse with friends, or wake up in the middle of the night thinking. Planning
involves both expanding and limiting options, locating the best strategy for the occasion at
hand, and focusing energy productively. Note that planning comes first, but also second
and third, for no matter how careful your first plans, the act of writing usually forces new

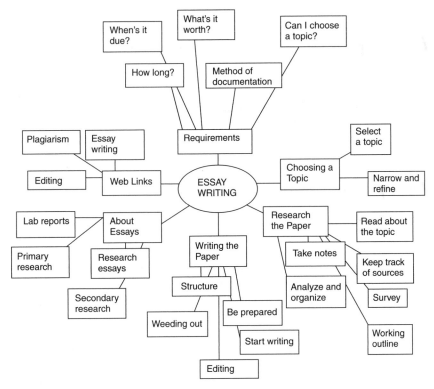

The elements of compositon

planning as you continue to think about why you are writing, what you are writing, and for whom.

Composing, as the term is used here, is the act of deliberately writing a paper with a purpose and audience in mind. It's what you do when you actually start writing a paper. First drafts are concerned with ideas, with getting the direction and concept of the piece of writing clear. Subsequent writing, which includes revising and editing, is concerned with making the initial ideas ever sharper, more precise and clearer. While most writers hope their first draft will be their final draft, it seldom is. While you try to make your early drafts as complete as possible, allow time for second and third drafts and maybe more. Sometimes it's hard to separate composing from the other stages of the writing process, so don't worry too much if they refuse to stay separate. In most serious writing, every phase of the process can be considered *recursive*—that is, moving back and forth almost simultaneously and maybe even haphazardly, from planning to revising to editing to drafting, back to planning, and so on.

Revising involves rewriting to make the purpose clearer, the argument stronger, the details sharper, the evidence more convincing, the organization more logical, the opening more inviting, the conclusion more satisfying. It helps to separate revising (sharpening ideas) from editing (sharpening sentences), yet the two tasks may not always be separable. Revising means re-seeing the drafted paper and thinking again about its direction, focus, arguments, and evidence. Revise before you edit so you don't invest time in sharpening sentences that later have to be eliminated.

Researching, like all these stages of writing, is likely to happen all the way through a serious piece of writing. The importance of research cannot be overstated: Serious writers need something to write about, and unless they are writing completely from memory, they need to locate ideas, authorities, specific information, and verifiable facts and figures. Even personal essays and experiential papers can benefit from researched information that substantiates and intensifies what the writer remembers. Whenever you write about unfamiliar subjects, you have two choices: to research and find things out, or to bluff with unsupported generalizations. Which kind of paper would you prefer to read? Which kind of writing will you profit by doing?

Editing is paying careful attention to the language used, striving for the most clarity and punch possible, trying to make a final draft say exactly what you want it to. Many writers edit partly to please themselves, so their writing sounds right to their own ears. At the same time, they edit hoping to please, satisfy, or persuade their intended readers. Careful editing means checking every word to see that it carries useful weight, every sentence to see that it follows effectively from the previous sentence and anticipates the one to follow. The last phase of editing is proofreading, to see that every word is spelled correctly and every punctuation mark is in the right place.

◆ WRITING 8

Study your own writing process as you work on one whole paper from beginning to end, taking notes in your journal to document your habits and practices. Write an analytic sketch describing the way you write and speculating about the origins of your current habits.

◆ SUGGESTIONS FOR WRITING AND RESEARCH

Individual

1. Select a topic that interests you and write about it in each of the three modes described in this chapter. First, begin with discovery writing to yourself, perhaps in a journal. Second, write a letter to communicate with somebody about this interest. Third, write creatively about it in a short poem, story, or play. Finally, describe your experience writing in these different modes.

2. Select a paper written recently for an instructor audience and explain how you would rewrite it for a publication, choosing either a student newspaper or a local magazine. Make notes about what elements should be changed: context, structure, tone, style, or purpose. Attach your revision notes to the paper and see if your instructor or classmates agree with your suggestions.

Collaborative

1. Select a topic that your whole writing group is interested in writing about. Divide your labor so that some of you do discovery writing, some do communicative writing, and some write creatively. With scissors and tape, combine your efforts into a single coherent, creative piece of college writing, making sure that some of every member's writing is included in the finished product. Perform a reading of this collage for the other groups; listen to theirs in return.

2. With your classmates, form interview pairs and identify local professional writers or professors who publish. Make an appointment with one of these practicing writers, interview him or her about the writing process he or she practices, and report back to the class. Write a collaborative report about writers in your community; make it available to other writing classes or interested faculty.

CHAPTER FIVE

Keeping Journals

Journal writing forces me to think about the problems I'm having with a paper. It's almost a relief, like talking to a friend. I have a conversation with myself and end up answering my own questions.

PETER

Journals allow people to talk to themselves without feeling silly. Writing in a journal helps college students think about what is happening in their personal and academic lives—an especially important activity for first-year students coping with a new, often bewildering and exciting environment. Sometimes students focus their journal writing narrowly, on the subject matter of a single discipline; at other times they speculate broadly, on the whole range of academic experience; at still other times they write personally, exploring their private thoughts and feelings.

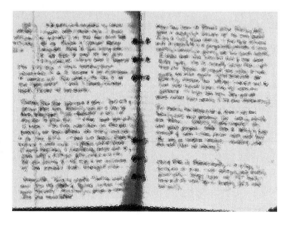

College instructors often require or recommend that students keep journals to monitor what and how they are learning. Just as often, however, students require journals of themselves, realizing that journals are useful and easy to keep whether they're handed in or not.

CHARACTERISTICS OF JOURNALS

In simplest terms, journals are daily records of people's lives (*jour* is French for "day"). Journals are sometimes called *diaries, daybooks, logs, learning logs,* or *commonplace books.* No matter what you call them, the entries written in them are likely to include whatever thoughts, feelings, activities, or plans are on your mind when you sit down to write. In this sense, a journal can be whatever you want it to be, recording whatever snippets of life you find interesting and potentially useful. Certain characteristics, however, remain true for most journals.

Sequence

You use a journal to capture your thoughts sequentially, from one day to the next, though you may not write in it every day. Over time the entries form a cumulative record of what's on your mind. Dating each entry allows you to compare ideas to later and earlier ones and provides an ongoing record of your constancy, change, or growth. You thus end up documenting your learning over the course of a semester or a project.

Audience

Journals are written to help writers rather than readers. A journal is a place to explore what's important, not to communicate information or ideas to someone else. While you may choose to share entries with readers whom you trust, that is not the reason you keep a journal. A journal assigned by an instructor who intends to read it may initiate an informal conversation between you and the instructor. As such, it has much in common with notes, letters, and other informal means of communication. Some instructors ask to see sample entries rather than read whole journals. In most cases, required journals receive credit but not specific grades.

Language

Journal writing is whatever writers want it to be. (The exception may be an assigned journal.) Your focus should be on *ideas* rather than on style, spelling, or punctuation. In journal writing, simply concentrate on what you want to say and use the word, spelling, or punctuation that comes most readily to mind.

Freedom

Journals are practice and discovery books: You can put new concepts into your own language, try out new lines of reasoning or logic, and not worry about completing every thought. If

something doesn't work the first time, you can try it again in subsequent entries—or abandon it entirely. In a journal, you always have the freedom to try again.

◆ WRITING 1

Describe your experiences or associations with journals. Have you ever kept one for
school before? In which class? With what result? Have you ever kept one on your own?
With what result? Do you still keep one? What is it like?

USING JOURNALS IN COLLEGE

Academic journals differ from diaries, daybooks, and private journals in important ways.
Whereas diaries may record any and all events of the writer's day, academic journals focus
more consistently on ideas under study in college.

Academic journals also differ in important ways from class notebooks, which record
the instructor's words rather than the writer's. Academic journals might be called "learning
logs" because they record the writer's own perceptions about the business of learning, including reactions to readings, impressions of class, and ideas for writing papers. They are
essentially a cross between private diaries and class notebooks. Like diaries, journals are
written in the first person about ideas important to the writer; like class notebooks, they focus
on a subject under study in a college course. I might diagram academic journals like this:

Diary → Academic journal ← Class notebook

Academic journals can be worthwhile in any class, because they help students become better thinkers and writers.

Journals in the Writing Class

Journals are often assigned in writing classes to help students discover, explore, advance, and
critique their specific writing projects and to help instructors monitor and informally assess
students' development as writers. In the following journal entry, John tells himself what to
do in the next draft of a paper describing his coaching of an eighth-grade girls' soccer team:

> 9/16 I'm going to try to use more dialogue in my paper. That is what I really think I
> was missing. The second draft is very dull. As I read it, it has no life. I should have
> used more detail.
>
> I'll try more dialogue, lots more, in draft #3. I'll have it take place at one of my prac-
> tices, giving a vivid description of what kids were like.
>
> I have SO MUCH MATERIAL. But I have a hard time deciding what seems more
> interesting.

John's entry is an excellent example of a writer critically evaluating himself and, on the basis
of that evaluation, making plans to change something.

Use your journal to record regularly what you are learning as you read the textbook,
participate in class discussion, read other student papers and models of good professional

writing, and review your own writing. Near the end of John's writing course, he reflected in his journal about what he'd learned so far.

> 11/29 I've learned to be very critical of my own work, to look at it again and again, looking for big and little problems. I've also learned from my writing group that other people's comments can be extremely helpful—so now I make sure I show my early drafts to Kelly or Karen before I write the final draft. I guess I've always known this, but now I actually do it.

◆ WRITING 2

Keep a journal for the duration of a writing project, recording in it all of your starts, stops, insights, and ideas related to the project. At the end, consider whether the journal presents a fair portrait of your own writing process.

Journals Across the Curriculum

Journals are good tools for learning any subject better. They are especially useful in helping you clarify the purposes of a course, pose and solve problems, keep track of readings, raise questions to ask in class, practice for exams, and find topics for paper assignments.

In science or mathematics, when you switch from numbers to words, you often see the problem differently. In addition, putting someone else's problem into your own words makes it your problem and so leads you one step further toward a solution. Ross made the following entry in a journal for a first-year biology course. He was trying to connect what he was learning in the class to what he knew from fishing.

> 10/7 I noticed that saltwater barracudas resemble freshwater pike, pickerel, and muskies. As a matter of curiosity, are these different species analogous—that is, equally successful forms but of different evolution, which converged toward similitude? Or are they of common heritage, homologous?

One of the best uses of a journal is to make connections between college knowledge and personal knowledge—each reinforces the other, and the connections often lead to greater total understanding. Once Ross finds the answer to his questions, he will be more likely to remember this information than information about which he cannot make personal connections.

When you record personal reflections in a literature or history journal, you may begin to identify with and perhaps make sense of the otherwise distant and confusing past. When you write out trial hypotheses in a social science journal, you may discover good ideas for research topics, designs, or experiments. Whether or not an instructor assigns a journal, keeping one will help you raise, reflect on, and answer your own questions in almost any course.

◆ WRITING 3

Think of a course you are taking that does not require a journal. Could you find a use for a journal in that class? What topics would you explore? Write about something in the course that you have not fully figured out. Or keep a journal for a week or two and see if it helps your understanding of the course. After doing so, consider how it worked. Did you find out something interesting? Explain.

Double-Entry Journals

A double-entry journal can help you separate initial observations from later, more reflective observations. To make such a journal, divide each page in a notebook with a vertical line down the middle. On the left side of the page, record initial impressions or data observations; on the right side, return as often as necessary to reflect on the meaning of what you first recorded.

While the idea of a double-entry journal originated in the sciences as a way for lab scientists to collect data at one time and to speculate about them later, these notebooks also serve well in other courses. In a literature class, for example, you can make initial observations about the plot of a story on the left, while raising questions and noting personal reflections on the right.

The example on page fifty-six is a sample journal entry by Susan, a first-year college student, who read Alice Walker's novel *The Color Purple* for the first time. In the left column, she recorded the plot; in the right column, she noted her personal reaction to what she was reading.

Susan took such careful notes in a double-entry journal because she intended to write an interpretive paper about the novel. You can see the value of a reader monitoring his or her reactions with such care, even noting which pages raise which questions. When Susan wrote her paper, these journal entries helped her to find a thesis and to locate particular passages in the novel to support her thesis.

◆ WRITING 4

Keep a double-entry journal for two weeks. On one side of the page, include notes from books you are reading or lectures you are attending. On the other side, write your own thoughts or reactions to those notes. At the end of two weeks, assess the value of this technique for your own understanding of the course material.

Personal Journals

In personal journals writers can explore their feelings about any aspect of their lives—being in college, prospective majors, getting along with a roommate, the frustration of receiving a low grade on a paper, the weekend party, or a new date. Anne, a student in a first-year writing class, put it this way:

Writing is a release, a way of expressing myself, and a way for me to be introspective. It helps me find meaning in my thoughts and gets me through hard times.

When you keep a journal in a writing class, it's a good idea to mark off a section for personal entries. Whether you share these with your instructor should be your choice. In the following example, Amy was writing more about herself than her writing class; however, she chose to share the entry with her instructor anyway.

11/12 I think I should quit complaining about being misunderstood . . . since I don't try very hard to be understandable, it's no wonder people get confused. I just get ticked because more people don't even seem to try to understand others. So many people talk instead of listening. (I think I'm scared of the ones who listen.)

◆ WRITING 5

Keep a personal journal for two weeks, writing faithfully for at least ten minutes each day. Write about your friends, family, future, work, money, frustrations, successes, failures, plans, dates, movies—whatever is on your mind. After two weeks, reread all of your entries and assess the value of such a journal to you.

EXPERIMENTING WITH JOURNALS

If you are keeping a journal for the first time, write often and regularly on a wide variety of topics, and take risks with form, style, and voice. Notice how writing in the early morning differs from writing late at night. Notice the results of writing at the same time every day, regardless of inclination or mood. Try to develop the habit of using your journal even when you are not in an academic environment. Good ideas, questions, and answers don't always wait for convenient times. Above all, write in your journal in your most comfortable voice, freely, and don't worry about someone evaluating you. The following selection of journal entries illustrates some of the ways journals can be especially helpful.

Inventing

Journals can help you plan and start any project by providing a place to talk it over with yourself. Whether it's a research paper, a personal essay, or a take-home exam, you can make journal notes about how to approach a project, where to start, or whom to consult before beginning a draft. Here are two entries from Peter's journal in which he tried to discover a research paper topic for his first-year writing class:

10/8 The first draft of this research paper is really difficult: how can you write about something you aren't even interested in? It was not a good idea to pick "legalization of marijuana" just because the issue came up in class discussion. I'm afraid my paper will be all opinion and no facts, because I really don't feel like digging for these facts—if there are any.

10/12 Well, I switched my research topic to something I'm actually interested in, a handicapped children's rehabilitation program right here on campus. My younger brother was born deaf and our whole family has pitched in to help him—but I've

Summary	What I think
pp. 3–12. Celie's mother is dying so her father starts having sex with her. She got pregnant by him twice, and he sold both of her babies.	Why did Celie's father sell her kids?
Celie's mother died and he got married again to a very young girl.	How could Mr. take Celie if he wanted Nettie so much?
Mr. is a man whose wife died and he has a lot of children. He wants to marry Celie's sister Nettie. Their father won't let him.	I think Celie's father is lowdown and selfish. A very cruel man.
He says Nettie has too much going for her so he lets him have Celie.	
pp. 13–23. Celie got married to Mr., and his kids don't like her. While Celie was in town she met the lady who has her kids. She was a preacher's wife. Nettie ran away and came to stay with Celie. Mr. still likes her and puts her out because she shows no interest in him. Celie tells her to go to the preacher's wife's house and stay with them because she was the only woman she saw with money.	I think it's wrong to marry someone to take care of your children and to keep your home clean.

I think Celie was at least glad to know one of her children was in good hands.

I am glad Nettie was able to get away from her Dad and Mr., hopefully the preacher & wife will take her in. |
| pp. 24–32. Shug Avery, Mr.'s old friend and also an entertainer, came to town. Mr. got all dressed up so he could go see her, he stayed gone all weekend. Celie was very excited about her. | How could he go and stay out with another woman all weekend? Why didn't he marry Shug?

Why was Celie so fascinated with Shug? |

Sample Page from Double-Entry Journal

never really studied what a college program could do to help. The basis of my research will be interviews with people who run the program—I have my first appointment tomorrow with Professor Stanford.

Sometimes planning means venting frustration about what's going wrong; at other times it means trying a new direction or topic. Peter does both. Journal writing is ultimately unpredictable: your writing doesn't come out neat and orderly, and sometimes it doesn't solve your problem, but your journal provides a place where you can keep trying.

Learning to Write

Part of the content of a writing course is the business of learning to write. In other courses, part of the content is learning to write papers about specific topics. You can use a journal to document how your writing is going and what you need to do to improve it. In the following example, Bruce reflects on his experience of writing a report:

> 10/3 I'm making this report a lot harder than it should be. I think my problem is I try to edit as I write. I think what I need to do is just write whatever I want. After I'm through, then edit and organize. It's hard for me though.

Bruce chastises himself for making his writing harder than need be but at the same time reminds himself about the process he learned in class that would help his report writing. Journals are good places to monitor your own writing process and document what helps you the most.

Writing to Learn

Journal writing can help you discover what you think. The act of regular writing clarifies thoughts and even causes new ones to develop. In that sense, journal writing is strategy for starting in new directions (see Chapter 6). In the following example, Julie, who kept a journal about all the authors she studied in her American literature course, noticed a disturbing pattern and wrote in her journal to make some sense of it:

> 5/4 So far, the first two authors we have to read have led tragic, unhappy lives. I wonder if this is just a coincidence or if it has something to do with the personality of successful writers. Actually, of all people, writers need a lot of time alone, by themselves, thinking and writing, away from other people, including, probably, close family members. The more I think about it, writers would be very difficult people to live with, that's it—writers spend so much time alone and become hard to live with. . . .

Julie used the act of regular journal writing to discover and develop ideas, make interpretations, and test hypotheses. Writing to learn requires you to trust that as you write, ideas will come—some right, some wrong; some good, some bad.

Questioning and Answering

A journal is a place to raise questions about ideas or issues that don't make sense. Raising questions is a fundamental part of all learning: The more you ask, the more you learn as you seek answers. In the following example, Jim wrote in his journal to figure out a quotation written on the blackboard in his technical writing class:

> 9/23 "All Writing Is Persuasive"—It's hard to write on my understanding of this quotation because I don't think that all writing is persuasive. What about assemblies for models and cookbook recipes? I realize that for stories, newspaper articles, novels, and so forth that they are persuasive. But is all writing persuasive? I imagine that for assemblies and so forth that they are persuading a person to do something a particular way. But is this really persuasive writing?

While Jim began by writing "I don't think that all writing is persuasive," he concluded that even assembly instructions "are persuading a person to do something a particular way." The writing sharpened the focus of Jim's questioning and made him critically examine his own ideas, leading him to reconsider his first response to the quotation.

Catching Insights

College is a good place to develop a wider awareness of the world, and a journal can help you examine the social and political climate you grew up in and perhaps took for granted. Jennifer used her journal to reflect on sexist language, recording both her awareness of sexist language in society as well as her own difficulty in avoiding it:

> 3/8 Sexist language is everywhere. So much so that people don't even realize what they are saying is sexist. My teacher last year told all the "mothers-to-be" to be sure to read to their children. What about the fathers? Sexist language is dangerous because it so easily undermines women's morale and self-image. I try my hardest not to use sexist language, but even I find myself falling into old stereotypes.

Evaluating Classes

Journals can be used to capture and record feelings about how a class is going, about what you are learning and not learning. In the following entry, Brian seemed surprised that writing can be fun:

> 9/28 English now is more fun. When I write, the words come out more easily and it's not like homework. All my drafts help me put together my thoughts and retrieve memories that were hidden somewhere in the dungeons of my mind. Usually I wouldn't like English, like in high school, but I pretty much enjoy it here. I like how you get to hear people's reactions to your papers and discuss them with each other.

Entries like this can help you monitor your own learning process. Instructors also learn from candid and freely given comments about the effects of their teaching. Your journal is one place where you can let your instructor know what is happening in class from your point of view.

Clarifying Values

Your journal can be a record of evolving insight as well as the tool to gain that insight. You might ask yourself questions that force you to examine life closely: "If my house were on fire and I could save only one object, what would it be?" or "If I had only two more days to live, how would I spend them?" I used my journal to wrestle with the next direction my life would take:

> 3/12 Do I really want to switch jobs and move to North Carolina? The climate is warmer—a lot longer motorcycle season—and maybe this time we'd look for a farm. But Laura would have to start all over with her job, finding new contacts in the public school system, and we'd both have to find new friends, new doctors, dentists, auto mechanics, get new driver's licenses.
>
> In truth, we really like Vermont, the size, the scale, the beauty, our house, and Annie is just starting college. Money and sunshine aren't everything. . . .

What you read here is only one entry from nearly a month's worth of writing as I tried to figure out what to do with an attractive job offer. In the end, and with the clarifying help of my journal, I stayed put.

Letting Off Steam

Journals are good places to vent frustration over personal or academic difficulties. College instructors don't assign journals to improve students' mental health, but they know that journals can help. Kenyon wrote about the value of the journal experience:

> 10/14 This journal has saved my sanity. It got me started at writing. . . . I can't keep all my problems locked up inside me, but I hate telling others, burdening them with my problems—like what I'm going to do with my major or with the rest of my life.

In many ways, writing in a journal is like talking to a sympathetic audience; the difference, as Kenyon noted, is that the journal is always there, no matter what's on your mind, and it never gives you grief.

Finding Patterns

The very nature of the journal—sequential, chronological, personal—lends it to synthesizing activities, such as finding patterns or larger structures in your learning over time. Rereading journal entries after a few weeks or months can provide specific material from which you can make generalizations and hypotheses. Each individual act of summary becomes a potential thread for weaving new patterns of meaning. Near the end of an American literature course, Maureen summarized the journal's cumulative power this way:

> 5/2 I feel that through the use of this journal over the weeks I have been able to understand certain aspects of each story by actually writing down what I like, and what I don't. . . . Many times I didn't even realize that something bothered me about a story until I put down my feelings in words. I wasn't even sure how I even felt about *The Sun Also Rises* until I kicked a few ideas around on paper. Now I plan to write my take-home exam about it. In short, this journal has really helped me understand this class.

Recording Change

Sometimes it's hard to see how a journal functions overall until you reread it at the end of a term and notice where you began and where you ended. All along your writing may have been casual and fast, your thoughts tentative, your assessments or conclusions uncertain. But the journal gives you a record of who you were, what you thought, and how you changed. Rereading a term's entries may be a pleasant surprise, as Jeff found out:

> 11/21 The journal to me has been like a one-man debate, where I could write thoughts down and then later read them. This seemed to help clarify many of my ideas. To be honest there is probably fifty percent of the journal that is nothing but B.S. and ramblings to fulfill assignments, but that still leaves fifty percent that I think is of importance. The journal is also a time capsule. I want to put it away and not look at it for ten or twenty years and let it recall for me this period of my life.

LETTERS FROM JOURNALS

Sometimes, instead of turning in your journal for an instructor to check, you will be asked to write a class letter to your instructor, addressing him or her personally, about issues related to the course—perhaps issues captured in your journal. What I like about this use of journals is that all your thoughts and insights remain private unless you choose to share them with a specific and known audience. An audience is the only real difference between a class letter and a journal entry—the former written to someone else, the latter to yourself.

As an instructor, I appreciate getting letters that are informal, personal, honest, and that contain some references to and insights about course materials: readings, class discussion, subject matter. In other words, I enjoy hearing from my own students about all the ideas for journal writing already explored in this chapter, the only difference being that these are intentionally shared with me. If you are asked to share letters with an instructor, consider the following:

1. Address your instructor personally, including references to common experience or shared ideas, single-space, and sign your name.
2. Focus on course ideas rather than your private life, but include incidents from your private life when they are relevant to course material.
3. Avoid being overly general: Include references to specific passages in the readings or specific incidents in the class.
4. Ask real questions or pose real problems that you hope to have answered.
5. Write informally, in your natural voice, but revise and edit enough so that your language is clear and coherent.

When I receive letters, I either write back a single letter to the whole class, quoting passages from different students so the whole class can be brought into the conversation, or I write brief responses on each letter and return every letter to the sender. I count the letters as I do journals, quantitatively: Students get credit for simply doing them, not grades on specific content.

Increasingly, my students and I share e-mail messages, which is a wonderfully quick and efficient way of conversing about specific ideas, questions, or problems related to the course. E-mail writing may resemble journal writing in that it is usually informal and unrevised; however, like talking on the telephone and writing letters, the addition of a specific audience means that even this most informal language needs to be clear, correct, and respectful. A loose version of the guidelines above would cover e-mail writing as well.

◆ SUGGESTIONS FOR WRITING AND RESEARCH

Individual

1. Select a writer in your intended major who is known for having written a journal (for example, Mary Shelley, Ralph Waldo Emerson, Virginia Woolf, or Anaïs Nin in literature; Leonardo da Vinci, Georgia O'Keeffe, or Edward Weston in the arts; B. F. Skinner or Margaret Mead in the social sciences; Charles Darwin or Marie Curie in the sciences). Study the writer's journals to identify the features that characterize them and the purpose they served. Write a report on what you find and share it with your class.

2. At the end of the semester, review your journal and do the following: (a) put in page numbers, (b) write a title for each entry, (c) make a table of contents, and (d) write an introduction to the journal explaining how it might be read by a stranger (or your instructor).

3. Review your journal entries for the past five weeks, select one entry that seems especially interesting, and write a reflective essay of several pages on it. How are they different? Which is better? Is that a fair question?

Collaborative

Have each student agree to bring a typed copy of one journal entry written during the term. Exchange entries in writing groups or in the whole class and discuss interesting features of the entries.

CHAPTER SIX

Strategies for Starting

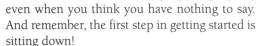

Get something down! The hardest part of writing is starting. Forget the introduction, skip the outline, don't worry about a thesis—just blast your ideas down, see what you've got, then go back more slowly and work on them.

AARON

Good writing depends on good ideas. When ideas don't come easily or naturally, writers need techniques for finding or creating them. Writers need to invent new ideas or discover old ones at all phases of the writing process, from finding and developing a topic to narrowing an argument and searching for good evidence. And knowing how to invent and discover ideas when none seems apparent is also the best antidote for writer's block, helping you get going

even when you think you have nothing to say. And remember, the first step in getting started is sitting down!

The main premise behind the techniques discussed in this chapter is "the more you write, the more you think." Language begets more language, and more language begets ideas, and ideas beget still more ideas. Virtually all writers have had the experience of starting to write in one direction and ending up in another; as they wrote, their writing moved their thinking in new directions—a powerful, messy, but ultimately positive experience and a good demonstration that the act of writing itself generates and modifies ideas. This occurs because writing lets people see their own ideas, and doing that, in turn, allows them to change those ideas. This chapter suggests ways to harness the creative power of language and make it work for you.

◆ WRITING 1

Describe the procedures you usually use to start writing a paper. Where do you get the ideas—from speaking? listening? reading? writing? Do you do anything special to help them come? What do you do when ideas don't come?

BRAINSTORMING

Brainstorming is systematic list making. You ask yourself a question and then list as many answers as you can think of. The point is to get lots of possible ideas on paper to examine and review. Sometimes you can do this best by setting goals for yourself: What are five possible topics for a paper on campus issues?

1. Overcrowding in campus dormitories
2. Prohibiting cars for first-year students
3. Date rape
4. Multiculturalism and the curriculum
5. Attitudes toward alcohol on campus

Sometimes you can brainstorm best by leaving the question open-ended: What do you already know about multiculturalism and the curriculum that interests you?

Racial diversity high among campus students
Racial diversity low among faculty
Old curriculum dominated by white male agenda
New curriculum dominated by young feminist agenda
How to avoid simplistic stereotypes such as those I've just written?

In making such lists, jotting down one item often triggers the next, as is seen above. Each item becomes a possible direction for your paper. By challenging yourself to generate a long list, you force yourself to find and record even vague ideas in concrete language, where you can examine them and decide whether or not they're worth further development.

FREEWRITING

Freewriting is fast writing. You write rapidly, depending on one word to trigger the next, one idea to lead to another, without worrying about conventions or correctness. Freewriting helps you find a focus by writing nonstop and not censoring the words and ideas before you have a chance to look at them. Try the following suggestions for freewriting:

1. Write as fast as you can about an idea for a fixed period of time, say five or ten minutes.
2. Do not stop writing until the time is up.

3. Don't worry about what your writing looks like or how it's organized; the only audience for this writing is yourself.

If you digress in your freewriting, fine. If you misspell a word or write something silly, fine. If you catch a fleeting thought that's especially interesting, good. If you think of something you've never thought of before, wonderful. And if nothing interesting comes out—well, maybe next time. The following five-minute freewrite shows John's attempt to find a topic for a local research project:

> I can't think of anything special just now, nothing really comes to mind, well maybe something about the downtown mall would be good because I wouldn't mind spending time down there. Something about the mall . . . maybe the street vendors, the hot dog guy or the pretzel guy or that woman selling T and sweatshirts, they're always there, even in lousy weather—do they like it that much? Actually, all winter. Do they need the money that bad? Why do people become street vendors—like maybe they graduated from college and couldn't get jobs? Or were these the guys who never wanted anything to do with college?

John's freewrite is typical: He starts with no ideas, but his writing soon leads to some. This kind of writing needs to be free, unstructured, and digressive to allow the writer to find thoughts wherever they occur. For John, this exercise turned out to be a useful one, since he ultimately wrote a paper about "the hot dog man," a street vendor.

LOOP WRITING

Loop writing is a sequenced set of freewrites. Each freewrite focuses on one idea from the previous freewrite and expands it. To loop, follow this procedure:

1. Freewrite for ten minutes to discover a topic or to advance the one you are working on.
2. Review your freewrite and select one sentence closest to what you want to continue developing. Copy this sentence, and take off from it, freewriting for another ten minutes. (John might have selected "Why do people become street vendors?" for further freewriting.)
3. Repeat step 2 for each successive freewrite to keep inventing and discovering.

ASKING REPORTERS' QUESTIONS

Writers who train themselves to ask questions are training themselves to find information. Reporters ask six basic questions about every news story they write: Who? What? Where? When? Why? and How? Following this set of questions leads reporters to new information and more complete stories.

1. Who or what is involved? (a person, character, or thesis)
2. What happened? (an event, action, or assertion)
3. Where did this happen? (a place, text, or context)
4. When did it happen? (a date or relationship)
5. Why did it happen? (a reason, cause, or explanation)
6. How did it happen? (a method, procedure, or action)

While these questions seem especially appropriate for reporting an event, the questions can be modified to investigate any topic:

What is my central idea?
What happens to it?
Where do I make my main point? On what page?
Are my reasons ample and documented?
How does my strategy work?

OUTLINING

Outlines are, essentially, organized lists. In fact, outlines grow out of lists, as writers determine which ideas go first, which later; which are main, which subordinate. Formal outlines use a system of Roman numerals, capital letters, Arabic numerals, and lowercase letters to create a hierarchy of ideas. Some writers prefer informal outlines, using indentations to indicate relationships between ideas.

When Carol set out to write a research essay on the effect of acid rain on the environment in New England, she first brainstormed a random list of areas that such an essay might cover.

What is acid rain?
What are its effects on the environment?
What causes it?
How can it be stopped?

After preliminary research, Carol produced this outline:

I. Definition of acid rain
II. The causes of acid rain
    A. Coal-burning power plants
    B. Automobile pollution
III. The effects of acid rain
    A. Deforestation in New England
        1. The White Mountain study
        2. Maple trees dying in Vermont
    B. Dead lakes

Note how Carol rearranged the second and third items in her original list to talk about causes before effects. The very act of making the outline encouraged her to invent a structure for her ideas. Moving entries around is especially easy if you are using a computer, because you can see many combinations before committing yourself to any one of them. The rules of formal outlining also cause you to search for ideas: If you have a Roman numeral I, you need a II; if you have an A, you need a B. Carol thought first of coal-burning power plants as a cause, then brainstormed to come up with another source of pollution.

Writing outlines is generative: In addition to recording your original thoughts, outlines actually generate new thoughts. Outlines are most useful if you modify them as you write in accordance with new thoughts or information.

CLUSTERING

A *clustering diagram* is a method of listing ideas visually to reveal their relationships. Clustering is useful both for inventing and discovering a topic and for exploring a topic once you have done preliminary research. To use clustering, follow this procedure:

1. Write a word or phrase that seems to be the focus of what you want to write about. (Carol wrote down *acid rain.*)
2. Write ideas related to your focus in a circle around the central phrase and connect them to the focus phrase. If one of the ideas suggests others related to it, write those in a circle around it. (Carol did this with her idea *solutions.*)

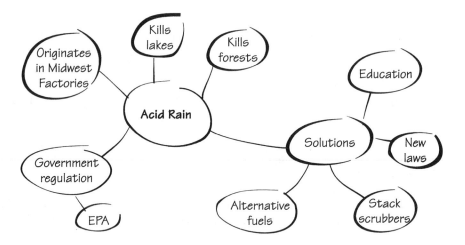

3. If one idea (such as *solutions*) begins to accumulate related ideas, start a second cluster with the new term in the center of your paper.

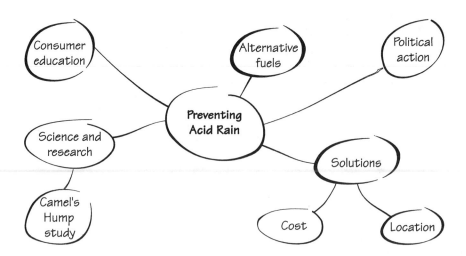

STARTING A DIALOGUE

One of the most powerful invention techniques is talking to a partner with the deliberate intention of helping each other find ideas. The directions are simple: Sit across from each other for five or ten minutes and talk about possible topics or approaches or ways of finding sources. It doesn't matter who starts or finishes, since the principle at work here is that oral language, like written language, begets ideas. At some point it will be helpful to write down what you are talking about so that you have a record to return to.

You can also start a deliberate dialogue by writing back and forth with a classmate. Each of you starts by posing a problem to solve; the other responds by offering a solution. Continue to exchange ideas, each time pushing harder to solve your classmate's problem as well as your own.

Suggestions for Invention and Discovery

1. Brainstorm a list of five possible topics to write about.
2. Freewrite for ten minutes about the most interesting topic on your list.
3. Loop back in your freewriting, selecting the most interesting or useful point, and freewrite again with that point as the focus.
4. Ask the reporter's questions about the topic.
5. Make an outline of a possible structure for your paper.
6. Cluster ideas about your topic; then cluster on a related idea that occurs during the initial clustering.
7. Talk with a partner for seven minutes; take turns helping each other find or advance one idea, seeing how fast you can go.

◆ WRITING 2

Pose a writing problem and try to solve it using at least three of the invention strategies described in this chapter. Which seems most helpful? If you still have a problem to solve, try several of the other techniques and see if they help.

◆ SUGGESTIONS FOR WRITING AND RESEARCH

Individual

Explain your own most useful invention technique for finding ideas. Explain your technique and support it with samples from your earlier papers. Give clear directions to teach other writers how to use it.

Collaborative

Find a common writing topic by having each person in the group or class select one of the invention and discovery techniques described in this chapter and practice using it for ten minutes. Make a collective list of the topic ideas generated this way. Then ask each individual to select one topic and write for another five minutes. Again make a list of topics and the important ideas generated about them. Discuss the ideas together and try to arrive at a consensus on a common writing topic.

CHAPTER SEVEN

Sharing and Responding

Listening to other people's criticism is really helpful, especially when they stop being too nice and really tell you what they think about your paper.

KELLY

All writing profits from help. Most published writing has been shared, talked over, revised, and edited by others somewhere along the way to make it as readable, precise, and interesting as it is. The published writing you read in books, magazines, and newspapers that is signed by individual authors is seldom the result of either one-draft writing or one-person work. This is not to say that authors do not write their own work. But even the best of writers begin, draft, and revise better when they receive suggestions from friends, editors, reviewers, teachers, and critics. This chapter explores specific ways to ask for help with your own writing as well as to provide it to others.

SHARING YOUR WRITING

Writers can ask for help at virtually all stages of the writing process. Sometimes they try out ideas on friends and colleagues while they are still planning or drafting. More often, however, writers ask for help while they are revising, as they try to make their ideas coherent and convincing, and while they are editing, as they try to make their language clear and precise. In addition, when a draft is nearly final, many writers ask for proofreading help, since most writers are their own worst proofreaders. Here are some suggestions for getting good help as you revise your writing.

Specify what you want. When you share a draft with a reader, specify what kind of help you are looking for. If you consider your draft nearly finished and want only a quick proofreading, it can be very frustrating if your reader suggests major changes you do not have time for or interest in. Likewise, if you share an early draft and want help organizing and clarifying ideas because you intend to do major rewriting, it is annoying to have your paper returned with sentences edited for wordiness, misspellings, and typographical errors. You can usually head off such undesirable responses by being clear about exactly what kind of help you want. If you do want a general reaction, say so, but be prepared to hear about everything and anything.

Ask specific questions. Tell your reader exactly what kinds of comments will help you most. If you wonder whether you've provided enough examples, ask about that. If you want to know whether your argument is airtight, ask about that. If you are concerned about style or tone, ask about that. Also mark in the margins your specific concerns about an idea, a phrase, a sentence, a conclusion, or even a title.

Ask global questions. If you are concerned about larger matters, make sure you identify what these are. Ask whether the reader understands and can identify your thesis. Ask whether the larger purpose is clear. Ask whether the paper seems right for its intended audience. Ask for general reactions about readability, style, evidence, and completeness. Ask whether your reader can anticipate any objections or problems other readers may have.

Don't be defensive. Whether you receive responses about your paper orally or in writing, pay close attention to them. You have asked somebody to spend time with your writing, so you should trust that that person is trying to be helpful, that he or she is commenting on your paper, not on you personally. While receiving oral comments, stay quiet, listen, and take notes about what you hear, interrupting only to ask for clarity, not to defend what your reader is commenting on. Remember, a first draft may contain information and ideas that are clear to you; what you want to hear is where they are less clear to someone else.

Maintain ownership. If you receive responses that you do not agree with or that you consider unhelpful, do not feel obliged to heed them. It is your paper; you are the ultimate judge of whether the ideas in it represent you. You will have to live with the results; you may, in fact, be judged by the results. Never include someone else's idea in your paper if you do not understand it or believe it.

◆ WRITING 1

Describe the best response to a piece of your writing that you remember. How old were you? What were the circumstances? Who was the respondent? Explain whether you think the response was deserved or not.

GIVING HELPFUL RESPONSES

When you are asked to respond to other writers' work, keep these basic ideas in mind.

Follow the golden rule. Give the kind of response to others' writing that you would like to receive on your own. Remember how you feel being praised, criticized, or questioned. Remember what comments help advance your own papers as well as comments that only make you defensive. Keeping those in mind will help you help others.

Attend to the text, not the person. Word your comments so that the writer knows you are commenting on his or her writing and not his or her person. Writers, like all people, have egos that can be bruised with careless or cruel comments. Attending to the text itself helps you avoid these problems. Point out language constructions that create pleasure as well as those that create confusion, but avoid commenting on the personality or intelligence of the writer.

Praise what deserves praise. Tell the writer what is good about the paper as well as what is not good. All writers will more easily accept critical help with weaknesses if you also acknowledge strengths. But avoid praising language or ideas that do not, in your opinion, deserve it. Writers can usually sense praise that is not genuine.

Ask questions rather than give advice. Ask questions more often than you give suggestions. You need to respect that the writing is the writer's. If you ask questions, you give the writer room to solve problems on his or her own. Of course, sometimes it is very helpful to give advice or to suggest alternatives when they occur to you. Use your judgment about when to ask questions and when to provide solutions.

Focus on major problems first. If you find a lot of problems with a draft, try to focus first on the major problems (which are usually conceptual), and let the minor ones (which are usually linguistic and stylistic) go until sometime later. Drafts that are too marked up with suggestions can overwhelm writers, making them reluctant to return to the job of rewriting.

◆ WRITING 2

What kind of response do you usually give to a writer when you read his or her paper? How do you know what to comment on? How have your comments been received?

RESPONDING IN WRITING

The most common written responses college students receive are those that instructors make in the margins or at the end of a paper, usually explaining how they graded the paper. Many of these comments—except the grade—are similar to those made by professional editors on manuscripts. In writing classes you will commonly be asked by classmates to read and write comments on their papers. Here are some suggestions to help you do that:

Use a pencil. Many writers have developed negative associations from teachers covering their writing in red ink, primarily to correct what's wrong rather than to praise what's right. If you comment with pencil, the message to the writer is more gentle—in fact, erasable—and suggests the comments of a colleague rather than the judgments of a grader.

Use clear symbols. If you like, you can use professional editing symbols to comment on a classmate's paper. Or you can use other symbols that any writer can figure out. For example, underline words or sentences that puzzle you and put a question mark next to them. Put brackets where a missing word or phrase belongs or around a word or phrase that could be deleted. Circle misspellings.

There are many advantages to written responses. First, writing your comments takes less time and is therefore more efficient than discussing your ideas orally. Second, written comments are usually very specific, identifying particular sentences, paragraphs, or examples that need further thought. Third, written comments leave a record to which the writer can refer later—after days, weeks, and even months—when he or she gets around to revising.

There are also disadvantages to writing comments directly on papers. First, written comments may invite misunderstandings that the respondent is not present to help clarify. Second, written comments that are too blunt may damage a writer's ego—and it's easier to unintentionally make such comments in writing than face to face. Third, written comments do not allow the writer and reader to clear up simple questions quickly and so risk allowing misinterpretations to persist.

◆ WRITING 3

Describe your most recent experience in receiving written comments from a reader. Were the comments helpful? Did the respondent use an approach similar to that detailed in this section or some other approach? In either case, were the reader's comments helpful?

RESPONDING THROUGH CONFERENCES

One-to-one conferences provide the best and most immediate help that writers can get. Sitting together, a reader and a writer can look at a paper together, read passages aloud, and ask both general and specific questions about the writing: "What do you want to leave me with at the end?" or "Read that again, there's something about that rhythm that's especially strong" or "Stop. Right there I could really use an example to see what you mean." Often an oral conference helps as a follow-up to written comments.

The suggestions for making effective written responses in the previous section also apply to oral conferences. In addition, here are a few other things to keep in mind:

Relax. Having your conference in a comfortable place can go a long way toward creating a friendly, satisfying discussion. Don't be afraid of digressions. Very often a discussion about a piece of writing branches into a discussion about the subject of the paper instead of the paper itself. When that happens, both writer and reader learn new things about the subject and about each other, some of which will certainly help the writer. Of course, if the paper is not discussed specifically, the writer may not be helped at all.

Ask questions. If you are the reader, ask follow-up questions to help the writer move farther faster in his or her revising. If you have written your responses first, the conference can be a series of follow-up questions, and together you can search for solutions.

Listen. If you are the writer, remember that the more you listen and the less you talk, the more you will learn about your writing. Listen attentively. When puzzled, ask questions; when uncertain, clarify misunderstanding. But keep in mind that your reader is not your enemy and that you and your work are not under attack, so you do not need to be defensive. If you prefer the battle metaphor, look at it this way: Good work will defend itself.

One advantage of one-to-one conferences is that they promote community, friendship, and understanding between writer and reader. Also, conferences can address both global and specific writing concerns at the same time. In addition, conferences allow both writer and reader to ask questions as they occur and to pursue any line of thought until both parties are satisfied with it. And finally, writer and reader can use their facial expressions, body language, and oral intonation to clarify misunderstandings as soon as they arise.

There are, however, a few disadvantages to one-on-one conferences. First, it is harder to make tough, critical comments face to face, so readers are often less candid than when they write comments. Second, conferring together in any depth about a piece of writing takes more time than communicating through written responses.

◆ WRITING 4

Confer with a writer about his or her paper, using some of the techniques suggested in this section. Describe in a journal entry how each technique worked.

RESPONDING IN WRITING GROUPS

Writing groups provide a way for writers both to give and receive help. When the group considers a particular writer's work, that writer receives multiple responses; the writer is also one respondent among several when another writer's work is considered.

All of the suggestions in previous sections about responding to writing apply, with appropriate modifications, to responding in writing groups. But writing groups involve more people, require more coordination, take more time, and, for many people, are less familiar. Here are some guidelines for organizing writing groups:

Form a group along common interests. Most commonly, writing groups are formed among classmates, often with the instructor's help, and everyone is working on the same or similar class assignments. Membership in a group may remain fixed over a semester, and members may meet every week or two. Or membership may change with every new assignment. Writing groups can also be created outside of class by interested people who get together regularly to share their writing.

Focus on the writing. The general idea for all writing groups is much the same: to improve one another's writing and encourage one another to do more of it. Writers pass out copies of their writing in advance or read it aloud during the group meeting. After members have read or heard the paper, they share, usually orally but sometimes in writing, their reactions to it.

Make your group the right size for your purpose. Writing groups can be as small as three or as large as a dozen. If all members are to participate, smaller groups need less time than larger groups and provide more attention to each member. Groups that meet outside of classroom constraints have more freedom to set size and time limits, but more than a dozen members will make it hard for each member to receive individual attention and will require several hours, which may be too long to sustain constructive group efforts.

Appoint a timekeeper. Sometimes group meetings are organized so that each member reads a paper or a portion of a paper. At other times a group meeting focuses on the work of only one member, and members thus take turns receiving responses. If papers are to be read aloud, keep in mind that it generally takes two minutes to read a typed, double-spaced page out loud. Discussion time should at least match the oral reading time for each paper. If group members are able to read the papers before the meeting, length is not as critical an issue because group time can be devoted strictly to discussion. Independently formed groups can experiment to determine how much they can read and discuss at each session, perhaps varying the schedule from meeting to meeting.

There are many advantages to discussing writing in groups. First, writing groups allow a single writer to hear multiple perspectives on his or her writing. Second, writing groups allow an interpretation or consensus to develop through the interplay of those perspectives; the result can be a cumulative response that existed in no single reader's mind before the session. Third, writing groups can give both writers and readers more confidence by providing each with a varied and supportive audience. Fourth, writing groups can develop friendships and a sense of community among writers that act as healthy stimuli for continuing to write.

One disadvantage is that groups meeting outside of class can be difficult to coordinate, set up, and operate, as they involve people with varied schedules. Also, at the outset, the multiple audiences provided by groups may be more intimidating and threatening to a writer than a single person responding.

♦ WRITING 5

Imagine a writing group you would like to belong to. What subjects would you write about? Whom would you invite to join your group? How often and where would you like to meet? Explain in a journal entry why you would or would not join a writing group voluntarily.

RESPONDING ELECTRONICALLY

In the event that you respond to classmates' papers via e-mail or by using the Web, you usually have two choices for response: (1) to mark the text itself with internal comments (using boldface type, italics, capital letters, or colors to distinguish your comments) and send it back, or (2) to send back a written response only, in which you generalize about the language in the text and your response. As an instructor, I have done both, depending on the time and circumstances. Here is what I might suggest:

- When you read classmates' discovery drafts, freewrites, and early drafts, send back summary responses with your reactions to the paper as a whole—what aspects are strong, where you have questions, and so on. Don't mark up the text itself to send back, since at the early stages, writers need to attend to the larger idea level of their texts and not so much to the specific language of sentences and paragraphs.
- When you read later drafts, it may be more helpful—so long as it is convenient and you have the time—to mark up the text itself with your questions and suggestions about specific paragraphs or sentences.

◆ SUGGESTIONS FOR WRITING AND RESEARCH

Individual

Recently a large body of literature has developed concerning the nature, types, and benefits of peer responses in writing. Go to the library and see what you can find about writing groups or peer response groups. Check, in particular, for work by Patricia Belanoff, Kenneth Bruffee, Peter Elbow, Anne Ruggles Gere, Thom Hawkins, and Tori Haring-Smith. Write a report to inform your classmates about your discoveries.

Collaborative

Form interview pairs and interview local published writers about the ways in which responses by friends, family, editors, or critics affect their writing. Share results orally or by publishing a short pamphlet.

CHAPTER EIGHT

Reflecting on Experience

Writing allows me to hold up a mirror to my life and see what clear or distorted images stare back at me.

Rick

Good stories occur everywhere and can be told about anything. They are as likely to occur in your own neighborhood as in some exotic locale. Potential stories happen daily; what makes potential stories actual stories is putting them into language, recounting them, orally or in writing. Good stories are entertaining, informative, lively, and believable; they will mean something to those who write them and to those who read them.

All stories, whether they're imagined (fiction) or true (nonfiction), are accounts of something that *happened*—an event or series of events, after which something or somebody is changed. Whether the story is "The Three Little Pigs" or *The Adventures of Huckleberry Finn* (both fiction), or Darwin's *The Voyage of the Beagle* or an account of your own canoe trip (nonfiction), it includes the following elements: a character (*who?*) to whom something happens (*what?*), in some place (*where?*), at some time (*when?*), for some reason (*why?*), told from a particular perspective (*how?*). In other words, any time you render a full account of a personal experience, you answer what we called "reporter's questions" in the previous chapter— the who, what, where, when, why, and how questions reporters ask themselves to make sure their reports of news stories are complete. Whether your story is engaging or not depends upon the subject, your interest in telling it, and the skill with which you weave together these story elements.

CHARACTER (WHO)

In personal experience writing, your main character is yourself, so try to give your readers a sense of who you are through your voice, actions, level of awareness, and description. The characters in a good story are believable and interesting; they come alive for readers. Study the elements that give life to characters in your story: voice, actions, insight, and detail.

Voice

In your own story, your language reveals who you are—playful, serious, rigid, loose, stuffy, honest, warm, or whatever. In the following excerpt, in which Beth relates her experience playing oboe during a two-hour Saturday morning orchestra rehearsal, we learn she's serious, fun-loving, impish, and just a little lazy:

> I love that section. It sounds so cool when Sarah and I play together like that. Now I can put my reed back in the water and sit back and listen. I probably should be counting the rests. Counting would mean I'd have to pay attention and that's no fun. I'd rather look around and watch everyone else sweat.

Actions

Readers learn something about the kind of person you are from your actions. For example, when Karen recalls her thoughts playing in a basketball tournament, we learn something of her insecurity, fears, and skills all at once:

> This time, don't be so stupid Karen—if you don't take it up court, you'll never get the ball. Oh, God, here I go. Okay, they're in a twenty-one—just bring it up—Sarah's alone—fake up, bounce pass—yes, she hits it! I got the assist!

Insight

One of the best ways to reveal who you are is to show yourself becoming aware of something, gaining a new way of seeing the world, a new insight. While such awareness can occur for apparently unexplainable reasons, it most often happens when you encounter new ideas or have experiences that change you in some way. In writing a paper about why she goes to the library to write a paper, Judith has the small but important insight about needing to feel centered and safe to write well:

> Like a dog who circles her bed three times before lying down, I circle the reading room looking for the right place to sit. I need to feel safe and comfortable so I can concentrate on mental activity. I find my place, an empty chair near a window, and slouch down into it, propping my legs on the low table in front. If my mother could see me, she'd reprimand me for not sitting up straight. I breathe deeply, close my eyes for a moment, and become centered, forgetting both last night's pizza and

~~tomorrow's philosophy exam. I need a few minutes to acclimate to this space, relax,~~
~~and feel safe before starting my work.~~

Telling Details

Describe yourself and other participants in your story in such a way that the details and facts help tell your story. A telling detail or fact is one that advances your characterization of someone without your having to render an obvious opinion. For example, you could characterize your little sister by pointing out the field hockey stick in the corner of her room, the photograph of the seventh-grade field hockey team on the wall, and the teddy bear next to her pillow. You could characterize her coach by pointing to the logo on her sweatshirt: "Winning isn't everything. It's the only thing."

◆ WRITING 1

Start to characterize yourself. Write four paragraphs, and in each one, emphasize one of these individualizing elements: voice, actions, awareness, and any telling details of your life. Select any or all that seem worthy of further exploration and write a few more paragraphs.

SUBJECT (WHAT)

People write about their personal experiences to get to know and understand themselves better, to inform and entertain others, and to leave permanent records of their lives. Sometimes people recount their experiences casually, in forms never intended for wide circulation, such as journals, diaries, and letters. Sometimes they write in forms meant to be shared with others, such as memoirs, autobiographies, or personal essays. In college, the most common narrative forms are personal experience essays.

Subjects for good stories know no limits. You already have a lifetime of experiences from which to choose, and each experience is a potential story to help explain who you are, what you believe, and how you act today. Here are some of the topics selected by a single first-year writing class:

- Playing oboe in Saturday orchestra rehearsals
- Counseling disturbed children at summer camp
- Picking strawberries on a farm
- Winning a championship tennis match
- Studying at the library
- Losing in a championship basketball game
- Solo camping as part of an Outward Bound experience
- Touring Graceland in Memphis, Tennessee
- Painting houses during the summer
- Working on an assembly line in a battery factory

When you write a paper based on personal experience, ask yourself: Which experience do I want to write about? Will anybody else want to read about it? Here are some suggestions.

Winning and Losing

Winning something—a race, a contest, a lottery—can be a good subject, since it features you in a unique position and allows you to explore or celebrate a special talent. At the same time, exciting, exceptional, or highly dramatic subjects, such as scoring the winning goal in a championship game or placing first in a creative writing contest, may be difficult to write about because they've been used so often that readers have very high expectations.

The truth is that in most parts of life there are more losers than winners. While one team wins a championship, dozens do not. So there's a large, empathetic audience out there who will understand and identify with a narrative about losing. Although more common than winning, losing is less often explored in writing because it is more painful to recall. Therefore, there are fresher, deeper, more original stories to tell about losing.

Milestones

Perhaps the most interesting but also the most difficult experience to write about is one that you already recognize as a turning point in your life, whether it's winning a sports championship, being a camp counselor, or surviving a five-day solo camping trip in midwinter. People who explore such topics in writing often come to a better understanding of them. Also, their very significance challenges writers to make them equally significant for an audience that did not experience them. When you write about milestones, pay special attention to the physical details that will both advance your story and make it come alive for readers.

Daily Life

Commonplace experiences make fertile subjects for personal narratives. You might describe practicing for, rather than winning, the big game, or cleaning up after, rather than attending, the prom. If you are accurate, honest, and observant in exploring a subject from which readers expect little, you are apt to pleasantly surprise them and draw them into your story. Work experiences are especially fruitful subjects, since you may know inside details and routines of restaurants and retail shops that the rest of us can only guess. For example, how long is it before McDonald's tosses its unsold hamburgers? How do florists know which flowers to order when?

A Caution about Love, Death, and Divorce

Several subjects that you may need to write about may not make good topics for formal papers that will be shared with classmates and instructors. For example, you are probably too involved in a love relationship to portray it in any but the rosiest terms; too close to the recent death of someone you care about to render the event faithfully; too angry, confused, or miserable to write well of your parents' divorce. Writing about these and other close or painful experiences in your journal or diary can be immensely cathartic, but there is no need to share them with others.

◆ WRITING 2

Make a list of a dozen experiences about which you could tell stories. Think of special insight you gained as well as commonplace events that were instructive or caused change. Share your list with classmates and find out which they would most like to hear about.

SETTING (WHERE)

Experiences happen in some place at some time, and good stories describe these settings. To describe a believable physical setting, you need to re-create on paper the sights, sounds, smells, and physical sensations that allow readers to experience it for themselves. In addition to telling details that support your plot or character development, try to include evocative details, colorful details of setting and character that will let your readers know you were really there. In the following example, Heather portrays details of the farm where she spent the summer picking strawberries:

> The sun is just barely rising over the treetops and there is still dew covering the ground. In the strawberry patch, the deep green leaves are filled with water droplets and the strawberries are big and red and ready to be picked. The patch is located in a field off the road near a small forest of Christmas trees. The white house, the red barn, and a checkerboard of fields can be seen in the distance. It is 5:30 A.M. and the day has begun.

The evocative details are those that appeal to your senses, such as sight, touch, and smell: *dew covering the ground, deep green leaves, strawberries . . . big and red, white house, red barn,* and *checkerboard of fields.*

The details of a setting reveal something essential about your story without your explaining them. For example, in telling a story about your sister, you might describe the physical objects in her room, which in turn describe important elements of her character: the hockey stick, soccer ball, gym bag, sweatpants, and baseball jersey, and the life-size posters of Tiger Woods and Jackie Joyner-Kersee. In other words, skillful description helps you "tell" the story without your telling it outright.

◆ WRITING 3

Describe in detail one of the settings in which your experience took place. Appeal to at least three senses, and try to include details that "tell" some of your story without needing further explanation or overt value judgments on your part.

SEQUENCE (WHEN)

In every story, events are ordered in some way. While you cannot alter the events that happened in your experience, as a writer you need to decide which events to portray and in what order to present them.

Selecting Events

You have dozens of places to start and end any story, and at each point along the way, many possible details and events worth relating. Your final selection should support the theme of your story. To decide which events to portray, figure out how much detail you intend to devote to each one. In writing about her basketball career, Karen could have told about her four years playing in high school or her senior year alone or one single game. Because she wanted to focus on a climactic point in great detail, she selected "even less"—she writes her entire six-page paper about the final six minutes of her final game.

In selecting events, consider using one of two strategies that writers commonly use to maintain reader interest: showing cause and effect, and building suspense. When writers recount an experience to show cause and effect, they pair one event (having an accident, meeting a person, taking a journey) with another event or events that were caused as a result (undergoing physical therapy, making a friend, learning a new language).

In using suspense, writers raise questions or pose problems but delay answering or solving them. If the writer can make the question interesting enough, the problem pressing enough, readers will keep reading to learn the answers or solutions—in other words, to find out what happens. Karen's paper asks indirectly, "What is it like to play a championship game from the perspective of a substitute player?"

Ordering Events

The most common way to sequence events is to use chronological order, presenting events in the sequence in which they happened. Chronological order can be straightforward, following a day from morning to night as Heather does in her narrative about picking strawberries. Chronology also orders one student's twenty-two days of Outward Bound. And chronology orders Karen's six minutes at the end of one basketball game. Sometimes, however, the order is deliberately broken up, so that readers are first introduced to an event in the present and then, later in the story, are allowed to see events that happened earlier in time through flashbacks. For example, the Outward Bound journal could start with his first day of solo camping and then, in another entry, flash back to the early days to explain how he got there. Such a sequence has the advantage of stimulating readers' interest by opening with a point of exceptional drama or insight.

◆ WRITING 4

Outline the sequence of events of your story in the order that makes the most sense. Is the arrangement chronological? If not, what is it? How do you decide which event to begin with? Which one to end with?

THEME (WHY)

We can talk about the "why" of a story on two levels: First, why did the events occur in the story? What motivated or caused them? Well-told stories will answer this question, directly or indirectly. But we can also ask the writer: "Of all the stories you could write, why did you write this one?" Or, more bluntly, every reader asks, at least tacitly: "So what? What's the meaning or significance of this story? What did I learn by reading it?" Well-told stories will also answer this question; readers will see and understand both why you wrote it and why they read it.

However, first drafts of personal experience narratives often do not reveal clear answers to these questions, even to the writers themselves. First drafts are for getting the events down on paper for writers to look at. In subsequent drafts, the meaning of these events—the theme—should become clearer. If it doesn't, the writer should drop the subject.

In experiential stories, the theme isn't usually explicitly stated in the first paragraph, as the thesis statement often is in expository or argumentative writing. Instead, storytellers may create a meaning that is not directly stated anywhere and that becomes clear only at the end of the narrative. Many themes fall into three broad categories: slices of life, insights, and turning points.

Slices of Life

Some stories simply let readers see what life is like for someone else. Such stories exist primarily to record the writer's memories and to convey information in an interesting way. Their primary theme is, "This is what my life is like." Beth's story of the Saturday orchestra rehearsal is a slice of life, as she chooses to focus on a common practice rather than a more dramatic performance. After using interior monologue for nine paragraphs, in the last paragraph she speaks to the readers directly, explaining what the meaning of music is in her everyday life.

> As hard as it is to get up every Saturday morning, and as hard as it is to put up with some people here, I always feel good as I leave rehearsal. A guest conductor once said, "Music sounds how feelings feel." It's really true. Music evokes emotions that can't be described on paper. Every human feeling can be expressed through music— sadness, love, hatred. Music is an international language. Once you learn it you can't forget it.

Insights

In contrast to the many but routine experiences that reveal slices of life is the single important experience that leads to a writer's new insight, change, or growth. Such an experience is deeply significant to the writer, and he or she makes sure that readers see the full value of the experience, usually by commenting explicitly on its meaning. The final paragraph of Karen's championship basketball game reveals just such an insight.

> It's over now, and I've stopped crying, and I'm very happy. In the end I have to thank—not my coach, not my team—but Walpole for beating us so badly that I got

to play. I can't get over it. I played. And my dream came true, I hit a three pointer in the Boston Garden.

Turning Points

Turning points are those moments in one's life when something happens that causes the writer to change or grow in some large or small way—more than routine, less than spectacular—perhaps somewhere in between slices of life and profound insights. In fact, many of the best personal experience stories have for themes a modest change or the beginning of growth. Although such themes may be implied throughout the story, they often become clear only in a single climactic moment or episode. Mary's camp counselor story shows her progress from insecurity to confidence in gaining the trust of a ten-year-old. The following excerpt takes place after she has rescued Josh from ridicule by other campers.

> He ran in and threw himself on my bed, crying. I held him, rubbing his head for over an hour. "I love you, Mary. You're the best big sister in the whole world and you're so pretty! I love you and don't ever want you to leave."

Reflections

In reflective writing, the main point of the paper may be conveyed only indirectly and nearly always emerges at the end rather than the beginning of the essay. That way, readers are drawn into the act of reflecting themselves and become more and more curious to find out what the writer thinks. In other words, reflective writers are musing, exploring, or wondering rather than arguing. In fact, reflective essays are most persuasive when least obviously instructive or assertive. And keep in mind that when you start to write about a track meet, paper route, or library trip, you may not realize what caused you to explore this particular memory. In other words, a writer may select to write about an object with only a vague idea of why it's attractive, interesting, or compelling. Commonly it's only through the act of recalling the details of a past event that you, the writer, find the nature of the attraction, interest, or compulsion.

When you retell a story about past events, sometimes you find out that more was on your mind than at first you realized. The event itself is one thing, but the meaning of the event becomes something else—and a reflective writer may deliberately share how that second-level or deeper meaning emerged in the act of storytelling. For example, in narrating a personal experience, a writer may step back and pause, saying to the reader, in effect, "Wait a minute, there's something else going on here—stop and consider." Such pauses are a sign that connections are being made—between the present and the past, the concrete and the abstract, the literal and the symbolic. It signals to the reader that the essay is about to move in a new and less predictable direction. Sometimes, such reflective pauses are accompanied by slight shifts in voice or tone as the writer moves in closer to what's really on his or her mind. The exact nature of these shifts will, of course, be determined by the point the writer wants to make.

In early drafts of her essay about studying at the library, it wasn't clear why Judith had selected this topic at all, as nothing of particular note seemed to happen. But in her final draft, new language emerged near the end of her essay that tipped off the reader—and perhaps the writer—to what had been on her mind all along:

Two weeks ago, a female student was assaulted not far from where I live—that's why I've taken to locking my door so carefully. I am beginning to understand the importance of feeling safe in order to be creative and productive. Here, in the library, I feel secure, protected from real violence and isolated from everyday distractions. There are just enough people for security's sake but not so many that I feel crowded. And besides, I'm surrounded by all these books, all these great minds who dwell in this hallowed space! I am comfortable, safe, and beginning to get an idea.

At the very end of a reflective essay, writers often return to the specific person, place, or thing that prompted the reflection in the first place. This brings about a sense of closure—if not for the topic itself, at least for this particular essay. When you read Judith's whole essay about her library experience at the end of this chapter, notice how she ends it.

◆ WRITING 5

Freewrite for ten minutes about the meaning of your story as you have written it so far, addressing some of these questions: What have you discovered about yourself? Were there any surprises? Does your story interest you? Why or why not? What do you want readers to feel or know at the end?

PERSPECTIVE (HOW)

When reporters ask themselves "How?" they mean "How did the news event happen?" However, in this chapter, "How?" means "How is the story told?"—from what vantage point, position, or perspective are you telling the story? Perspective addresses the question "How close—in time, distance, or spirit—are you to the experience?" Do you write as if it happened long ago or yesterday? Do you summarize what happened or put readers at the scene? Do you explain the experience or leave it a mystery? In other words, you can control, or at least influence, how readers respond to a story by controlling the perspective from which you tell it.

Point of View

Authorial perspective is established largely by point of view. Using the first person (*I*) puts the narrator right in the story as a participant. This point of view is usually the one used in personal experience writing, as Beth and Karen do in earlier examples.

The third person (*he* or *she*) establishes a distinction between the person narrating the events and the person experiencing them and thus tends to depersonalize the story. This perspective is more common in fiction, but it has some uses in personal essays as well. In the following example, for instance, Karen opens her personal experience essay from the imagined perspective of the play-by-play announcer who broadcasts the championship game; the point of view is first person, but from the perspective of a third person:

2:15 Well folks, it looks as if Belmont has given up, the coach is preparing to send in his subs. It has been a rough game for Belmont. They stayed in it during the first quarter, but Walpole has run away with it since then. Down by twenty with only six minutes left, Belmont's first sub is now approaching the table.

Verb Tense

Verb tense establishes the time when the story happened or is happening. The tense used to relate most of the events in a story is called the *governing tense*. Personal experience stories are usually set in either the past or the present.

Once Upon a Time: Past Tense

The most natural way to recount a personal experience is to write in the past tense; whatever you're narrating did happen sometime in the past. Lorraine uses the past tense to describe an automobile ride with her Native American grandfather to attend a tribal conference:

> I sat silently across from Grandfather and watched him slowly tear the thin white paper from the tip of the cigarette. He gathered the tobacco in one hand and drove the van with the other. I memorized his every move as he went through the motions of the prayer, which ended when he finally blew the tobacco out of the window and into the wind.

Even though the governing tense for your personal narrative may be the past tense, you may still want to use other tenses for special purposes.

Being There: Present Tense

The present tense provides the illusion that the experience is happening at the moment; it leaves no time for your reflection. This strategy invites readers to become involved with your story as it is happening and invites them to interpret it for themselves.

If you want to portray yourself thinking rather than talking—in what is called interior monologue—you may choose to use fragment sentences and made-up words since the flow of the mind doesn't obey conventional rules of language. For example, when Beth describes her thoughts during orchestra rehearsal, she writes an interior monologue; we hear her talking to herself while trying to blow her oboe. Note how she provides clues so that we understand what is going on around her.

> No you don't really mean that, do you? You do. Rats. Here we go. . . . Pfff . . . Pfff . . . Why isn't this playing? Maybe if I blow harder . . . HONK!! Great. I've just made a total fool of myself in front of everyone. Wonderful.

◆ WRITING 6

Write one page of a possible story using the first person, past tense, and a second page using the first person, present tense. From which perspective do you prefer to tell the story? Why?

SHAPING THE WHOLE PAPER

The finished draft of Judith's personal reflective essay, "Writing in Safety," opens and closes with a walk to and from the library. It has a loosely narrative pattern and is written in the present tense to convey a sense of the events unfolding as we read them. Her essay tells a very simple story, since it's mainly about walking and sitting down. The journey emerges as a mental, almost spiritual, quest for safety—safety in which to think and create without fear. At the same time, the physical dimensions of her journey and the attention to descriptive detail make her journey believable.

Writing in Safety

Judith Woods

It is already afternoon. I fiddle with the key to lock the apartment door after me. I am not accustomed to locking doors. Except for the six months I spent in Boston, I have never lived in a place where I did not trust my neighbors. When I was little, we couldn't lock our farmhouse door; the wood had swollen and the bolt no longer lined up properly with the hole, and nobody ever bothered to fix it. I still remember the time our baby-sitter, Rosie, hammered the bolt closed and we had to take the door off the hinges to get it open.

I heft the book bag onto my shoulder and walk up College Street toward the library. As I pass and am passed by other students, I scrutinize everything around me, hoping to be struck with a creative idea for a topic for my English paper. Instead, my mind fills with a jumble of disconnected images, like a bowl of alphabet soup: The letters are there, but they don't form any words. Campus sidewalks are not the best places for creativity to strike.

Approaching the library, I see skateboarders and bikers weaving through students who talk in clusters on the library steps. A friendly dog is tied to a bench, watching for its owner to return. Subjects to write about? Nothing strikes me as especially interesting, and besides, my heart is still pounding from the walk up the hill. I wipe my damp forehead and go inside.

Inside the smoke-colored doors, the loud and busy atmosphere vanishes, replaced by the soft, soothing hum of air-conditioning and the hushed sound of whispering voices. The repetitive sound of the copy machine has a calming effect as I look for a comfortable place in which to begin my work.

I want just the right chair, with a soft cushion, and a low sturdy table for a leg rest. The chairs are strategically positioned with comfortable personal space around each one, so you can stretch your arms fully without touching a neighbor. I notice that if there are three chairs in a row, the middle one is always empty. If seated at a table, people sit staggered so they are not directly across from one another. People seem to respect each other's need for personal space.

Like a dog who circles her bed three times before lying down, I circle the reading room looking for the right place to sit. I need to feel safe and comfortable so I can concentrate on mental activity. Some students, however, are too comfortable. One boy has moved two chairs together and covered himself with his coat, and he is asleep in a fetal position. A girl sits at a table, head down, dozing like we used to do in first grade.

I find my place, an empty chair near a window, and slouch down into it, propping my legs on the low table in front. If my mother could see me, she'd reprimand me for not sitting up straight. I breathe deeply, close my eyes for a moment, and become centered, forgetting both last night's pizza and tomorrow's philosophy exam. I need a few minutes to acclimate to this space, relax, and feel safe before starting my work.

Two weeks ago, a female student was assaulted not far from where I live—that's why I've taken to locking my door so carefully. I am beginning to understand the importance of feeling safe in order to be creative and productive. Here, in the library, I feel secure, protected from real violence and isolated from everyday distractions. There are just enough people for security's sake but not so many that I feel crowded. And besides, I'm surrounded by all these books, all these great minds who dwell in this hallowed space! I am comfortable, safe, and beginning to get an idea.

Hours later—my paper started, my exam studied for, my eyes tired—I retrace the path to my apartment. It is dark now, and I listen closely when I hear footsteps behind, stepping to the sidewalk's edge to let a man walk briskly past. At my door, I again fumble for the now familiar key, insert it in the lock, open the door, turn on the hall light, and step inside. Here, too, I am safe, ready to eat, read a bit, and finish my reflective essay.

◆ SUGGESTIONS FOR WRITING AND RESEARCH

Individual
Reflect on a personal experience drawing on the work you did in writings 2–6 in this chapter. Find a subject that intrigues you, but that you have not fully figured out yet. Plan to write this narrative in several drafts, each one exploring a different aspect of your experience.

Collaborative
As a class, write the story of your writing class so far in the semester. Each class member contributes one chapter (one page) to this tale. Each member chooses any moment (funny, momentous, boring, routine) and describes it so that it stands on its own as a complete episode. Choose two class members to collect all the short narrative chapters and weave them into a larger narrative with a beginning, middle, and end.

CHAPTER NINE

Profiling Self and Others

*I am the son of a man who does not know who Mick Jagger is, but can recite the
names of all the state capitals in alphabetical order.*

JEREMY

Ｈow do you write about your own
past, present, and future? How much
does your current identity depend upon
your past or anticipate your future? And
how do you represent the character or
identity of other people in writing?
Three of the four assignments in this
chapter let you construct in writing a
limited but substantial version of yourself: An *autobiography* asks you to explore how you became who you are
today; a *language autobiography* focuses
on your specific development as a user
of language; and a *career profile* asks you
to build upon both past and present to
anticipate an interesting future. The
chapter concludes with suggestions for
profiling other people.

WRITING AUTOBIOGRAPHY

It is presumptuous, of course, for most people to write an autobiography while still in college, with so much life still ahead. However, it may be useful to use your enrollment in college as a life marker—a point of reflection—to examine how your pre-college years have shaped the person you are today.

In order to write even a partial autobiography, it helps to remember and then examine the important influences that come to mind: family, home life, neighborhood environment, school, favorite activities (hobbies, sports, clubs), political and religious experiences, and so on. It also helps to research your past by interviewing those who have watched you grow up: parents, siblings, relatives, teachers, neighbors, and friends. And it helps to dig, too, among saved artifacts that offer clues to your development: journals, diaries, letters, report cards, photographs, letters, posters, toys, scrapbooks, and the like. Following are a number of approaches to experiment with or help you get started.

Artifacts

Explore a dimension of your growing up based on something you once valued—a present from someone, something you saved up money to purchase, or an object that played an important role in the past. When you recall this artifact, describe it in as much concrete detail as you can so that others who did not grow up with you can see it. In the following example, Sara writes about a journal she kept as a child:

> When I was in fifth grade, I used to keep a journal that I would write in every day. Its shiny red cover was decorated with yellow sunflowers and it had my initials embossed in gold in the corner—SAH. It also had a lock and key so my older sisters couldn't read it. I would write freely in it about being happy or sad, or about adventures with my girlfriend, Molly, or sometimes I just wrote when I felt lonely. I stopped writing in it when I was in sixth grade, because then I started having boyfriends.

Interests

Write a version of yourself based on what you care about most passionately. Think about old interests that carry through to the present as well as more recent interests (playing guitar, collecting sports cards, running, ballet) and describe them as well as explore the reason they fascinate you. In the following example, Rene focuses on so common an activity as playing cards:

> I have always been a card player. I have played with family, friends, boyfriends, and strangers. I have played by myself and with as many as ten or twelve people. Card playing is an exercise in skill and chance, a social event, and a creative act. I say creative because on more than one occasion I've invented my own games—though you won't find them in *The Complete Hoyle*. When I meet someone who doesn't play cards, I look at them with suspicion—what's wrong with you I think, not liking to play cards is not natural.

Quotations

Write a version of yourself based on what somebody has said about you. Sometimes when you overhear people talking about you, you gain insight into how others in the world perceive you. Think about overheard conversations, the way your parents characterize you, what friends have said, or what a teacher has written on a report card. In the following example, Joy seems rather pleased that she was often described as a handful when she was young:

> I was what some people would call a problem child. When I talk to my aunt or grand-mother about my younger years, they just shake their heads and say, "You were a pisser, that's for sure." But they also smile when they say it, so it couldn't have been that bad.

Snapshots

One of the most daunting aspects of writing an autobiography or self-profile of any kind is our own complexity as human beings. While some of us may be said to have one clearly dominant characteristic that stands out above others, most of us see ourselves as more complicated than that, made up of multiple and even contradictory selves, making it especially difficult to write unified and coherent portraits of ourselves. One way to solve the coherence problem is to write in a form that allows you to celebrate multiplicity without pretending to unity and to portray contradictions without resolving them.

Writing prose snapshots is just such a form, allowing writers to compose their autobiographies through a collection of short prose pictures or verbal snapshots. Each individual snapshot focuses on one dimension of self the way a single photograph captures one particular scene. At the same time, a collection of such verbal episodes, carefully juxtaposed against others, tells a larger, more complete story the way a collection of photographs in an album or exhibit tells a larger story.

 Consider a single prose snapshot as an autonomous paragraph of a few sentences or a hundred words, but separated from preceding and following snapshots by white space rather than transitional phrases. Each snapshot tells its own small story, and each may be followed by another snapshot telling either a related or a quite different story. An accumulation of such snapshots allows writers to present complex versions of self in a brief amount of space and time. Here, for example, are three of thirteen snapshots from Becky's personal portrait:

- My mother grew up in Darien, Connecticut, a Presbyterian. When she was little, she gave the Children's Sermon at her church.

- My father grew up in Cleveland, Ohio, a Jew. When I went away to college, he gave me the Hebrew Bible he received at his Bar Mitzvah.

- The only similarity between my parents' families is freckles. They both have them, which means I get a double dose. Lucky me. My mother once told me that freckles are "*angels' kisses*." Lucky me.

Note that Becky explores her conflicting religious heritage as well as her common freckle inheritance by briefly but carefully juxtaposing mother against father. She covers a lot of ground with a few sentences, allowing the reader to figure out the transitions without writing them in herself.

◆ WRITING 1

Make a list of five episodes in your life, each of which reveals something about who you are or what you value. Arrange these episodes in two different ways: first, chronologically, with earliest episode first, most recent last. Then arrange according to significance, with least important first, most important last. Which way would you prefer telling your story?

WRITING A LANGUAGE AUTOBIOGRAPHY

In many ways, getting a college education is getting a language education, learning course by course, new vocabulary, new meanings, and new ideas. Consequently, one of the most interesting types of autobiography to write is one that focuses on your growth and development as a user of language. Such "language autobiographies" focus on those moments when you learned something connected with language—reading, writing, speaking, listening. Such studies need not be limited to verbal languages, as other languages such as music, mathematics, visual, and body languages also have much to teach. You would go about constructing a language autobiography in the same way as any autobiography but now limiting your investigation to those experiences and episodes that shed light on you as a reader, writer, and speaker.

To construct a language autobiography, list all the possible places and episodes where you remember language making a special impact on you—home, neighborhood, school, hobbies, sports, clubs, and so forth. Also, list the books, films, television shows, and song lyrics that you remember most vividly as well as any stories, poems, and lyrics you may have written yourself.

Time Line

One way to begin a language autobiography is to create a time line. Draw a vertical line on a sheet of paper. On one side write a chronological list of all the books you remember reading in school, and on the other side, make a similar chronology of readings (including being read to) at home. Expand the entries on either side of the line by adding in other episodes of language learning—keeping a journal, writing letters, entering a short story contest, and so on, as Figure 9.1 illustrates. Include age or grade in parentheses next to each entry.

Time Line

Personal	School

Read to: Dr. Seuss--lots (age 4?)
        The Giving Tree
        Good Night, Moon	

Winnie the Pooh	Learn to write a paragraph (2nd grade)
	Learn cursive (3rd)
The Jungle Book (9)	
Letters to Mike (10)	
	Where the Red Fern Grows (6th)

Write and perform play: *The Moon Man*
        (Summer Festival
        of the Arts)	

Write story about Mars (12)	
Catcher in the Rye (13)	*The Diary of Anne Frank* (8th)
	Presentation of moon study in biology class (10th)
Keep personal journal (15) *Story of Michael Jordan*	Paper on *Caged Bird* read aloud in class Keep basketball diary
Letter to editor published (17)	Two poems published in school paper (11th)
	Research paper on Ecuador (12th)
College entrance essay (successful!)	

Figure 9.1   Time line

Research

Research will add an element of persuasive authenticity to this project. First, plan to talk—in person, on the telephone, via e-mail—with your parents, aunts, uncles, and brothers or sisters in the event they remember something about the "young you" growing up that you do not. Next, browse among the books in your current bookshelf as well as among any childhood books still available, and make a list of the titles that most influenced you. Finally, dig—at home or in your own school files—among your own literate artifacts, and look again at old school reports, report cards, stories, poems, journals, or letters to the editor—any written documents that provide clues to early language influences or habits.

It makes good sense to write this paper in chronological order, beginning with earliest influences and working forward to watch yourself develop. However, consider reversing chronology or using flashbacks if that way of telling your story seems more interesting to you. Megan, for example, began her language autobiography by recounting a trip home to rummage through the attic looking for artifacts:

> I took great pains to discover my first creative writing. Luckily, my mother has saved boxes of drawings, class pictures, and old stories from my kindergarten year on in our attic. I found two Big Chief writing tablets from first grade, a story about my summer vacation from second grade, and the complete manuscript of my first novel from fifth grade.

Artifacts

Once you've located a poem, letter, or journal entry from the past, you need to decide how to use it: If you simply mention it, you are suggesting it is notable but not very important. If you summarize it, you are suggesting the content is important, but there's no need to see the document itself. If you reproduce it, you are telling us the artifact itself reveals more than a summary would. In the sample below, Susan includes a complete poem written in elementary school when she was seven years old.

> My Special Tree
>
> My special tree is very old.
> It is large and green and in our yard.
> It is a maple tree.
> Birds fly in and out of its leaves.
> It has a big curved branch.
> I hang on tight and swing.

In fact, Susan's language autobiography is composed of fourteen artifacts solely from her elementary years, ages five through eleven. She prefaces the collection with this introduction:

> The truth and honesty of my childhood writing is the centerpiece of my language autobiography. In rummaging through my essays, research papers, stories, poems, and even journal entries from later years, I realized my true voice was already shaped by the time I entered seventh grade. I am now fourteen years older than the earliest sample included here, but it speaks for me as well now as it did then.

As a reader I infer that the simplicity of childhood dreams and pleasures is still very much alive in this now more experienced college student. Because Susan's paper is made up almost entirely of her own early writing, neither edited nor explained, I must do most of the interpretive work, a method which works so long as the material is self-explanatory. However, many times when a writer refers to an old poem or mentions a book, we don't understand its importance unless the writer tells us. Here, for example, when Kate writes about her first encounter with classical literature, she is explicit about why it was so important:

> When I was in sixth grade, we were assigned *The Odyssey*. It was the thickest book I'd ever tried to read, so it seemed like a big deal. How could I possibly read so many pages—here were at least 200? I trudged home with it in my backpack, feeling its weight, grumpily calculating how long it would take to read it. But I ended up reading it hungrily—Homer's beautiful writing drew me in to the most ghastly and majestic stories I'd ever experienced. Good literature had affected me for the first time.

◆ WRITING 2

List five artifacts from five different years that reveal something significant about your life as a language user. Write a paragraph about each one, describing it and explaining its significance. When you are able, retrieve these artifacts, study them closely, and expand your paragraphs accordingly.

COMPOSING A CAREER PROFILE

This identity assignment involves exploring who you intend to become next by exploring either potential college majors or out-of-college careers. If you know what you want to pursue as life work, it makes the most sense to investigate and report on that; if you are undecided about either career or major, it makes good sense to explore those toward which you are leaning or most attracted. If you are more uncertain than that, uncertain even about why you are in college or what to major in, this assignment could be your chance to give voice to that confusion and look more closely at possible resolutions.

Whatever your college goals, you might start with a close look at your own past work experiences as well as at any other firsthand experience with what seem to be attractive careers. You also might explore how you selected a college to attend as well as a discipline in which to major. Any of these initial investigations will be relevant to what you intend to do next with your life. For this paper, plan to include a substantial amount of research into possible careers or majors as well as to look closely at your own past experience and interests.

Where You Came From

Your past interests, hobbies, and successes often anticipate your college major as well as your life work. Even in those instances where you encounter whole new fields in college, from engineering to social work, the origins of your new interest are often evident in past activities. In the following example, Chris outlines a childhood dream.

As far back as I can remember, I wanted to be a weather reporter. If I couldn't be a professional sailboat racer, I wanted to be a weatherman. I never had any desire to be the guy on TV, but I wanted to know what the guy on TV knows.

Early on in his paper, Chris also explores impediments to pursuing this dream.

One day, when I was in eighth grade, my teacher told me I had to drop back from the regular math group to the slower math group. Math was not my strong suit. But when obtaining a degree in meteorology—the degree you need to be a weather reporter I got the same answer every time: "You need lots of math."

Where You Are

If you're interested in finding out what certain jobs or professions are like, look in the phone book and find out where, in your community, people actually practice this work. If you want to research the global dimensions of this career, your local library or bookstore will have occupation guidebooks to read. And if you want to find out how your college or university could help prepare you, talk to professors in the disciplines that interest you as well as visit your career counselor or job placement service.

To find out firsthand whether or not even to attempt to major in meteorology, Chris set up an appointment with Paul Sisson of the National Weather Service in Burlington, Vermont, whom he interviewed in person:

I asked several questions, eventually getting around to my fear of math. "Yes, you have to be pretty proficient in math to survive meteorology. If you can't survive calculus, you won't be able to survive the rest." I looked across at Paul in his blue oxford shirt, navy knit tie, pressed khakis, and boat shoes with a combination of respect, envy, and hopelessness.

But in spite of his difficulty with math, writing this paper became a way for Chris to explore his fascination with weather more deeply and resolve what next to do about it:

In a way I'd never considered before, my desire to be a meteorologist stems from my desire to help people since the ability to predict severe weather can help everyone from airline pilots to farmers to flood victims. More than ever, I realize that this is what I want to do with my education. I believe my desire to learn will help me overcome my difficulties with mathematics.

◆ WRITING 3

Write about where you currently stand in terms of college major or career choice. Include the names of people you might talk to or places you might visit to gather more information. When you finish writing, plan to set up appointments with the most available prospects.

Sample Snapshot Autobiography

The following highly focused autobiography portrays Rebecca Rabin's mixed religious heritage, strong commitment to Protestantism, and current participation in Christian rituals. Each individual snapshot focuses on a single small event in her life and actually tells a small story, complete with beginning, middle, and punch line. At the same time, the cumulative effect of these thirteen snapshots reveals Rebecca's broad tolerance, education, and interest in a spirituality that goes well beyond separate religious creeds. This theme emerges as one experience is juxtaposed against another, past tense against present tense, without editorializing, allowing readers to supply the connective tissue by filling in the white spaces for themselves.

I Know Who I Am

Rebecca Rabin

- My mother grew up in Darien, Connecticut, a Presbyterian. When she was little, she gave the Children's Sermon at her church.
- My father grew up in Cleveland, Ohio, a Jew. When I went away to college, he gave me the Hebrew Bible he received at his Bar Mitzvah.
- The only similarity between my parents' families is freckles. They both have them, which means I get a double dose. Lucky me. My mother once told me that freckles are "angels' kisses." Lucky me.
- When my parents married and decided to have kids, they agreed to raise them Christian. Thus, I was brought up Presbyterian. According to Jewish tradition and law, Judaism is passed on via a person's mother. Thus I am not a Jew.
- I have attended First Presbyterian Church of Boulder, Colorado, for most of my life. When I was baptized, Reverend Allen said: "Becky is being baptized here today, brought by her believing mother and her unbelieving—but supportive—father."
- When I was little, I was terrified of the darkness. Sometimes, I would wake up in the night and scream. It was my mother who came in to comfort me, smoothing my hair, telling me to think of butterflies and angels.
- I once went through this stage in which I was quite certain I was meant to be Greek Orthodox. That was one my parents couldn't quite understand. My fascination came from watching a movie that had an Eastern Orthodox wedding with the bride wearing beautiful flowers.
- I have always said my prayers before going to bed. Lying silently in the dark, talking to God. Like the disciples in the Garden of Gethsemane, I have been known to fall asleep while praying. Now I pray on my knees, it is harder to doze off that way.
- My father's sister's family is Orthodox Jewish. Things in their house are very different from things in our house. They have two of everything: refrigerators, sinks, dish sets, and dishwashers. When I go there, though, I always feel comfortable in the most basic way—as if my heart says, Oh yes, this is where I belong.
- I am not afraid of the dark anymore. Except sometimes, when I wake up in a sweaty panic, certain there's an axe murderer in my room. My father, the Jewish psychiatrist, says that nightmares are from going to sleep before your brain

has sufficiently wound down from a busy day. He says reading before sleeping will cure that.

- When I am in Vermont, I attend North Avenue Alliance Church. I chose it because it is big, like my church at home. The last two Sundays I have sung solos. The first time, I sang "Amazing Grace." The second time, I sang "El Shaddai," which is partly in Hebrew. In church, my heart says, Oh yes, this is where I belong.

- I wear a cross around my neck. It is nothing spectacular to look at, but I love it because I bought it at the Vatican. Even though I am not a Catholic, I am glad I bought it at the Pope's home town. Sometimes, when I sit in Hebrew class, I wonder if people wonder, "What religion is she, anyway?"

- From a very early age I have always known exactly what I wanted: To live in a safe world. To worship freely. To sing. I know what I believe. I know who I am. I know where I'm going.

PROFILING PEOPLE

The purpose of profiling a person is to capture his or her essence on paper. Good profiles generally focus on a single aspect of the subject's life or personality and make some sort of comment on it. In short, a good profile tells a story about its subject.

Profiles are usually about people other than the writer, but you, the writer, are ultimately in control. You decide what to include, what to omit, how to describe the subject and his or her surroundings, where to begin, and where to end. However, the ultimate purpose of a profile is to convey a sense of who your subject is. You must develop a portrait that is essentially true.

Profiles lie on a spectrum between two related forms, informal interviews and more formal biographies. Like interviews, profiles include direct conversations with living people. Like biographies, they make use of other sources of information about the subject. Profiles, such as those published in popular magazines, are usually longer and more focused than interviews, but they are considerably shorter than biographies.

Profiles can be written about virtually any person willing to hold still long enough to reveal something about him- or herself. Members of the campus community are usually willing subjects: classmates, professors, librarians, cafeteria workers, resident assistants, alumni staff, and coaches, to name some of the obvious ones. In addition, the local community contains other potential subjects: shopkeepers, street vendors, police officers, city administrators, and various local characters of good and ill repute. Relatives make good profile subjects because they are usually more than willing to cooperate, and the knowledge resulting from the profile will contribute to your family history.

Research Information

The profile examples in this chapter are taken from profiles of classmates, easy subjects to locate and who represent varied backgrounds and interests. The elements that comprise an effective profile, however, are fairly similar for any subject. A note of caution: It's very

difficult to profile, with any objectively at all, a subject with whom you're romantically involved.

BACKGROUND.   To write an effective profile, learn as much about your subject as possible. Finding background information requires good research skills. You must take advantage of all the available sources of information and follow up on new leads wherever you find
them.

INTERVIEWS.   Talking with your subject often is the best place to start. In addition to
providing valuable background information, he or she can give you leads to further information. If you are profiling a classmate, interview him or her for ten or fifteen minutes to
get started. For other subjects, call ahead and set up a time to meet.

PUBLIC INFORMATION.   If your subject has a résumé, ask to see it. If your subject has
published something—whether a letter to the editor or a book—get a copy. If your subject
has made a speech or taken a public stand, find a record of it. If the person has been the
subject of an interview or biography, read it to see what previous writers have found out.

WRITING SAMPLES.   A rich source of recent background information is your subject's
writings—especially if your subject is a student. Assigned papers or essay tests will tell you
something of the person's intellectual interests, but journals or letters may reveal more personal information.

FRIENDS AND ACQUAINTANCES.   An obvious source of background information is the
people who know, live, and work with your subject. Each conversation you have with a
friend or acquaintance of your subject is itself a small interview. Good questions to ask are
fairly obvious: what is this person like? How did you come to know each other? What do
you most often do together? Whom does this person admire? What does this person want
to do or become next?

PHYSICAL CHARACTERISTICS.   Often the first thing we notice about people is what they
look like—their appearance. In the early stages of developing a profile, take brief notes on
every aspect of your subject's appearance; as you get to know your subject, details that capture his or her individuality and personality. Remember to use words that express size,
shape, color, texture, and sound. Be sure to describe clothing, habits or gestures, and physical characteristics. Pam can capture Mari Anne's appearance by employing all three types
of information:

> While sitting at her desk, Mari Anne keeps twirling her hair to help her think and
> relax. She is dressed in solid colors, black and red, and has a dozen bracelets on her
> right arm. She smiles as if nervous, but as I got to know her, I found that smile al-
> ways on her face. She is five feet two inches tall, has naturally curly brown hair, a
> dark complexion, and dark brown eyes, and is always smiling.

Pam's description tells readers much about Mari Anne's tastes (solid colors, lots of
jewelry) and personality (friendly but perhaps a little high-strung). By mentioning Mari
Anne's nervous hair twisting at the beginning of the description and her nervous smile a bit
later, Pam makes readers see the subject as nervous.

At the same time, take note of the interview setting. If the interview takes place in a neutral space, the setting provides a realistic backdrop. If the interview setting is a person's room or apartment, record the details that tell the most about your subject's special interests. Settings can be described on their own or subtly and indirectly along with the action of the interview, as Beth does here:

> Becky sits cross-legged at the foot of the bottom bunk on her pink and green home-made quilt. She leans up against the wall and runs her fingers through her brown shoulder-length hair. The sounds of James Taylor's "Carolina on My Mind" softly fill the room. Posters of John Lennon, James Dean, and Cher look down on us from the walls.

Beth includes a rich number of sight words about Becky's home away from home—describing bed, posture, person, posters, and room—letting the detail contribute to the portrait of the person. By including the James Taylor song as well as the three posters, she allows readers to make inferences about what these say about Becky's tastes. Beth slips in the setting details quietly so as not to detract attention from the subject herself.

◆ WRITING 4

As an exercise, sit with a classmate and each spend five to ten minutes taking notes on physical appearance, facial expression, and dress. Also capture briefly some details of the place in which you are both sitting. Write one to two pages organizing these physical details to convey a dominant impression.

Subjects Speak for Themselves

Allow people to reveal information about themselves through their own words. The easiest way to conduct an interview is to schedule a sit-down conversation, in a comfortable setting, perhaps over coffee, and get to know your subject informally, jotting down quick notes as you talk. In all but the most informal interviews, come with prepared questions. Following are questions you might ask a classmate in developing a profile, though you'd change what you ask depending on who your subject is and the purpose of your profile.

- Where did you grow up? What was it like?
- What do your parents do for a living?
- Do you have any brothers or sisters? What are they like? How are you similar to or different from them?
- How do you spend your free time?
- What kinds of jobs have you held?
- What are your favorite books, movies, or recordings?
- How did you come to be where you are today?
- What do you intend to do next?

If you can plan subsequent interviews, narrow your questions to a more limited range of interests. For example, if your first interview revealed that photography is your subject's favorite hobby, in your second interview focus several questions on his or her involvement with photography. Your profile will succeed according to the amount of detailed information you get your subject to reveal through interviews. After the interview with Becky, Beth wrote the following narrative from her tape transcript:

> Finally, after minutes of silence she says, "I don't ever remember my father ever living in my house, really. He left when I was three and my sister was just a baby, about a year old. My mom took care of us all. Forever, it was just Mom, Kate, and me. I loved it, you know? Just the three of us together."

Beth is aware that if she can capture the small details of Becky's childhood along with her teenage conversational style (*like, you know*), Becky's story will be all the more plausible—which in turn will make the profile more lively and readable.

Point of View

The point of view from which you write will do much to establish the tone and style of your profile. In the first-person point of view, the writer (*I*) has a presence in the story (*I met Sarah sitting in the coffee shop.*). In the third-person point of view, the writer is absent, and the subject is the sole focus (*Sarah sat in the coffee shop.*). Many profiles are actually written in a combination of first person and third person, with most of the focus on the subject, but with occasional references to the writer's presence.

◆ WRITING 5

Write one page of a profile in the first person, then repeat the same page, but use third person, being sure, at some point, to let your subject speak. What difference do you notice writing in the first versus third person? Which do you prefer? Why?

Theme

Ultimately, profiles tell stories about people. Profile writers select the details and dialogue and background information that tell the story they want to tell about their subject. Most often, that story builds as the profile progresses so that the last page or paragraph focuses on the most important point the writer wants to make about the subject. This central theme can be revealed *explicitly,* with the writer telling readers what to think, or *implicitly,* with the evolution of the profile making the theme clear.

For example, Pam concludes her profile of Mari Anne with her own explicit judgment on what the realities of college life have done to Mari Anne's passion, gymnastics.

> [Mari Anne says,] "I want to be able to judge [gymnastics] here at college, so I will still have to pass part two of the exam. I would especially like to judge creative matches that show each gymnast's unique ability." As of now Mari Anne has not had time to fit gymnastics into her schedule. She is too busy trying to keep up with her studies. But you can bet that next year will find her on the floor or behind the judge's table; Mari Anne has too much passion for the sport to stay out for very long.

In contrast, Beth never suggests what readers should think of Becky, letting her subject's words end the profile, thus allowing readers to make their own inferences about who Becky is and what she stands for.

"I think that because I didn't have my dad, we're closer to my grandparents. Because Mom was so young and they helped us out all the time. They gave us property to build a house and everything. So we're a lot closer because she could always count on them. That's the most important thing, you know, being able to count on people."

◆ WRITING 6

In the profile you are writing, would you like your theme to emerge explicitly or implicitly? Try one version with an explicit statement summarizing your subject, then another version concluding with dialogue or descriptive language most likely to suggest, but not your theme.

SHAPING THE WHOLE PAPER

Beth Devino's finished draft of her profile "Becky" is presented here. Notice that Beth chose to shape the profile as if it took place at one sitting in Becky's dormitory room; in fact, she interviewed Becky at several different times and places over several weeks. Beth removes herself almost completely from the profile, letting Becky's own words do most of the characterizing—though at times she also presents information from the dormitory setting and her own summary of background information.

Notice the focus on trust and dependability, which develops early in the profile and carries through to the concluding words that express Becky's attitudes toward men. The final line makes a very strong ending, but be aware that the writer, not her subject, created this ending. Over the course of several interviews, Becky talked about a wide range of subjects, including sports, teacher education, and college life. It was Beth who shaped these many conversations into a coherent essay with a beginning, a middle, and an end.

Becky
Beth Devino

Becky sits cross-legged at the foot of the bottom bunk on her pink and green homemade quilt. She leans up against the wall and runs her fingers through her brown shoulder-length hair. The sound of James Taylor's "Carolina on My Mind" softly fills the room. Posters of John Lennon, James Dean, and Cher look down on us from the walls. Becky stares at the floor and scrunches her face as if she is thinking hard.

Finally, after minutes of silence she says, "I don't ever remember my father ever living in my house, really. He left when I was three and my sister was just a baby, about a year old. My mom took care of us all. Forever, it was just Mom, Kate, and me. I loved it, you know? Just the three of us together."

Becky smiles and continues, "And I remember little things, you know, like we would all sleep together in Mom's bed. We'd all climb in. Little things like, I remember one night there was a bat in the house and Mom is afraid of bats and I was only, like, five, and Mom climbed under the covers with my little sister and I had to go down and call my grandmother to get the bat out of the house.

"But I'm really proud of my mother for bringing up my sister and me on her own. She had to work, sometimes two jobs, and she worked really hard. I don't remember a sad time then, ever. I had the happiest childhood. You know, some of my friends who have whole families complain about fights with their parents, but I have no complaints about anything. I never felt like I needed anything or that I lacked anything."

Becky pauses, hugging her knees close to her chest, rocking slightly. "Hmmm," she mumbles. She traces her lips with the back of her fingernail. "Oh, I always do this when I'm thinking or I'm upset—now I'm just thinking."

Becky Harris grew up in West Granville, a small town where people knew and supported each other. She came to the university to major in elementary education: "I really think those early years are so crucial, when children are first learning how to live in and trust the world."

On campus, she lives in Connors Hall, with Trish, a roommate from Maine who is fast becoming a best friend. Trish agrees, saying, "Outside of classes, we do everything together, share tapes, run on the weekends, borrow clothes, and talk late almost every night. The posters? She put those up. I really like them."

Becky offers me a cup of herbal tea, then makes a cup for herself and resumes her place on the bed. "Anyway, Mom and I have the strangest relationship. It's like we're friends—she's my mom, but we're friends more than she's my mom because, when my dad left, I kinda had to grow up overnight and take care of my sister 'cause my mom was working so much. I mean, she never left us alone or anything, but I had to do things. I had to learn to dress myself and all those little things really fast, earlier than lots of kids because she didn't have time for both of us.

"Oh! I have this watch bear. I put it over my bed, somewhere where it can watch me all the time." She gets up from the bed and slides across the linoleum floor to her desk to pick up the little white stuffed animal. "Two years ago, I lost Watch Bear. For almost three whole days, and I didn't have anybody watching over me. But I found him, he was under the bed. I brought him with me to college to sit on my desk to watch over me and to make sure I'm safe like he did when I was little."

Becky carefully places Watch Bear against the wall near her and continues, "Anyway, I hope that if I were ever in the same situation as my mom, I could be as strong as she. 'Cause that would scare me to have a car and this brand new house that they just built and have to take care of everything. 'Cause my dad never paid any money, never a cent of child support, ever in his life to us.

"I've seen him maybe three or four times in ten or twelve years. Once two years ago, at Thanksgiving, I saw him, and that was when he had just gotten remarried, and I met his wife. I really liked her a lot and I really liked their kids. I got along with them, but you know, I don't think of him as part of my family. I don't even really think of him as my father, really. I mean biologically, but that's all. I used to get really sad sometimes that I didn't have a dad. But I don't feel like I've missed any-thing in my life, ever. I'd rather have my mother happy than to have her live with someone just to make a whole family 'cause I think we had a whole family.

"My mother has never said a bad thing about my father, ever, in her life. And if it was me who got dumped with two children, I would just—would always be bad-talking, I'm sure. She never wanted us to hate him and wanted us to have the op-portunity to get to know him if we wanted to when we could choose to. When he called and asked us to go to Thanksgiving with him a few years ago, I didn't want to, but Mom really encouraged us to 'cause she said maybe he's going to reach out and try to change his ways and be your dad. So we went. Kate, my sister, who was just a year when he left, never knew him at all. She was very uncomfortable there, but I talked to him a little bit."

Becky pauses and traces her lips again. "I used to have really bad feelings to-wards men in general. Like, I didn't trust them at all 'cause I thought that, you know, they were all sort of like him; you couldn't count on them for anything. I just don't think there's. . . . I get so mad that there's people that would just leave someone with children—especially their own, you know? I'm better now. I have a boyfriend and I trust him a lot, but I question everything he does. When he makes commitments I don't really think he's going to come through, you know? I wonder about that a lot because—I don't really have a reason to distrust all men but, you know?

"I think that because I didn't have my dad, we're closer to my grandparents. Be-cause Mom was so young and they helped us out all the time. They gave us prop-erty to build a house and everything. So we're a lot closer because she could always count on them. That's the most important thing, you know, being able to count on people."

◆ SUGGESTIONS FOR WRITING AND RESEARCH

Individual

1. Explore your identity by selecting one of the four types of autobiographical writing discussed in this chapter—autobiography, language autobiography, self-portrait, or career profile. Write an impressionistic first draft based on remembered experiences. Write a researched second draft based on artifacts or interviews. Write a snapshot-shaped third draft, mixing memory and research in a structure that pleases you.
2. Write a profile of a classmate, collecting as many kinds of information collecting as possible. In doing this assignment, plan to write several drafts and share these with your subject. Listen to his or her response to your profile, and take those comments into account when writing your final draft. Keep in mind the golden rule of profile writing: Do unto your subject as you would want him or her to do unto you.

Collaborative

1. Compile a class book of autobiographical sketches that includes a contribution from each class member. Elect a team of editors who will collect, compile, introduce, and produce these essays. Ask your instructor to write an afterword explaining the assignment. (For more information on publishing class books, see Chapter 21.)
2. Write a collaborative profile of your class. First, discuss what a class profile might be like: Would it be a collection of individual profiles arranged in some order? Or would it consist of written bits and pieces about people, places, and events, arranged as a verbal collage? Would there be a place for visual components in this class profile? Would you want to challenge other writing classes to develop similar profiles and share them with one another?

CHAPTER TEN

Explaining Things

When I give directions to somebody about how to find some place, it's much easier to draw a map than write it out in words. I mean, with words you have to be so precise but with a map you just draw lines.

JANE

To explain something is to make it clear to somebody else who wants to understand it. Explaining is fundamental to most acts of communication and to nearly every type of writing, from personal to argumentative and research writing. Explanatory writing is also a genre unto itself: a newspaper feature examining the ins and outs of baseball card collecting, a magazine article explaining the extinction of dinasaurs, an Internet site clarifying the difference between socialism and communism, a textbook on the French Revolution, a recipe for chili, or a laboratory report.

WRITING TO EXPLAIN

Explanatory writing (also called *expository* or *informational* writing) answers questions such as these:

- What is it?
- What does it mean?
- How does it work?
- How is it related to other things?
- How is it put together?
- Why did it happen?
- What will its consequences be?

To write a successful explanation, you need to find out first what your readers *want to know*, then what they *already know* and what they *don't know*. If you are able to determine—or at least make educated guesses about—these audience conditions, your writing task becomes clear. When you begin to write, keep in mind three general principles that typify much explanatory writing: (1) it focuses on the idea or object being explained rather than on the writer's beliefs and feelings: (2) it often—not always—states its objective early in what might be called an informational thesis; and (3) it presents information systematically and logically.

In writing classes, explanation usually takes the form of research essays and reports that emphasize informing rather than arguing, interpreting, or reflecting. The assignment may be to "describe how something works" or to "explain the causes and effects" of a particular phenomenon. This chapter explains how to develop a topic, articulate your purpose, and use strategies appropriate for your audience.

◆ WRITING 1: EXPLORATION

How good are you at explaining things to people? What things do you most commonly find yourself explaining? What is the last thing you explained in writing? How did your audience receive your explanation?

FINDING A TOPIC

Topics with a limited, or specific, scope are easier to explain carefully and in detail than topics that are vague, amorphous, or very broad. For example, general subjects such as mountains, automobiles, or music sound systems are so broad that it's hard to know where to begin. However, a specific aspect of sound systems, such as compact discs (CDs) is easier. Within the subject of CDs, of course, there are several topics as well (design, manufacturing process, cost, marketing, sound quality, comparison to tape and vinyl recordings, etc.). If your central question focuses on how CDs are manufactured, you might well address some of these other issues (cost, marketing, comparison) as well, but only in so far as they illuminate and advance your focus on manufacturing. Effective explanations are detailed and developed, include examples, and are focused around a central question ("How are CDs made?" or "How do CDs differ from LPs?"). Of course, there may be other questions to be answered along the way ("How do CDs work?" "Why do CDs cost so much?"), but these are secondary.

Once you have a focused topic on a central question, you need to assemble information. If you're not an expert yourself, you'll need to consult authorities on the topic. Even if you are already an expert, finding supporting information from other experts will help make your explanation clear and authoritative. Keep your audience in mind as you begin your research. You don't want to waste time researching and writing about things your audience already knows or issues that are beyond the scope of your focused topic.

◆ WRITING 2

What would you like to explain? for what purpose? to whom? If you're not sure, do some freewriting or journal writing to help you discover a question.

DEVELOPING A THESIS

The **thesis** statement in an explanatory paper is simply the writer's declaration of what the paper is about. Stating a thesis early in an explanatory work lets readers know what to expect and guides their understanding of the information to be presented. In explanatory writing, the thesis states the answer to the implied question your paper sets out to address: What is it? How does this work? Why is this so?

QUESTION   **What's the cultural significance of fairy tales and cartoons?**
THESIS   **Fairy tales and cartoons are a subtle means of indoctrinating children with cultural values.**

The advantage of stating a thesis in a single sentence is that it sums up the purpose of your paper in a single idea that lets readers predict what's ahead. Another way to state a single-sentence thesis is to convey an image, analogy, or metaphor that provides an ongoing reference point throughout the paper and gives unity and coherence to your explanation—a good image keeps both you and your readers focused.

QUESTION   **How are the offices of the city government connected?**
THESIS   **City government offices are like an octopus, with eight fairly independent bureaus as arms and a central brain in the mayor's office.**

The thesis you start with may evolve as you work on your paper—and that's okay. For example, suppose the more you learn about city government, the less like an octopus and the more like a centipede it seems. So, your first thesis is really a **working thesis,** and it needs to be tentative, flexible, and subject to change; its primary function is to keep your paper focused to guide further research.

◆ WRITING 3: APPLICATION

Write out a working thesis for the topic you are explaining. If you are addressing a *when* or *how* question, find a controlling image or analogy that will hold all of the elements together.

USING STRATEGIES TO EXPLAIN

Good strategies that can be used to explain things include defining, describing, classifying and dividing, analyzing causes and effects, and comparing and contrasting. Which strategy you select depends on the question you are answering as well as the audience to whom you are explaining. You could offer two very different explanations to the same question depending on who asked it. For example, if asked "Where is Westport Drive?" you would respond differently to a neighbor familiar with local reference points ("One block north of Burger King") than to a stranger who would not know where Burger King was either. With this caution in mind and considering who is the receiver of the explanation, here is a brief overview of possible strategies:

QUESTION	STRATEGY
What is it?	Define

Example: *A fairy tale is a story about fairies, giants, dwarfs, etc. that takes place in imaginary places.*

What does it mean?	Define

Example: The story of "Three Little Pigs" is a children's story that celebrates the work ethic.

What are its characteristics?	Describe

Example: *Animated cartoons are hand drawings made to move.*

How is it related to other things?	Compare and contrast

Example: *Fairy tales and cartoons convey cultural values to children in the same way that novels and plays convey cultural values to adults.*

How is it put together?	Classify and divide

Example: *An animated cartoon is composed of many individual images combined to tell a story.*

To what group does it belong?	Classify and divide

Example: *Cartoons, fairy tales, and nursery rhymes comprise an important part of children's literature.*

Why did it happen?	Analyze cause and effect

Example: *The strong wind can blow down the straw house because straw is not a substantial building material.*

What will its consequences be?	Analyze cause and effect

Example: *If you build a house of brick, it will withstand strong winds and not fall down.*

If your paper is on a tightly focused topic and answers a narrow, simple question, you may need to use only one strategy. More often, however, you will have one primary strategy that shapes the paper as a whole and several secondary strategies that can vary from paragraph to paragraph or even sentence to sentence. For example, to explain why the government has raised income taxes, your primary strategy would be to analyze cause and effect, but you might also need to define terms such as *income tax*, to classify the various types of taxes, and to compare and contrast raising income taxes to other budgetary options. In fact, almost every explanatory strategy makes use of other strategies: How, for example, do you describe a process without first dividing it into steps? How can you compare and contrast without describing the things compared and contrasted?

Defining

To define something is to identify it, to set it apart so that it can be distinguished from similar things. Writers need to define any terms central for reader understanding in order to make points clearly, forcefully, and with authority.

Formal **definitions** are what you find in a dictionary. They usually combine a general term with specific characteristics:

> A computer is a programmable electronic device [*general term*] that can store, retrieve, and process data [*specific characteristics*].

Usually, defining something is a brief preliminary step accomplished before you move on to a more important part of the explanation. When you need to define something complex or difficult or when your primary explanatory strategy is definition, you will need an extended definition consisting of a paragraph or more. This was the case with Mark's paper explaining computers, in which he defined each part of a typical computer system. After defining the central processor unit (CPU), he defined computer memory:

> Computer storage space is measured in units called "Kilobytes" (K). Each K equals 1,024 "bytes" or approximately 1,000 single typewriter characters. So 1 K equals about 180 English words, or a little less than half of a single-spaced typed page, or maybe three minutes of fast typing.
>
> Personal computers are now measured in "gigibytes" (GB) which is a thousand "megabytes" (MB), each of which equal 1,048,567 bytes (or 1,000 K), which translates into approximately 400 pages of single-spaced type. One gigabyte, then, equals approximately 400,000 pages of single-spaced type.

Describing

To describe a person, place, or thing means to create a verbal image so that readers can see what you see; hear what you hear; or taste, smell, and feel what you taste, smell, and feel. In other words, effective descriptions appeal to the senses. Furthermore, good descriptions contain enough sensory detail for readers to understand the subject, but not so much as to distract or bore them. Your job, then, is to include just the right amount of detail so that you put readers in your shoes.

To describe how processes work is more complicated than describing what something looks like: In addition to showing objects at rest, you need to show them in sequence and motion. You need to divide the process into discrete steps and present the steps in a logical order that will be easy for readers to follow. This is easier to do with simple processes, such as making a peanut butter and jelly sandwich, than for complex processes, such as manufacturing an automobile.

To help orient your readers, you may also want to number the steps, using transition words such as *first, second,* and *third.* In the following example, taken from an early draft of his paper, Keith describes the process of manufacturing compact discs:

> CDs start out as a refrigerator-sized box full of little plastic beads that you could sift your hands through. They are fed into a giant tapered corkscrew—a blown-up version

of an old-fashioned meat grinder. As the beads pass down the corkscrew, they are slowly melted by the heated walls.

At the bottom of their descent is a "master recording plate" onto which the molten plastic is pressed. The plastic now resembles a vinyl record, except that the disc is transparent. The master now imprints "pits," rather than grooves, around the disc, the surface resembling a ball of Play-Doh after being thrown against a stucco wall—magnified five thousand times.

Comparing and Contrasting

To compare two things is to find similarities between them; to contrast is to find differences. **Comparing and contrasting** at the same time helps people understand something two ways: first, by showing how it is related to similar things, and second, by showing how it differs. College assignments frequently ask you to compare and contrast two authors, books, ideas, and so on.

People usually compare and contrast things when they want to make a choice or judgment about them: books, food, bicycles, presidential candidates, political philosophies. For this reason, the two things compared and contrasted should be similar: You'll learn more to help you vote for president by comparing two presidential candidates than one presidential candidate and a senate candidate; you'll learn more about which orange to buy by comparing it with other oranges (*navel, mandarin*) than with apples, plums, or pears. Likewise, it's easiest to see similarities and differences when you compare and contrast the same elements of each thing. If you describe one political candidate's stand on gun control, describe the other's as well; this way, voters will have a basis for choosing one over the other.

Comparison-and-contrast analysis can be organized in one of three ways: (1) a *point-to-point analysis* examines one feature at a time for both similarities and differences; (2) a *whole-to-whole analysis* first presents one object as a whole and then the other as a whole: (3) a *similarity-and-difference analysis* first presents the similarities, then the differences between the two things, or vice versa.

Use a point-to-point or similarity-and-difference analysis for long explanations of complex things, such as manufacturing an automobile, in which you need to cover everything from materials and labor to assembly and inspection processes. But use a whole-to-whole analysis for simple objects that readers can more easily comprehend. In the following whole-to-whole example, a student explains the difference between Democrats and Republicans:

> Like most Americans, both Democrats and Republicans believe in the twin values of equality and freedom. However, Democrats place a greater emphasis on equality, believing equal opportunity for all people to be more important than the freedom of any single individual. Consequently, they stand for government intervention to guarantee equal treatment in matters of environmental protection, minimum wages, racial policies, and educational opportunities.
>
> In contrast, Republicans place greater emphasis on freedom, believing the specific rights of the individual to be more important than the vague collective rights of the masses. Consequently, they stand for less government control in matters of property ownership, wages and the right to work based strictly on merit and hard work, and local control of schools.

Note how the writer devotes equal space to each political party, uses neutral language to lend academic authority to his explanation, and emphasizes the differences by using parallel examples as well as parallel sentence structure. The careful use of several comparison-and-contrast strategies makes it difficult for readers to miss his point.

An *analogy* is an extended comparison which shows the extent to which one thing is similar in structure and/or process to another. Analogies are effective ways of explaining something new to readers, because you can compare something they are unfamiliar with to something they already know about. For example, most of us have learned to understand how a heart functions by comparing it to a water pump. Be sure to use objects and images in analogies that will be familiar to your readers.

Classifying and Dividing

People generally understand short more easily than long, simple more easily than complex. One way to help readers understand a complicated topic is to **classify and divide** it into simpler pieces and to put the pieces in context.

- To *classify* something, you put it in a category or class with other things that are like it:

  Like whales and dolphins, sea lions are aquatic mammals.

- To *divide* something, you break it into smaller parts or subcategories:

  An insect's body is composed of a head, a thorax, and an abdomen.

Most readers have a difficult time remembering more than six or seven items at a time, so explaining is easier when you organize a long list into fewer logical groups, as in the preceding example. Also be sure that the categories you use are meaningful to your readers, not simply convenient for you as a writer.

Analyzing Causes and Effects

Few things happen all by themselves. Usually, one thing happens because something else happened; then it, in turn, makes something else happen. You sleep because you're tired, and once you've slept, you wake up because you're rested, and so on. In other words, you already know about cause and effect because it's a regular part of your daily life. A **cause** is something that makes something else happen; an **effect** is the thing that happens.

Cause-and-effect analyses are most often assigned for college papers to answer *why* questions: Why are the fish dying in the river? The most direct answer is a *because* statement:

Fish are dying *because* oxygen levels in the lake are too low.

The answer, in other words, is a thesis, which the rest of the paper must defend and support:

There are three reasons for low oxygen level . . .

Cause-and-effect analyses also try to describe possible future effects:

If nitrogen fertilizers were banned from farmland that drains into the lake, oxygen levels would rise, and fish populations would be restored.

Unless there is sound, widely accepted evidence to support the thesis, however, this sort of analysis may lead to more argumentative writing. In this example, for instance, farmers or fertilizer manufacturers might complicate the matter by pointing to other sources of lake pollution—outboard motors, paper mill effluents, urban sewage runoff—making comprehensive solutions harder to reach. Keep in mind that most complex situations have multiple causes. If you try to reduce a complex situation to an overly simple cause, you are making the logical mistake known as *oversimplification.*

◆ WRITING 4: APPLICATION

Decide which of the five strategies described in this section best suits the primary purpose of the explanatory paper you are drafting. Which additional or secondary strategies will you also use?

ORGANIZING WITH LOGIC

If you explain to your readers where you're taking them, they will follow more willingly; if you lead carefully, step by step, using a good road map, they will know where they are and will trust you.

Your method of organization should be simple, straightforward, and logical, and it should be appropriate for your subject and audience. For example, to explain how a stereo system works, you have a number of logical options: (1) you could start by putting a CD in a player and end with the music coming out of the speakers; (2) you could describe the system technically, starting with the power source to explain how sound is made in the speakers; (3) you could describe it historically, starting with components that were developed earliest and work toward the most recent inventions. All these options follow a clear logic that, once explained, will make sense to readers.

◆ WRITING 5: APPLICATION

Outline three possible means of organizing the explanatory paper you are writing. List the advantages and disadvantages of each. Select the one that best suits your purpose and the needs of your audience.

MAINTAINING A NEUTRAL PERSPECTIVE

First, you need to understand that absolute neutrality or objectivity is impossible when you write about anything. All writers bring with them assumptions and biases that cause them to view the world—including this explanatory project—in a particular way. Nevertheless, your explanations will usually be clearer and more accessible to others when you present them as fairly as possible, with as little bias as possible—even though doing this, too, will depend on who your readers are and whether they agree or disagree with your biases. In general, it's more effective to emphasize the thing explained (the object) rather than your personal beliefs and feelings. This perspective allows you to get information to readers as quickly and efficiently as possible without you, the writer, getting in the way.

To adopt a neutral perspective, write from the third-person point of view, using the pronouns *he, she,* and *it.* Keep yourself in the background unless you have a good reason not to, such as explaining your personal experience with the subject. In some instances, adopting the second-person *you* adds a friendly, familiar tone that keeps readers interested.

Be fair; present all the relevant information about the topic, both things you like about it and things you dislike. Avoid emotional or biased language. Remember that your goal is not to win an argument, but to convey information.

SHAPING THE WHOLE PAPER

In the following paper, Katie Moll discovered an unexpected and disturbing controversy surrounding the television cartoon show, *The Smurfs.* The essay records her step-by-step attempt to explain and understand the truth about her favorite childhood program. Here is an instance where information found on the Internet first created a problem to solve, then provided the solution. Katie's essay concludes with a personal postscript that poses interesting questions for all who rely on Web-based research.

The Smurfs as Political Propaganda

Katie Moll

Saturday morning cartoons were a large part of my childhood. They brought enjoyment and laughter, and they sometimes taught moral lessons. I grew up surrounded by shows like *Fraggle Rock, Rainbow Brite, The Jetsons,* and *Reading Rainbow.* My personal favorite, however, was *The Smurfs,* a cartoon focused on a village of small blue elf-like creatures that lived in mushrooms and were always content with their lives. Much to my despair, they were taken off the air after the 1980s.

It wasn't until about a year ago that the Smurfs were brought to my attention again, when I chose to attend a theme party dressed as one of the Smurf character such as Brainy, Handy, or Smurfette. However, after checking party stores around, I could find no costumes. When I checked the Internet for Smurf costumes, I found more than I bargained for, as Web sites popped up with titles such as "Sociopolitical Themes in the Smurf" and "Papa Smurf Is a Communist." How could they make such claims about my favorite cartoon? And then I wondered, could this be true? Was *The Smurf* television show really political propaganda?

To check this story further, I searched the Web with the keyword "Smurfs," which took me to "The Smurfs Official Site" at <www.smurf.com/homepage.html>. It had nothing about the communist theory, but then again, why would it? This was the home page promoting the cartoon, so I doubted it would slander the program. However, I did obtain useful background information on the origin of The Smurfs. The creator of the Smurf characters was Peyo, the pen name of Pierre Culliford, who lived and worked in Brussels, Belgium. The Smurfs first appeared as a comic strip in 1958. It was not until 1981 that the The Smurfs became an animated television series designed by the team of William Hanna and Joseph Barbera. Nothing on the Smurf home page suggested that either Peyo or Hanna-Barbera had subversive intentions, so I began to think the theory was a complete hoax. But I wanted to find out more.

Papa Smurf wears red pants

Then, amidst a jumble of commercial topics, I found a Web site called "The Smurfs as a Paradigm for Communist Society" that suggested, "The Smurfs were actually a well-devised piece of communist propaganda to erode American society from within" (Gozer, para 2). Five points of comparison between the Smurf cartoon show and a Russian communist society make the author's case: (1) Papa Smurf, the wise leader of the Smurf community, looks like Karl Marx and (2) wears red pants; (3) all Smurfs work according to their ability and receive according to their needs; (4) the villain, Gargamel, acts like a greedy capitalist; and (5) his cat, Azreal, represents "third-world despotisms that are clinging onto the coattails of first-world capitalism." He concludes, saying, "these five points provide very strong evidence pointing to the conclusion that the TV show 'The Smurfs' is indeed a paradigm for communist society" (para 8). "Strong evidence"? It is hard to take this 500-word Web site very seriously. It is short; the supporting detail in each paragraph is sketchy; some of the arguments (Papa Smurf as Karl Marx!) are far-fetched; and the author is not accountable, providing no name and no credentials, though an e-mail address <9620080@cc.wwu.edu> is included. However, a second Web site, Sociopolitical Themes in *The Smurfs* by J. Marc Schmidt, outlines in much more detail the basis for a Marxist interpretation: "Unlike many other cartoons, or indeed other television programmes, The Smurfs is about an entire society and its interactions with itself and with outsiders, rather than the adventures of a few characters. Hence, I believe it is, in short, a political fable, in much the same way that *The Lion, the Witch and the Wardrobe* was a fable about Christianity. Rather than Christianity, however, The Smurfs is about Marxism. (para 2)"

Note that Schmidt does not label *The Smurfs* "propaganda," but describes the cartoon series in the same terms as other respected "political fables" such as those by C. S. Lewis, something to be studied or learned from rather than be brainwashed by. In Schmidt's words, "I am not accusing *The Smurfs* of being some kind of subversive kiddie propaganda" (para 3).

Schmidt believes Peyo to be a socialist rather than a card-carrying communist, calling the Smurf village "a Marxist utopia" rather than a police state like the old Soviet Union (para 5). The evidence Schmidt assembles is thoughtful and far more convincing than Gozer's hasty claims. For example, he points out that Smurf village is "a perfect model of a socialist commune or collective" (para 5), that "the Smurfs are all completely equal" (para 6), that "everyone is equally a worker and an owner" (para 7), and that "they wear the same kind and colour of clothes" (para 9).

I found the Schmidt Web site to be quite convincing. For one thing, all that he says about the Smurfs and Smurf village matches what I remember about the show. Once he points out those similarities, I can see his point. For another thing, the Schmidt article on the Web site is carefully written, with clear explanations and concrete examples. In addition, Schmidt includes his whole name along with an e-mail address <j_marc_s@hotmail.com>—an indication that he is willing to be responsible for his ideas. Because of the way Schmidt spells certain words (programme and colour), a first reading of his site suggests that his English is British rather than American, in which case he may have more objective distance from the cartoon show than an American author would.

However, when I looked at a third Web site that addressed this propaganda issue, "Papa Smurf Is a Communist," I became confused again. At first glance, this site seemed to have been written from an angry capitalist perspective, upset that communist connections are hidden in the children's cartoon. Even the feel of this Web page was different, with a menacing black background and dark red letters as opposed to the more neutral tones on the other Web sites. At first, I was annoyed by its aggressive tone, but when I read it a second time, I found myself laughing. This Web site is not serious at all! Instead, it is making obvious fun of the communist propaganda theory, as the following excerpt illustrates:

> Yes, that is correct, Papa Smurf and all of his little Smurf minions are not the happy little characters Hanna-Barbera would have us believe! The cartoon was really created by the Russian government in order to indoctrinate the youngest members of Western society with communist beliefs and ideals, thus destroying their resistance to the imminent Russian invasion that was to occur when this generation (my generation) grew up.

When I read "imminent Russian invasion," I said wait a minute. While it is true that during the Cold War many Americans feared a nuclear war with Russia, I didn't think anyone actually feared an invasion. And when he claimed that the word Smurf was an acronym standing for "Small Men Under Red Father" I found myself laughing again. And in yet another passage, this anonymous author argues that Papa Smurf resembles Stalin more than Marx:

> I feel that Stalin is most likely the man that Papa Smurf was modeled after. Marx believed more in the system of socialism, not communism. What is the difference, you may ask? Well, under both systems everything is supposedly shared equally among all members of the society; however, under the socialist system there are free elections for the leadership of the society, whereas under the communist system there are no elections. I sure as hell don't remember Papa Smurf being [an] elected leader. . . . [but] Stalin's appearance also highly resembles that of Papa Smurf. His beard may not be as perfect as that of Marx, but look at that round face! (para 7)

The author does not reveal his or her identity but does provide an e-mail address <commiesmurfs@hotmail.com> to which readers can respond, along with twenty reader responses printed at the end of the site such as these two:

- "Your page was one of the funniest things I have read in a long time! Great job on it—I especially like the shot [an image on the Web page] of Papa Smurf with the hammer and sickle in his hat!"
- "The site made me open my eyes and realize that communism only exists not in society but in most of our pop culture as well. Being concerned, I am now proposing 'CASCO' (Canadians Against Smurf Communism) to rid the evils of the Smurfs on Sunday mornings; they are shown on a regular basis in Canada. Spread the news."

To make sense of three different Web sites, each pointing to similarities between *The Smurfs* and Marxism, I looked more carefully at the sequence in which the sites were created. Who, in other words, started this comparison? Fortunately, each site was dated. The brief Gozer site was created in September 1997. The anonymous and obvious parody, "Papa Smurf," was created in March of the same year—six months *earlier* than Gozer—so the parody was first. The only serious site, Schimidt's, was not created until sometime in 1998 (exact month not available). In other words, the most obvious parody of the cartoon show, the anonymous "Papa Smurf," seemed to start a small chain reaction, with the Gozer site second and Schmidt's last.

Curious to see whether there were any connections among the three Web sites, I sent e-mail queries to each site. I never heard from the anonymous creator of the earliest site, "Papa Smurf," but I received responses from the other two authors. J. Marc Schmidt responded promptly, identifying himself as a high school teacher living in Sydney, Australia (hence the British spellings), and explaining that he created his site after attending a museum exhibit on cartoon animation in which he found hard-to-believe interpretations of many animated shows. Schmidt writes, "I started thinking more and more about socialism, and eventually the idea just clicked. Anyway, for good or bad, that incomprehensible blurb was the seed, which led me to write an essay called 'Sociopolitical Themes in the Smurfs.' I turned it into a Web site and put it on the Internet."

The author of the Gozer site also responded, providing his real name, Eric Lott, but asking me not to give out his personal e-mail address. Lott writes: "In honest truth, it was/is not intended as a parody. Personally, I am an anarcho-socialist. I began thinking this up . . . and developed it into a monologue. Most people I gave [it] to found it quite amusing."

After reading the comic, the amusing, and the serious interpretations of the socialist Smurfs, I realized I had to take another look at the cartoon myself. I obtained a copy of one Smurf episode by borrowing it from a friend's younger sister (who else would collect such videotapes?) and tried to watch it with an open mind, as if I were young again.

This untitled episode portrayed Smurfette in danger of being captured by the cat, Azreal, but rescued just in time by Papa and the other Smurfs. After having read all the political ideas about The Smurfs, however, I found it difficult to watch an episode with an open mind. As soon as it was over, I began seeing possible socialist connections myself. For example, when Papa Smurf rounds up the rescue team, is he a communist dictator taking charge? When the villain, Gargamel, orders his cat to catch Smurfette, is he a capitalist dictator delegating his dirty jobs to the workers? Is the chase scene a reminder of the constant war between the free world and communism? Does the color red symbolize communism?

It was then I also realized that I could take virtually any children's story and make it mean something else. Do Santa Claus and Little Red Riding Hood wear red because they are communists? Do Santa's elves make toys because they are slaves? Is the Big Bad Wolf a greedy capitalist? While these interpretations are possible, I don't believe they were ever intended by the creators of these stories.

Postscript

Browsing the Internet after writing this paper, I found an interpretation of the popular children's television show Teletubbies, suggesting that one of the Teletubbies characters is a homosexual role model. According to "Parents Alert: Tinky Winky Comes Out of the Closet," an article published in the February 1999 edition of the National Liberty Journal—a newsletter edited and published by the Rev. Jerry Falwell—"Tinky Winky has the voice of a boy yet carries a purse . . . is purple—the gay-pride color; and his antenna is shaped like a triangle—the gay-pride symbol" (qtd. in Reed). At this point, however, I stopped reading. Who really cares whether it's possible that Tinky Winky is gay—or a Marxist, for that matter? Not me.

Thinking about my Smurf investigation now, I think the real topic was neither *The Smurfs* nor the Marxists, but what I found out about the Internet itself. First, for anybody with access to a computer, the Internet is the greatest medium ever devised for the unlimited practice of free speech. Second, the Internet is also the greatest repository of both fact and fiction ever devised—but there's nobody to tell you for sure which is which, sometimes not even the author! This idea clearly needs further investigation and elaboration, but to tell the truth, I don't have the time. I'll leave that topic, along with the Teletubbies, for my next paper.

Works Cited

Gozer. The Smurfs as a Paradigm for Communist Society. 27 Sep. 1997. 7 Oct. 2001 <http://www.ac.wwu.edu/~n9620080/smurf.html>.

Lott, Eric. Personal e-mail. 4 Dec. 2001.

Papa Smurf Is a Communist. 16 Mar. 1997. 8 Oct. 2001 <http://geocities.com/CapitolHill/Lobby/1709>.

Reed, David. "Falwell's Newspaper Attempts to Label Teletubbies Character as Gay." 10 Feb. 1999. 9 Nov. 2001 <http://www.sfgate.com/cgibin/article.cgi?file=/news/archive/1999/02/10/national0333EST0476.DTL>.

Schmidt, J. Marc. Sociopolitical Themes in the Smurfs. 7 Oct. 1998. 8 Oct. 2001<http://www.geocities.com/Hollywood/Cinema/3117/sociosmurf2. htm>.—. Personal e-mail. 3 Dec. 2001.

The Smurfs Official Site. 2005. 7 Oct. 2001 <http://www.smurf.com/homepage.html>.

Teletubbies. PBS kids. 2005. 8 Nov. 2001 <http://pbskids.org/teletubbies. html>.

2444 words

◆ SUGGESTIONS FOR WRITING AND RESEARCH

Individual

1. Write a paper explaining any thing, process, or concept. Use as a starting point an idea you discovered in writing 2. When you have finished one draft of this essay, look back and see whether there are places where your explanation could be improved through use of one of the explanatory strategies explained in this chapter.
2. Select a writer of your choice, fiction or nonfiction, who explains things especially well. Read or reread a passage of explanatory writing in his or her work and write an essay in which you analyze and explain the effectiveness of the explanation you find there.

Collaborative

Form writing groups based on mutual interests; agree as a group to explain the same thing, process, or concept. Write your explanations separately and then share drafts, comparing and contrasting your different ways of explaining. For a final draft, either (1) rewrite your individual drafts, borrowing good ideas from others in your group, or (2) compose a collaborative single paper with contributions from each group member.

CHAPTER ELEVEN

Arguing For and Against

When I argued against federal gun control laws with my roommates, it was pretty easy to convince them I was right, but when I wrote the same arguments in my English paper, my writing group challenged every point I made and kept asking for more evidence, more proof. Do you have to have evidence for everything you write?

Argument is deeply rooted in the American political and social system, in which free and open debate is the essence of the democratic process. Argument is also at the heart of the academic process, in which scholars investigate scientific, social, and cultural issues, hoping through the give-and-take of debate to find reasonable answers to complex questions. Argument in the academic world, however, is less likely to be about winning or losing—as it is in political and legal systems—than about changing minds or altering perceptions about knowledge and ideas.

Argument as rational disagreement, rather than as quarrels and contests, most often occurs in areas of genuine uncertainty about what is right, best, or most reasonable. In disciplines such as English, history, and philosophy, written argument commonly takes the form of interpretation, in which the meaning of an idea or text is disputed. In disciplines such as political science, engineering, and business, arguments commonly appear as position papers in which a problem is examined and a solution proposed.

The purpose of writing argument papers is to persuade other people to agree with a particular point of view. Arguments focus on issues about which there is some debate; if there's no debate, there's no argument. College assignments commonly ask you to argue one side of an issue and defend your argument against attacks from skeptics.

WRITING TO CHANGE PEOPLE'S MINDS

In a basic position paper assignment, you are asked to choose an issue, argue a position, and support it with evidence. Sometimes your investigation of the issue will lead you beyond polar positions toward compromise—a common result of real argument and debate in both the academic and political worlds. In other words, such a paper may reveal that the result of supporting one position (**thesis**) against another (**antithesis**) is to arrive at yet a third position (**synthesis**), which is possible now because both sides have been fully explored and a reasonable compromise presents itself. This chapter explains the elements that constitute a basic position paper: an arguable issue, a claim and counterclaim, a thesis, and evidence.

Issues

An issue is a controversy, something that can be argued about. For instance, mountain bikes and cultural diversity are things or concepts, not in themselves issues. However, they become the foundation for issues when questions are raised about them and controversy ensues.

ISSUE   **Do American colleges adequately represent the cultural diversity of the United States?**

ISSUE   **Should mountain bikes be allowed on wilderness hiking trails?**

These questions are issues because reasonable people could answer them in different ways; they can be argued about because more than one answer is plausible, possible, or realistic.

Virtually all issues can be formulated, at least initially, as yes/no questions about which you will take one position or the other: pro (if the answer is yes) or con (if the answer is no).

ISSUE   **Should mountain bikes be allowed on trails in Riverside Park?**

PRO   **Yes, they should be allowed to share pedestrian trails.**

CON   **No, they should not be allowed to share trails with pedestrians.**

Claims and Counterclaims

A **claim** is a statement or assertion that something is true or should be done. In arguing one side of an issue, you make one or more claims in the hope of convincing an audience to believe you. For example, you could make a claim that calls into question the educational experience at Northville College:

CLAIM   **Northville College fails to provide good education because the faculty is not culturally diverse.**

Counterclaims are statements that oppose or refute claims. You need to examine an opponent's counterclaim carefully in order to refute it or, if you agree with the counterclaim, to argue that your claim is more important to making a decision. For example, the following counterclaim might be offered against your claim about the quality of Northville College education:

COUNTERCLAIM   **The Northville faculty is good scholars and teachers; therefore, their cultural backgrounds are irrelevant.**

You might agree that "Northville faculty *are* good scholars and teachers" but still argue that the education is not as good as it would be with more diversity. In other words, the best arguments provide not only good reasons for accepting a position but also good reasons for doubting the opposition. They are made by writers who know both sides of an issue and are prepared for the arguments of the opposition.

Thesis

In an argument, the major claim your paper makes is your **thesis:**

THESIS   **Northville College should enact a policy to make the faculty more culturally diverse by the year 2010.**

In taking a position, you may make other claims as well, but they should all work to support this major claim or thesis:

CLAIM   **The faculty is not culturally diverse now.**

CLAIM   **A culturally diverse faculty is necessary to provide a good education for today's students.**

CLAIM   **The goal of increased cultural diversity by the year 2010 is achievable and practical.**

In arguing a position, you may state your thesis up front, with the remainder of the paper supporting it (*thesis first*), or you may state it later in the paper after weighing the pros and cons with your reader (*delayed thesis*). As a writer, you can decide which approach is the stronger rhetorical strategy after you fully examine each claim and the supporting evidence. Each strategy, thesis first or delayed, has its advantages and disadvantages (see 9f).

Evidence

Evidence makes a claim believable. **Evidence** consists of facts, examples, or testimony that supports a claim. For example, to support a claim that Northville College's faculty lacks cultural diversity, you might introduce the following evidence:

EVIDENCE   **According to the names in the college catalog, 69 of 79 faculty members are male.**

EVIDENCE   **According to a recent faculty survey, 75 of 79 faculty members are Caucasian or white.**

EVIDENCE   **According to Carmen Lopez, an unsuccessful candidate for a position in the English department, 100 percent of the faculty hired in the last ten years have been white males.**

Most arguments become more effective when they include documentable source material; however, shorter and more modest argument papers can be written without research and can profitably follow a process similar to that described here.

◆ WRITING 1

An issue debated by college faculty is whether or not a first-year writing course should be required of all college students. Make three claims and three counterclaims about this issue. Then select the claim you most believe in and write an argument thesis that could form the basis for a whole essay.

FINDING AN ISSUE

You'll write better and have a more interesting time if you select an issue that interests you and about which you still have real questions. A good issue around which to write a position paper will meet the following criteria:

- It is a real issue about which there is controversy and uncertainty.
- It has at least two distinct and arguable positions.
- Resources are available to support both sides.
- It is manageable within the time and scope of the assignment.

In selecting an issue to research and write about, consider both national and local issues. You are likely to see national issues explained and argued in the media:

- Are SAT scores a fair measure of academic potential?
- Should handgun ownership be outlawed in the United States?
- Does acid rain kill forests?

The advantages of national issues include their extensive coverage by television and radio, national newspapers such as *The New York Times* and *Washington Post,* and national newsmagazines. The broad coverage of national news is likely to provide evidence and supporting claims from many sources. In addition, you can count on your audience's having some familiarity with the subject. The disadvantage is that it may be difficult to find local experts or a site where some dimension of the issue can be witnessed.

Local issues derive from the community in which you live. You will find these issues argued about in local newspapers and on local news broadcasts:

- Should a new mall be built on the beltway?
- Should mountain bikes be allowed in Riverside Park?
- Should Northville College require a one-semester course introducing students to diverse American cultures?

The advantage of local issues is that you can often visit a place where the controversy occurs, interview people who are affected by it, and find generous coverage in local news media. The disadvantage is that the subject won't be covered in the national news. Evidence and claims in support of your thesis may be more limited.

Perhaps the best issue is a national issue (hikers versus mountain bikers) with a strong local dimension (this controversy in a local park). Such an issue will enable you to find both national press coverage and local experts.

♦ WRITING 2: APPLICATION

Make a list of three national and three local issues about which you are concerned. Next, select the three issues that seem most important to you and write each as a question with a yes or no answer. Finally, note whether each issue meets the criteria for a good position paper topic.

ANALYZING AN ISSUE

The most demanding work in writing a position paper takes place *after* you have selected an issue but *before* you actually write the paper. To analyze an issue, you need to conduct enough research to explain it and identify the arguments of each side.

In this data-collecting stage, treat each side fairly, framing the opposition as positively as you frame the position. Research as if you are in an honest debate with yourself. Doing so may even cause you to switch sides—one of the best indications of open-minded research. Furthermore, empathy for the opposition leads to making qualified assertions and heads off overly simplistic right-versus-wrong arguments. Undecided readers who see merit in the opposing side respect writers who acknowledge an issue's complexity.

Context

Provide full context for the issue you are writing about, as if readers know virtually nothing about it. Providing **context** means answering these questions: What is this issue about? Where did the controversy begin? How long has it been debated? Who are the people involved? What is at stake? Use a neutral tone, as Issa does in the essay on pages 133–137 in discussing the mountain bike trail controversy:

> With all these new riders, there is a need for places to ride, and this is where the wilderness trail controversy begins. The mountain bike is designed to be ridden on dirt trails, logging roads, and fire trails in backwoods country. However, other trail users who have been around much longer than mountain bikers prefer to enjoy the woods at a slow, leisurely pace. They find the rapid and sometimes noisy two-wheel intruders unacceptable. . . .

Claims For (Pro)

List the claims supporting the pro side of the issue. Make each claim a distinctly strong and separate point, and make the best possible case for this position, identifying by name the most important people or organizations that hold this view. Issa makes the following claims for opening up wilderness trails to mountain bikes:

1. All people should have the right to explore the wilderness so long as they do not damage it.
2. Knobby mountain bike tires do no more damage to hiking trails than Vibram-soled hiking boots.

3. Most mountain bike riders are respectful of the wilderness and courteous to other trail users.

Claims Against (Con)

List the claims supporting the con side of the issue—the counterclaims. It is not important to have an equal number of reasons for and against, but you do want an approximate balance.

1. Mountain bike riders ride fast, are sometimes reckless, and pose a threat to slower moving hikers.
2. Mountain bike tires damage trails and cause erosion.

Annotated References

Make an alphabetical list on note cards or computer files of the references you consulted during research, briefly identifying each according to the kind of information it contains. The same article may present claims from both sides as well as provide context. Following are two of Issa's annotated references:

Buchanan, Rob. "Birth of the Gearhead Nation." Rolling Stone 9 July 1992: 80-85. Marin Co. CA movement advocates more trails open to mountain bike use. Includes history. (pro)

Schwartz, David M. "Over Hill, Over Dale on a Bicycle Built for . . . Goo." Smithsonian June 1992: 74-84. Discusses the hiker vs. biker issue, promotes peaceful coexistence; includes history. (pro/con)

Annotating your list of references allows you to check and rearrange your claims at any time during the writing process. In addition, if you write and organize your references now, your reference page will be ready to go when you've finished writing your paper.

♦ WRITING 3: APPLICATION

Select one of the issues you are interested in, establish the necessary context, and make pro and con lists similar to those described in this section, including supporters of each position. Make the best possible case for each position.

◆ TAKING A POSITION

Once you have examined the two positions fairly, weigh which side is the stronger. Select the position that you find more convincing and then write out the reasons that support this position, most compelling reasons last. This will be the position you will most likely defend; you need to state it as a thesis.

Start with a Thesis

Formulate your initial position as working thesis early in your paper-writing process. Even though it is merely something to start with, not necessarily to stick with, it serves to focus your initial efforts in one direction and it helps you articulate claims and assemble evidence to support it.

WORKING THESIS   **Hikers and mountain bikers should cooperate and support each other in using, preserving, and maintaining wilderness trails.**

Writers often revise their initial positions as they reshape their paper or find new evidence. Your working thesis should meet the following criteria:

- It can be managed within your confines of time and space.
- It asserts something specific.
- It proposes a plan of action.

◆ WRITING 4: APPLICATION

Take a position on the issue you have identified. Formulate a working thesis that you would like to support. Test your thesis against the criteria listed for good theses.

DEVELOPING AN ARGUMENT

Your argument is the case you will make for your position, the means by which you will try to persuade your readers that your position is correct. Good arguments need solid and credible evidence and clear and logical reasoning.

Assembling Evidence

A claim is meaningless without evidence to support it. Facts, examples, inferences, informed opinion, and personal experience all provide believable evidence.

Facts are verifiable and agreed upon by everyone involved regardless of personal beliefs or values. Facts are often statistical and recorded in some place where anybody can look them up:

Water boils at 212 degrees Fahrenheit.

Northville College employed 79 full-time faculty and enrolled 1,143 full-time students in 1999.

Five hundred Japanese-made "Stumpjumper" mountain bikes were sold in the United States in 1981, while over five million Stumpjumpers were sold in 1991.

Examples can be used to illustrate a claim or clarify an issue. If you claim that many wilderness trails have been closed to mountain biking, you can mention examples you know about:

The New Jersey trails at South Mountain, Eagle Rock, and Mills Park have all been closed to mountain bikes.

Facts and examples can, of course, be misleading and even wrong. For hundreds of years malaria was believed to be caused by "bad air" rather than, as we know today, by a parasite transmitted by mosquitoes; however, for the people who believed the bad-air theory, it was fact.

Inferences are generalizations based on an accumulation of a certain number of facts. For example, if you attend five different classes at Northville College and in each class you find no minority students, you may infer that there are no minority students on campus. However, while your inference is reasonable, it is not a fact, since your experience does not allow for your meeting all the students at the college.

Facts are not necessarily better or more important than inferences; they serve different purposes. Facts provide information, and inferences give that information meaning.

Sometimes inference is all that's available. For example, statistics describing what "Americans" believe or do are only inferences about these groups based on information collected from a relatively small number of individuals. To be credible, however, inferences must be reasonable and based on factual evidence.

Expert opinion makes powerful evidence. A forest ranger's testimony about trail damage caused by mountain bikes or lug-soled hiking boots reflects the training and experience of an expert. A casual hiker making the same observation is less believable. To use expert opinion in writing arguments, be sure to cite the credentials or training that makes this person's testimony "expert."

Personal testimony is based on direct personal experience. When someone has experienced something firsthand, his or her knowledge cannot easily be discounted. If you have been present at the mistreatment of a minority student whether as the object or an observer of the incident, your eyewitness testimony will carry weight, even though you are not a certified expert of any kind. To use personal testimony effectively, provide details that confirm for readers that you were there and know what you are talking about.

Reasoning Effectively

To build an effective argument, consider the audience you must persuade. If you were writing about the mountain bike controversy and taking a pro-biker position, for example, you would ask yourself these questions:

- Who will read this paper? Members of an environmentally conscious hiking club? members of a mountain bike club? your instructor?
- Where do I think my readers stand on the issue? Hikers are often opposed to mountain bikes, and mountain bikers are not, but you would need more information to predict your instructor's position.
- How are their personal interests involved? Hikers want the trails quiet and peaceful; bikers want to ride in the wilderness, and your instructor may or may not care.
- What evidence would they consider convincing?
- A hiker would need to see convincing examples of trails not being damaged by mountain bike use; bikers would accept anecdotal testimony of good intentions, and you're still not sure about your instructor.

The more you know about the audience you're trying to sway, the easier it will be to present your case. If your audience is your instructor, you'll need to make inferences about his or her beliefs based on syllabus language, class discussion, assigned readings, or personal habits. For example, if your instructor rides a mountain bike to work, you may begin to infer one thing; if he or she assigns Sierra Club readings in the course, you infer something else; and if the instructor rides a mountain bike *and* reads Sierra Club publications, well, you've got more homework ahead. Remember that inferences based on a single piece of evidence are often wrong; find out more before you make simple assumptions about your audience. And sometimes audience analysis doesn't work very well when an instructor, in an effort to help you learn to develop a persuasive position paper, assumes a deliberately skeptical role, no matter which side of an issue you support. It's best to assume you will have a critical reader and to use the best logic and evidence available. Following are some ways to marshal careful and substantial evidence.

FIRST, ESTABLISH YOUR CREDIBILITY.   Demonstrate to your audience that you are fair and can be trusted. Do this by writing in neutral, not obviously biased, language—avoid name-calling. Also do this by citing current sources by respected experts—and don't quote them out of context. Do this also by identifying elements that serve as common ground between you and the audience—be up front and admit when the opposite side makes a good point.

CREDIBLE   **Northville College offers excellent instruction in many areas; however, its offerings in multicultural education would be enhanced by a more diverse faculty.**

LESS CREDIBLE   **Education at Northville College sucks.**

SECOND, USE LOGIC.   Demonstrate that you understand the principles of reasoning that operate in the academic world: Make each claim clearly and carefully. Make sure you have substantial, credible evidence to support each claim. Make inferences from your evidence with care; don't exaggerate or argue positions that are not supported by the evidence. Use **logic** to infer reasonable relationships between pieces of evidence.

LOGICAL   **Because 75 of 79 faculty members are white and 69 of 79 are male, hiring more blacks, Hispanics, Native Americans, and women, when they are available, would increase the cultural diversity of the faculty.**

ILLOGICAL   **Because most of the Northville faculty are white men, they must be racists and should be sent to another country.**

THIRD, APPEAL TO YOUR AUDIENCE'S EMOTIONS.   It's fair to use means of persuasion other than logic to win arguments. Write with vivid details, concrete language, and compelling examples to show your audience a situation that needs addressing. It is often helpful, as well, to adopt a personal tone and write in friendly language to reach readers' hearts as well as minds.

EMOTIONAL APPEAL   **When Bridgett Jones, the only black student in Philosophy 1, sits down, the desks on either side of her remain empty. When her classmates choose partners for debate, Bridgett is always the last one chosen.**

◆ WRITING 5

Develop an informal profile of the audience for your position paper by answering the questions posed in this section. Make a list of the kinds of evidence most likely to persuade this audience.

ORGANIZING A POSITION PAPER

To organize your paper, you need to know your position on the issue: What is the main point of your argument? In other words, move from a *working thesis* to a *final thesis*: Confirm the working thesis that's been guiding your research so far, or modify it, or scrap it altogether and assert a different one. You should be able to articulate this thesis in a single sentence as the answer to the yes/no question you've been investigating.

> THESIS   **Wilderness trails should be open to both mountain bikers and hikers.**
> THESIS   **Wilderness trails should be closed to mountain bikes.**

Your next decision is where in this paper you should reveal your thesis to the reader—in your opening or strategically delayed until later?

Thesis-First Organization

Leading with a thesis, the most common form of academic argument, tells readers from the beginning where you stand on the issue. One good way to organize a thesis-first argument is to make the remainder of the essay defend your claim against counterclaims, support your thesis with evidence, and close with a restatement of your position. In this organization, your thesis occupies both the first and last position in the essay, making it easy for your readers to remember.

1. *Introduce and explain the issue.*   Make sure there are at least two debatable sides. Pose the question that you see arising from this issue; if you can frame it as a yes/no, for/against construction, both you and your reader will have the advantage throughout your answer of knowing where you stand.

   Minority students, supported by many majority students at Northville College, have staged a week-long sit-in to urge the hiring of more minority faculty across the curriculum. Is this a reasonable position? Should Northville hire more minority faculty members?

2. *Assert your thesis.*   Your thesis states the answer to the question you have posed and establishes the position from which you will argue. Think of your thesis as the major claim the paper will make.

   Northville College should enact a policy to make the faculty more culturally diverse as soon as reasonably possible.

   Writers commonly state their thesis early in the paper, at the conclusion of the paragraph that introduces the issue.

3. *Summarize the counterclaims.*   Before elaborating on your own claims, explain the opposition's counterclaims. Doing that gives your own argument something to focus on—and refute—throughout the rest of the paper. Squeezing the counterclaims between the thesis (2) and the evidence (5) reserves the strongest places—the opening and closing—for your position.

COUNTERCLAIM 1   **Northville College is located in a white middle-class community, so its faculty should be white and middle-class also.**

COUNTERCLAIM 2   **The Northville faculty are good scholars and teachers; therefore, their race is irrelevant.**

4. *Refute the counterclaims.*   Look for weak spots in the opposition's argument, and point them out. Use your opponent's language to show you have read closely but still find problems with the claim. To refute counterclaim 1, you could make a statement like this:

> If the community in which the college is located is "white middle-class," all the more reason to offer that diversity in the college.

Your refutation is often stronger when you acknowledge the truth of some of the opposition's claims (demonstrating your fairness) but point out the limitations as well. To refute counterclaim 2, you could say this:

> It's true that Northville College offers excellent instruction in many areas; however, its instruction in multicultural education would be enhanced by a more diverse faculty.

5. *Support your claims with evidence.*   Spell out your own claims clearly and precisely, enumerating them or being sure to give each its own full-paragraph explanation, and citing supporting evidence. This section will constitute the longest and most carefully documented part of your essay. The following evidence supports the thesis that Northville needs more cultural diversity:

> According to the names in the college catalog, 69 of 79 faculty members are male.

> According to a recent faculty survey, 75 of 79 faculty members are white.

> According to Carmen Lopez, an unsuccessful job candidate for a position in the English department, all faculty hired in the last ten years have been white males.

6. *Restate your position as a conclusion.*   Near the end of your paper, synthesize your accumulated evidence into a broad general position, and restate your original thesis in slightly different language.

> While Northville College offers a strong liberal arts education, the addition of more culturally diverse faculty members would make it even stronger.

Delayed-Thesis Organization

Using the delayed-thesis type of organization, you introduce the issue and discuss the arguments for and against, but you do not obviously take a side until late in the essay. In this way, you draw readers into your struggle to weigh the evidence, and you arouse their curiosity about your position. Near the end of the paper, you explain that after carefully considering both pros and cons, you have now arrived at the most reasonable position.

Concluding with your own position gives it more emphasis. The following delayed-thesis argument is derived from the sample student essay at the end of this chapter.

1. *Introduce the issue and pose a question.*   Both thesis-first and delayed-thesis papers begin by establishing context and posing a question. Following is the question for the mountain bike position paper:

   Should mountain bikes be allowed on wilderness trails?

2. *Summarize the claims for one position.*   Before stating which side you support, explain how the opposition views the issue:

   To traditional trail users, the new breed of bicycle [is] alien and dangerous, esthetically offensive, and physically menacing.

3. *Refute these claims.*   Still not stating your own position, point out your difficulties with believing this side:

   Whether a bicycle—or a car or horse for that matter—is "alien and . . . esthetically offensive" depends on your personal taste, judgment, and familiarity. And whether it is "dangerous" depends on how you use it.

   In addition, you can actually strengthen your position by admitting that in some cases the counterclaims might be true:

   While it's true that some mountain bikers—like some hikers—are too loud, mountain biking at its best respects the environment and promotes peace and conservation, not noise and destruction.

4. *Summarize the counterclaims.*   You are supporting these claims and so they should occupy the most emphatic position in your essay, last:

   Most mountain bikers respect the wilderness and should be allowed to use wilderness trails.

5. *Support your counterclaims.*   Now give your best evidence; this should be the longest and most carefully documented part of the paper:

   Studies show that bicycle tires cause no more erosion or trail damage than the boots of hikers and far less than horses' hooves.

6. *State your thesis as your conclusion.*   Your rhetorical strategy is this: After giving each side a fair hearing, you have arrived at the most reasonable conclusion.

   It's clear that mountain bikers don't want to destroy trails any more than hikers do. The surest way to preserve America's wilderness areas is to establish strong cooperative bonds among the hikers and bikers, as well as those who fish, hunt, camp, canoe, and bird-watch, and encourage all to maintain the trails and respect the environment.

◆ WRITING 6: APPLICATION

Make two outlines for organizing your position paper, one with the thesis first, the other with a delayed thesis. Share your outlines with your classmates and discuss which seems more appropriate for the issue you have chosen.

SHAPING THE WHOLE PAPER

In the following paper, Issa explores whether or not mountain bikers should be allowed to share wilderness trails with hikers. In the first part of the paper he establishes the context and background of the conflict; then he introduces the question his paper will address: "Is any resolution in sight?" Note his substantial use of sources, including the Internet and interviews, cited in the MLA documentation style (see Chapter 55). Issa selects a delayed-thesis strategy, which allows him to air both sides of the argument fully before revealing his solution, a compromise position: So long as mountain bikers follow environmentally sound guidelines, they should be allowed to use the trails. Finally, note the use of selected photos to illustrate the essay. While photos are not essential to Issa's argument, the visual information adds depth, increases credibility, makes the paper more attractive to read, and suggests a serious commitment to the assignment on the part of the student.

On the Trail: Can the Hikers Share with the Bikers?
By Issa Sawabini

The narrow, hard-packed dirt trail winding up the mountain under the spreading oaks and maples doesn't look like the source of a major environmental conflict, but it is. On the one side are hikers, environmentalists, and horseback riders who have traditionally used these wilderness trails. On the other side, looking back, are the mountain bike riders sitting atop their modern steeds wanting to use them too. But the hikers don't want the bikers, so trouble is brewing.

The debate over mountain bike use has gained momentum recently because of the increased popularity of this form of bicycling. Technology has made it easier for everyone to ride these go-anywhere bikes. These high-tech wonders incorporate

exotic components including quick gear-shifting derailleurs, good brakes, and a more comfortable upright seating position—and they can cost up to $2,000 each (Kelly 104). Mountain bikes have turned what were once grueling hill climbs into casual trips, and more people are taking notice.

Mountain bikes have taken over the bicycle industry, and with more bikes come more people wanting to ride in the mountains. The first mass-produced mountain bikes date to 1981, when 500 Japanese "Stumpjumpers" were sold; by 1983 annual sales reached 200,000; today the figure is 8.5 million. In fact, mountain biking is second only to in-line skating as the fastest-growing sport in the nation: "For a sport to go from zero to warp speed so quickly is unprecedented," says Brian Stickel, director of competition for the National Off Road Bicycle Association (Schwartz 75).

With all these new riders, there is a need for places to ride, and this is where the wilderness trail controversy begins. The mountain bike is designed to be ridden on dirt trails, logging roads, and fire trails in backwoods country. However, other trail users who have been around much longer than mountain bikers prefer to enjoy the woods at a slow, leisurely pace. They find the rapid and sometimes noisy two-wheel intruders unacceptable: "To traditional trail users, the new breed of bicycle [is] alien and dangerous, esthetically offensive and physically menacing" (Schwartz 74).

"The problem arises when people want to use an area of public land for their own personal purpose," says Carl Newton, forestry professor at the University of Vermont. "Eventually, after everyone has taken their small bit of the area, the results can be devastating. People believe that because they pay taxes for the land, they can use it as they please. This makes sense to the individual, but not to the whole community." Newton is both a hiker and a mountain biker.

When mountain bikes first came on the scene, hikers and environmentalists convinced state and local officials to ban the bikes from wilderness trails (Buchanan 81; Kelly 104). The result was the closing of many trails to mountain bike use: "Many state park systems have banned bicycles from narrow trails. National Parks prohibit them, in most cases, from leaving the pavement" (Schwartz 81). These trail closings have separated the outdoor community into the hikers and the bikers. Each group is well organized, and each group believes it is right. Is any resolution in sight?

The hikers and other passive trail users have a number of organizations, from conservation groups to public park planning committees, who argue against allowing mountain bikes onto narrow trails traditionally traveled only by foot and horse in the past. They believe that the wide, deeply treaded tires of the mountain bikes cause erosion and that the high speeds of the bikers startle and upset both hikers and horses (Hanley; Schwartz 76).

The arrival of mountain bikes during the 1980s was resisted by established hiker groups, such as the Sierra Club, which won debate after debate in favor of closing wilderness trails to mountain bike activities. The younger and less well organized biking groups proposed compromise, offering to help repair and maintain trails in return for riding rights, but their offers were ignored. "Peace was not given a chance. Foes of the bicycle onslaught, older and better connected, won most of the battles, and signs picturing a bicycle crossed with a red slash began to appear on trailheads all over the country" (Schwartz 74).

In Millburn, New Jersey, trails at South Mountain, Eagle Rock, and Mills Park have all been closed. Anyone caught riding a bike on the trails can be arrested and fined up to $100. Local riders offered an amendment calling for trails to be open Thursday through Sunday, with the riders helping maintain the trails on the other days. The amendment was rejected. According to hiker Donald Meserlain, the bikes "ruin the tranquillity of the woodlands and drive out hikers, bird watchers, and strollers. It's like weeds taking over the grass. Pretty soon we'll have all weeds" (Hanley).

Many areas in western New York, such as Hunter's Creek, have also been closed to mountain bike use. Anti-biking signs posted on trails frequently used by bicyclists caused a loud public debate as bike riding was again blamed for trail erosion.

Until more public lands are opened to trail riding, mountain bikers must pay fees to ride on private land, a situation beneficial to ski resorts in the off season: "Ski areas are happy to open trails to cyclists for a little summer and fall income" (Sneyd). For example, in Vermont, bike trails can be found at the Catamount Family Center in Williston, Vermont, as well as at Mount Snow, Killington, Stratton, and Bolton Valley. At major resorts, such as Mount Snow and Killington, ski lifts have actually been modified to the top of the mountains, and each offers a full-service bike shop at its base.

However, the real solution to the conflict between hikers and bikers is education, not separation. In response to the bad publicity and many trail closings, mountain bikers have banded together at local and national levels to educate both their own member bike riders and the nonriding public about the potential alliance between these two groups (Buchanan 81).

The largest group, the International Mountain Bike Association (IMBA), sponsors supervised rides and trail conservation classes and stresses that mountain bikers are friends, not enemies of the natural environment. "The IMBA wants to change the attitude of both the young gonzo rider bombing downhill on knobby tires and the mature outdoorsman bristling at the thought of tire tracks where boot soles alone did tread" (Schwartz 76). IMBA published guidelines it hopes all mountain bikers will learn to follow:

1. Ride on open trails only.
2. Leave no trace.
3. Control your bicycle.
4. Always yield trail.
5. Never spook animals.
6. Plan ahead. (JTYL)

The New England Mountain Bike Association (NEMBA), one of the largest East Coast organizations, publishes a home page on the Internet outlining goals: "NEMBA is a not-for-profit organization dedicated to promoting land access, maintaining trails that are open to mountain bicyclists, and educating riders to use those trails sensitively and responsibly. We are also devoted to having fun" (Koellner).

At the local level, the Western New York Mountain Bike Association (WNYMBA) educates members on proper trail maintenance and urges its members to cooperate with local environmentalists whenever possible. For instance, when angry cyclists continued to use the closed trail at Hunter's Creek, New York, WNYMBA used the Internet (see insert) to warn cyclists against continued trail use: "As WNYMBA wishes to cooperate with Erie County Parks Department to the greatest extent possible on the use of trails in open parks, WNYMBA cannot recommend ignoring posted signs. The first IMBA rule of trail is 'ride on open trails only' " (JTYL). As of the summer of 2005, Hunter's Creek remains closed to mountain bike use, and all serious mountain bikers in the western New York region respect this.

Educated mountain biking, like hiking and horseback riding, respects the environment and promotes peace and conservation, not noise and destruction. Making this case has begun to pay off, and the battle over who walks and who rides the trails should now shift in favor of peaceful coexistence. "Buoyed by studies showing that bicycle tires cause no more erosion or trail damage than the boots of hikers, and far less than horses' hooves, mountain bike advocates are starting to find receptive ears among environmental organizations" (Schwartz 78).

Even in the Millburn, New Jersey, area, bikers have begun to win some battles, as new trails have recently been funded specifically for mountain bike use: "After all," according to an unnamed legislator, "the bikers or their parents are taxpayers" (Hanley).

The Wilderness Club now officially supports limited use of mountain bikes, while the Sierra Club also supports careful use of trails by riders so long as no damage to the land results and riders ride responsibly on the path. "In pursuit of happy trails, bicycling organizations around the country are bending backward over their chain stays to dispel the hell-on-wheels view of them" (Schwartz 83).

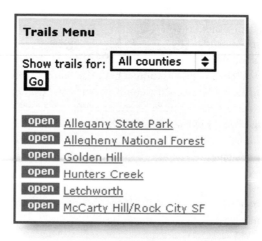

Trails Menu

Show trails for: All counties ⬍
Go

 open Allegany State Park
 open Allegheny National Forest
 open Golden Hill
 open Hunters Creek
 open Letchworth
 open McCarty Hill/Rock City SF

Education and compromise are the sensible solutions to the hiker/biker standoff. Increased public awareness as well as increasingly responsible riding will open still more wilderness trails to bikers in the future. It's clear that mountain bikers don't want to destroy trails any more than hikers do. The surest way to preserve America's wilderness areas is to establish strong cooperative bonds among the hikers and bikers, as well as those who fish, hunt, camp, canoe, and bird-watch, and to encourage all to maintain the trails and respect the environment.

Works Cited

Buchanan, Rob. "Birth of the Gearhead Nation." *Rolling Stone* 9 July 1992: 80–85.

Hanley, Robert. "Essex County Mountain Bike Troubles." *The New York Times* 30 May 1995: B4. JTYL (ed.) *Western New York Mountain Bike Association Home Page.* Western New York Mountain Bike Association. 4 Oct. 1995 <http://128.205.166.43/public/wnymba/wnymba.html>.

Kelly, Charles. "Evolution of an Issue." *Bicycling* May 1990: 104–105.

Koellner, Ken (ed.) *New England Mountain Bike Association Home Page.* 19 Aug. 1995. New England Mountain Bike Association. 30 Sep. 1995 <http://www.ultranet.com/~kvk/nemba.html>.

Newton, Carlton. Personal interview. 13 Nov. 2004.

Schwartz, David M. "Over Hill, Over Dale on a Bicycle Built for . . . Goo." *Smithsonian* June 1992: 74–84.

Sneyd, Ross. "Mount Snow Teaching Mountain Biking." *Burlington Free Press* 4 Oct. 1992. E1.

Western New York Mountain Bike Association (WNYBA) Home Page. 1 May 2005. WNYBA, 9 July 2005.

◆ SUGGESTIONS FOR WRITING AND RESEARCH

Individual

1. Write a position paper on the issue you have been working with in writings 2–6. Follow the guidelines suggested in this chapter, using as much research as you deem appropriate.
2. Write a position paper on an issue of interest to your class. Consider topics such as (1) student voice in writing topics, (2) the seating plan, (3) the value of writing groups versus instructor conferences, or (4) the number of writing assignments.

Collaborative

1. In teams of two or three, select an issue: divide up the work so that each group member contributes some work to (1) the context, (2) the pro argument, and (3) the con argument (to guarantee that you do not take sides prematurely). Share your analysis of the issue with another group and receive feedback. Finally, write your position papers individually.
2. Follow the procedure for the first collaborative assignment, but write your final position paper collaboratively.

CHAPTER TWELVE

Interpreting Texts

When I read, I've learned to ask a lot of questions, such as who's telling the story? What's the character like? Why does a certain action happen? What do symbols mean? Things like that. But I never find as much meaning in the stories as my teachers do.

DIANE

To interpret a text is to explain what it means. To interpret a text also implies that the text can be read in more than one way—your interpretation is your reading; others may read it differently. The word *text* implies words, writing, books; however, virtually all works created by human beings can be considered as texts open to interpretation—films, music and dance performances, exhibits, paintings, photographs, sculptures, advertisements, artifacts, buildings, and even whole cultures. Perhaps the most popular forms of interpretive writing are published reviews of movies, music, books, and the like.

In college, the most common form of interpretive essay assignment is to write analytical essays about reading assignments in humanities and social science courses. Since words can mean more than one thing, texts composed of written words have multiple meanings: They can mean different things depending on who is reading them, and there is no one right answer.

To find out what a poem, essay, play, or story means, you need to hear it, look at its language, examine how it is put together, compare it with similar things, notice how it affects you, and keep asking why.

WRITING TO INTERPRET

The best texts to select for an interpretive assignment are those that are most problematic— texts whose meaning seems to you somewhat slippery and elusive—since these give you, the interpreter, the most room to argue one meaning against another. Your job is to make the best possible case that your interpretation is reasonable and deserves attention.

A typical assignment may be to interpret a poem, story, essay, or historical document—a complex task that draws upon all of your reasoning and writing skills: You may have to describe people and situations, retell events, and define key terms, analyze passages, and explain how they work, perhaps by comparing or contrasting the text with others. Finally you will argue for one meaning rather than another—in other words, develop a thesis, and defend this thesis with sound reasoning and convincing evidence.

This chapter explores numerous ways of developing textual interpretations, using for illustrative purposes Gwendolyn Brooks' poem "We Real Cool." Brooks' poem is especially useful because it is short, quickly read, yet full of potential meanings. Our questions about this text, as well as the strategies for finding answers, are virtually the same as we would use with any text—fiction, nonfiction, or poetry.

Read, now, the following poem by Gwendolyn Brooks, and follow along as we examine different ways of determining what it means.

We Real Cool*

THE POOL PLAYERS
SEVEN AT THE GOLDEN SHOVEL

We real cool. We
Left school. We

Lurk late. We
Strike straight. We

Sing sin. We
Thin gin. We

Jazz June. We
Die soon.

◆ WRITING 1

After reading "We Real Cool," freewrite for ten minutes to capture your initial reaction. Ask yourself questions such as these: What did it remind me of? Did I like it? Do I think I understand it? What emotions did I feel?

EXPLORING A TOPIC

A good topic for an interpretive essay addresses a question that has several possible answers. If you think the text is overly simple, you will have no real need to interpret it. In addition, choose a topic that interests or intrigues you; if it doesn't, chances are it won't interest or intrigue your readers either.

No matter what text you are interpreting, however, you need to figure out what it means to you before you can explain it well to someone else. Plan to read it more than once,

*"We Real Cool" from BLACKS by Gwendolyn Brooks. The Third World Press, 1987. Reprinted by permission.

first to understand what it's like, where it goes, what happens literally. As you read, mark passages that interest or puzzle you. Read the text a second time, more slowly, making marginal notes or journal entries about the interesting, questionable, or problematic passages. As you do this, look for answers and solutions to your previous concerns, rereading as many times as necessary to further your understanding. In selecting a text to interpret, ask yourself these questions:

> Can this text be read in more than one way?
> What are some of the different ways of reading it?
> With which reading do I most agree?
> Where are the passages in the text that support this reading?
> Whom does my interpretation need to convince? (Who is my audience?)

◆ WRITING 2

Select a text that you are interested in interpreting. Choose a work of fiction, nonfiction, poetry, or drama that you find interesting and enjoyable, yet that has about it elements you do not fully understand, and then write out the answers to the questions above. Do not at this time worry about developing any of these answers thoroughly.

IDENTIFYING INTERPRETIVE COMMUNITIES

How you read and interpret a text depends on who you are. Who you are depends on the influences that have shaped you—the communities to which you belong. All of us belong to many communities: families, social and economic groups (students or teachers, middle or working class), organizations (Brownies, Boy Scouts, Democrats, Masons), geographic locales (rural or urban, North or South), and institutions (school, church, fraternity). Your membership in one or more communities determines how you see and respond to the world.

The communities that influence you most strongly are called *interpretive communities;* they influence the meaning you make of the world. People who belong to the same community that you do are likely to have similar assumptions and therefore are likely to interpret things as you would. If you live in an urban black community, jazz and rap music may be a natural and constant presence in your life; if you live in a rural white community, country and western music may be the norm; at the same time, as a member of either group you might also belong to a larger community that surrounds itself with classical music. All this means is that people who belong to different communities are likely to have different—not better or worse—perspectives from yours.

Before writing an interpretive essay, it is helpful to ask, "Who am I when writing this piece?" You ask this to examine the biases you bring to your work, for each of us sees the world—and consequently texts—from our own particular vantage point. Be aware of your age, gender, race, ethnic identity, economic class, geographic location, educational level, political or religious persuasion. Ask to what extent any of these identities emerges in your writing.

College is, of course, a large interpretive community. Various smaller communities exist within it called disciplines—English, history, business, art, and so on. Within any discipline there are established ways of interpreting texts. Often when you write an interpretive essay, you will do so from the perspective of a traditional academic interpretive community. Take care to follow the conventions of that community, whether you are asked to write a personal interpretation or an analytical interpretation.

Whether or not you deliberately identify yourself and your biases in your essay depends on the assignment you are given. Some assignments ask you to remove your personal perspective as much as possible from your writing; others ask that you acknowledge and explain it, while still others fall somewhere in between.

◆ WRITING 3

Make a list of all the interpretive communities to which you belong. Annotate your list, putting an asterisk next to those that seem to have the greatest influence on how you think or act and note how this influence manifests itself.

Personal Interpretation

In writing from a personal or subjective perspective, the interpreter and his or her beliefs and experiences are part of the story and need to be both expressed and examined. In examining "We Real Cool," for instance, you may bring your background into your writing to help your reader understand why you view the poem as you do. You may compare or contrast your situation to that of the author or characters in the text. Or you might draw upon particular experiences that cause you to see the poem in a particular way. For example, Mitzi Fowler's response (reprinted at the end of this chapter) begins with memories inspired by the poem:

> Gwendolyn Brooks's "We Real Cool" is a sad poem. It reminds me of the gang in high school who used to skip classes and come back smelling of cigarette smoke and cheap liquor—not that I knew it was cheap back then.

It is increasingly common for good interpretive essays to include both analytical and personal discussions, allowing you to demonstrate your skill at closely reading texts while acknowledging your awareness of the subjective nature of virtually all interpretive acts. To move in a more analytic direction, Mitzi would need to quote and discuss more lines directly from the poem, as she does later in her essay:

> These "cool" dropouts paid for their rebellion in drug overdoses, jail terms, police shootouts, and short lives. They "Die soon," so we never know where else their adventurous spirits might have taken them.

Analytical Interpretation

In analyzing a text, writers often focus on the content and deliberately leave themselves, the interpreters, in the background, minimizing personal presence and bias. If you are asked to write this way—to avoid first-person pronouns or value judgments—do your best to focus on the text and avoid language that appears biased. In reality, of course, authors reveal their presence by the choices they make: what they include, what they exclude, what they emphasize, and so on. But when you are aware of your inescapable subjectivity, aware that your own situation affects the inferences and judgments you make about others, this awareness will help you keep your focus on the subject and off yourself.

In writing about "We Real Cool," for example, your first reaction may be more personal than analytical, focusing on your own emotions by calling it a sad poem, as Mitzi does, or by expressing value judgments about the poem's characters:

> I think these guys are stupid, cutting their lives short drinking, stealing, and fighting.

However, a more analytical response would be to drop the first person ("I think") and the judgment ("these guys are stupid") and to focus more closely on the text itself, perhaps quoting parts of it to show you are paying close attention:

> The speakers in the poem, "The Pool Players," cut their lives short by hanging out at "The Golden Shovel," fighting, drinking, stealing, and perhaps worse.

There is no formula for arriving at or presenting an interpretation in essay form, but readers, especially English instructors, will expect you to address and explain various elements of the text that usually contribute substantially to what it means.

◆ WRITING 4

Examine more closely the text you have selected to interpret. In one paragraph, write out your initial and personal impressions of what this text means to you—why it interests you. In another paragraph, list those elements or features of the text that pose problems or raise questions that you'd like to answer.

DEVELOPING AN INTERPRETATION

Convincing interpretive essays commonly, but not always, include the following information:

1. An overview of the text, identifying author, title, and genre and briefly summarizing the whole text
2. A description of form and structure
3. A description of the author's point of view
4. A summary of the social, historical, or cultural context in which the work was written
5. An assertion or thesis about what the text means—your main business as an interpreter

Your thesis is a clear, concise statement that identifies your interpretation, on which the readers then expect you to elaborate. While some interpretive essays include all of the above information, essays more commonly will emphasize some aspects while downplaying others.

Identify and Summarize the Text

All interpretive essays should begin by answering basic questions: What genre is this text—poem, play, story, or essay? What is its title? Who is the author? When was it published? In addition, all such essays should provide a brief summary of the text's story, idea, or information. Summarize briefly, logically, and objectively to provide a background for what else you plan to say about the text, as in this example:

> "We Real Cool," a poem by Gwendolyn Brooks, condenses the life story of pool-playing high school dropouts to eight short lines and foreshadows an early death on the city streets.

Explain the Form and Organization

To examine the organizational structure of a text, ask: How is it put together? Why start here and end there? What connects it from start to finish? For example, by repeating words, ideas, and images, writers call attention to them and indicate that they are important to the meaning of the text. No matter what the text, some principle or plan holds it together and gives it structure. Texts that tell stories are often organized as a sequence of events in chronological order. Other texts may alternate between explanations and examples or between first-person and third-person narrative. You will have to decide which aspects of the text's form and organization are most important for your interpretation. The following example pays close attention to Brooks's overall poetic structure:

> The poem consists of a series of eight three-word sentences, each beginning with the word "We." The opening lines "We real cool. We / left school" explain the characters' situation. The closing lines "We / Jazz June. We / Die soon" suggest their lives will be short.

Describe the Author's Perspective

Authorial perspective is the point of view from which the text is presented. In an article, essay, textbook, or other work of nonfiction, you can expect the author to write about truth as he or she sees it—just as we are doing in this textbook, trying to explain writing according to our own beliefs about writing. However, in a work of poetry, fiction, or drama the author's point of view may be quite different from that of the character(s) who narrate or act in the story. If you can describe or explain the author's perspective in your interpretive essay, you provide readers with clues about the author's purpose. For example, Kelly Sachs' essay (reprinted at the end of this chapter) opens by making a distinction between Brooks, the poet, and her characters, "Seven at the Golden Shovel":

> Gwendolyn Brooks writes "We Real Cool" from the point of view of members of a street gang who have dropped out of school to live their lives hanging around pool halls—in this case "The Golden Shovel." These guys are semiliterate and speak in slangy street lingo that reveals their need for mutual support in their mutually rebellious attitude toward life.

What he doesn't say, but clearly implies, is that Brooks herself is a mature and highly skilled user of formal English, and that in the poem she adopts the persona or mask of semiliterate teenagers in order to tell their story more effectively.

Place the Work in Context

What circumstances (historical, social, political, biographical) produced this text? How does this text compare or contrast with another by the same author or a similar work by a different author? No text exists in isolation. Each was created by a particular author in a particular place at a particular time. Describing this context provides readers with important background information and indicates which conditions you think were most influential. "We Real Cool" could be contextualized this way:

> "We Real Cool" was published in 1963, a time when the Civil Rights Movement was strong and about the time that African Americans coined the phrase "Black is beautiful." The poem may have been written to remind people that just because they were black did not mean they necessarily led beautiful lives.

Explain the Theme of the Text

In fiction, poetry, and reflective essays, the main point usually takes the form of an implicit theme, which in academic writing you might call a thesis, either stated or unstated. A main reason for writing an interpretive essay is to point out the text's theme. Examine what you think is the theme in the text. Ask yourself: So what? What is this really about? What do I think the author meant by writing this? What problems, puzzles, or ideas seem interesting? Good topics arise from material in which the meaning is not obviously stated.

When you write an interpretation from an objective or analytical perspective, you make the best case possible that, according to the evidence in the text itself, this is what the text means. In analytical writing, you generally state your thesis (about the text's theme) early in the essay, as Kelly does here about "We Real Cool" at the end of his first paragraph:

> The speakers in the poem, "We," celebrate what adults would call adolescent hedonism—but they make a conscious choice for a short intense life over a long, safe, and dull existence.

When you write from a subjective or personal perspective, you make it clear that your interpretation is based on your own emotional reactions and memories as much as on the content of the text, and that other readers will necessarily read it differently. The controlling idea or theme of Mitzi's subjective interpretation of "We Real Cool" is revealed in her first sentence, which the rest of the essay supports.

> "We Real Cool" . . . reminds me of the gang in high school who used to skip classes and come back smelling of cigarette smoke and cheap liquor—not that I knew it was cheap back then.

Support Your Interpretation

Analytical interpretations are usually built around evidence from the text itself: Summarize larger ideas in your own language to conserve space; paraphrase more specific ideas also in your own words; and quote directly to feature especially colorful or precise language. If you include outside information for supportive, comparative, or contrastive reasons, document carefully where it came from. Most of the preceding examples referred to specific lines in the poem, as does this passage from Kelly's essay:

> Instead of attending school or finding employment, these seven "Lurk late," "Strike straight," "Sing sin," "Thin gin," and "Jazz June"—actions that are illegal, frowned upon by society, or harmful to other people. This is a bunch of kids to watch out for. If you see them coming, cross the street.

Subjective interpretations also include textual evidence, but often passages from the text are cited as prompts to introduce the writer's own memories, associations, or personal ideas. The more specific and concrete your examples, the better.

> I think everybody who ever went to a public high school knows these guys—at least most of them were boys—who eventually "Left school" altogether and failed to graduate. They dressed a little differently from the rest of us—baggier pants, heavier boots, dirtier shirts, and too long hair never washed. And if there were girls—too much makeup or none at all.

◆ WRITING 5

Look once more at the text you plan to interpret, and make brief notes about each of the elements described in this section. Which elements do you already know something about? Which ones require further research?

Interpreting Different Genres

The brief examples we've been looking at in this chapter are all based on a single short poem. Many of the texts you may choose to interpret will be longer and in genres other than poetry. If you are interpreting a work of fiction or nonfiction, or something else altogether such as an art exhibit, a concert, or a film, the basic elements of interpretation discussed here still apply, but there will be important differences.

Poetry

Of all language genres and forms, poetry exhibits the most intensive, deliberate, and careful use of language. With certain exceptions, poetic texts are far shorter than even short stories or one-act plays. Consequently, when interpreting poems, pay special attention to specific words, phrases, and lines; quote lines, phrases, and words exactly to support your points; and familiarize yourself with the basic poetic terms you learned in high school: line, stanza, rhyme, rhythm, meter, metaphor, and image.

Fiction

To write about a novel or short story, explain how the main elements function: the narrator (who tells the story), plot (what happens in the story), one or more characters (who are acting or being acted upon), setting (where things are happening), and theme (the meaning of the story). Be sure to keep in mind that the author who writes the story is different from the characters in the story, and that what happens in the story is different from the meaning of the story.

Drama

Plays are a special kind of fiction meant to be acted out upon a stage; consequently, all the elements of fiction apply, except that since the characters are acting out the story, a narrator is seldom present. In drama, the setting is limited to what is contained on the stage. You usually do not have access to what the characters are thinking—the actors need to speak out loud or with body language to reveal themselves, so the actors who play the parts are crucial to the play's success; consequently, if you interpret a play that you see performed, you have more information to work with than a play listened to or read silently. Remember, too, that plays are structured according to acts, which are, in turn, divided into scenes. When you quote from drama, identify first the act (V), then the scene (iii), finally the line or lines, for example, *Hamlet* V.iii, 24–29.

Film

Fictional films are discussed in terms similar to those used for written fiction and drama (plot, character, setting, theme). However, additional elements also come into play: camera angles, special effects, and unlimited settings. Because of the complexity of orchestrating all of these elements, the film director rather than the screenwriter is often considered the "author" of a film.

Nonfiction

The elements of a nonfiction essay are similar to those of a fictional story, except that everything in the text is supposed to have really happened. For this reason, the author and the narrator of the story are one and the same. Informational nonfiction—essays, reports, and textbook chapters—is also meant to be believed; here you might say that "ideas" and "arguments" must be strong and well supported to be believed. When interpreting nonfiction, pay special attention to the author's theme or thesis, and to whether it is well supported or not. Note, too, any interesting developments in tone, style, form, or voice.

Other Media

In interpreting other kinds of texts—paintings, photographs, sculptures, quilts, concerts, buildings, and so on—always explain to your reader the basic identifying features, be they verbal, visual, musical, or something else: What is it? What is its name or title? Who created it? What are its main features? Where is it? When did it take place?

GLOSSARY OF LITERARY TERMS

In writing interpretations of literary texts, the following terminology is commonly used:

Alliteration   The repetition of initial consonant sounds. ("On the *bald* street *breaks* the *blank* day.")

Antagonist   A character of force opposing the main character (the *protagonist*) in a story.

Climax   A moment of emotional or intellectual intensity or a point in the plot where one opposing force overcomes another and the conflict is resolved.

Epiphany   A flash of intuitive understanding by the narrator or a character in a story.

Figurative language   Language that suggests special meanings or effects such as metaphors or similes; not literal language. ("She stands like a tree, solid and rooted.")

Imagery   Language that appeals to one of the five senses; especially language that reproduces something the reader can see. ("His heart was an open book, pages aflutter and crackling in the wind.")

Metaphor   A direct comparison between two things. ("He is a fox.")

Narrator   Someone who tells a story; a character narrator is a part of the story (such as Huckleberry Finn) while an omniscient narrator tells a story about other people.

Persona   A mask, not the author's real self, worn by the author to present a story or poem.

Plot   The sequence of events in a story or play.

Point of view   The vantage point from which a story or event is perceived and told.

Protagonist   The main character or hero of a plot.

Rhyme   The repetition of sounds, usually at the ends of lines in poems, but also occurring at other intervals in a line (*moon, June, noon*).

Rhythm   The rise and fall of stressed sounds within sentences, paragraphs, and stanzas.

Simile   An indirect comparison using the words *as* or *like*. ("He is like a fox.")

Symbol   An object that represents itself and something else at the same time. A black rose is both a rose of a certain color and the suggestion of something evil or deathlike.

Theme   The meaning or thesis of a text.

SHAPING THE WHOLE PAPER

This chapter concludes with two sample interpretive papers from which some of the foregoing illustrations have been taken. The first one might be called an *objective* or *critical* essay, while the other might be called a *subjective* or *personal* essay.

Analytic Response to "We Real Cool"

Kelly Sachs writes a brief analytical interpretation of "We Real Cool," called "High Stakes, Short Life," keeping himself in the background, writing in the third-person point of view. He presents his thesis early and supports it afterward with frequent quotations from the text, amplifying and explaining it most fully in his last paragraph.

High Stakes, Short Life

Kelly Sachs

Gwendolyn Brooks writes "We Real Cool" (1963) from the point of view of the members of a street gang who have dropped out of school to spend their lives hanging around pool halls—in this case "The Golden Shovel." These guys are semiliterate and speak in slangy street lingo that reveals their need for mutual support in their mutually rebellious attitude toward life. The speakers in the poem, "We," celebrate what adults would call adolescent hedonism—but they make a conscious choice for a short intense life over a long, safe, and dull existence.

For the "Seven at the Golden Shovel," companionship is everything. For many teenagers, fitting in or conforming to a group identity is more important than developing an individual identity. But for these kids, none of whom excelled at school or had happy home lives, their group is their life. They even speak as a group, from the plural point of view, "We," repeated at the end of each line; these seven are bonded and will stick together through boredom, excitement, and death.

From society's point of view, they are nothing but misfits—refusing to work, leading violent lives, breaking laws, and confronting polite society whenever they cross paths. Instead of attending school, planning for their future, or finding work, these seven "Lurk late," "Strike straight," "Sing sin," "Thin gin," and "Jazz June." Watch out for this bunch. If you see them coming, cross the street.

However, the most important element of their lives is being "cool." They live and love to be cool. Part of being cool is playing pool, singing, drinking, fighting, and messing around with women whenever they can. Being cool is the code of action that unites them, that they celebrate, for which they are willing to die.

The poet reveals their fate in the poem's last line. Brooks shows that the price of coolness and companionship is higher than most people are willing to pay. In this culture, the fate of rebels who violate social norms is an early death ("We / Die soon"), but to these seven, it is better to live life to the fullest than hold back and plan for a future that may never come. They choose, accept, and celebrate their lives, and "Die soon."

Personal Response to "We Real Cool"

In the following essay, "Staying Put," Mitzi Fowler writes about her personal reaction to Brooks' poem, describing how it reminds her of her own high school experience. Mitzi's theme, the sad lives of ghetto gangs, opens and closes the essay and provides the necessary coherence to hold it together. While she quotes the text several times, her primary supportive examples come from her own memories.

Staying Put

Mitzi Fowler

Gwendolyn Brooks's "We Real Cool" is a sad poem. It reminds me of the gang in high school who used to skip classes and come back smelling of cigarette smoke and cheap liquor—not that I knew it was cheap back then. I think everybody who ever went to a public high school knows these guys—at least most of them were boys—who eventually "Left school" altogether and failed to graduate. They dressed a little differently from the rest of us—baggier pants, heavier boots, dirtier shirts, and too long hair never washed—and if there were girls, too much makeup or none at all.

They had their fun, however, because they stayed in their group. They came late to assemblies, slouched in their seats, made wisecracks, and often ended up like the characters in *The Breakfast Club,* in detention after school or Saturday morning.

And no matter how straight-laced and clean-cut the rest of us were, we always felt just a twinge of envy at these careless, jaunty rebels who refused to follow rules, who didn't care if they got detentions, who didn't do homework, and whose parents didn't care if they stayed out all night. I didn't admit it very often—at least not to my friends—but some part of me wanted to have their pool hall or whatever adventures, these adult freedoms they claimed for themselves. However, I was always afraid—chicken, they would have said—of the consequences, so I practiced piano, did my algebra, and stayed put.

Then I think of the poem's last line and know why I obeyed my parents (well, most of the time), listened to my teachers (at least some of them), and stayed put (if you don't count senior cut day). These "cool" dropouts paid for their rebellion in drug overdoses, jail terms, police shootouts, and short lives. They "Die soon," so we never know where else their adventurous spirits might have taken them. In the end, this poem just makes me sad.

◆ SUGGESTIONS FOR WRITING AND RESEARCH

Individual

1. Write an interpretive essay about a short text of your choice. Write the first draft from an analytic stance, withholding all personal judgments. Then write the second draft from a personal stance, including all relevant private judgments. Write your final draft by carefully blending elements of your first and second drafts.
2. Locate at least two reviews of a text (book, recording, exhibit) with which you are familiar, and analyze each to determine the reviewer's critical perspective. Write your own review of the text, and agree or disagree with the approach of the reviewers you analyzed. If you have a campus newspaper, consider offering your review to the editor for publication.

Collaborative

As a class or small group, attend a local concert, play, or exhibition. Have each student take good notes and, when he or she returns home, write a review of this event that includes both an interpretation and a recommendation that readers attend it (or not). Share these variations on the same theme with others in your class or group and explore the different judgments that arise as a result of different perspectives.

CHAPTER THIRTEEN

Writing Creative Nonfiction

> *I spend all my time in college writing factual reports, essays, and term papers—I'm afraid I'll graduate never having had the chance to write about what I really care about.*
>
> KELSEY

Creative nonfiction is a term that describes nonfiction that is exciting to read. Well-known works of creative nonfiction include Sebastian Junger's *The Perfect Storm*, Jon Krakaur's *Into Thin Air*, and Terry Tempest Williams' *Refuge*, to name a few recent books. Shorter pieces are published regularly in popular literary magazines, especially in *The New Yorker, Harpers,* and *The Atlantic Monthly*, but also in *Sports Illustrated, Rolling Stone,* and *The Wall Street Journal*—the front page feature essay. Writers of creative nonfiction commonly borrow stylistic and formal techniques from the fast-paced visual narratives of film and television as well as from the innovative language of poetry, fiction, and drama— these influences encouraging a multi-faceted, multidimensional prose style to keep pace with the multifaceted and multidimensional world in which we live. In short, many current nonfiction prose writers find the traditions of continuity, order, consistency, and unity associated with conventional prose insufficient to convey the chaotic

truths of the postmodern world. This chapter examines some of the writing strategies associated with alternative or experimental prose and suggests appropriate venues within the academic curriculum in which such prose strategies could be useful. (Many of the ideas presented here were first articulated by Winston Weathers in his groundbreaking book *An Alternate Style: Options in Composition* [Hayden, 1980].)

LISTS

Lists can break up and augment prose texts in useful, credible, and surprising ways. Lists of names, words, numbers add variety, speed, depth, and humor to texts. And lists are everywhere we look, as Joan Didion illustrates in making the case that Las Vegas weddings are big business in this excerpt from "Marrying Absurd":

> There are nineteen such wedding chapels in Las Vegas, intensely competitive, each offering better, faster, and, by implication, more sincere services than the next: Our Photos Best Anywhere, Your Wedding on a Phonograph Record, Candlelight with Your Ceremony, Honeymoon Accommodations, Free Transportation from Your Motel to Courthouse to Chapel and Return to Motel, Religious or Civil Ceremonies, Dressing Rooms, Flowers, Rings, Announcements, Witnesses Available, and Ample Parking.

Didion's list of competitive wedding services convinces us she has observed carefully; she is not making this stuff up. Without her saying it, we see some level of absurdity in the way this town promotes marriage.

Lists need not be clever so much as purposeful. That is, you include a list of names, items, quotations, and so on to show readers you know what you're talking about: You have done your homework, read widely or observed carefully, taken good notes, and made sense from what you've found. Lists deepen a text by providing illustrations or examples. And they add credibility by saying, in effect, "Look at all this evidence that supports my point."

On the printed page, sometimes lists are presented simply as lists, not embedded in prose paragraphs. Such is the case in *Blue Highways: A Journey into America*, when author William Least Heat-Moon overhears people describing the desert as full of "nothing."

> Driving through miles of nothing, I decided to test the hypothesis and stopped somewhere in western Crockett County on the top of a broad mesa, just off Texas 29 . . . I made a list of nothing in particular:
>
> 1. mockingbird
> 2. mourning dove
> 3. enigma bird (heard not saw)
> 4. gray flies
> 5. blue bumblebee
> 6. two circling buzzards (not yet boys)
> 7. orange ants
> 8. black ants
> 9. orange-black ants (what's been going on?)

  10. three species of spiders

  11. opossum skull

  12. jackrabbit (chewed on cactus)

  13. deer (left scat)

  14. coyote (left tracks)

Heat-Moon's list continues through thirty items, ending this way:

  28. earth

  29. sky

  30. wind (always)

Itemized lists such as this change the visual shape of prose and call extra attention to the items listed; in this case, Heat-Moon is being mildly humorous by using a list to "prove" there is always something, even in nothing.

When Craig, a student in my advanced writing class, examined sexist stereotypes in children's toys, he made the following list of dolls and accessories on a single shelf at a local Woolworth's store:

> To my left is a shelf of Barbies: Animal Lovin' Barbie, Wet 'n Wild Barbie, Barbie Feelin' Pretty Fashions, Barbie Special Expressions (Woolworth Special Limited Edition), Super Star Barbie Movietime Prop Shop, Step 'n Style Boutique, My First Barbie (Prettiest Princess Ever), Action Accents Barbie Sewing Machine, Barbie Cool Times Fashion, Barbie and the All-Stars, Style Magic Barbie, a Barbie Ferrari, and tucked away in a corner, slightly damaged and dusty, Super Star Ken.

This list simply documents by name the products on the toy shelf, actually adding a dimension of authenticity and believability to the writer's case that, yes, the Barbie image and influence on children is considerable.

Creating an extended list is a bold, even audacious move, breaking up prose sentences, surprising readers and therefore picking up their interest, engagement, involvement. The purposeful use of lists may make readers pause to note the change in the form of words on the page; at the same time, lists allow readers to pick up speed—reading lists is fast.

However, lists that are quick to read may not be quick to write; an effective list that appears to be written by free association may, in fact, have been laboriously constructed as the writer ransacked his memory or her thesaurus for words, then arranged and rearranged them to create the right sound or sense effect.

◆ SNAPSHOTS

Writing prose snapshots is analogous to constructing and arranging a photo album composed of many separate visual images. Photo albums, when carefully assembled from informative snapshots, tell stories with clear beginnings, middles, and endings, but with lots of white space between one picture and the next, with few transitions explaining how the photographer got from one scene to the next. In other words, while photo albums tell stories, they do so piecemeal, causing the viewer to fill in or imagine what happened between shots. Or think of snapshots as individual slides in a slide show or pictures in an exhibition—each the work of the same maker, each a different view, each by some logic connected, the whole a story.

Prose snapshots function the same way as visual snapshots, each connected to the other by white space and leaps of reader logic and faith, the whole making self-explanatory story structure. Or you might imagine written snapshots as a series of complete and independent paragraphs, each a whole thought, without obvious connections or careful transitions to the paragraph before or after.

Sometimes individual snapshots are numbered to suggest deliberate connectedness; other times each is titled, to suggest an ability to stand alone, as are chapters within books; sometimes they appear on a page as block paragraphs, the reading alone revealing the lack of transitions, the necessity for active reader interpretation. As such, they are satisfying for fast readers, each containing a small story unto itself, the whole a larger story, in part of the reader's making.

Margaret Atwood writes snapshots to emphasize the dangers of men's bodies in the following passage from her essay "Alien Territory" (1983):

> **The history of war is a history of killed bodies. That's what war is: bodies killing other bodies, bodies being killed.**
>
> **Some of the killed bodies are those of women and children, as a side effect you might say. Fallout, shrapnel, napalm, rape and skewering, anti-personnel devices. But most of the killed bodies are men. So are most of those doing the killing.**
>
> **Why do men want to kill the bodies of other men? Women don't want to kill the bodies of other women. By and large. As far as we know.**
>
> **Here are some traditional reasons: Loot. Territory. Lust for power. Hormones. Adrenaline high. Rage. God. Flag. Honor. Righteous anger. Revenge. Oppression. Slavery. Starvation. Defense of one's life. Love; or, a desire to protect the men and women. From what? From the bodies of other men.**
>
> **What men are most afraid of is not lions, not snakes, not the dark, not women. What men are most afraid of is the body of another man.**
>
> **Men's bodies are the most dangerous things on earth.**

Note how the white space between one snapshot and another gives readers breathing space, time out, time to digest one thought before supping at the next. The white space between snapshots actually exercises readers' imaginations, as they participate in constructing some logic that makes the text make sense—the readers themselves to supply the connectives, construct the best meaning, which, nevertheless, will be very close to what skillful authors intend.

Snapshots allow busy writers to compose in chunks, in five- and ten-minute blocks between appointments, schedules, classes, or coffee breaks. And, as we've seen, five or ten or twenty chunks—reconsidered, rearranged, revised—can tell whole stories. (For examples of students composing in snapshots, see an excerpt from Paige Kaltsas' essay later in this chapter and Rebecca's complete essay at the end of Chapter 9.)

While it's fun to write fast, random, and loose snapshots, the real secret to a successful snapshot essay is putting them together in the right order—some right order—some pattern that, by the end, conveys your theme as surely as if you had written straight narration or exposition. Writing snapshots on a computer is especially fun, since you can order and reorder indefinitely until you arrive at a satisfying organization. Composing snapshot essays on three-by-five-inch cards also works. In either case, assemble and arrange as you would pictures in a photo album, playfully and seriously: Begin at the beginning, alternate themes, begin in the middle, alternate time, begin with flashbacks, alternate voices, consider frames, alternate fonts, reinforce rhythms, experiment with openings and closings, change type, and try different titles.

PLAYFUL SENTENCES

No matter what your form or style, sentences are your main units of composition, explaining the world in terms of subjects, actions, and objects, suggesting that the world operates causally: Some force (a subject) does something (acts) that causes something else to happen (an object). English prose is built around complete and predictable sentences such as those in which this paragraph and most of this book are written. Sometimes, however, writers use sentences in less predictable, more playful ways, which we will explore here.

Fragment sentences suggest fragmented stories. Stories different from the stories told by conventional subject-verb-object sentences. Fragmented information. Fragment sentences, of course, can be used judiciously in conventional writing—even academic writing—so long as the purpose is crystal clear and your fragment is not mistaken for fragmentary grammatical knowledge. However, alternate-style writers use fragments audaciously and sometimes with abandon to create the special effects they want. A flash of movement. A bit of a story. A frozen scene. Fragments force quick reading, ask for impressionistic understanding, suggest parts rather than wholes. Like snapshots, fragments invite strong reader participation to stitch together, to move toward clear meaning.

Fragment sentences suggest, too, that things are moving fast. Very fast. Hold on! Remember the snapshot passage from Margaret Atwood's "Alien Territory"? Note that she uses fragments to emphasize the sharp dangers of men's bodies:

> **Some of the killed bodies are those of women and children, as a side effect you might say. Fallout, shrapnel, napalm, rape and skewering, anti-personnel devices. But most of the killed bodies are men. So are most of those doing the killing.**
>
> **Why do men want to kill the bodies of other men? Women don't want to kill the bodies of other women. By and large. As far as we know.**

Atwood's fragments make the reader notice sharply the brutal and jarring truths she is writing about. In this example, the lack of conventional connections between words mirrors the disconnectedness she sees in her subject: men, violence, and war. Notice, too, that some of her fragments illustrate another use of lists.

Write fragments in such a way that your reader knows they are not mistakes. Not ignorance. Not sloppiness or printer error or carelessness. Purposeful fragments can be powerful. Deliberate. Intentional. Careful. Functional. And usually brief. (See the student samples of collage writing later in this chapter.)

Labyrinthine sentences tell stories different from either conventional or fragment sentences. In fact, a labyrinthine sentence is quite the opposite of the fragment sentence because it seems never to end; it won't quit, but instead it goes on and on and on, using all sorts of punctuational and grammatical tricks to create compound sentences (you know, two or more independent clauses joined by a comma and a conjunction such as *and* or *but*) and complex sentences (you know these, too: one independent clause with one or more dependent clauses) and is written to suggest, perhaps, that things are running together and are hard to separate—also to suggest the "stream of consciousness" of the human mind, in which thoughts and impressions and feelings and images are run together without an easy separation into full sentences or paragraphs complete with topic sentences—the power (and sometimes confusion) of which you know if you have read James Joyce or Virginia Woolf or William Faulkner or Toni Morrison.

Or James Agee, who in the following passage imaginatively enters the thoughts of the people he is profiling in *Let Us Now Praise Famous Men* (1941), the poor Alabama tenant farmers:

> But I am young; and I am young and strong and in good health; and I am young and pretty to look at; and I am too young to worry; and so am I for my mother is kind to me; and we run in the bright air like animals, and our bare feet like plants in the wholesome earth: the natural world is around us like a lake and a wide smile and we are growing: one by one we are becoming stronger, and one by one in the terrible emptiness and the leisure we shall burn and tremble and shake with lust, and one by one we shall loosen ourselves from this place, and shall be married, and it will be different from what we see, for we will be happy and love each other, and keep the house clean, and a good garden, and buy a cultivator, and use a high grade of fertilizer, and we will know how to do things right; it will be very different:) (?:)

Agee's long connected sentence creates the run-together, wishful, worried, desperate internal dream of his subjects in a way a conventional paragraph could not. Notice, too, that punctuation and grammar are mostly conventional and correct—even though at the end, they are used in unexpected ways to suggest something of the confusion and uncertainty these people live with daily.

You may also write run-on or fused sentences—where punctuation does not function in expected ways the missing period before this sentence is an example of that. However, such writing more often suggests error than experiment, so be careful. I use both fragments and labyrinthine sentences to create certain effects, since each conveys its information in an unmistakable way; but I never, deliberately, write with run-on sentences, and when I encounter them as a reader, they make me suspicious.

REPETITION/REFRAIN

Writers repeat words, phrases, or sentences for emphasis. They repeat words to remind us to think hard about the word or phrase repeated. They repeat words to ask us to attend and not take for granted. They repeat words to suggest continuity of idea and theme. They repeat words to hold paragraphs and essays together. And, sometimes, they repeat words to create rhythms that are simply pleasing to the ear.

The following paragraph opens Ian Frazier's book-length study *The Great Plains*:

> Away to the Great Plains of America, to that immense Western shortgrass prairie now mostly plowed under! Away to the still empty land beyond newsstands and malls and velvet restaurant ropes! Away to the headwaters of the Missouri, now quelled by many impoundment dams, and to the headwaters of the Platte, and to the almost invisible headwaters of the slurped up Arkansas! Away to the land where TV used to set its most popular dramas, but not anymore! Away to the land beyond the hundredth meridian of longitude, where sometimes it rains and sometimes it

doesn't, where agriculture stops and does a double take! Away to the skies of the
sparrow hawks sitting on telephone wires, thinking of mice and flaring their tail
feathers suddenly, like a card trick! Away to the airshaft of the continent, where
weather fronts from two hemispheres meet and the wind blows almost all the time!
Away to the fields of wheat and milo and Sudan grass and flax and alfalfa and nothing! Away to parts of Montana and North Dakota and South Dakota and Wyoming
and Nebraska and Kansas and Colorado and New Mexico and Oklahoma and Texas!
Away to the high plains rolling in waves to the rising final chord of the Rocky
Mountains!

Frazier's singing chant invites us, in one sweeping passage, to think about the Great Plains
as geography, biology, history, and culture. Along the way he uses fragments and lists and a
plentitude of exclamation marks to invite readers to consider this arid and often overlooked
part of America.

While *refrain* is a term more often associated with music, poetry, and sermons, it is a
form of repetition quite powerful in prose as well. A refrain is a phrase repeated throughout a text to remind readers (or listeners) of an important theme. For example, the phrase
"I have a dream" is a refrain in Martin Luther King's famous speech by the same name. In
"Report from the Bahamas," June Jordan reflects upon her experience as a black woman
being waited on by black maids and waiters while staying at the Sheraton British Colonial
Hotel. Throughout the essay Jordan returns to a phrase to remind herself, as well as the
reader, of her troubled and complicated situation as a black feminist writer. The refrain is
repeated six times at different points throughout the essay. Here are the first four, which
occur within a span of six pages:

> This is my consciousness of race as I unpack my bathing suit in the Sheraton British
> Colonial.
>
> This is my consciousness of class as I try to decide how much money I can
> spend on Bahamian gifts for my family back in Brooklyn.
>
> This is my consciousness of race, class, and gender identity as I notice the fixed
> relations between these other Black women and myself.
>
> This is my consciousness of race, class, and gender identity as I collect wet tow-
> els, sunglasses, wristwatch, and head towards a shower.

Repetition and refrains, along with lists, snapshots, fragments, and labyrinthine sentences, are all stylistic devices that add an emotional dimension to the otherwise factual
material of nonfictional prose—without announcing, labeling, or dictating what those emotions need be. The word play of alternate-style composing allows nonfictional prose to convey themes more often conveyed only through more obviously poetic forms.

DOUBLE VOICE

Good nonfiction writing usually (I'd like to say *always* but don't dare) expresses something
of the writer's voice. But all writers are capable of speaking with more than one voice (how
many more?)—or maybe with a single voice that has wide range, varied registers, multiple
tones, and different pitches. No matter how you view it, writers project more than one voice
from piece to piece of writing—sometimes within the same piece.

In any given essay, a writer may try to say two things at the same time. Sometimes writers question their own assertions (as in the previous paragraph); sometimes they say one thing out loud and think another silently to themselves (again, see the previous paragraph); sometimes they say one thing that means two things; sometimes they express contradictions, paradoxes, or conundrums; and sometimes they establish that most of us have more than one voice with which to speak.

Double voices in a text may be indicated by parentheses—the equivalent of an actor speaking an "aside" on the stage (see what I mean?) or in a film. The internal monologue of a character may be revealed as voice-over or through printed subtitles while another action is happening on screen. Or by changes in the size or *type font,* a switch to *italics,* **boldface,** or CAPITAL LETTERS signaling a switch in the writer's voice. Or the double voice may occur without distinguishing markers at all. Or it may be indicated by simple paragraph breaks, as in the following selection from D. H. Lawrence in his critical essay on Herman Melville's *Moby Dick* from *Studies in Classic American Literature,* where he uses fragments, repetition, and double voice:

> **Doom.**
>
> **Doom! Doom! Doom! Something seems to whisper it in the very dark trees of America.**
>
> **Doom of what?**
>
> **Doom of our white day. We are doomed, doomed. And the doom is in America. The doom of our white day.**
>
> **Ah, well, if my day is doomed, and I am doomed with my day, it is something greater than I which dooms me, so I accept my doom as a sign of the greatness which is more than I am.**
>
> **Melville knew. He knew his race was doomed. His white soul, doomed. His great white epoch, doomed. Himself doomed. The idealist, doomed. The spirit, doomed.**

Here, Lawrence critiques Melville by carrying on a mock dialogue with himself, alternating his caricature of Melville's voice with his own whimsical acceptance of Melville's gloomy prophecy. Lawrence's essay seems written to provoke readers into reassessing their interpretations of literary classics, and so he provokes not only through the questions he raises but through his style as well. Note his poetic use of repetition and sentence fragments that contribute to his double-voice effect.

Double voice may also be offset spatially, in double columns or alternating paragraphs, as my student Paige Kaltsas did in trying to capture the experience of running a 26.2-mile marathon. She alternated voices in separate stanzas (one double stanza for each mile). The following example is from her third set of stanzas, where her first voice is in the race (present tense) while her second voice is remembering the training (past tense):

> Mile 3: Make sure you are going the right pace. Slow down a little, you're going too fast. Let people pass you. Don't worry, they will burn out and you'll glide by later. Don't make a mistake.

> My typical training week went like this:

> Monday: a two-mile warm-up at a slow pace; then three miles at a faster pace; finally, two miles slowing down, cooling off. After: a leg strength workout.
>
> Tuesday: a medium long run, ten miles at a medium pace.

Wednesday: the dreaded speed workouts at the track, with mile runs alternating with quarter-mile sprints. Afterwards, nausea and arm and leg strength workouts.

COLLAGE

Collages are more often associated with visual than verbal art, but creative nonfiction writers borrow freely from other media, especially in this age of the Internet and its combined verbal-visual style. Even my own journal has elements of a collage when I use it as a scrapbook, taping in photos or clippings wherever I find white space, thus creating meaningful—if only to me—juxtapositions. However, collage writing has been used to more deliberate effect in the novels of John Dos Passos—a technique since borrowed by Tom Wolfe, Hunter S. Thompson, and others in what may be called "new journalism" or "literary nonfiction." Dos Passos, a writer of both fiction and nonfiction, began his essay "The Death of James Dean" (1959) with quotations taken from newspaper headlines, then continued using fragments, repetition, and double voices along the way.

> **TEEN-AGE DANCES SEEN THREATENED BY PARENTS FAILURE TO COOPERATE MOST OFFENDERS EMULATE ADULTS**
> James Dean is three years dead but the sinister adolescent still holds the headlines.
> James Dean is three years dead;
> but when they file out of the close darkness and breathed out air of the second-run motion picture theatres where they've been seeing James Dean's old films
> they still line up;
> the boys in the jackboots and the leather jackets, the boys in the skintight jeans, the boys in broad motorbike belts,
> before mirrors in the restroom
> to look at themselves
> and see
> James Dean;

Collage techniques may also be used to write collaboratively, with multiple authors contributing not only multiple voices but also multiple perspectives. In the following example, taken from a last-day-of-class writing exercise, my students wrote snapshots of their semester-long experience in this writing course, some of them looking all the way back to the first day of class, where, as an introductory exercise, we spent the entire time writing notes to each other in silence.

1. First day of class. I walk in early (I'm always early) only to find "Silence" written on the blackboard. Never had this Toby guy before. Instead of saying anything, he uses the overhead projector to tell us what to do: "On a sheet of paper, write a note to a classmate, introduce yourself, then pass it." Not a word spoken the whole class. Silent chaos. But also a way of showing us the importance of voice in writing. Weird, not one word the whole 75 minutes. (Paul)

2. Shhh! The instructor writes on the board "No talking." What the hell? I think to myself. A writing class and nobody talks, everybody writes. I get it. (Mary)

3. First day of class. I arrive ten minutes late, couldn't find the building. No one speaks. Everyone is writing. I get reprimanded for asking the girl next to me what's going on. I get reprimanded for asking the teacher what's going on. I figure it out and leave class partly annoyed, partly amused. (Brad)

ELECTRONIC STYLE

Computer graphics programs included in conventional word-processing programs now allow writers to create varied page layouts with different fonts and styles. They make experimental writing easier, more possible, and more likely than at any other time in the history of print technology.

Images from the Web inserted from word-processing programs now enliven many college papers and are something most instructors enjoy so long as they enhance or amplify the content they accompany and the content is solid, not fishy.

It is now common for instructors to receive college papers that resemble professionally published articles in sophisticated journals. In one example from a recent writing class about the phenomenon of "slam poetry," Gabe Krechmer designed his first page to resemble a page in popular journalism (see p. 160).

E-mail messages are also written in a loose style that I hesitate to call creative nonfiction, but which include similar elements of fun, such as emoticons ☺. And the convention of fast typing emerged with e-mail messages, which have come to be regarded as somewhere in between informal telephone messages and informal letters.

> **the original word processing programs for e-mail correspondence were limited in their revision and editing capabilities, so that if you were typing on line 8 and you noticed an error in line 1, you had to erase all the text back to the error in order to fix it. so people just said, to heck with it, let the error go—which created a fast, loose, informal style in which typos, spelling mistakes, and lapses in punctuation simply came with the territory. the priority in e-mail correspondence has become speed and practicality, with most e-mail messages never being printed on paper at all. even with better and faster word-processing programs, the loose informal style of e-mail writing continues today. it is common, for example, for e-mail writers to use no capital letters or to invent unorthodox punctuation)**

A WORD OF CAUTION

Wise writers will master both conventional and unconventional styles and formats, using each as occasion and audience demand. Proficiency in one format is a poor excuse for sloppiness or neglect of the other. Creative nonfiction or alternate-style techniques, used carefully and judiciously on selected writing tasks, are fun to write and enjoyable to read, and they may be able to convey the emotional and aesthetic dimension of ideas difficult to convey in conventional prose. At the same time, such stylistic devices are easy to overuse and exaggerate, resulting then in predictable, routine, or overly cute expressions that lose the very edge they are trying to achieve, and that made them effective in the first place. Check with your instructor before submitting an unconventional paper in response to a conventional assignment.

What Is Slam Poetry, Anyway?
Gabriel Krechmer

There is something about poetry slam that can leave you utterly confused. I have done a good amount of public speaking in my life. I have been a teacher's assistant for several classes. I know Those eyes decide if you rise to the challenge or fail miserably; I understand the responsibility of having all eyes pointing at you, evaluating your every move. Those eyes can be especially taxing on your self-esteem. This is what flowed through my mind when I arrived at the Rhombus gallery for my introduction with Slam.

"We are at the testing zone of consciousness . . . we are at the moment of democratization of art. And it is the tongue of the slam that wants to tickle your inner-eardrum."
—*Bob Holman, New York City Slammaster*

"Greetings!" the woman yells, her arms flinging up into the air, "and thank you all for returning, and thank you all for joining us. My name is Kathy, and I am fortunate enough to be your slam mistress tonight!"

Shouts of approval come from all around. Kathy has crazy, curly black hair and wears a green dress. She looks like she stepped out of a Grateful Dead show, complete with bloodshot eyes.

Finding the gallery itself was not an easy task. It's housed in one of gray stone buildings that you easily dismiss and pass on by, having no consequence to your daily life.

Much like the genre itself, the building remains incognito. It took me forty-five minutes, walking up and down College Street, to find the place.

No big signs, no fancy lighted lettering, just a piece of eight-and-a-half-by-eleven piece of paper, colored hospital green, loosely taped next to the door, proclaiming the night's events:

! ! Poetry Slam ! !
Rhombus Gallery
With Special Guests
Friday at 8 p.m.
Donations Appreciated.

On the first floor of the building resides a gift card shop, charmingly named *Initially Yours*. The Rhombus gallery lives and breathes on the upper floors. The gallery itself is located not on the second floor or first floor, but in between the two: on the mezzanine. This seemed to parallel the genre's place in the literary world. I was late and forced to wait a bit before I could get in. Intermission came and people left and I soon entered the threshold of the actual gallery, which was straight out of the 1960's. The walls were antiseptic white; pieces of local artwork hung here and there. The window trim was more of that hospital green. The ceiling was composed of one-by-one acoustic tiles with three sets of track lights, all focused on the stage: a five-foot-by-three-foot area painted black centered adjacent to the front wall. The philosophies of the gallery's era lent themselves to the poets it hosted.

◆ SUGGESTIONS FOR WRITING AND RESEARCH

Individual

1. Select one or more of the following techniques to compose your next essay: lists, snapshots, fragment sentences, labyrinthine sentences, repetition, double voice, and collage.
2. Recast an essay previously written in one or more of the alternative-style techniques above. Compare and contrast the effects created by each version.

Collaborative

As a class, compose a collaborative collage profile of your class, piecing together writing from each classmate in one thematically consistent text.

CHAPTER FOURTEEN

Writing Essay Examinations

When you write essay exams, you can throw all the process stuff out the window—there just isn't time to brainstorm, revise, edit, and all. So what are the tricks to good one-draft writing?

ANGEL

Essay examinations typically require students to sit and compose responses to instructors' questions at a single sitting for fifty minutes or more. So, Angel's right, there isn't much room for the careful writing you're able to do when you've a few days to devote to the

process of exploring, researching, revising, or editing. You'll do well if you already have pretty good off-the-cuff writing skills, but if you don't there are a few tricks that might help you get better. Keep in mind that instructors assign essay exams instead of "objective" tests (multiple choice, matching, true/false) because they want to see you go beyond identifying facts and, instead, demonstrate a mastery of larger course concepts in your own language.

Of course, the best preparation for taking an essay exam is to acquire a thorough knowledge of the subject matter, which means if you've attended class, read assigned texts, and completed other assignments, you should be in good shape. If you've taken good notes, kept journals, annotated readings, and discussed course material with other students, you should be in even better shape. So, while there is no substitute for a thorough knowledge of the course subject, certain writing strategies may enhance your presentation of information. This brief chapter outlines suggestions for writing under examination pressure.

WHAT ARE THE BEST STRATEGIES?

Read Before You Write

You've heard this before, but we'll say it once more: Before answering a single question, quickly read over the whole exam to assess its scope and focus. Figure out how much time you'll have for each question and stick to that estimate if you can. If you are given a choice among several questions, select questions that, taken together, demonstrate your knowledge of the whole course rather than answering two on pretty much the same topic. Finally, decide which questions you are best prepared to answer, and respond to those first. Answering questions you know relaxes you, warms you up intellectually, and gives you confidence to tackle the tougher ones.

Attend to Direction Words

Take a moment to analyze each question before you write: Read it several times, then underline the direction word that identifies your task to keep you on track.

Define or *identify* asks for the distinguishing traits of a term, subject, or event, but does not require an interpretation or judgment. Use appropriate terminology learned in the course. For example, the question *Define John Locke's concept of tabula rasa* is best answered by using some of Locke's terminology along with your own.

Describe may ask for a physical description (*the setting of a play*) or it may request an explanation of a process, phenomenon, or event (*the culture and practices of the mound builders*). Answering description questions requires specific detail and apt examples.

Summarize asks for an overview or a synthesis of the main points. If asked to *summarize the impact of the Battle of Gettysburg,* hit the highlights, but don't get bogged down in details.

Compare and contrast asks that you point out both similarities and differences, between two or more subjects, so be sure to do both.

Analyze asks that you write about a subject in terms of its component parts. If asked to *analyze the typical seating plan of a symphony orchestra,* examine part at a time.

Interpret asks you to explain the meaning of something. If asked to *interpret a Flannery O'Connor short story,* focus on the theme you think most important and provide relevant quotations from the text to back you up.

Explain asks what causes something (*List three causes of the Civil War*), how something works (*How are compact disks are manufactured?*), or what something means (*Explain the function of color in the work of Picasso.* Note that while the first two examples call for value-neutral responses, the third really asks for interpretation. So, *explain,* like *discus,* is really a catch-all term that requires careful attention on your part.

Evaluate, like *critique,* asks for a judgment based on clearly articulated analysis and reasoning (*Evaluate this questionnaire and eliminate weak questions*). Back up your evaluation with good reasons, which may include citing other's opinions that support your own.

Discuss, like *explai*n or *comment,* is a general request, which allows you considerable latitude. If asked to *discuss the effects of monetarist economic theories on current Third World development,* you should be using terms and ideas found in the course readings and lectures, though it is implied that you will add your own insights as well.

WHAT MAKES GOOD ANSWERS?

Instructors give essay exams to find out how much students know about course content and how expertly they can discuss it, which suggests that a written answers should use course concepts in a clearly organized and appropriate way. If they were interested in testing only for specific facts and information, they could give true/false or multiple-choice tests.

Therefore, the best essay answers will be accurate but also highly focused, carefully composed, and easy to follow. The following are two examples of answers to an essay question from a music history examination. Which do you think is the better answer?

Explain the origin and concept of neoclassicism, and identify a significant composer and works associated with the development of this music.

ESSAY 1

Neoclassicism in music is a return to the ideas of the classical period of earlier centuries. It is dry and emphasizes awkward and screeching sounds and does not appeal to the listener's emotions. It does not tell a story, but presents only a form. It is hard to listen to or understand compared to more romantic music such as Beethoven composed. Neoclassical music developed in the early part of the twentieth century. Stravinsky is the most famous composer who developed this difficult music.

ESSAY 2

Neoclassical music developed as a reaction against the romantic music of the nineteenth century. Stravinsky, the most famous neoclassical composer, took his style and themes from the eighteenth-century classical music of Bach, Handel, and Vivaldi rather than Beethoven or Brahms. Stravinsky emphasizes technique and form instead of story or image, with his atonal compositions appealing more to the intellect than the emotions. "Rite of Spring" (1913) and "Symphony of Psalms" (1940) are good examples.

Both answers are approximately the same length, and both are approximately correct. However, the second answer is stronger for the following reasons: It is more carefully organized (from general to specific); it includes more information (names, works, dates); it uses more careful disciplinary terms (*technique, form, image*); and it answers all parts of the question (the first answer omits the titles of works). It also does not digress into the writer's personal value judgments (that neoclassical music "is hard to listen to"), which the question did not ask for.

TRICKS OF THE ESSAY-ANSWER TRADE

Jot a Word Outline

Take one or two minutes per question to make a word outline of your answer. If asked to compare and contrast three impressionist painters, decide in advance which three you will write about and in which order. Then, jot that brief organizational strategy in margins of the test booklet or your paper to help focus information and present it in a logical rather than haphazard order.

Lead with a Thesis

The surest way to receive full credit on an essay question is to answer the question briefly and directly in your first sentence. In other words, if possible, state your answer as a thesis statement which the rest of your essay explains, supports, and defends (here, again, outlining will help). In examination writing, it's usually—though not always—better to be direct and explicit than creative and implicit.

Remember the Five-Paragraph Strategy

A five-paragraph essay is often taught in high school as a way to write a satisfying, if formulaic, short essay. To write one, you open with a broad, general first paragraph that states your main idea or thesis. You follow with three more specific paragraphs that support this main idea. You conclude by returning to the broad theme with which you started. While I don't think this formula is very good for writing interesting essays, it's actually pretty handy for rapidly organizing an essay exam answer, as it gives you an easy template to follow while wrestling with ideas on the spot in a short period of time.

Include Details, Examples, and Illustrations

Good writing contains specific information that lets readers see for themselves the evidence for your position. Use as many supportive specifics as you can, so in studying, memorize names, titles, dates, and ideas so you can recall them accurately when needed. Individual facts alone are not worth much, but when used as evidence along with strong reasoning, these specifics make the difference between mediocre and good answers.

Provide Context

In answering a question posed by an instructor who is an expert in the field, it is tempting to assume no context is needed. However, since you are being asked to demonstrate how much *you* understand, treat each question as an opportunity to show how thoroughly you know the subject. Explain, if ever so briefly, concepts, terms, and background information that amplifies your answer.

Use Disciplinary Language

Use, define, explain, and correctly spell all technical terms used in the course. Essay exams implicitly test your facility with the language the discipline as well as explicitly test your knowledge of its concepts.

STRATEGIES FOR WRITING ESSAY EXAMINATIONS

1. Read first and block your time so that you know what you're being asked to do and approximately how much time you should spend on each question.
2. Choose your essay questions carefully. The essay questions you answer should allow you to write on what you know best. Don't repeat answers but use this as an occasion show a broad range of course knowledge.
3. Focus on direction words. For each question you have chosen, it is important to recognize what your instructor is really asking, for this understanding enables you to answer the question successfully.
4. Plan and outline each essay. Prepare a single word outline of your answer by identifying the key points you need to make in the best order to make them.
5. Lead with a thesis to illustrate your confidence in knowing the answer and setting out to prove it.
6. Include details, examples, illustrations—the evidence that shows your mastery of the subject matter. Even include short powerful quotations where relevant, citing each by author, title, and date. To help you remember, focus on key words and jot them in the margins near your answer.
7. Use the discipline's terms and methods. Enter into the conversation of a particular discipline by using its accepted terms and methods.
8. Provide context but stay focused. Explain all your points as if your audience did not have the understanding your teacher does, but keep all your information focused on simply answering that one question. If you know more than time allows you to tell, end your answer with an outline of key points that you would discuss if you had more time.
9. If you've got a few minutes at the end of writing, proofread! You'll always find a few small things, but maybe you'll find something pretty important that needs correcting.

◆ SUGGESTIONS FOR WRITING AND RESEARCH

Individual

In preparation for an essay examination in one of your courses, conduct an analytical reading of your course syllabus, asking questions such as:

- In reading the descriptive overview of the course, which words seem most important?
- What are the main subheadings into which the course is divided?
- How much time is allocated for each subdivision of course content?
- What is the title or stated agenda of each scheduled class?
- How would you describe the voice of the syllabus (stern, authoritarian, loose, relaxed, etc.)?
- What specific tasks do course assignments ask you to do?

On the basis of this analysis, outline the most important issues, concepts, and information which you should study for the upcoming exam.

Collaborative

Form a small study group of students who are taking the same course, and first, do an individual analysis of the syllabus as described above. Then, pool your answers and see if additional answers emerge about the relative importance of some topics compared to others. (A successful conclusion to either of these exercises, of course, will be the measure of how well you do taking the examination.)

PART THREE

REVISING
AND EDITING

CHAPTER FIFTEEN

Strategies for Revision

Writing. I'm more involved in it. But not as attached. I used to really cling to my writing and didn't want it to change. Now I can see the usefulness of change. I just really like my third draft, but I have to let it go. I can still enjoy my third draft and make an even better fourth.

KAREN

A first draft is a writer's first attempt to give shape to an idea, argument, or experience. Occasionally, this initial draft is just right and the writing is done. More often, however, the first draft shows a general direction that needs further thinking and redirecting. An unfocused first draft, in other words, is not a mistake but rather a start toward a next, more focused draft.

No matter how much prior thought writers give to a particular paper, once they begin composing, the draft begins to shift, change, and develop in unexpected ways. Each act of writing produces new questions and insights to be incorporated into the emerging piece of writing. While inexperienced writers view revising as an alien activity that doesn't come easily, experienced writers view revising as the primary way of developing thoughts to be shared with others.

UNDERSTANDING REVISING

The terms *revising, editing,* and *proofreading* may seem similar, but there is good reason to understand each as a separate process, each contributing to good finished writing.

Revising is re-seeing, rereading, and rethinking your thoughts on paper until they fully match your intention. Mentally, it's conceptual work focused on units of meaning larger than the sentence. Physically it's cutting, pasting, crossing out, and rewriting until the ideas are satisfying.

Editing, in contrast, is changing language more than ideas. It's primarily stylistic work, where writers test each word or phrase to see that is accurate, appropriate, necessary, generally sentence-level work.

Proofreading is checking a manuscript for accuracy and correctness. It is the last phase of the editing process, completed after conceptual and stylistic concerns have been addressed. Proofreaders review spelling, punctuation, capitalization, and usage to make sure no careless mistakes continue to the final draft.

Try to revise before you edit so you don't waste time on passages that later get cut from your manuscript. At the same time, it's especially easy to violate this guideline, as writers are always circling back through the stages, editing when know they should be revising and vice versa. Nonetheless, you will save time if you revise before editing and edit before proofreading.

◆ WRITING 1

Describe any experience you've had with revising papers: Was it for a school assignment or some writing on your own? Why did you revise? How many drafts did you do? Were you pleased? Was your audience?

ASKING REVISION QUESTIONS

To begin revising, return to the basic questions of purpose, audience, and voice: Why am I writing? to whom? in what voice?

Questions of purpose. It is often easier to see your purpose—or lack thereof—most clearly after you have written a draft or two. Ask: Why am I writing this paper? Do all parts of the paper advance this purpose? What is my rhetorical strategy: to narrate, explain, interpret, argue, reflect, or something else?

Questions of audience. Make sure your paper is aimed accurately at your readers by asking: What does my audience know about this subject? What does my audience need to know to understand the point of my paper? What questions or objections do I anticipate my audience raising? (Try to answer these questions as you revise.)

Questions of voice. Make sure your paper satisfies you. Revise so you say what you intend in the voice you intend by reading out loud and asking, Which passages sound like me speaking and which don't? (Enjoy those that do; fix those that don't.)

♦ WRITING 2

Describe your approach to writing a paper from the time it's assigned to the time you hand it in. Do you do any of the prerevision work described above? Which of these general strategies makes sense in view of your current writing habits?

CREATING TITLES

Titles catch the attention of readers and provide a clue to the paper's content. If a title doesn't suggest itself in the writing of your paper, try one of these strategies:

- Use one strong short phrase from your paper.
- Present a question that your paper answers.
- State the answer to the question or issue your paper will explore.
- Use a clear or catchy image from your paper.
- Use a famous quotation.
- Write a one-word title (or a two-word title, a three-word title, and so on).
- Begin your title with the word *On*.
- Begin your title with a gerund (*-ing* word).

USING REVISION STRATEGIES

You cannot revise if you haven't first written, so write early and leave time to revise later. Good college papers are seldom written in one draft the night before they are due. When you plan in advance, you'll have the opportunity to take advantage of some of the dozen **revision strategies** other writers have found useful. While they won't all work for you all the time, some will be useful at one time or another.

1. *Impose early due dates.*   Write the due date for a final draft on your calendar; then fool yourself a little by adding in earlier, self-imposed due dates for first, second, or third drafts. Your self-imposed intermediate due dates will guarantee you the time you need to revise well.
2. *Establish distance.*   Let your draft sit for a while, overnight if possible; then reread it to see whether it still makes sense. A later reading allows you to see whether there are places that need clarification, explanation, or development that you did not see close up. You can gain distance also by reading your draft aloud—hearing instead of seeing it—and by sharing it with others and listening to their reactions.
3. *Reconsider everything.*   Reread the whole text from the beginning: Every time you change something of substance, reread again to see the effect of these changes on other parts of the text. If a classmate or instructor has made comments on some parts of the paper and not on others, do not assume that only the places where there are comments need revision.

4. *Believe and doubt.*   Reread your draft twice, first as if you wanted to believe everything you wrote (imagine a supportive friend), putting check marks in the margins next to passages that create the most belief—the assertions, the discussion, the details, the evidence. Next, reread your draft as if you were suspicious and skeptical of all assertions, putting question marks next to questionable passages. Be pleased with the check marks, and answer the question marks.

5. *Test theme and evidence.*   When you make changes in theme or thesis, review the whole manuscript to make sure all parts remain consistent. When you find multiple bit of evidence to support your major idea, keep in mind that facts make the strongest evidence. Inferences based on accumulated facts are also powerful; however, opinion can be strong or weak depending on the source.

6. *Make a paragraph outline.*   The most common unit of thought in a paper is the paragraph, a group of sentences set off from other groups because they focus on the same main idea. A paragraph outline creates a map of your whole paper that shows whether the organization is effective or needs changing. Number each paragraph and write a phrase describing its topic or focus. Check to make sure each subject of each paragraph leads logically to the next.

7. *Create a new file for each revision.*   Each time you revise a draft, give that version a new number (e.g., draft 1, 2, etc.) so that you automatically save your earlier draft in a separate file. That way, if you become unhappy with your revisions, you can always return to the earlier copy.

8. *Review hard copy.*   When revising with a computer, print out hard copies of your drafts on scrap paper and see how they read. Hard copy lets you scan several pages at a time and quickly flip pages in search of certain patterns or information.

9. *Rewrite introductions and conclusions.*   Once started, papers grow and evolve in unpredictable ways: An opening that seemed appropriate in an earlier draft may no longer fit. The closing that once nicely ended the paper may now fail to do so. Examine both introduction and conclusion to be sure they actually introduce and conclude. (See also Chapter 17.)

10. *Listen for your voice.*   In informal and semiformal papers—in fact, in most college papers—your language should sound like a real human being speaking. Read your paper aloud and see whether the human being speaking sounds like you. If a formal style is requested, the language should sound less like you in conversation and more like you giving a presentation—fewer opinions, more objectivity, no contractions.

11. *Let go.*   View change as good, not bad. Many writers become overly attached to the first words they generate, proud to have found them, now reluctant to abandon them. Learn to let your words, sentence, and even paragraphs go. Trust that new and more appropriate ones will come.

12. *Start over.*   Sometimes the best way to revise is to start fresh. Review your first draft, then turn it face down and start again. Starting over generates your best writing, as it doesn't lock you into old constructions, eliminates dead-end ideas, and opens up new possibilities. (Many writers have discovered this fact accidentally, by losing a file on a computer and thus being forced to reconstruct; almost every one of them will tell you they wrote a better draft because they started over.)

◆ WRITING 3

Look over the suggestions for revision in this section. Which of them have you used in the past? Which seem most useful to you now? Which seem most farfetched?

◆ SUGGESTIONS FOR WRITING AND RESEARCH

Individual
Select any paper that you previously wrote in one draft but that you believe would profit from revision. Revise the paper by following some of the revision strategies and suggestions in this chapter.

Collaborative
As a class, brainstorm favorite revision strategies and write these on a board or overhead projector screen. Put check marks by those used by most students. Put asterisks next to any ideas not already mentioned in this chapter. Promise yourself to use at least one new strategy next time you revise a paper.

CHAPTER SIXTEEN

Focused Revision

*I never realized before that in revising you can do drafts from totally different per-
spectives and keep experimenting with your ideas. When you write the final draft, it
could be totally different from how you expected it to come out in the beginning.*

GARY

*I want my audience to feel like they're actually attending the game, that they're sit-
ting just behind the bench, overhearing Coach telling us how to defend against the
in-bounds pass, and I can do this if I just close my eyes while I write and remember
being there—I can put you at the game.*

KAREN

Have you ever found yourself running out of ideas, energy, or creativity on what seemed to be a perfectly good topic for a paper? Have you ever been told to rewrite, revise, review, redo, rethink a paper, but didn't know exactly what those suggestions meant? Have you ever written a paper you thought was carefully focused and well researched but was also dull and lifeless?

Odds are you're not alone. When anyone writes a first draft—especially on an assigned topic to which he or she has given little prior thought—it's easy to summarize rather than analyze, to produce generalities and ignore specifics, to settle for clichés rather than invent fresh images, to cover too much territory in too little time. In fact, most first drafts contain more than their share of summary, generalization, superficiality, and cliché, since most first-draft writers are feeling their way and still discovering their topic. In

175

other words, it's seldom a problem if your first draft is off the track, wanders a bit, and needs refocusing. However, it is a problem if, for your second draft, you haven't changed it.

The best way to shape a wandering piece of writing is to return to it, reread it, slow it down, take it apart, and build it back up again, this time attending more carefully to purpose, audience, and voice. Celebrate first-draft writing for what it is—a warm-up, a scouting trip—but plan next to get on with your journey in a more deliberate and organized fashion. Sometimes you already know—or your readers tell you—exactly where to go. Other times, you're not sure and need some strategies to get you moving again. This chapter offers four specific strategies for restarting, reconceiving, and refocusing a stuck paper.

LIMITING

Broad topics lead to superficial writing. It's difficult to recount a four-week camping trip, to explain the meaning of *Hamlet,* or to solve the problems of poverty, crime, or violence in a few double-spaced pages. You'll almost always do better to cover less ground in more pages. Instead, can you *limit* your focus to one pivotal day on the trip? Can you explain and interpret one crucial scene? Can you research and portray one real social problem in your own back yard?

Limit Time, Place, and Action

When a first draft attempts to describe and explain actions that took place over many days, weeks, or months, try limiting the second draft to actions that took place on one day, on one afternoon, or in one hour. Limiting the amount of time you write about automatically limits the action (what happened) and place (where it happened) as well. For example, in the first draft of a paper investigating the homeless in downtown Burlington, Vermont, Dan began with a broad sweep:

> In this land of opportunity, freedom takes on different meaning for different people. Some people are born to wealth, others obtain it by the sweat of their brows, while average Americans always manage to get by. But others, not so fortunate or talented, never have enough food or shelter to make even the ends of their daily lives meet.

While there is nothing inherently wrong with this start, neither is there anything new, interesting, or exciting. The generalizations about wealth and poverty tell us only what we already know; there are no new facts, information, or images to catch our attention and hold it for the pages still to come.

Before writing his second draft, Dan visited the downtown area, met some homeless people, and observed firsthand the habits of a single homeless man named Brian; then he limited his focus and described what he witnessed on one morning:

> Dressed in soiled blue jeans and a ragged red flannel shirt, Brian digs curiously through an evergreen bush beside a house on Loomis Street. His yellow mesh baseball cap bears no emblem or logo to mark him a member of any team. He wears it low, concealing any expression his eyes might disclose. After a short struggle, he emerges from the bush, a Budweiser can in hand, a grin across his face. Pouring out

the remaining liquid, he tosses the can into his shopping cart among other alu-
minum, glass, and plastic containers. He pauses, slides a Marlboro out of the crum-
pled pack in his breast pocket, lights it, and resumes his expedition.

While only one small act happens in this revised first paragraph—the retrieving of a single
beer can—that act anticipates Dan's story of how unemployed homeless people earn money.
By starting with a single detailed—and therefore convincing—scene, Dan writes more about
less; in the process, he teaches his readers specific things about people he originally labeled
"not so fortunate or talented." By describing instead of evaluating or interpreting this scene,
he invites readers to make their own inferences about what it means. In other words, writing one specific, accurate, nonjudgmental scene asks readers to interpret and therefore engage more deeply in the text.

Limit Scope

In the process of Dan's researching and writing, the scope of his paper became progressively
more restricted: In draft one, he focused on the homeless in America; in draft two, he focused on the homeless in downtown Burlington; in draft three, he focused on those homeless people who collect cans for income. From his initial limitation in time came a consequent
limitation in scope, and a distinct gain in specificity, detail, and reader interest.

One technique for limiting the scope of any type of paper is to identify the topic of
any one page, paragraph, or sentence in which something important or interesting is introduced. Begin your next paper with that specific topic, focusing close now and limiting
the whole draft to only that topic. For example, in a paper arguing against the clear-cutting
of forests, focus on one page describing the cutting of Western red cedar in one specific
place; limit the next whole draft to that single subject. In a paper examining the exploita-
tion of women in television advertising, focus on one paragraph describing a single soda ad;
limit the next whole draft to that single subject. In a paper examining your high school soccer career, focus on one sentence describing the locker room after the loss of an important
game. When you limit scope, you gain depth.

◆ WRITING 1

Devote a portion of your journal or class notebook exclusively to exploring the revision
possibilities of one paper. For your first entry, reread the paper you intend to revise, and
limit either the time or scope that you intend to cover in the second draft.

ADDING

A sure way to increase reader interest in a paper, and your own interest as well, is to *add* new
and specific material to that overly general first draft. Whether you are arguing about the
effects of mountain bikes on the wilderness, explaining the situation of the homeless people downtown, or interpreting the poems of Gwendolyn Brooks, it is your job to become
the most informed expert on this subject in your writing class. It's your job to read the

necessary articles, visit the appropriate places, interview the relevant people who will make you the authority to write the paper. On first drafts, neither your instructor nor classmates expect you to be this authority; on subsequent drafts, their expectations increase.

Add Expert Voices

The surest way to locate new information to add to next drafts is to read widely and listen carefully. Get to the library and locate sources that supplement and substantiate your own knowledge. Enlist the support of experts by citing them in your paper, identifying who they are and why they should be listened to. Also get out into the field and talk to people who are the local experts on your subject. Quote these experts, too, and include their voices in your next draft.

Although textual quotations are helpful and expected in academic papers, they are seldom so locally specific or lively as interview quotations from local people. In many instances where little may have been published on local issues, the only way to get up-to-date local information is from talking to people. Quoting people directly not only adds new and credible information to your paper, it invariably adds a sense of life as well. For example, as Dan continued his story of Burlington's homeless people, he interviewed a number of people, such as police officer Pat Hardy, who had firsthand knowledge of the homeless can collectors:

> "They provide a real service to the community," he explains. "You'd see a lot more cans and bottles littering the streets if they weren't out here working hard each day. I've never had a problem with any of them. They are a real value."

While Dan himself could have made the same observation, it has greater authority and life coming from a cop on the beat.

In another instance, a team of first-year students collaborated to write a profile of the local Ronald McDonald House, a nonprofit organization providing free room and board for the families of hospital patients. In their first draft, they researched the local newspaper for introductory information on the origins of this institution. It was useful information, but without much life:

> The McDonald's corporation actually provided less than 5 percent of the total cost of starting the Ronald McDonald House. The other 95 percent of the money came from local businesses and special-interest groups.

For their second draft, the group interviewed the director of the Ronald McDonald House and used her as an additional and more current source of information. In fact, they devoted the entire second draft to material collected through interviews with the director and staff at the house. In the following sample, the director substantiates the information from the initial newspaper story but adds more specific, local, and lively details.

> "Our biggest problem is that people think we're supported by the McDonald's corporation. We have to get people to understand that anything we get from McDonald's is just from the particular franchise's generosity—and may be no more than is donated by other local merchants. Martins, Hood, and Ben and Jerry's provide much of the food. McDonald's is not obligated to give us anything. The only reason we use their name is because of its child appeal."

The final profile of the Ronald McDonald House included information ranging from newspaper and newsletter stories to site descriptions and interviews with staff, volunteers, and family.

Add Details

If you quickly review this chapter's samples of revision by *limiting* and *adding,* you will notice the increase in specific detail. Focusing close, interviewing people, and researching texts all produce specific information, which adds both energy and evidence to whatever paper you are writing. In the can-collecting paper, the visual details make Brian come alive—*soiled blue jeans, red flannel shirt, yellow mesh baseball cap, Budweiser can, Marlboro.* In the Ronald McDonald revisions, the newspaper statistics add authority (*5 percent of the total cost*) while the interview information adds specificity (*Martins, Hood, and Ben and Jerry's*), both of which help explain the funding of this nonprofit organization.

◆ WRITING 2

Identify texts, places, or people that contain information relevant to your paper topic and go collect it. If you are writing a paper strictly from memory, close your eyes and visit this place in your imagination: Describe the details and re-create the dialogue you find there.

SWITCHING

Another strategy for focusing a second or third draft is deliberately to alter your customary way of viewing and thinking about this topic. One sure way to change how you see a problem, experience, story, issue, or idea is to *switch* the perspective from which you view it (the point of view), the language in which you portray it (the verb tense), or the audience for whom you are writing.

Switch Point of View

Switching the point of view from which a story, essay, or report is written means changing the perspective from which it is told. For example, in recounting personal experience, the most natural point of view is the first person (*I, we*) as we relate what happened to us. Here Karen writes in the first person in reporting her experience participating in the Eastern Massachusetts women's basketball tournament.

> We lost badly to Walpole in what turned out to be our final game. I sat on the bench most of the time.

However, Karen opened the final draft of her personal experience basketball narrative with a switch in point of view, writing as if she were the play-by-play announcer broadcasting the game at the moment, in this case moving to third person *and* adopting a new persona as well:

> Well folks, it looks as if Belmont has given up; the coach is preparing to send in his subs. It has been a rough game for Belmont. They stayed in it during the first quarter, but Walpole has run away with it since then. Down by twenty with only six minutes left, Belmont's first sub is now approaching the table.

In her final draft, Karen opened from the announcer's point of view for one page, then switched for the remainder of the paper to her own first-person perspective, separating the two by white space. Karen's switch to announcer is credible (she *sounds* like an announcer); if she chose to narrate the same story from the perspective of the bouncing basketball, it might seem silly.

In research writing, as opposed to personal narrative, the customary point of view for reporting research results is third person (*he, she, it*) to emphasize the information and deemphasize the writer. For example, the profile of the Ronald McDonald House begins, as you might expect, with no reference to the writers of the report:

> The Ronald McDonald House provides a home away from home for out-of-town families of hospital patients who need to visit patients for extended periods of time but cannot afford to stay in hotels or motels.

However, in one of their drafts, the writers switched to first person and wrote a more personal and impressionistic account explaining their feelings about reporting on this situation. While the impressionistic draft did not play a large part in the final profile, some of it remained purposefully in their final draft as they reported where they had had difficulties.

> In this documentary, we had a few problems with getting certain interviews and information. Since the house is a refuge for parents in distress, we limited the kinds of questions we asked. We didn't want to pry.

Switch Tense

Switching verb tense means switching the time frame in which a story or experience occurs. While the present tense is a natural tense for explaining information (see the Ronald McDonald example above), the most natural tense for recounting personal experience is the past tense, as we retell occurrences that happened sometime before the present moment—the same tense Karen adopted in the first draft of her basketball essay. However, her final draft is written entirely in the present tense, beginning with the announcer and continuing through to the end of her own narrative.

> It's over now, and I've stopped crying, and I'm very happy. In the end I have to thank—not my coach, not my team—but Walpole for beating us so badly that I got to play.

The advantage of switching to the present tense is that it lets you reexperience an event, and doing that, in turn, allows you to reexamine, reconsider, and reinterpret it—all essential activities for successful revision. At the same time, readers participate in the drama of the moment, waiting along with you to find out what will happen next. The disadvantage is that the present tense is associated with fiction—it's difficult or impossible to write while you're doing something else, like playing basketball. It's also difficult to reflect on experience if you're pretending it's occurring as you write.

Switch Sides

Another way to gain a new revision perspective is to switch sides in arguing a position: Write your first draft supporting the "pro" side, then write a second draft supporting the "con" side. For example, Issa, a dedicated mountain bike enthusiast, planned to write in favor of opening up more wilderness trails for use by mountain bikers. However, before writing his final draft, he researched the arguments against his position and wrote from that point of view:

> The hikers and other passive trail users argue against allowing mountain bikes onto narrow trails traditionally traveled only by foot and horse. They point out that the wide, deeply treaded tires of the mountain bikes cause erosion and that the high speeds of the bikers startle and upset both hikers and horses. According to hiker Donald Meserlain, the bikes "ruin the tranquillity of the woodlands and drive out hikers, bird watchers, and strollers" (Hanley 4).

For the writer, the main advantage of switching sides for a draft may be a better understanding of the opposition's point of view, making for a more effective argument against it in the final draft.

For his final draft, Issa argues his original position in favor of mountain bikes, but he does so with more understanding, empathy, and effectiveness because he spent a draft with the opposition. His final draft makes it clear where he stands on the issue:

> Educated mountain biking, like hiking and horseback riding, respects the environment and promotes peace and conservation, not noise and destruction. Making this case has begun to pay off, and the battle over who walks and who rides the trails should now shift in favor of peaceful coexistence. Buoyed by studies showing that bicycle tires cause no more erosion or trail damage than the boots of hikers, and far less than horses' hooves, mountain bike advocates are starting to find receptive ears among environmental organizations (Schwartz 78).

The tone of the mountain bike essay is now less strident and more thoughtful—an approach apparently brought about by his spending time seriously considering the objections of the opposition. (See Chapter 11 for the complete essay.)

Another switch that pays good dividends for the writer is changing the audience to whom the paper is being written. In college writing situations, the final audience always includes the instructor, so such a change may simply be a temporary but useful fiction. Had a draft of the mountain bike essay been aimed at the different constituencies mentioned in the essay—the Sierra Club, mountain bicycle manufacturers, property owners, or local newspapers—the writer might have gained a useful perspective in attempting to switch language and arguments to best address this more limited readership. Likewise, drafts of various papers written to young children, empathetic classmates, skeptical professors, or sarcastic friends may also provide useful variations in writer perspective.

◆ WRITING 3

Write in your journal about a past experience, using the present tense and/or third-person point of view. Then reread the passage and describe its effect on you as both writer and reader.

TRANSFORMING

To *transform* a text is to change its form by casting it into a new form or genre. In early drafts, writers often attend closely to the content of their stories, arguments, or reports but pay little attention to the form in which these are presented, accepting the genre as "school paper" only. However, recasting ideas and information into different and more public genres presents them in a different light. The possibilities for representing information in different genres are endless, since anything can become anything else. Consequently, keep in mind that some transformations are useful primarily to help you achieve a fresh perspective during the revision process, while others are more appropriate for presenting the information to readers.

In the world outside of college, it is actually common for research information to be reported in different genres to different audiences. For example, in a business or corporate setting, the same research information may be conveyed as a report to a manager, a letter to a vice president, a pamphlet for the stockholders, and a news release for public media—and show up still later in a feature article in a trade publication or newspaper. As in the working world, so in college: Information researched and collected for any paper can be presented in a variety of forms and formats.

Transform Personal Experience from Essay to Journal

The journal form encourages informal and conversational language, creates a sense of chronological suspense, is an ideal form for personal reflection, substitutes dates for more complex transitions, and proves especially useful for conveying experience over a long period of time. For example, after several essay-like narratives written from a past-tense perspective, Jeff used the journal format to tell the story of his month-long camping trip with the organization Outward Bound. Following is an excerpt, edited for brevity, in which he describes his reactions to camping alone for one week, using a mix of past and present tenses:

> Day 14 I find myself thinking a lot about food. When I haven't eaten in the morning, I tend to lose my body heat faster than when I don't. . . . At this point, in solo, good firewood is surprisingly tough to come by. . . .
>
> Day 15 Before I write about my fifth day of solo, I just want to say that it was damn cold last night. I have a –20 degree bag, and I froze. It was the coldest night so far, about –25. . . .
>
> Day 17 I haven't seen a single person for an entire week. I have never done this before, and I really don't want to do it again—not having anyone to talk to. Instead of talking, I write to myself. . . . If I didn't have this journal, I think I would have gone crazy.

Transform to Letters

An issue might be illuminated in a lively and interesting way by being cast as a series or exchange of letters. Each letter allows a different character or point of view to be expressed. For example, Issa's argumentative paper on mountain bike use in wilderness areas could be represented as a series of letters to the editor of a local paper arguing different sides of the controversy: from the perspective of a hiker, a horseback rider, a mountain bike rider, a forest ranger, a landowner, among others.

Transform to a Documentary

Radio, film, and television documentaries are common vehicles for hearing news and information. Virtually any research paper could be made livelier by being cast as a documentary film or investigative feature story. Full research and documentation would be required, as for formal academic papers; however, writers would use the style of the popular press rather than the MLA or APA. In fact, the final form of the profile of the Ronald McDonald House was written as a script for *Sixty Minutes* and opened with a Mike Wallace–type of reporter speaking into a microphone:

> Smith: Hello, this is John Smith reporting for *Sixty Minutes*. Our topic this week is the Ronald McDonald House. Here I am, in front of the house in Burlington, Vermont, but before I go inside, let me fill you in on the history of this and many other houses like it.

The final paper included sections with the fictional Smith interviewing actual staff members as well as some sections presented neutrally from the camera's point of view:

> Toward the back of the house, three cars and one camper are parked in an oval-shaped gravel driveway. Up three steps onto a small porch are four black plastic chairs and a small coffee table containing a black ashtray filled with cigarette butts.

Transform to a Book with Chapters

Teams of student writers can collaborate on writing short books with "chapters" exploring issues of common interest. Such a form could include a table of contents, preface, foreword, afterword, introduction, and so on. For example, Dan's report on the life of a can collector could become one chapter in a collaborative "book" investigating how the homeless live:

1. Housing for the Homeless
2. Dinner at the Salvation Army
3. Shopping at Goodwill
4. Brian: Case Study of a Can Collector
5. Winter Prospects

Transform to a Magazine Article

If you are investigating consumer products, such as mountain bikes and CD's, consider writing the final draft as a report for *Consumer Reports*. If you are investigating an issue such as homelessness, write it as an article for *Time* or *Newsweek*. Likewise, a campus story on the Greek system could be aimed at the campus newspaper or the profile of a classmate in the style of *People* magazine or *The New Yorker*. Before writing the final draft, be sure to study the form and conventions of the periodical for which you are writing.

Transform to a Talk-Show Debate

An especially good genre for interpretive or argumentative papers would be a debate, conversation, or panel discussion. For example, students recently wrote a paper as a debate on the advantages versus disadvantages of clear-cutting timber: On one side were the environmentalists and tourist industry, on the other side the paper companies and landowners; each side had valid points in its favor. The debate format was real, as it echoed very closely a similar debate in Congress.

Transform to Any Medium of Expression

The possibilities for reshaping college papers are endless: song, play, poem, editorial, science fiction story, laboratory report, bulletin, brochure, television or radio commercial, public address, political speech, telephone conversation, e-mail exchange, World Wide Web page, poster, "Talk of the Town" for *The New Yorker,* sound bite, environmental impact statement, conference paper, video game, philosophical debate, or bar stool argument.

◆ WRITING 4

Propose a transformation for a paper you are writing or have recently written. List the advantages and disadvantages of this transformation. Recast your paper (or a part of it) in the new genre and describe the effect.

EXPERIMENTATION VERSUS CONVENTION

Standard *academic conventions* are accepted ways of doing certain things, such as using an objective voice in research reports and placing the thesis first in position papers. These conventions have evolved over time for good reasons. When carefully done, they transmit ideas and information clearly and predictably, thereby avoiding confusion and misunderstanding. Although in many cases these conventions work well, successful writers sometimes invent unorthodox strategies and experiment with new or alternative forms to better express new or complicated ideas. In order to decide whether a conventional or experimental form is preferable in any part of your paper, try both to see which more appropriately presents your ideas in their best light. Sometimes an act as simple as changing time, tense, point of view, or genre can effectively change the impact of a piece of writing.

The strategies described in this chapter are useful revising tools because they force writers to re-see the events in different languages and from different perspectives. Writing in new forms is also intriguing, exciting, and fun—which is often what writers need after working long and hard to put together a first draft.

When and under what circumstances should you limit, add, switch, or transform? While there are no rules, you might try using these strategies whenever you feel stuck or in need of new energy or insight. But be sure to weigh gains and losses whenever you use new focusing techniques.

Disregarding academic conventions in early drafts should seldom be a problem; however, disregarding them in final drafts could be if it violates the assignment, so check with your instructor. Be sure that in gaining reader attention in this way, you do not lose credibility or cause confusion.

♦ SUGGESTIONS FOR WRITING AND RESEARCH

Individual

1. Write the first draft of a personal experience paper as a broad overview of the whole experience. Write the second draft by limiting the story to one day or less of this experience. Write the third draft using one of the other techniques described in this chapter: adding, switching, or transforming. Write the final draft in any way that pleases you.
2. Write the first draft of a research-based paper as an overview of the whole issue with which you intend to deal. In the second draft, limit the scope to something you now cover in one page, paragraph, or sentence. In the third draft, adopt one of the focused revision strategies described in this chapter: adding, switching, or transforming. For your final draft, revise in any way that pleases you.

Collaborative

1. For a class research project, interview college instructors in different departments concerning their thoughts about transforming academic papers into other genres. Write up the results in any form that seems useful.
2. As a class, compile a catalog in which you list and describe as many alternative forms for college papers as you can.

CHAPTER SEVENTEEN

Openings and Closings

I could start this essay just about anywhere at all, by telling you about the background, by stating the thesis, by telling a funny story, or even by rambling, which is what I usually do. Where do you think I should start?

WENDY

M y advice, Wendy, is to lead with your best punch. Make your opening so strong your reader feels compelled to continue. Make your closing so memorable that your reader can't forget it.

Readers pay special attention to openings and closings, so make them work for you. Start with titles and lead paragraphs that grab readers' attention and alert them to what is to come; end with closings that sum up and reinforce where they've been. This chapter looks closely at how these special paragraphs function and how you can make these paragraphs stronger through skillful editing.

◆ OPENINGS

Openings orient your reader. Your first paragraph—in fact, your whole first page—sets readers up for the rest of the reading journey. Here you provide the first clues about your subject, purpose, and voice and invite your audience to keep reading.

Good opening paragraphs are seldom written in first drafts. Often, it's not until you've finished a draft or two that you know exactly what your paper says and does. So when your paper is nearly finished, return to your first page, read it again, and edit carefully. The following examples of effective openings are taken from the student papers reproduced earlier in this textbook; all of them were rewritten at the editing stage.

186

Open with a Conflict

If your paper is about conflict, sometimes it's best to open by directly spelling out what that conflict is. Identifying a conflict captures attention by creating a kind of suspense: Will the conflict be resolved? How will it be resolved? Issa's exploration of the conflict between hikers and mountain bikers opens this way:

> The narrow, hard-packed dirt trail winding up the mountain under the spreading oaks and maples doesn't look like the source of a major environmental conflict, but it is. On the one side are hikers, environmentalists, and horseback riders who have traditionally used these wilderness trails. On the other side, looking back, are the mountain bike riders sitting atop their modern steeds who want to use them too. But the hikers don't want the bikers, so trouble is brewing.

This essay argues, ultimately, in favor of opening wilderness trails to mountain biking; however, Issa uses a delayed-thesis organizational pattern, exploring both sides of the conflict without giving away his own position on the conflict—the opening tells us that *trouble is brewing,* but we don't know how it will be resolved. (To read Issa's complete essay, see Chapter 11.)

Open with a Thesis

Argumentative and interpretive papers commonly open with a clear thesis statement that the rest of the paper will support. Opening with your thesis is the most direct way of telling your reader what the paper will be about. The reader may agree with you and want to see how you support your case, or the reader may disagree and want to find holes in your argument, or the reader may start off neutral and read to see whether or not your paper is believable and persuasive. Following is the first paragraph from Kelly's essay interpreting a poem by Gwendolyn Brooks:

> Gwendolyn Brooks writes "We Real Cool" (1963) from the point of view of the members of a street gang who have dropped out of school to live their lives hanging around pool halls—in this case "The Golden Shovel." These guys are semiliterate and speak in slangy street lingo that reveals their need for mutual support in their mutually rebellious attitude toward life. The speakers in the poem, "We," celebrate what adults would call adolescent hedonism—but they make a conscious choice for a short, intense life over a long, safe, and dull existence.

While you will need to read Brooks' short poem to fully understand Kelly's argument, this opening passage states Kelly's position about the subjects—who are also the narrators—of the poem: "they make conscious choices for a short intense life over a long, safe, and dull existence."

Thesis stating, like summary writing, is among the most difficult of all writing tasks and for that reason is most easily and clearly written only when you are thoroughly familiar with your subject, which is seldom the case with early drafts. Consequently, openings such as Kelly's above are commonly written after the rest of the paper is completed. (To read Kelly's complete interpretive essay, see Chapter 12.)

Open with a Story

Most readers enjoy stories. Professional writers often open articles with anecdotes to catch readers' attention. The following first paragraph is from Judith's reflective essay about finding a safe place to study in the library. Only in her last draft did she decide to start at the door, in present tense, locking up as she leaves to walk to the library:

> It is already afternoon. I fiddle with the key to lock the apartment door after me. I am not accustomed to locking doors. Except for the six months I spent in Boston, I have never lived in a place where I did not trust my neighbors. When I was little, we couldn't lock our farmhouse door; the wood had swollen, and the bolt no longer lined up properly with the hole, and nobody ever bothered to fix it. I still remember the time our babysitter, Rosie, hammered the bolt closed and we had to take the door off the hinges to get it open.

Stories not only need to catch attention; they need to set up or foreshadow the paper to follow. In Judith's case, the theme and content of her paper emerged through several drafts, so it was only in the final draft that she discovered a personal story about locked doors to anticipate the theme of safety in the rest of the paper. (To read Judith's complete essay, see Chapter 8.)

Open with a Specific Detail

Specific details appeal to readers' visual sense and help them see situations and settings. In early drafts, Beth opened her profile of Becky with Becky speaking; only in this latest version did she decide to set the physical scene first, letting Becky's manner and surroundings characterize her right from the start:

> Becky sits cross-legged at the foot of the bottom bunk on her pink and green homemade quilt. She leans up against the wall and runs her fingers through her brown shoulder-length hair. The sound of James Taylor's "Carolina on My Mind" softly fills the room. Posters of John Lennon, James Dean, and Cher look down on us from her walls. Becky stares at the floor and scrunches her face as if she were thinking hard.

Details need to be specific and interesting, but they also need to be purposeful and to advance the paper one way or another. It turns out that Becky is a nineties college student living in a room dominated by musical and visual icons from the fifties and sixties. The details anticipate an important theme in this profile—the subject's closeness to her mother and her mother's values, which are rooted in decades past rather than present. (To read Beth's complete profile, see Chapter 9.)

Open with a Quotation

Although Beth decided not to open with her subject talking, an opening quotation can be an effective hook. Readers enjoy hearing the voices of people on the subject of the piece. The following paragraph was Beth's original opening; she moved it to the second paragraph, adding the transitional first sentence to link the two paragraphs. (It would work equally well as her opening, since it introduces the reader to Becky's lively and interesting human voice, after which we expect more talk about her early years growing up "forever" with her mother and sister.)

> "I don't ever remember my father ever living in my house, really. He left when I was three and my sister was just a baby, about a year old. My mom took care of us all. Forever, it was just Mom, Kate, and me. I loved it, you know. Just the three of us together."

Sometimes it's just a matter of personal preference in deciding where to start. That, of course, is what editing is all about: trying one thing, then another, looking at options, in the end selecting the one that you think is best.

Open with Statistics

Statistics that tell a clear story are another form of opening that suggests immediately that the writer has done his or her homework. Statistics catch attention when they assert something surprising or answer in numbers something the reader has been wondering about. The more dramatic your statistics are, the more useful they are to open your paper. In the following example, Elizabeth opens a research essay about unethical marketing practices with statistics more reassuring than dramatic.

> A recent Gallup poll reported that 75% of Americans consider themselves to be environmentalists (Smith & Quelch, 1993). In the same study, nearly half of the respondents said they would be more likely to purchase a product if they perceived it to be environmentally friendly or "green." According to Smith and Quelch (1993), since green sells, many companies have begun to promote themselves as marketing products that are either environmentally friendly or manufactured from recycled material. Unfortunately, many of these companies care more about appearance than reality.

Statistics are used here to establish a norm—that most Americans care about the environment—and then to examine the way in which clever, but not necessarily truthful, advertisers exploit that norm. (To read Elizabeth's complete research essay, see Research Reference 2.)

Open with a Question

Questions alert readers to the writer's subject and imply that the answer will be forthcoming in the paper. Every paper is an answer to some implicit or explicit question. Look at the examples above: Issa's mountain bike essay asks, "Can mountain bikes peacefully coexist with hikers on wilderness trails?" Kelly's interpretative paper asks, "What is the meaning of the poem 'We Real Cool'?" Judith's reflection on the comfort of libraries asks, "What has scholarship to do with safety?" Beth's profile asks, "What is Becky like?" And Elizabeth's research essay asks, "How do advertisers exploit the environmental movement?" In other words, the question that drives the paper is implicit, not directly stated.

In contrast, sometimes it's most effective to pose your question explicitly in the title or first paragraph so that readers know exactly what the report is about or where the essay is going, as Gabe did by titling his paper "What Is Slam Poetry, Anyway?" (See the sample page in Chapter 13.)

Open at the Beginning

In narrative writing, sometimes the best opening is where you think things started. In the following autobiographical snapshot, Rebecca opens a portrait of herself with brief portraits of her parents:

> My mother grew up in Darien, Connecticut, a Presbyterian. When she was little, she gave the Children's Sermon at her church. My father grew up in Cleveland, Ohio, a Jew. When I went away to college, he gave me the Hebrew Bible he received at his Bar Mitzvah.

Since the theme of Rebecca's self-profile is her devotion to an eclectic blend of religion, it seems right that she begin by focusing on the mixed religious heritage derived from her parents. (To read Rebecca's complete essay, see Chapter 9.)

We have just looked at eight different openings from eight effective essays, each effective in its own way. All eight strategies are good ones, fairly commonly used. None is necessarily better or worse than another, as each reflects a different intention. If we examine eight more essays, we might find still another set of opening strategies. Keep in mind that the first opening you write is just that, an initial opening to get you started. If it's effective, you may decide to keep it, but don't be afraid to return to that opening once the essay is complete and see if a new approach might better suit the direction your essay has finally taken.

◆ WRITING 1

Recast the opening of a paper you are currently working on, using one or more of the suggestions in this section: a conflict, a thesis, a story, a specific detail, a quotation, an interesting statistic, or a provocative question. For your final draft, use the opening that pleases you most.

CLOSINGS

Closings are final impressions. Your concluding sentences, paragraphs, or the entire last page are your final chance to make the point of your paper stick in readers' minds. The closing can summarize your main point, draw a logical conclusion, speculate about the issues you've raised, make a recommendation for some further action, or leave your reader with yet another question to ponder.

After writing and revising your paper, attend once more to the conclusion, and consider whether the final impression is the one you want. You may discover that an earlier paragraph makes a more suitable ending, or you may need to write a new one to conclude what you've started. The following examples of effective closings are from student papers reproduced in this textbook.

Close with an Answer

If your paper began by asking a question, and the rest of the paper worked at answering that question, it makes good sense to close with an answer—or at least the summary of your answer, reminding readers where they started some pages ago. For example, consider Gabe's opening question, which is also the title of his paper: "What is slam poetry, anyway?" Following that question, Gabe explored answers by attending a slam poetry reading, interviewing people about what it meant, and searching the Internet for both its history and definitions. After digesting several different answers, Gabe concluded with this summary sentence:

> So, in the end, slam poetry proves to be simply another kind of poetry reading, with this difference: the audience and the performer are one and the same.

This conclusion closes the frame of Gabe's paper, satisfying the reader (and writer) by answering the paper's central question. Of course, the real exploration of the meaning of slam poetry occurs on the way to this one-sentence answer, the whole paper providing a more carefully detailed answer than any single sentence could provide.

Close by Completing a Frame

An effective way to end some papers is to return deliberately to the issue or situation with which you began—to frame the body of your paper with an opening and a closing that mirror each other. Judith uses a frame in her paper about personal safety, returning in the closing to the setting of the opening—her front door:

> Hours later—my paper started, my exam studied for, my eyes tired—I retrace the path to my apartment. It is dark now, and I listen closely when I hear footsteps behind, stepping to the sidewalk's edge to let a man walk briskly past. At my door, I again fumble for the now familiar key, insert it in the lock, open the door, turn on the hall light, and step inside. Here, too, I am safe, ready to eat, read a bit and finish my reflective essay.

Close with a Resolution

Many argumentative papers present first one side of an issue and then the other side, then conclude by agreeing with one side or the other. This is the case in Issa's essay about the conflict between hikers and mountain bikers, where he concludes by suggesting that more education is the only sensible resolution to the problem:

> Education and compromise are the sensible solutions to the hiker/biker standoff. Increased public awareness as well as increasingly responsible riding will open still more wilderness trails to bikers in the future. It's clear that mountain bikers don't want to destroy trails any more than hikers do. The surest way to preserve America's wilderness areas is to establish strong cooperative bonds among the hikers and bikers, as well as those who fish, hunt, camp, canoe, and bird-watch, and to encourage all to maintain the trails and respect the environment.

The most successful resolution to many conflicts is not an either/or conclusion but an enlightened compromise where both sides gain. Issa manages to accomplish this by siding with mountain bikers but, at the same time, suggesting they need to change some of their actions to gain further acceptance by the opposition. In any case, it is especially important to edit carefully at the very end of your paper so that your last words make your best case.

Close with a Recommendation

Sometimes writers conclude by inviting their readers to do something—to support some cause, for example, or take some action. This strategy is especially common in papers that argue a position or make a case for or against something. Such papers seek not only to persuade readers to believe the writer but to act on that belief. In the following closing, Elizabeth asks consumers to be more careful:

> Consumers who are genuinely interested in buying environmentally safe products and supporting environmentally responsible companies need to look beyond the images projected by commercial advertising in magazines, on billboards, and on television. Organizations such as Earth First! attempt to educate consumers to the realities by writing about false advertising and exposing the hypocrisy of such ads ("Do people allow," 1994), while the Ecology Channel is committed to sharing "impartial, unbiased, multiperspective environmental information" with consumers on the Internet (Ecology, 1996). Meanwhile the Federal Trade Commission is in the process of continually upgrading truth-in-advertising regulations (Carlson et al., 1993). Americans who are truly environmentally conscious must remain skeptical of simplistic and misleading commercial advertisements while continuing to educate themselves about the genuine needs of the environment.

Along with asking consumers to be more careful in the future, this closing reveals that further action is being taken by watchdog groups, suggesting those who are careful will have powerful allies on their side.

Close with a Speculation

In papers relating personal experience, reflection, or speculation, the issues you raise have no clear-cut conclusions or demonstrated theses. In these papers, then, the most effective conclusion is often one in which you admit some uncertainty, as Zoe does at the end of her investigation of what steps she should take to become a photographer's assistant for her summer job—her first step toward becoming a professional photographer.

> So I'll keep sitting around hoping for a break. I can't guarantee that this research method for landing an internship will work; it still remains to be tried and tested. To my knowledge, there is no foolproof formula for a successful start. Like everybody else before me, I'm creating my own method as I go along.

The casualness in such a paragraph, as if it were written off the cuff, is often deceptive. While that is the effect Zoe wanted to create, this paragraph emerged only late in her drafting process, and when it did, she edited and reedited it to achieve just the effect she wanted.

Close by Restating Your Thesis

In thesis-driven papers, it's often a good idea to close by reminding readers where you began, what you were trying to demonstrate in the first place. In Andrew's literary research paper, he concludes by restating the power of Thoreau's concept of freedom:

Practical or not, Thoreau's writings about freedom from government and society have inspired countless people to reassess how they live their lives. Though unable to live as he advocated, readers everywhere remain inspired by his ideal, that one must live as freely as possible.

Restating a thesis is especially important in longer research-based papers where a lot of information has to be digested along the way. (To read Andrew's complete paper, see Research Reference 1.)

Close with a Question

Closing with a question, real or rhetorical, suggests that things are not finished, final, or complete. Concluding by admitting there are things you, the author, still do not know creates belief because most of us live with more questions than answers. In the following example, Rebecca ends with a question that is tongue-in-cheek and serious at the same time:

> I wear a cross around my neck. It is nothing spectacular to look at, but I love it because I bought it at the Vatican. Even though I am not a Catholic, I am glad I bought it at the Pope's home town. Sometimes, when I sit in Hebrew class, I wonder if people wonder, "What religion is she, anyway?"

Throughout her essay, Rebecca has presented herself and her commitment to religion in cryptic terms, suggesting perhaps that she herself is still not sure what she is or where her mixed religious heritage will take her. Closing with the bemused question above seems appropriate to her intentions. (To read Rebecca's complete essay, see Chapter 9.)

As with openings, so with closings—there are no formulas to follow, just a variety of possibilities that you'll need to weigh with your audience and purpose in mind. Since closing is a last impression, be willing to revise and edit carefully, and be willing to try more than once to get it just right.

◆ WRITING 2

Recast the closing of a current draft using one or more of the suggestions in this section: a summary, a logical conclusion, a real or a rhetorical question, a speculation, a recommendation, or the completion of a frame. In the final draft, use the closing that pleases you most.

FINDING THE TITLE

Finally, after revising and editing to your satisfaction, return to your title and ask, "Does it work?" You want to make sure it sets up the essay to follow in the best possible way, both catching readers' attention and providing a clue for the content to follow. One good strategy for deciding on a title is to create a list of five or ten possibilities and then select the most suitable one. Play with words, arranging and rearranging them until they strike you as just right. Many writers spend a great deal of concentrated time on this task because titles are so important.

In my own case, when I was casting about for a title for this book, I happened to be riding my motorcycle late one chilly October night on the interstate highway between Binghamton and Albany, New York. I was cold and knew I had a good hour before arriving at my destination, so to forget the cold, I set about brainstorming titles and came up with "Writing to Discover" or "The Discovering Writer." As I thought about them, I decided to keep the word *writing* but to move away from *discover* toward *work,* and so I played with "The Writer Working," "Working Writers," "The Writer at Work," "Work and the Writer," and finally *The Working Writer.* Work hard to find the words that seem about right, and play with them until they form a construction that pleases you.

The following suggestions may help you find titles:

- Use one good sentence from your paper that captures the essence of your subject.
- Ask a question that your paper answers.
- Use a strong sense word or image from your paper.
- Locate a famous line or saying that relates to your paper.
- Write a one-word title (a two-word, a three-word title, and so on).
- Make a title from a gerund (an *-ing* word, such as *working*).
- Make a title starting with the word *on* and the name of your topic.
- Remain open at all times to little voices in your head that make crazy suggestions and copy these down.

◆ WRITING 3

Using some of the strategies described in this section, write five titles for a paper you are currently working on. For the final draft, use the title that pleases you most.

CHAPTER EIGHTEEN

Working Paragraphs

Paragraphs tell readers how writers want to be read.
WILLIAM BLAKE

W hile there are no hard-and-fast rules for editing, there are important points to keep in mind as your essay nears completion. Once you are satisfied with the general shape, scope, and content of your paper, it's time to stop making larger conceptual changes—to stop revising—and start attending to smaller changes in paragraphs, sentences, and words—to begin editing. When you edit, you shape these three elements (paragraphs, sentences, and words) so that they fulfill the purpose of the paper, address the audience, and speak in the voice you have determined is appropriate for the paper.

THE WORK OF PARAGRAPHS

Most texts of a page or more in length are subdivided by indentations or breaks—called paragraphs—that serve as guideposts, or as William Blake puts it, "that tell readers how writers want to be read." Readers expect paragraph breaks to signal new ideas or directions; they expect each paragraph to have a single focus as well and to be organized in a sensible way; and they expect clear transition markers to link one paragraph to the next.

In truth, however, there are no hard-and-fast rules for what makes a paragraph, how it needs to be organized, what it should contain, or how long it should be.

I could, for instance, start a new paragraph here (as I have just done), leaving the previous sentence to stand as a single-sentence paragraph and so call a little extra attention to it. Or I could connect both that sentence and these to the previous paragraph and have a single five-sentence paragraph to open this section.

Most experienced writers paragraph intuitively rather than analytically; that is, they indent almost unconsciously, without thinking deliberately about it, as they develop or emphasize ideas. Sometimes their paragraphs fulfill conventional expectations, presenting a single well-organized and -developed idea, and sometimes they serve other purposes—for example, creating pauses or breathing spaces or points of emphasis.

The following paragraphs, many of which are excerpts from student papers that have already appeared in previous chapters, do different kinds of work, and although each is a good example, none is perfect. As you study them, bear in mind that each is *illustrative,* not *definitive,* of various purposes and organization.

WRITING WELL-ORGANIZED PARAGRAPHS

Unity: Stick to a Single Idea

Paragraphs are easiest to write and easiest to read when each one presents a single idea, as most of the paragraphs in this textbook do. The following paragraph opens Kelly's interpretive essay:

> Gwendolyn Brooks writes "We Real Cool" (1963) from the point of view of the members of a street gang who have dropped out of school to spend their lives hanging around pool halls—in this case "The Golden Shovel." These guys are semiliterate and speak in slangy street lingo that reveals their need for mutual support in their mutually rebellious attitude toward life. The speakers in the poem, "We," celebrate what adults would call adolescent hedonism—but they make a conscious choice for a short, intense life over a long, safe, and dull existence.

The opening sentence focuses on "the point of view of the members of a street gang" and the sentences that follow continue that focus on "these guys" and "the speakers." (To read Kelly's complete essay, see Chapter 12.)

Focus: Write a Topic Sentence

One of the easiest ways to keep each paragraph focused on a single idea is to include a *topic sentence* in it, announcing or summarizing the topic of the paragraph, with the rest of the sentences supporting that main idea. Sometimes topic sentences conclude a paragraph, as in the previous example, where the topic sentence is also the thesis statement for the whole essay. More commonly, however, the topic sentence introduces the paragraph, as in the next example from Issa's essay on mountain biking:

> Mountain bikes have taken over the bicycle industry, and with more bikes come more people wanting to ride in the mountains. The first mass-produced mountain bikes date to 1981, when five hundred Japanese "Stumpjumpers" were sold; by 1983 annual sales reached 200,000; today the figure is 8.5 million. In fact, mountain biking is second only to in-line skating as the fastest growing sport in the nation: "For a sport to go from zero to warp speed so quickly is unprecedented," says Brian

Stickel, director of competition for the National Off Road Bicycle Association (Schwartz 75).

The sentences after the first one support and amplify the topic sentence, explaining the rapid growth of mountain bikes, from *five hundred Japanese "Stumpjumpers"* to *8.5 million today*. (To read Issa's complete essay, see Chapter 11.)

Most of the following examples have topic sentences, and all focus on single subjects. Note, however, that not all paragraphs need topic sentences. For example, if a complicated idea is being explained, a new paragraph in the middle of the explanation will create a pause point. Sometimes paragraph breaks are inserted to emphasize an idea, like my own one-sentence paragraph earlier, which is a topic and a support sentence all in one. Additionally, paragraphs in a personal experience essay seldom have a deliberate topic sentence since these sorts of essays are seldom broken into neat topics (see, for example, Judith's paragraph below). Nevertheless, in academic writing, there is great reverence for topic sentences because they point to clear organization and your ability to perform as an organized and logical thinker within the discipline. Thus, when you write academic papers, attend to topic sentences.

◆ WRITING 1

Examine the paragraphs in a recent draft, and pencil in brackets around those that stick well to a single idea. Put an X next to any sentences that deviate from the main idea in a paragraph, and note whether you want to delete that sentence or use it to start a new paragraph. Finally, underline each topic sentence. If a paragraph does not have one, should it? If so, write it.

Order: Follow a Recognizable Logic

On first drafts, most of us write sentences rapidly and paragraph intuitively. However, when we revise and edit, it pays to make certain that paragraphs work according to a recognizable logic. There are dozens of organizational patterns that make sense. Here we look at five of them: free association, rank order, spatial, chronological, and general to specific.

When ideas are organized according to *free association,* one idea triggers the next because it is a related one. Free association is especially common in advancing a narrative, as in a personal experience essay. It is quite fluid and suggestive and seldom includes topic sentences. In the following paragraph, Judith allows the first act of locking a door to trigger memories related to other locked doors.

It is already afternoon. I fiddle with the key to lock the apartment door after me. I am not accustomed to locking doors. Except for the six months I spent in Boston, I have never lived in a place where I did not trust my neighbors. When I was little, we couldn't lock our farmhouse door; the wood had swollen, and the bolt no longer lined up properly with the hole, and nobody ever bothered to fix it. I still remember the time our babysitter, Rosie, hammered the bolt closed and we had to take the door off the hinges to get it open.

Notice that Judith uses a reverse chronological arrangement to order her associations; that is, she moves backward from the present—first to Boston, then to childhood—thereby using one pattern to strengthen another, helping us still further to follow her. (To read Judith's complete essay, see Chapter 8.)

When ideas are arranged by *rank order,* that is, order of importance, the most significant idea is reserved for the end of the paragraph. The writer leads with the idea to be emphasized least, then the next most important, and so on. This paragraph is commonly introduced by a topic sentence alerting readers that an orderly list is to follow. Here is a paragraph from Kelly's essay interpreting "We Real Cool" where he explains the values of the narrators of the poem:

> However, the most important element of their lives is being "cool." They live and love to be cool. Part of being cool is playing pool, singing, drinking, fighting, and messing around with women whenever they can. Being cool is the code of action that unites them, that they celebrate, for which they are willing to die.

Kelly explains three dimensions of being cool, making sure he concludes the paragraph with his most important point: first, being cool includes "[living] and [loving] to be cool," second, that it includes "playing pool, singing, drinking," and so on; and third, that it is their "code of action . . . for which they are willing to die." (To read Kelly's complete essay, see Chapter 12.)

When ideas are arranged *spatially,* each is linked to the next. Thus, the reader's eye is drawn through the paragraph as if through physical space. For example, a writer might describe a landscape by looking first at the field, then the forest, then the mountain, then the sky. In the following paragraph, Beth begins by showing Becky in the spatial context of her dormitory room; her description moves from bed to walls to floor:

> Becky sits cross-legged at the foot of the bottom bunk on her pink and green home-made quilt. She leans up against the wall and runs her fingers through her brown shoulder-length hair. The sound of James Taylor's "Carolina on My Mind" softly fills the room. Posters of John Lennon, James Dean, and Cher look down on us from her walls. Becky stares at the floor and scrunches her face as if she were thinking hard.

Becky's subtle, silent actions carry readers through the paragraph as Beth describes her sitting, leaning, listening, and staring—actions that set up the next paragraph in her paper in which Becky speaks. (To read Beth's complete essay, see Chapter 9.)

When ideas or facts are arranged *chronologically,* they are presented in the order in which they happened, with the earliest first. Sometimes it makes sense to use *reverse chronology,* listing the most recent first and working backward in time. The following paragraph from a collaborative research paper illustrates forward chronology; it begins with the first microbrewery and then moves to a full-fledged brewers' festival five years later.

> According to Shaw (1990) the home brewing revolution did not begin in Vermont until February 1987 when Stephan Mason and Alan Davis opened Catamount Brewery, which offered golden lager, an amber ale, and a dark porter as well as several seasonal brews. This was only the beginning. In September 1992, the first Vermont Brewers Festival was held at Sugarbush Resort. Sixteen breweries participated and the forty-plus beers present ranged from American light lagers to German-style bock and everything in between. The beers included such colorful names as Tall Tale Pale Ale, Black Fly Stout, Slopbucket Brown Ale, Summer Wheat Ale, Avid Barley Wee Heavy, and Hickory Switch Smoked Amber Ale.

Notice that starting in the middle of the paragraph, another supportive pattern is at work here: the pattern of general to specific. It is unlikely that the first draft of this paragraph contained these mutually supportive organizational patterns; careful editing made sure the final draft did.

A *general to specific pattern* begins with an overall description or general statement and moves toward a description of smaller, more specific details. In the preceding paragraph, the general idea is "all breweries"; the specific idea is "Catamount beer." Notice, too, the pattern in Elizabeth's essay on questionable environmental advertising:

> Some companies court the public by mentioning environmental problems and pointing out that they do not contribute to those problems. For example, the natural gas industry describes natural gas as an alternative to the use of ozone-depleting CFC's ("Don't you wish," 1994). However, according to Fogel (1985), the manufacture of natural gas creates a host of other environmental problems from land reclamation to the carbon-dioxide pollution, a major cause of global warming. By mentioning problems they don't cause, while ignoring ones they do, companies present a favorable environmental image that is at best a half truth, at worst an outright lie.

The opening sentence introduces the general category, "environmental problems," and the following sentences provide a particular example, "the natural gas industry." (To read Elizabeth's complete essay, see Chapter 30.)

Note, too, that *specific to general*, the reverse of the previous pattern, is also common and has a recognizable logic. For example, the environmental paragraph could have opened with the description of a specific abuse by a specific company and closed by mentioning the general problem illustrated by the specific example. The point here, as it is in all writing, is to edit carefully for a pattern that's recognizable and logical so that you lead your readers through the paper in ways that match their expectations.

◆ WRITING 2:

Review a near-final draft of a paper you are working on, and identify the organizational pattern in each paragraph. Do you find a pattern to your paragraphing? Identify paragraphs that contain a single idea carefully developed and paragraphs that need to be broken into smaller paragraphs. What editing changes would you now make in light of this review?

HELPING THE READER

So far, most of this discussion has focused on structures within paragraphs. When editing, it's important to know how to rewrite paragraphs to improve essay readability. However, you can improve readability in other ways as well. One of them is to break up lengthy paragraphs.

Paragraph breaks help readers pause and take a break while reading, allowing them, for example, to imagine or remember something sparked by the text and yet find their place again with ease. Breaking into a new paragraph can also recapture flagging attention, especially important in long essays, reports, or articles where detail sometimes overwhelms readers. And you can emphasize points with paragraph breaks, calling a little extra attention to what follows.

TRANSITIONS BETWEEN PARAGRAPHS

Your editing is not finished until you have linked the paragraphs, so that readers know where they have been and where they are going. In early drafts, you undoubtedly focused on getting your ideas down and paid less attention to clarifying relationships between ideas. Now, as you edit your final draft, consider the elements that herald transitions: words and phrases, subheads, and white spaces.

Words and Phrases

Writers often use transitional expressions without consciously thinking about them. For example, in writing a narrative, you may naturally use sequential transition words to indicate a chronology: *first, second, third; this happened, next this happened, finally this happened;* or *last week, this week, yesterday, today.* Here are some other transitional words and phrases and their functions in paragraphs:

- *Contrast or change in direction:*   but, yet, however, nevertheless, still, at the same time, on the other hand
- *Comparison or similarity:*   likewise, similarly
- *Addition:*   and, also, then, next, in addition, furthermore, finally
- *Summary:*   finally, in conclusion, in short, in other words, thus
- *Example:*   for example, for instance, to illustrate, specifically, thus
- *Concession or agreement:*   of course, certainly, to be sure, granted
- *Time sequence:*   first, second, third; (1), (2), (3); next, then, finally, soon, meanwhile, later, currently, eventually, at last
- *Spatial relation:*   here, there, in the background, in the foreground, to the left, to the right, nearby, in the distance, above, below

There is no need to memorize these functions or words; you already know and have used all of them and usually employ them quite naturally. When reworking your final draft, though, be sure you have provided transitions. If you haven't, work these words in to alert your readers to what's coming next.

Alternative Transitional Devices

Other common devices that signal transitions include subheadings, lines, alternative typefaces, and white spaces. The first two are more common in textbooks and technical reports; the latter two may appear in any text, including literary-style essays. When you edit your final draft, consider whether using any of these techniques would make your ideas clearer.

Subheads

To call extra attention to material or to indicate logical divisions of ideas, some writers use subheads. They are more common in long research papers, technical reports, and laboratory analyses and less common in narrative essays. They are essential in textbooks, such as this one, for indicating divisions of complex material.

Lines

Blocks of text can be separated by either continuous or broken dashes (———) or asterisks (*****), which signify material clearly to be set off from other material. In technical writing, for example, material may even be boxed in by continuous lines to call special attention to itself. In a *New Yorker* research essay or short story, a broken line of asterisks may suggest a switch in time, place, or point of view.

Alternative Typefaces

Writers who use computers can change fonts with ease. When they use alternative typefaces, they are indicating a transition or a change. In a narrative or essay, *italics* may suggest someone talking or the narrator thinking. A switch to a smaller or larger typeface may signal information of less or more importance.

White Space

You can indicate a sharp break in thought between one paragraph and the next by leaving an extra line of space between them (although the space break does not tell the reader what to expect next). When I use a space break, I am almost always suggesting a change in direction more substantial than a mere paragraph indentation; I want readers to notice the break and be prepared to make a larger jump than a paragraph break signals. In a narrative essay, I may use the space to suggest a jump in time (the next day, week, or year); in argumentative writing, to begin a presentation of an opposing point of view; in an essay, to introduce another voice. White space, in other words, substitutes for clear transition words and subheadings but does not explicitly explain the shift.

When I work on early drafts, I may use some of these transition or separation devices to help me keep straight the different parts of what I'm writing. In final drafts, I decide which devices will help my readers as much as they have helped me, and I eliminate those that no longer work. In other words, paragraphs and transitions are as useful for me when I'm drafting as they will be later for my readers. (For more ideas on alternate transitions, see Chapter 13.)

◆ WRITING 3

When you edit a final draft, look carefully at your use of transitional devices. Identify those that are doing their work well; add new ones where appropriate.

CHAPTER NINETEEN

Working Sentences

> *Teachers are always nitpicking about little things, but I think writing is*
> *for communicating, not nitpicking. I mean, if you can read it and it makes sense,*
> *what else do you want?*
>
> OMAR

Editing is about nitpicking. It's about making your text read well, with the most possible sense. After the ideas are in order and well supported, your job is to polish the paragraphs, sentences, and individual words so that they shine. Then you correct to get rid of all the "nitpicky" errors in punctuation, spelling, and grammar. In other words, you attend to editing *after* your ideas are conceptually sound, carefully supported, skillfully organized, and fairly well aimed at your readers. (Even now, it doesn't hurt to review it once more to make sure it represents your voice and ideas in the best way possible.)

As in editing paragraphs, there is no one best way to go about editing sentences. You edit in such a way that you remain, as much as possible, in control of your text. (As you probably know by now, texts have a way of getting away from all of us at times. Editing is how we try to get control back!) At the same time you're wrestling for final control of a text for yourself, you're also anticipating reader needs. In this sense, sentence editing is your final balancing act, as you work to please yourself and your readers.

EDITING FOR CLARITY, STYLE, AND GRACE

To effect maximum communication, edit your sentences first for clarity, making sure each sentence clearly reflects your purpose. Also edit to convey an appropriate style for the occasion, that is, the formality or informality of the language. And at perhaps the highest level, edit to convey grace—some sense that this text is not only clearly written, by you, but that it is also particularly well written—what we might call elegant or graceful.

While I can explain this loose hierarchy as if these several levels are easily distinguished, in fact, they are not, and they mix and overlap easily. For instance, in writing the chapters for this text I have tried to edit each chapter, paragraph, and sentence with all three goals in mind, demanding that all my language be clear, hoping that my style is friendly, and trying to make my sentences graceful—knowing that, in many cases, grace has proved beyond my reach. The remainder of this chapter will examine the fine tuning of words and phrases that make clear, stylistically appropriate, and sometimes graceful sentences.

◆ WRITING 1

Reread a near-final draft of one of your papers, and draw a straight vertical line next to places where your text seems especially clear. Draw a wavy line next to passages where the style sounds especially like you. And put an asterisk next to any passages that you think are especially graceful. Exchange drafts with a classmate and see if you agree with each other's assessment.

THE WORK OF SENTENCES

Sentences are written in relation to other sentences, so most of our attention thus far has been on larger units of composition, from whole texts on down to individual paragraphs. This chapter focuses on strategies for strengthening sentences. In editing, first look at the effect of particular words within sentences, especially nouns, verbs, and modifiers. Second, consider the importance of rhythm and emphasis in whole sentences. And finally, learn to identify and avoid the common problems of wordiness, clichés, jargon, passive constructions, and biased language.

WRITE WITH CONCRETE NOUNS

Nouns label or identify persons (*man, Gregory*), animals (*dog, golden retriever*), places (*city, Boston*), things (*book, The Working Writer*), or ideas (*conservation, Greater Yellowstone Coalition*). General nouns name general classes or categories of things (*man, dog, city*); concrete nouns refer to particular things (*Gregory, golden retriever, Boston*). Notice that concrete nouns (not just any dog, but a golden retriever) appeal more strongly to a reader's senses (I can see the dog!) than abstract nouns do and create a more vivid and lively reading experience.

Here is an example of a paragraph composed primarily of general nouns (underlined in the passage):

> Approaching the library, I see lots of <u>people</u> and <u>dogs</u> milling about, but no subjects to write about. I'm tired from my walk and go inside.

When Judith described a similar scene for her essay on personal safety, she used specific nouns (which are underlined) to let us see her story sharply:

Approaching the library, I see <u>skateboarders</u> and <u>bikers</u> weaving through <u>students</u> who talk in clusters on the library steps. A <u>friendly black dog</u> is tied to a bench watching for its master to return. Subjects to write about? Nothing strikes me as especially interesting and, besides, my heart is still pounding from the walk up the hill. I wipe my <u>damp forehead</u> and go inside.

Judith could have gone even further (writers always can) in using concrete nouns. She could have named the library, described some individual students, identified the dog, and described the bench. None of these modifications would have changed the essential meaning of the sentences, but each would have added a dimension of specific reality—one of the key ways writers convince readers that what they are writing about is true or really happened.

WRITE WITH ACTION VERBS

Action verbs *do* something in your sentences; they make something happen. *Walk, stride, run, jump, fly, hum, sing, sail, swim, lean, fall, stop, look, listen, sit, state, decide, choose,* and *conclude*— all these words and hundreds more are action verbs. Static verbs, in contrast, simply *appear* to describe how something *is*. Action verbs, like concrete nouns, appeal to the senses, letting readers see, hear, touch, taste, or smell what is happening. They create more vivid images for readers, drawing them more deeply into the essay.

In the following passage, the conclusion to Judith's reflective essay, notice how action verbs (underlined) help you see clearly what is going on:

Hours later—my paper started, my exam studied for, my eyes tired—I <u>retrace</u> the path to my apartment. It is dark now, and I <u>listen</u> closely when I <u>hear</u> footsteps behind, stepping to the sidewalk's edge to let a man <u>walk</u> briskly past. At my door, I again <u>fumble</u> for the now familiar key, <u>insert</u> it in the lock, <u>open</u> the door, <u>turn on</u> the hall light, and <u>step</u> inside. Here, too, I am safe, ready to eat, <u>read</u> a bit, and <u>finish</u> my reflective essay.

Judith also uses several static verbs (*is, am*) in other places; these verbs describe necessary states of being, carrying a different kind of weight. When they are used among action verbs, they do good work. But the paragraph gets its life and strength from the verbs that show action. (To read Judith's complete essay, see Chapter 8.)

Editing for action verbs is one of the chief ways to cut unneeded words, thus increasing readability and vitality. Whenever you find one of the following noun phrases (in the first column) consider substituting an action verb (in the second column):

reach a decision	decide
make a choice	choose
hold a meeting	meet
formulate a plan	plan
arrive at a conclusion	conclude
have a discussion	discuss
go for a run	run

USE MODIFIERS CAREFULLY AND SELECTIVELY

Well-chosen modifiers can make both nouns and verbs more concrete and appealing to readers' senses. Words that modify—describe, identify, or limit—nouns are called *adjectives* (*damp* forehead); words that amplify verbs are called *adverbs* (listen *closely*). Modifiers convey useful clarifying information and make sentences vivid and realistic.

In the previous example paragraph, Judith could have added several more modifiers to nouns such as *man* (*tall, thin, sinister*) and *door* (*red, heavy, wooden*). And she could have used modifiers with verbs such as *retrace* (*wearily, slowly*) and *fumble* (*nervously, expectantly*). Judith's writing would not necessarily benefit by these additions, but they are further possibilities for her to examine as she edits her near-final sentences. Sometimes adding modifiers to sentences distracts from rather than enhances a paragraph's purpose. And that's what editing is all about: looking carefully, trying out new possibilities, settling for the effect that pleases you most.

Not all modifiers are created equal. Specific modifiers that add descriptive information about size, shape, color, texture, speed, and so on appeal to the senses and usually make writing more realistic and vivid. General modifiers such as the adjectives *pretty, beautiful, good,* and *bad* can weaken sentences by adding extra words that do not convey specific or vital information. And the adverbs *very, really,* and *truly* can have the same weakening effect because they provide no specific clarifying information.

◆ WRITING 2

Review a near-final draft, and mark all concrete nouns (underline once), action verbs (underline twice), and modifiers (circle). Then place parentheses around the general nouns, static verbs, and general modifiers. Reconsider these words, and edit appropriately.

FIND A PLEASING RHYTHM

Rhythm is the pattern of sound sentences make when you read them out loud. Some rhythms sound natural—like a person in a conversation. Such sentences are easy to follow and understand and are usually pleasing to the ear. Others sound awkward and forced, make comprehension difficult, and offend the ear. It pays to read your sentences out loud and see if they sound like a real human being talking. To make sentence clusters sound better, use varied sentence patterns and parallel construction.

Varied sentence patterns make sentence clusters clear and enjoyable for readers. Judith effectively varied her sentences—some long, some short, some simple, some complex. For example, note the dramatic effect of following a lengthy compound sentence with a short simple sentence (made up of short words) to end the paragraph above: "Nothing strikes me as especially interesting and, besides, my heart is still pounding from the walk up the hill. I wipe my damp forehead and go inside."

Parallelism, the repetition of a word or grammatical construction within a sentence, creates symmetry and balance, makes an idea easier to remember, and is pleasing to the ear. The following sentence from Brendan's essay demonstrates the pleasing rhythmic effect of parallel construction: "A battle is being waged between environmental conservationists, who support the reintroduction of wolves, and cattle ranchers and Western hunters, who oppose it." The parallelism is established by repetition of the word *who* plus a verb; the verbs, opposite in meaning, provide additional dramatic effect.

In the following example, the repetition of the word *twice* establishes a rhythm and contributes as well to the writer's point about costs: "A CD may be twice as expensive as a cassette tape, but the sound is twice as clear and the disc will last forever."

PLACE THE MOST IMPORTANT POINT LAST

As in paragraphs, the most emphatic place in sentences is last. You achieve the best effect by placing information that is contextual, introductory, or less essential earlier in the sentence and end with the idea you most want readers to remember. Sometimes you write first-draft sentences with emphatic endings, but often such emphasis needs to be edited in. Notice the difference in emphasis in the following version of the same idea:

> **Angel needs to start now if he wants to have an impact on his sister's life.**
> **If Angel wants to have an impact on his sister's life, he has to start now.**

The second sentence is much more dramatic, emphasizing the need for action on Angel's part.

The next two sentences also illustrate the power of placing what you consider important at the end of the sentence:

> **Becky stares at the floor and scrunches her face as if she were thinking hard.**
> **As if she is thinking hard, Becky stares at the floor and scrunches up her face.**

The first sentence emphasizes Becky's concentration. To end with Becky's scrunching up her face diminishes the emphasis on her thinking.

In the following sentence, Judith uses end-of-sentence emphasis for a transitional purpose: "I wipe my damp forehead and go inside." The ending forecasts the next paragraph—in which Judith goes inside the library. To reverse the actions would emphasize the damp forehead instead of Judith's entrance into the library.

One more example from Judith's essay suggests how emphasis at the end can increase and then resolve suspense: "It is dark now, and I listen closely when I hear footsteps behind, stepping to the sidewalk's edge to let a man walk briskly past." At first we are alarmed that footsteps are coming up behind the writer—as Judith wants us to be. Then we are relieved that a man passes harmlessly by—as Judith also wants us to be. The end of the sentence relieves the tension and resolves the suspense.

◆ WRITING 3

Examine the sentences in a recent draft for rhythm and end-of-sentence emphasis by reading the draft out loud, listening for awkward or weak spots. Edit for sentence variety and emphasis as necessary.

EDIT WORDY SENTENCES

Cut out words that do not pull their weight or add meaning, rhythm, or emphasis. Sentences clogged with unnecessary words cause readers to lose interest, patience, and comprehension. Editing sentences for concrete nouns, action verbs, and well-chosen modifiers will help you weed out unnecessary words. Writing varied and emphatic sentences helps with this task too. Look at the following sentences, which all say essentially the same thing:

- In almost every situation that I can think of, with few exceptions, it will make good sense for you to look for as many places as possible to cut out needless, redundant, and repetitive words from the papers and reports, paragraphs and sentences you write for college assignments. (48 words)
- In most situations it makes good sense to cut out needless words from your college papers. (16 words)
- Whenever possible, omit needless words from your writing. (8 words)
- Omit needless words. (3 words)

The forty-eight-word-long first sentence is full of early-draft language; you can almost see the writer finding his or her way while writing. The sixteen-word sentence says much the same thing, with only one-third the number of words. Most of this editing simply cut out unnecessary words. Only at the end were several wordy phrases condensed: "from the papers and reports, paragraphs and sentences you write for college assignments" was reduced to "from your college papers."

That sixteen-word sentence was reduced by half by rephrasing and dropping the emphasis on college writing. And that sentence was whittled down by nearly two-thirds, to arrive at the core three-word sentence, "Omit needless words."

The first sentence was long-winded by any standard or in any context; each of the next three might serve well in different situations. Thus, when you edit to make language more concise, you need to think about the overall effect you intend to create. Sometimes the briefest construction is not the best one for your purpose. For example, the three-word sentence is more suited to a brief list than to a sentence of advice for this book. To fit the purposes of this book, in fact, I might write a fifth version on needless words, one including more of my own voice:

> **I prefer to read carefully edited papers, where every word works purposefully and pretty much pulls its own weight. (19 words)**

In this sentence, I chose to include *I* to emphasize my own preference as a teacher and reader and to add the qualifying phrase *pretty much* to impart a conversational tone to the sentence.

In the following example, one of Judith's effective paragraphs has been deliberately padded with extra words, some of which might have existed in earlier drafts:

> It is now several hours later, almost midnight, in fact. I have finally managed to get my paper started and probably overstudied for my exam. My eyes are very tired. I get up and leave my comfortable chair and walk out of the library, through the glass doors again, and retrace the path to my apartment. Since it is midnight, it is dark, and I nervously listen to footsteps coming up behind me. When they get too close for comfort, I step to the sidewalk's edge, scared out of my wits, to let a man walk

briskly past. When I am finally at my door, I again fumble for the now familiar key, insert it in the lock, open the door, turn on the hall light, and step inside. Here, too, I am safe, ready to eat leftover pizza, study some more for my exam, and finish my reflective essay.

Now compare this with Judith's final version for simplicity, brevity, smoothness, and power. (To see Judith's complete essay, see Chapter 8.)

Hours later—my paper started, my exam studied for, my eyes tired—I retrace the path to my apartment. It is dark now, and I listen closely when I hear footsteps behind, stepping to the sidewalk's edge to let a man walk briskly past. At my door, I again fumble for the now familiar key, insert it in the lock, open the door, turn on the hall light, and step inside. Here, too, I am safe, ready to eat, read a bit, and finish my reflective essay.

The best test of whether words are pulling their own weight and providing rhythm, balance, and emphasis is to read the passage out loud and let your ear tell you what is sharp and clear and what could be sharper and clearer.

EDIT CLICHÉS

Clichés are phrases we've heard so often before that they no longer convey an original or individual thought. In the wordy paragraph above, the phrase "scared out of my wits" is a cliché. As you edit, note whether you remember hearing the same exact words before, especially more than once. If so, look for fresher language that is your own. Common clichés to avoid include the following:

> throwing the baby out with the bath water
> a needle in a haystack
> the last straw
> better late than never
> without further ado
> the handwriting on the wall
> tried and true
> last but not least
> lay the cards on the table
> jump-start the economy

Each of these phrases was once new and original and attracted attention when it was used; now when we read or hear these phrases, we pay them no conscious mind and may even note that the writer or speaker using them is not very thoughtful or original.

EDIT PASSIVE CONSTRUCTIONS

A construction is passive when something is done to the subject rather than the subject's doing something. *The ball was hit by John* is passive. *John hit the ball* is active. Not only is the first sentence needlessly longer by two words, but also it takes readers a second or two longer to understand since it is a roundabout way to make an assertion. Writing that is larded up with such passive construction lacks vitality and is tiresome to read.

Most of the example paragraphs in this book contain good examples of active constructions: *I retrace . . . I get up . . . Becky sits . . . Greg attributes. . . .*

EDIT BIASED LANGUAGE

Your writing should not hurt people. As you edit, make sure your language doesn't discriminate against categories of people based on gender, race, ethnicity, social class, or sexual orientation.

Eliminate Sexism

Language is sexist when it includes only one gender. The most common occurrence of sexist language is the use of the word *man* or *men* to stand for *human being* or *people*—which seems to omit *women* from participation in the species. Americans have been sensitized to the not-so-subtle bias against women embedded in our use of language.

It is important to remember that many thoughtful and powerful English-language works from the past took masculine words for granted, using *man, men, he, him,* and *his* to stand for all members of the human race. Consider Thomas Jefferson's "All men are created equal" and Tom Paine's "These are the times that try men's souls." Today we would write "All people are created equal" or "These are the times that try our souls"—two of several possible fixes for this gender nearsightedness. When you read older texts, recognize that the composing rules were different then, and the writers are no more at fault than the culture in which they lived.

As you edit to avoid sexist language, you will notice that the English language does not have a gender-neutral third-person singular pronoun to match the gender-neutral third-person plural (*they, their, them*). We use *he* (*him, his*) for men and *she* (*her, hers*) for women. In the sentence "Everybody has his own opinion," the indefinite pronoun *everybody* needs a singular pronoun to refer to it. While it is grammatically correct to say "Everybody has *his* own opinion," the sentence seems to exclude women. But it is grammatically incorrect to write "Everybody has *their* own opinion," although *their* is gender neutral. In editing, be alert to such constructions and consider several ways to fix them:

- Make the sentence plural so it reads "*People* have *their* own opinions."
- Include both pronouns: "Everybody has *his* or *her* own opinion."
- Eliminate the pronoun: "Everybody has *an* opinion."
- Alternate masculine and feminine pronouns throughout your sentences or paragraphs, using *she* in one paragraph and *he* in the next.

In my own writing, I have used all of these solutions at one time or another. The rule I most commonly follow is to use the strategy that makes for the clearest, most graceful writing.

Avoid Stereotypes

Stereotypes lump individuals into oversimplified and usually negative categories based on race, ethnicity, class, gender, sexual preference, religion, or age. You know many of these terms. The kindest are perhaps "Get out of the way, old man" and "Don't behave like a baby." I am willing to set these down in this book since we've all been babies and we're all growing older. The other terms offend me too much to write.

The mission of all institutions of higher learning is to teach students to read, write, speak, and think critically, which means treating each situation, case, problem, or person individually on its own merits and not prejudging it by rumor, innuendo, or hearsay unsupported by evidence or reason. To use stereotypes in academic writing will label you as someone who has yet to learn critical literacy. To write with stereotypes in any setting not only reveals your ignorance but hurts people.

PROOFREAD

The last act of editing is *proofreading,* the process of reading your manuscript word for word to make sure it is correct in every way. Here are some tips to help you in this process:

- Proofread for typing and spelling errors first by using a spelling checker on your computer, if you have one. But be aware that computers will *not* catch certain errors, such as omitted words or mistyping (for example, *if* for *of*). So you must also proofread the old-fashioned way—by reading slowly, line by line, word by word.
- Proofread for punctuation by reading your essay out loud and looking for places where your voice pauses, comes to a full stop, questions, or exclaims. Let your verbal inflections suggest appropriate punctuation (commas, periods, question marks, and exclamation points, respectively). Also review Chapter 20, paying special attention to the use of commas, the most common source of punctuation errors.
- Proofread the work of others, and ask others to proofread for you. It's easy when reading your own writing to fill in missing words and read through small errors; you're much more likely to catch such errors in someone else's writing. We are all our own worst proofreaders; ask somebody you trust to help you.
- Proofread as a whole class: Tape final drafts on the wall, and roam the class with pencils reading one another's final drafts, for both pleasure and correctness.

◆ WRITING 4

Examine a recent draft for wordiness, clichés, passive constructions, and biased language. Edit as necessary according to the suggestions in this section. Proofread before you hand in or publish the paper.

CHAPTER TWENTY

Punctuating Sentences

Punctuation marks tell readers how written sentences are meant to be read. When people speak, they "punctuate" their sentences by pausing, raising or lowering their voices, speeding up or slowing down their delivery, gesturing with hands, wrinkling their faces, rolling their eyes, and the like. So, when they write, they attempt to approximate these oral and visual cues by small marks in the middle and at the end of sentences—*periods, question marks, exclamation points, commas, colons, semi-colons,* and so on. In other words, if you want people to understand your written texts, in the way you intend for them to be understood, learn the conventions and punctuate with care. The following brief guide explains the most common uses of the most common punctuation marks. If you have further questions or need more detail, consult a grammar handbook or a dictionary.

Period *stops sentences and abbreviates words.*

1. Use a period to end a sentence that is a statement, a mild command, or an indirect question.

   The administration has canceled classes.

   Do not attempt to drive to school this morning.

   We wondered who had canceled classes.

2. Use a period for certain abbreviations.

> Dr. Joan Sharp
>
> Ms. Amy Bowen
>
> 6:30 A.M.

3. Do not use periods to abbreviate most words in formal writing or in acronyms.

> He made $200 per week [*not* wk.].
>
> He worked for the FBI [*not* F.B.I.].

Question mark *ends a direct question and indicates uncertainty in dates.*

1. Use a question mark to end a direct question.

> Where is Times Square?
>
> She asked, "What time is it?"

2. Use a question mark to indicate uncertainty in a date.

> The plays of Francis Beaumont (1584?–1616) were as popular as Shakespeare's plays.

Exclamation point *ends an emphatic or emotional sentence.*

Use an exclamation point to end a sentence that is emphatic or conveys strong emotion.

> What a mess!
>
> "Ouch! That hurts!" he shouted.

Comma *alerts readers to brief pauses within sentences.*

1. Use a comma before a coordinating conjunction joining independent clauses.

> We must act quickly, or the problem will continue.

2. Use a comma after an introductory element.

> After we attend class, we'll eat lunch.
>
> Whistling, he waited for his train.

3. Use a comma around nonrestrictive modifiers (modifiers that are not essential to the meaning of the sentence).

> Cats, which are nocturnal animals, hunt small rodents.

4. Use a comma between items in a series.

   He studied all of the notes, memos, letters, and reports.

5. Use a comma to set off parenthetical elements or transitional expressions.

   Surprisingly enough, none of the bicycles was stolen.

6. Use a comma to set off attributory words with direct quotations.

   "Time will prove us right," he said.

7. Use a comma with numbers, dates, titles with names, and addresses.

   The sign gave the city's population as 79,087.

   She was born on June 19, 1976.

   Joyce B. Wong, M.D., supervised the CPR training.

   His new address is 169 Elm Street, Boston, Massachusetts 02116.

Semicolon *joins independent clauses and connects items in a complex series.*

1. Use a semicolon between independent clauses not joined with a coordinating conjunction.

   The storm raged all night; most of us slept fitfully, if at all.

2. Use semicolons between items in a series that contain internal commas.

   The candidates for the award are Maria, who won the essay competition; Elaine, the top debater; and Shelby, who directed several student productions.

Colon *introduces lists, summaries, and quotations and separates titles and subtitles.*

1. Use a colon to introduce a list.

   Writers need three conditions to write well: time, ownership, and response.

2. Use a colon before a summary or explanation.

   He had only one goal left: to win the race.

3. Use a colon to formally introduce a quotation in text or to introduce a long in-dented quotation.

   He quoted Puck's final lines from *A Midsummer Night's Dream:* "Give me your hands, if we be friends, / And Robin shall restore amends."

4. Use a colon to separate a title and subtitle.

Blue Highways: A Journey into America

Apostrophe *indicates possession, forms certain plurals, and forms contractions.*

1. Use an apostrophe to indicate possession in a noun or indefinite pronoun.

Jack's brother

anyone's guess

2. Use an apostrophe to form the plural of a word used as a word and the plural of letters.

She wouldn't accept any *if*'s, *and*'s, or *but*'s.

The word *occurrence* is spelled with two *r*'s.

3. Use an apostrophe to replace missing letters in contractions.

I can't means I won't.

Quotation marks *indicate direct quotations and certain titles.*

1. Use quotation marks around words quoted directly from a written or spoken source.

She said, "It really doesn't matter anymore."

Who wrote, "Fourscore and seven years ago"?

2. Use quotation marks for titles of stories, short poems, book chapters, magazine articles, and songs.

"Barn Burning" (short story)

"To an Athlete Dying Young" (poem)

"Finding Your Voice" (book chapter)

"Symbolism in Shakespeare's Tragedies" (magazine article)

"A Day in the Life" (song)

3. Place periods and commas inside closing quotation marks. Place semicolons and colons outside closing quotation marks. Place question marks and exclamation points inside or outside quotation marks depending on the meaning of the sentence.

After Gina finished singing "Memories," Joe began to hum "The Way We Were."

The sign read "Closed": There would be no cold soda for us today.

"Would you like some fruit?" Phil asked.

I can't believe you've never read "The Lottery"!

Parentheses *enclose nonessential or digressive but useful information.*

Use parentheses to enclose nonessential information: explanations, examples, asides.

In 1929 (the year the stock market crashed) he proposed to his first wife.

He graduated with high honors (or so he said) and found a job immediately.

Dashes *enclose nonessential information and indicate abrupt changes of direction.*

Use dashes to enclose nonessential information and to indicate contrast or a pause or change of direction.

At first we did not notice the rain—it began so softly—but soon we were soaked.

Nothing is as exciting as seeing an eagle—except maybe seeing two eagles.

Ellipsis points *indicate the omission of words in a direct quotation.*

Use ellipsis points (three dots) to indicate where you have omitted words in a direct quotation from a written or spoken source.

"We the People of the United States, in Order to form a more perfect Union . . . do ordain and establish this Constitution for the United States of America."

Brackets *indicate changes to or comments on a direct quotation.*

Use brackets when you make changes to or comments on a direct quotation.

E. B. White describes a sparrow on a spring day: "Any noon, in Madison Square [in New York City], you may see one pick up a straw in his beak."

CHAPTER TWENTY-ONE

Portfolios and Publishing

Revised and edited final drafts are written to be read. At the minimum, your audience is your instructor; at the maximum, it's the whole world—an audience now made possible by everyone's access to the Internet. In writing classes, the most common audience, in addition to the instructor, includes the other students in the class itself. This final Chapter explores three common avenues of presenting your work in final form via writing portfolio, class book, and World Wide Web.

DESIGNING DOCUMENTS FOR PUBLICATION

When the substance of a paper has been drafted, revised, and edited to your satisfaction, your final choice is one of format: How should the finished text be presented? To complete an assigned paper, many students just print out what's on the screen and call it done, essentially letting the computer's default settings make all the choices. However, conscious attention to a document's design actually contributes to a reader's understanding and enjoyment of a text, so it pays to select good paper, set appropriate margins, select font shape and size, and evaluate your use of headings, white space, and graphics. The most effective design is often simple, clear, and logical, while calling the least attention to itself.

Most effective designs begin traditional and expected formats so that readers are alerted to your intentions from the start. You may, of course, experiment with creative variations on the expected and traditional, but do so carefully and for good reason. Note that in many cases, it is not necessary to read the information in a document to understand its general purpose, audience, and situation. Glance, for example, at the expected designs of four conventional documents (Figure 21.1) and notice how rapidly each form tells us, generally, what type of communication to expect.

Each of the illustrated forms telegraphs its general intention in the first place, simply by how it appears to the viewer, even before it is read.

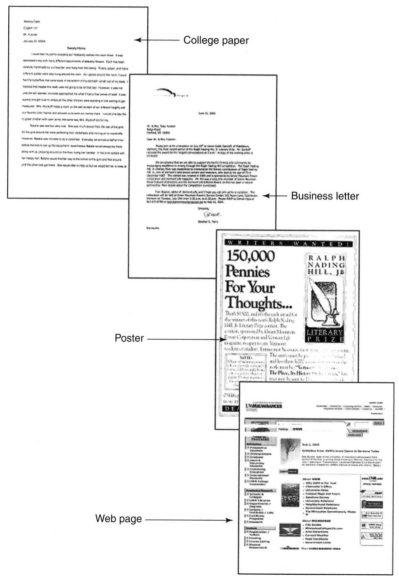

College paper

Business letter

Poster

Web page

Figure 21.1

- The purpose of the **college paper** is to demonstrate that a certain kind and amount of learning has taken place. The audience is the instructor who assigned the paper and therefore must read it. The situation demands a document that is clear and legible, but not necessarily brief or visually exciting.
- The purpose of the **business letter** is to convey information clearly and succinctly. The audience is an individual who expects to find out the business of the letter in a short amount of time. The situation demands a document in a predictable format that gets quickly to the point.
- The purpose of the **poster** is to call attention to a specific event. The audience can be anyone willing to stop and notice the message posted on bulletin board or telephone pole. The situation demands a document with text and graphics that catch attention and deliver information briefly and clearly.
- The purpose of the **Web page** is to present information about a general subject plus cues to where additional more specific information can be found. The audience is curious about the subject, but competing sites invite immediate attention as well. The situation demands a document with text and graphics that invite further investigation, information available at the site. (This discussion will be continued later in the chapter.)

In other words, over the years, writers have learned to shape document features to achieve rhetorical effects that address audience needs. And over the years, audiences have learned to rely on these features to help them understand what authors intend. Before printing your college paper for presentation in a writing portfolio, in a class book, or on a class or personal Web site, let tradition and convention work for you. The following guidelines apply for printing traditional college papers:

- *Expectations.*   Put expected information in expected places (name, title, date on first page; reference or bibliography page at the end, etc.).
- *Paper and ink.*   For printed copy, use good fresh paper and strong black ink.
- *Typeface.*   Select a readable typeface (11–12 point) in standard style (New Times Roman, Courier, or Ariel—something reasonable).
- *Line space.*   Double-space all information, including indented material and reference pages.
- *Margins.*   Use standard margins (1" all around)
- *Paragraphs.*   Indent five spaces or use block paragraphs that are not indented, but separated from each other by white space.
- *Word space.*   Allow one space after each word; after end punctuation, and commas, semicolons, or colons. Do not space between words and quotation marks, parentheses, or brackets.
- *Titles.*   Center titles, double space above first line, bold optional, do not underline or put in quotation marks.
- *White space.*   Separate sections or parts with white space to mark breaks in direction or category.
- *Headings and subheadings.*   Use appropriate headings and subheadings to call attention to different areas or directions in your paper.
- *Special features.*   Use *italics,* underlining, **boldface,** and color sparingly and to clear purpose.
- *Images.*   Integrate visual images smoothly within text pages.

- *Boxes and sidebars.*   Consider placing useful but not central information in sidebars or boxes.
- *Labels.*   Include labels under all images, graphs, charts, and sidebars so readers understand why they are included.
- *Lists.*   Use bullets and numbers to call attention to material best presented in lists.

To learn more information about designing documents with creative flourishes, consult the specialized information available online at http://desktoppublishing.com/ open.html> or <http://desktoppub.about.com/>.

PREPARING WRITING PORTFOLIOS

In simplest terms, a *writing portfolio* is a collection of your writing contained within a single binder or folder. This writing may have been done over a number of weeks, months, or even years; it may be organized chronologically, thematically, or according to quality. A private writing portfolio may contain writing that you wish to keep for yourself; in this case you decide what's in it and what it looks like. However, a writing portfolio assigned for a class will contain writing to be shared with an audience to demonstrate your writing and reasoning abilities. One kind of writing portfolio, accumulated during a college course, presents a record of your work over a semester and will be used to assign a grade. Another type of portfolio presents a condensed, edited story of your semester's progress in a more

narrative form. In addition, portfolios are often requested by prospective employers in journalism and other fields of professional writing; these samples of your best work over several years may determine whether or not you are offered a job as a writer or editor.

Course Portfolios

The most common type of portfolio assigned in a writing course contains the cumulative work collected over the semester plus a cover letter in which you explain the nature and value of these papers. Sometimes you will be asked to assign yourself a grade based on your own assessment. The following suggestions may help you in preparing a course portfolio:

1. **Make your portfolio speak for you.**   If your course portfolio is clean, complete, and carefully organized, that's how you will be judged. If it's unique, colorful, creative, and imaginative, that, too, is how you'll be judged. So, too, will you be judged if your folder is messy, incomplete, and haphazardly put together. Before giving your portfolio to somebody else for evaluation, consider whether it reflects how you want to be presented.

2. **Include exactly what is asked for.**   If an instructor wants three finished papers and a dozen sample journal entries, that's the minimum your course portfolio should contain.

If an employer wants to see five samples of different types of writing, be sure to include five samples. Sometimes you can include more than asked for, but never include less.

3. **Add supplemental material judiciously.**   Course portfolios are among the most flexible means of presenting yourself. If you believe that supplemental writing will present you in a better light, include that too, but only after the required material. If you include extra material, attach a note to explain why it is there. Supplemental writing might include journals, letters, sketches, or diagrams that suggest other useful dimensions of your thinking.

4. **Include perfect final drafts.**   At least make them as close to perfect as you can. Show that your own standard for finished work is high. Final drafts should be printed double-spaced on one side only of high-quality paper, be carefully proofread, and follow the language conventions appropriate to the task—unless another format is requested.

5. **Demonstrate growth.**   This is a tall order, of course, but course portfolios, unlike most other assessment instruments, can demonstrate positive change. The signal value of portfolios in writing classes is that they allow you to demonstrate how a finished paper came into being. Consequently, instructors commonly ask for early drafts to be attached to final drafts of each paper, the most recent on top, so they can see how you followed revision suggestions, how much effort you invested, how many drafts you wrote, and how often you took risks. To build such a record of your work, date every draft of each paper and keep it in a safe place.

6. **Demonstrate work in progress.**   Course portfolios allow writers to present partially finished work that suggests future directions and intentions. Both instructors and potential employers may find such preliminary drafts or outlines as valuable as some of your finished work. When you include such tentative drafts, be sure to attach a note explaining why you still believe it has merit and in which direction you want to take it.

7. **Attach a table of contents.**   For portfolios containing more than three papers, attach a separate table of contents. For those containing only a few papers, embed your table of contents in the cover letter.

8. **Organize your work with clear logic.**   Three methods of organization are particularly appealing:

- *Chronological order.*   Writing is arranged in order, beginning the first week, ending the last week, with all drafts, papers, journal entries, letters, and such fitting in place according to the date written. Only the cover letter (see below) is out of chronological order, serving as an introduction to what follows. This method allows you to show the evolution of growth most clearly, with your latest writing—presumably the best—presented at the end.
- *Reverse chronological order.*   The most recent writing is up front and the earliest writing at the back. In this instance, the most recent written document—the cover letter—is in place at the beginning of the portfolio. This method features your latest (and best) work up front and allows readers to trace back through the history of how it got there.
- *Best-first order.*   You place your strongest writing up front and your weakest in back. Organizing a portfolio this way suggests that the work you consider strongest should count most heavily in evaluating the semester's work.

Unless otherwise specified, arrange your work in a three-ring binder as you collect it during the term, so you can add and delete as you choose, making the best possible case for yourself. Work collected this way can then be bound in a simple cover for presentation at term's end or left in the binder. In either case, put your name and address on the outside cover for easy identification.

9. **Write a careful and honest cover letter.**   Include a cover letter. For many instructors, the cover letter will be the most important part of your course portfolio since it represents your own most recent assessment of the work you completed over the semester. A cover letter serves two primary purposes: (1) an introduction describing and explaining the portfolio's contents and organization, including accounts of any missing or unusual pieces to be found therein; and (2) a self-assessment of the work, from earliest to latest draft of each paper, and from earliest to latest work over the course of the semester. The following excerpt is from Kelly's letter describing the evolution of one paper:

> In writing the personal experience paper, I tried three different approaches, two different topics, and finally a combination of different approaches to my final topic. My first draft [about learning the value of money] was all summary and didn't show anything actually happening. My second draft wasn't focused because I was still trying to cover too much ground. At this point, I got frustrated and tried a new topic [the hospital] but that didn't work either. Finally, for my last draft, I returned to my original topic, and this time it worked. I described one scene in great detail and included dialogue, and I liked it better and so did you. I am pleased with the way this paper came out when I limited my focus and zeroed in close.

The following excerpt describes Chris's assessment of her work over the whole semester:

> As I look back through all the papers I've written this semester, I see how far my writing has come. At first I thought it was stupid to write so many different drafts of the same paper, like I would beat the topic to death. But now I realize that all these different papers on the same topic all went in different directions. This happened to some degree in the first paper, but I especially remember in my research project, when I interviewed the director of the Ronald McDonald House, I really got excited about the work they did there, and I really got involved in the other drafts of that paper.

◆ **Guidelines for Creating Course Portfolios**

1. Date, collect, and save in a folder all papers written for the course.
2. Arrange papers in chronological, reverse chronological, or qualitative order, depending on the assignment.
3. In an appendix, attach supplemental writing such as journal excerpts, letters, class exercises, quizzes, or other relevant writing.
4. Review your writing and compose a cover letter explaining the worth or relevance of the writing in the portfolio: Consider the strengths and weaknesses of each individual paper as well as those of the entire collection. Provide a summary statement of your current standing as a writer as your portfolio represents you.
5. Attend to the final presentation: Include all writing in a clean, attractive folder; organize contents logically; attach a table of contents; write explanatory memos to explain unusual materials; and make sure the portfolio meets the minimum specifications of the assignment.

I have learned to shorten my papers by editing and cutting out needless words. I use more descriptive adjectives now when I'm describing a setting and try to find action verbs instead of "to be" verbs in all of my papers. I am writing more consciously now—I think that's the most important thing I learned this semester.

Story Portfolios

A *story portfolio* is a shorter, more carefully edited and focused production than a cumulative course portfolio. Instead of including a cover letter and all papers and drafts written during the term as evidence for self-assessment, a story portfolio presents the evolution of your work and thought over the course of the semester in narrative form. In a story portfolio, you include excerpts of your papers insofar as they illustrate points in your development as a writer. In addition, you include excerpts of supplemental written records accumulated at different times during the semester, including the following:

- Early and dead-end drafts of papers
- Journal entries
- Lecture and discussion notes
- In-class writing and freewriting
- Comments on papers from your instructor
- Letters to or from your instructor
- Comments from classmates about your papers

In other words, to write a story portfolio, you conduct something like an archeological dig through the written remains of your work in a class. By assembling this evidence in chronological order and choosing the most telling snippets from these various documents, you write the story that explains, amplifies, or interprets the documents included or quoted. The best story portfolios commonly reveal a theme or set of issues that run from week to week or paper to paper throughout the semester. As you can see, a story portfolio is actually a small research paper, presenting a claim about your evolution as a writer with the evidence coming from your own written sources.

I encourage students to write their story portfolios using an informal voice as they might in a journal or letter. However, some students choose a more formal voice. Some prefer to write in the third person, analyzing the semester's work as if they did not know the writer (themselves). I also encourage them to experiment with the form and structure of their story portfolios, so that some present their work as a series of dated journal entries or snapshots while others write a more fluid essay with written excerpts embedded as they illustrate this or that point. Following are a few pages from Karen's story portfolio that illustrate one example of such a portfolio:

> When I entered English 1, I was not a confident writer and only felt comfortable writing factual reports for school assignments. Those were pretty straightforward, and personal opinion was not involved. But over the course of the semester I've learned that I enjoy including my own voice in my writing. The first day of class I wrote this in my journal:
>
> > *8/31 Writing has always been hard for me. I don't have a lot of experience writing papers except for straightforward things like science re-*

*ports. I never did very well in English classes, usually getting B's and
C's on my papers.*

But I began to feel a little more comfortable when we read and discussed the
first chapter of the book—a lot of other students besides me felt the same way, pretty
scared to be taking English in college.

Our first assignment was to write a paper about a personal experience that was
important to us. At first, I couldn't think where to start, but when we brainstormed
topics in class, I got some good ideas. Three of the topics listed on the board were
ones I could write about:

- excelling at a particular sport (basketball)
- high school graduation
- one day in the life of a waitress

I decided to write about our basketball season last year, especially the last game
that we lost. Here is a paragraph from my first draft:

> *We lost badly to Walpole in what turned out to be our final game. I sat
> on the bench most of the time.*

As I see now, that draft was all telling and summary—I didn't show anything happening that was interesting or alive. But in a later draft I used dialogue and wrote
from the announcer's point of view, and the result was fun to write and my group
said fun to read.

> *Well folks, it looks as if Belmont has given up, the coach is preparing to
> send in his subs. It has been a rough game for Belmont. They stayed in
> it during the first quarter, but Walpole has run away with it since then.
> Down by twenty with only six minutes left, Belmont's first sub is now
> approaching the table.*

You were excited about this draft too, and your comment helped me know where to
go next. You wrote:

> *Great draft, Karen! You really sound like a play-by-play announcer—
> you've either been one or listened closely to lots of basketball games.
> What would happen if in your next draft you alternated between your
> own voice and the announcer's voice? Want to try it?*

This next excerpt comes from a story portfolio that included twelve pages of discussion and writing samples and concluded with this paragraph:

> *I liked writing this story portfolio at the end of the term because I
> can really see how my writing and my attitude have changed. I came
> into class not liking to write, but now I can say that I really do. The
> structure was free and we had plenty of time to experiment with dif-
> ferent approaches to each assignment. I still have a long way to go,
> especially on my argumentative writing, since neither you nor I liked
> my final draft, but now I think I know how to get there: rewrite,
> rewrite, rewrite.*

◆ GUIDELINES FOR CREATING STORY PORTFOLIOS

1. Assemble your collected writing in chronological order, from the beginning to the end of each paper, from beginning to end of the semester.
2. Reread all your informal work (in journals, letters, instructor comments) and highlight passages that reflect the story of your growth as a writer.
3. Reread all your formal work (final papers, drafts) and highlight passages that illustrate your growth as a writer. Note especially if a particular passage had evolved over several drafts in the same paper—these would show you learning to revise.
4. Arrange all highlighted passages in order and write a story that shows how one passage connects to another, and the significance of each passage.
5. Before writing your conclusion, reread your portfolio and identify common themes or ideas or concerns that have occurred over the semester; include these in your portfolio summary.

PUBLISHING CLASS BOOKS

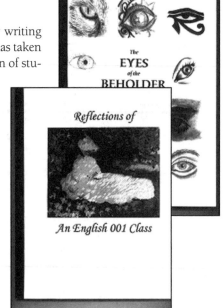

Publishing a class book is a natural end to any writing class—or any class in which interesting writing has taken place. A class book is an edited, bound collection of student writing, usually featuring some work from each student in the class. The compilation and editing of such a book is commonly assigned to class volunteers, who are given significant authority in designing and producing the book. It is a good idea for editors to discuss book guidelines with the whole class so that consensus guidelines emerge. I suggest that class editors do the following.

Define editorial mission. Usually students ask for camera-ready copy from classmates to simplify and speed the publishing process. However, editors may want to see near-final drafts and return with comments; or they may wish to set up class editorial boards to preview or screen near-final drafts; or they may wish to leave this role with the instructor.

Divide editorial responsibilities. Class books are best done by editorial teams consisting of two or more students who arrange among themselves the various duties described above.

Establish manuscript guidelines. Discuss with the class what each submitted paper should look like, arrive at a consensus, and ask for camera-ready copy to speed production and decrease the editors' work load. The editors should specify the following:

- double- or single-spaced typing
- type face
- font size
- margins: top and bottom, right and left
- justified or not
- title font and size
- position of author name

Set page limits. Each student may be allowed a certain number of single- or double-spaced pages. Since printing charges are usually made on a per-page basis, page length discussion is related to final publication cost.

Set deadlines. This is usually set so published copies can be delivered on the last class day or next-to-last class day (this latter allowing for reading and discussing the book on the last class day).

Organize the essays. Arrange the collected essays according to some ordering principle; this may depend upon how many essays there are and what kinds of writing was done during the term. For example, students may have written (1) personal profiles, (2) feature stories, and (3) reflective essays; should there be a separate section for each? How should the essays be arranged within each section?

Write an introduction. The most significant editorial work is writing an introduction to contextualize the class book, explain its development, and describe the contents. Introductions vary in length from a paragraph to several pages.

Prepare a table of contents. Include essay title, author's name, and page number on which the essay is to be found. (And remember to paginate the manuscript, by hand if necessary.)

Ask the instructor to write an afterword or preface. Instructors may write about the assignment objectives, impressions of the essays, or reactions to the class; they may add any other perspective that seems relevant to the book.

Collect student writer biographies. Most class books conclude with short (fifty to one hundred word) biographies of the student writers, which may be serious, semi-serious, or comical, depending on class wishes.

Design a cover. The editor(s) may commission a classmate to do the artwork or take it on themselves. Covers can be graphic or printed, black and white or color. (Color and plastic covers usually cost more.)

Estimate publishing cost. The editors are responsible for exploring (with local print shops such as Kinko's or Staples, or the college print shop) the cost of producing a certain number of copies of class books (for example, 60 pages at $0.05 each, plus color cover at $1 each, plus binding at $0.50 each equals $4.50 per book); often the local college print shop will sell the books to the students, freeing the instructor from handling the money. Alternatively, the editors may ask the class to assemble the book—each student could be asked to bring in twenty copies of his or her essay to be collated and bound with the rest.

Lead a class discussion. The final responsibility of class editors is to stimulate a class discussion on theme, format, and voice as represented by the class book or its various sections. I try to arrange for this to happen during the last class. Class responsibilities here include both a careful reading of their own book and bringing cookies and cider to facilitate the discussion.

SUGGESTIONS FOR DISCUSSING CLASS BOOKS

Asking students to read the finished books with the following questions in mind is likely to lead to a lively in-class discussion about the writing in the book

- Which is your favorite title and why?
- Which essay, besides your own, is your favorite and why?
- What ideas or techniques did you learn from classmates' essays?
- In which essays are graphics used most effectively?
- In your own essay, what is your favorite passage?
- In your own essay, what would you still like to change?

Since editors do a significant amount of work in compiling their classmates' writing, I usually excuse them from making oral reports or leading class discussions—which the rest of the students do during the term.

Finally, when I assign editors to design and publish a class book, I make it clear that the paper published in the book is the final draft of that particular paper; when reading student portfolios at term's end, it is in the class book that I find the final drafts of one or more essays.

DESIGNING WEB PAGES

Web pages should be designed using many of the same principles as paper text pages, with readable fonts, clear titles and headings, generous use of white space, and careful organization. However, while most printed texts are meant to be read from beginning to end, start to finish, in what might be described as a linear pattern, Web pages—especially first or home pages—are often merely attractive outlines that direct viewers/readers to more specific and detailed information contained at other places (links) on the site or to other sites. In that sense, a Web page has a logical, but not a linear, organization that commonly contains design elements associated with posters and brochures. Like these other more visual media, well-designed Web pages invite readers to scan and jump around rather than read straight, top to bottom, beginning to end. When viewers "read" a Web page, their eyes are often hit with a lot of information simultaneously, as titles, headings, text, graphics, technical images, and color all vie for attention at once. In a well-designed page, pertinent information will jump out and the viewer may choose what specific information to peruse next.

While the possibilities for catching viewer attention on a Web page are greater than on text-only pages (such as this book), the probability of holding viewer attention for any length of time is actually less. Viewers seldom like to read long blocks of text on a computer screen or even to scroll down to second and third pages to find what they're looking for. This means that Web page designers need to be judicious in what they include on a single Web screen, and make sure that everything on the screen serves a purpose and does its job.

Outline. Construct an outline to highlight the most important ideas and subordinate the lesser ones. With the scope of your page clear, you can begin composing in headings and subheadings as well as in chunks or blocks of writing (like verbal snapshots). Since your aim is not to invite readers to read straight through for a long single reading, don't worry about verbal transitions in a conventional sense—readers can choose to read background information first, or skip to conclusions, or deviate to a side topic.

Compose in chunks. Arrange your outline in a logical and highly visible pattern on a single page, for these entries will become links to more detailed information. Each heading will become a link to further information composed in chunks or block paragraphs explaining each concept in greater detail—each block now content of a link with additional information and images for the reader to delve into (see Figure 21.2 for a home page followed by more detailed links.)

Link with logic. Using links, any Web page can be "next to" any other page or any number of other pages. For example, look at the *home page* for the University of Wisconsin–Milwaukee, which has been set up to direct the interested viewer to various aspects of UWM life—different clusters of information are grouped around main headings such as *"Admissions," "Academics and Research,"* and *"Students,"* among others. Subheadings under each main head identify links to lead to more specific information. For example, under *Admissions,* you could click on the links *Prospective Students, Undergraduate, Graduate,* and so on. This is a process that many of you reading this book know well—how to read and navigate Web pages, especially those dealing with college admissions. So all you need to know in order to design your own Web page is the logic of formal outlining. In other words, to create your own Web site with links to related information, first create an outline with main heads and subheads and a logic will quickly emerge suggesting what links to put where. From there, you select appropriate and attractive font sizes and images, and your page begins to take shape.

The Logic of Web Page Design

Logging on to the Home Page of the University of Wisconsin—Milwaukee allows prospective students to complete an online application by clicking on relevant links in right margin of each successive Web page.

UWM Home Page

Prospective Students Page (found in right margin of Home Page)

Requirements for Admission

Page (found in right margin of Prospective Students Page)

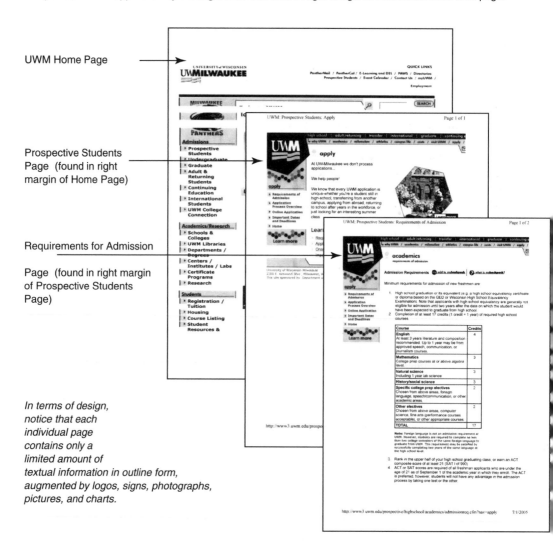

In terms of design, notice that each individual page contains only a limited amount of textual information in outline form, augmented by logos, signs, photographs, pictures, and charts.

Figure 21.2

Online Tutorials for Constructing Web Pages

To learn the specifics of Web page design and creation, go online and follow one of the many detailed tutorials available at sites identified in the box.

ONLINE HTML GUIDES/TUTORIALS/REFERENCES

- **NCSA—A Beginner's Guide to HTML**
  <http://www.ncsa.uiuc.edu/General/Internet/WWW/HTMLPrimerAll.html>
- **HTML Teaching Tool** from WebMonkey.
  <http://hotwired.lycos.com/webmonkey/teachingtool/index.html>
- **Yale Web Style Guide**
  <http://info.med.yale.edu/caim/manual>
- **WebPagesThatSuck.com:** Learn good Web design by looking at bad design.
  <http://www.webpagesthatsuck.com>
- **"How Users Read on the Web"** by Jacob Nielsen
  <http://www.useit.com/alertbox/9710a.html>
- **The Alertbox: Current Issues in Web Usability**
  <http://www.alertbox.com>

PART FOUR

RESEARCH ACROSS THE DISCIPLINES

CHAPTER TWENTY-TWO

Writing and Research Across the Disciplines

Good *writing* satisfies the expectations of an audience in form, style, and content. But different audiences come to a piece of writing with different expectations, so writing that is judged "good" by one audience may be judged "less good" by another. Although all college instructors value good writing, each area of study has its own set of criteria by which writing is judged. For instance, the loose form, informal style, and speculative content of a reflective essay that please an English instructor might not please an anthropology instructor, who expects form, style, and assertions to follow the more formal structures established in that discipline.

In like manner, careful *research*, conducted according to the scope and method of each given discipline, is a precondition for good research writing. This chapter provides a broad outline of the differences and similarities of writing and research techniques across the curriculum.

HOW THE DISCIPLINES DIFFER

As a rule, knowledge in the humanities focuses on texts and on individual ideas, speculations, insights, and imaginative connections. Interpretation in the humanities is thus relatively subjective. Accordingly, writing and research in the humanities are characterized by personal involvement, lively language, and speculative or open-ended conclusions.

In contrast, knowledge in the social and physical sciences is likely to focus on data and on ideas that can be verified through observing, measuring, and testing. Interpretation in these disciplines needs to be objective. Accordingly, writing and research in the social and physical sciences emphasizes inferences based on the careful study of data and downplays the personal opinion and speculation of the writer.

But boundaries between the disciplines are not absolute. For example, at some colleges history is considered one of the humanities, while at others it is classified as a social science. Geography is a social science when it looks at regions and how people live, but it is a physical science when it investigates the properties of rocks, glaciers, and climate. Colleges of business, engineering, health, education, and natural resources all draw on numerous disciplines as their sources of knowledge.

The field of English alone includes not only the study of literature but literary theory and history, not only composition but creative and technical writing. In addition, English departments often include linguistics, journalism, folklore, women's studies, Afro-American studies, and sometimes speech, film, and communications. In other words, within even one discipline, you might be asked to write several distinct types of papers: personal experience essays for a composition course, interpretations for a literature course, abstracts for a linguistics course, short stories for a creative writing course. Consequently, any observations about the different kinds of knowledge and the differing conventions for writing about them are only generalizations. The more carefully you study any one discipline, the more complex it becomes, and the harder it is to make a generalization that doesn't have numerous exceptions.

Formal differences exist among the styles of research writing for different disciplines, especially in the conventions for documenting sources. Each discipline has its own authority or authorities, which provide rules about such issues as spelling of technical terms and

DISCIPLINE	STYLE
Languages and literature	Modern Language Association (MLA) (see Chapter 29)
Social sciences	American Psychological Association (APA) (see Chapter 30)
Humanities	*Chicago Manual of Style* (CMS)
Sciences	
Life sciences	Council of Science Editors (CSE)
Chemistry	American Chemical Society (ACS)
Physics	American Institute of Physics (AIP)
Business	Varies (see Chapter 30)
Education	Varies (see Chapter 30)
Journalism	Associated Press (AP)
Medicine	American Medical Association (AMA)

Figure 22.1

preferred punctuation and editing mechanics, as well as documentation style. In addition, if you write for publication in a magazine, professional journal, or book, the publisher will have a *house style,* which may vary in some details from the conventions listed in the authoritative guidelines for the discipline in which you are writing. Figure 22.1 lists the sources of style manuals for various disciplines.

WHAT THE DISCIPLINES HAVE IN COMMON

Regardless of disciplinary differences, certain principles of writing and research hold true *across* the curriculum.

KNOWLEDGE.   Each field of study attempts to develop knowledge about a particular aspect of the physical, social, or cultural world in which we live. For example, the physical sciences observe nature to learn how it works, while history and anthropology examine civilizations over time, sociology looks at human beings in groups, and psychology attempts to explain the operation and development of the individual human mind. In writing for a particular course, keep in mind the larger purpose of the field of study, especially when selecting, introducing, and concluding your investigation.

METHOD.   Each field has accepted methods of investigation. Perhaps the best known is the scientific method, used in most of the physical and social sciences. One who uses the scientific method first asks a question, then poses a possible answer (a hypothesis), then car-

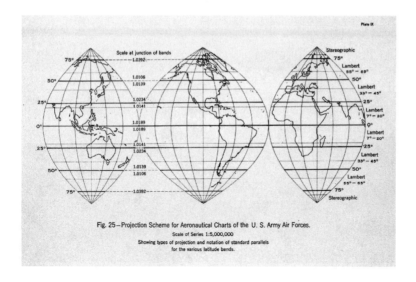

Fig. 25—Projection Scheme for Aeronautical Charts of the U. S. Army Air Forces.
Scale of Series 1:5,000,000
Showing types of projection and notation of standard parallels
for the various latitude bands.

ries out experiments in the field or laboratory to test this answer, and finally, if it cannot be disproved, concludes that the hypothesis is correct. However, while research in the social sciences follows this scientific pattern, some disciplines, such as anthropology, rely instead on the more personal approach of ethnographic study. Literary research may be formal, historical, deconstructive, and so on. It is important to recognize that every discipline has its accepted—and its controversial—methods of study. Any conclusions you discuss in your writing should reflect that awareness.

EVIDENCE.   In every field, any claim you make about the subject of your study needs to be supported by evidence. If, in order to identify an unknown rock, you scrape it with a known rock in the geology laboratory, the scratch marks of the harder rock on the softer will be part of your evidence to support your claims about the unknown rock. If you analyze Holden Caulfield on the basis of his opening monologue in *The Catcher in the Rye,* his words will be evidence to support your interpretation. If you conduct a survey of students to examine college study habits, counting and collating your findings will be evidence to support your conclusions. In other words, although the *nature* of evidence varies greatly from one discipline to another, the *need* for evidence is constant. In some cases, when you need to support an assertion, you will consult certain sources for evidence and will need to have clear documentation for these sources. (Chapters 29 and 30 provide detailed guidelines for documenting sources in the most frequently used disciplines.)

ACCURACY.   Each field values precision and correctness, and each has its own specialized vocabulary for talking about knowledge. Writers are expected to use terms precisely and to spell them correctly. In addition, each discipline has developed formats in which to report information. When you write within a discipline, you should know the correct form in which to communicate a literary analysis in English, a research report in sociology, or a laboratory report in biology. Each discipline also values conventional correctness in language. Your writing will be most respected when it reflects standard use of grammar, punctuation, and mechanics.

◆ SUGGESTIONS FOR WRITING AND RESEARCH

Individual

Examine the syllabi of two courses you are taking in two different disciplines, looking closely at the printed rationale, readings, and assignments. Make an outline of the differences you notice that seem to be discipline based. Also note any disciplinary similarities you find. Then using evidence from the syllabi, write a paper explaining why one discipline's scope and methods align more closely with your interests and beliefs.

Collaborative

Join with a classmate who is interested in the same major you are, and together interview several instructors in that discipline to find out what attracted them to that particular field of study and where they see that field evolving in the future. Write individual papers or collaborate on a single paper in which you explain the nature and future of the discipline in which you plan to major, including information from college catalogue and course syllabi as well as instructor interviews.

CHAPTER TWENTY-THREE

Strategies for Conducting Research

This isn't my best writing. To write this paper we had to have at least fifteen references from ten different sources, and I was really struggling to find that many, and in the end I just sort of stuck them in to get it done with. You really shouldn't read this paper.

MEGAN

Before agonizing too long over your next research project, stop to consider what, exactly, research entails. Keep in mind that in your nonacademic life you conduct practical research of one kind or another every time you search the want ads for a used car, browse through a library in search of a book, or read a movie review. You may not make note cards or report the results in writing, but whenever you ask questions and then systematically look for answers, you are conducting research.

In college, the research you conduct is academic rather than practical. In other words, it's designed to result in a convincing paper rather than a purchase or an action. Academic research is part of the writing process for most of your papers.

You rarely begin writing an explanation, argument, or interpretation already knowing all the facts and having all the information you'll need: To fill in the gaps in your knowledge, you conduct research. In fact, one type of assignment, the research essay, is specially designed to introduce you to the process of conducting research and writing a paper based on your findings. Research essays are generally longer, require more extensive research, use a more formal style and format, and take more time than other papers.

Meaningful research results from real questions that you care to answer. It's exciting work. And if you're not now excited about something, once you start engaging in research activities you may surprise yourself. Take a tour of your library and find out what's there; get on the Internet and explore the resources of the World Wide Web; above all, start thinking, writing, and talking to people about ideas, and exciting things will happen.

PRACTICAL RESEARCH

Let me tell you about the last time I did research of a substantial nature—I bought a new motorcycle. I don't buy new cars, or even new houses, but riding motorcycles is a special passion of mine and this time I wanted to buy a new motorcycle—the latest, smoothest, best-handling, most powerful motorcycle available. I'd recently moved to a home in a rural setting where I had to travel two miles on a gravel road coming or leaving. I discovered that my large touring motorcycle, heavy with narrow handlebars and small wheels, felt especially precarious on this road, so I explored purchasing a lighter motorcycle that would give me more control on gravel as well as asphalt roads. Finding the right machine meant shopping carefully, which meant asking good questions: What kind of motorcycle was best for both rough road riding and long-range touring? What make and model was most reliable? How much would it cost? (How much could I afford?) Who were the best dealers? And so on.

To locate and purchase this new motorcycle I worked to answer all these questions and more; here's how I remember the process.

Over a period of several months I talked to people who knew a lot about motorcycles—some old friends, the mechanic who serviced my old motorcycle, and a neighbor who owned a variety of machines.

I also subscribed to *Motorcyclist* and *Rider* magazines, finding the latter more interesting since it focuses on a wider range. The more I read, the more familiar I became with current terminology (ABS, telelever, paralever), brands (BMW, Yamaha, Harley-Davidson), models (roadsters, off-road, dual sport), and performance data (roll-on speed, braking distance). On a corner of my desk, I piled the most useful magazines with many dog-eared pages.

I also visited my local library—not the larger one at the university—to browse through other magazines to which I did not personally subscribe: *Motorcycle Consumer News* I found particularly helpful, and so made photocopies of the most relevant articles, underlined key findings, made notes in the photocopy margins, and explored my progress in my personal journal.

I also visited the local chapter of the BMW Motorcycle Club, meeting more people who seemed to be expert motorcyclists (all, of course, recommending BMWs); I also bought a copy of *BMW Motorcycle Owners News*.

I rented the video *On Any Sunday* (1972), considered by many to be the best film ever made about motorcycles, and watched it three times—this more to feed my passion than to help select a motorcycle to purchase. As far as research goes, I'd call this step filling in context and helping maintain momentum, since watching the film never played a role in my finished research.

I approached the owner of Frank's Motorcycle Shop and asked about the virtues of certain models, especially the new two-cylinder BMW R1200GS and the three-cylinder Triumph Tiger 955i—both dual-sport models apparently at home on dirt roads as well as paved highways. I was allowed a test ride on each, and found each quite exciting. I also checked out the local dealers who sold Honda and Yamaha motorcycles and listened to sales pitches explaining the features of their best dual-sport machines, but found neither dealer willing to give me test rides.

Narrowing my choice to the BMW vs. the Triumph, I logged onto both factory Web sites—BMW at <ww.motoplex.com> and Triumph at <http://www.triumph.co.uk>—and read several comparative reviews online of the BMW vs. the Triumph <www.motorcycle-

usa.com> in which the BMW had the edge in performance while the Triumph had the edge in price. I also found two magazines (*Rider, Cycle World*) that named the R1200GS "Bike of the Year"—and that interested me a lot.

After weighing the relative merits of performance vesus price and based on a large amount of reading and some faith in the reviews I read—I returned to Frank's Motorcycle Shop and purchased the R12000GS, a decision about which I've never been sorry.

◆ WRITING 1

What research outside of school settings have you conducted recently? Think about major changes, moves, or purchases that required you to ask serious questions. Also think about any explorations you've made on site, through interviews, in a library or on the World Wide Web. Choose one of these recent research activities and list the sources you found, the questions you asked, and any steps you took to answer them. Finally, what was the result of this research?

THE RESEARCH PROCESS

While the search for motorcycle knowledge is practical rather than academic, it serves nevertheless to introduce a process common to many research projects, argumentative or informational, in school or out.

1. **The researcher has a genuine interest in the topic.**   It's difficult to fake curiosity, but it's possible to develop it. My interest in motorcycles was long-standing, but the more I investigated, the more I learned and the more I still wanted to know. Some academic assignments will allow you to pursue issues that are personally important to you; others will require that you dive into the research first and generate interest as you go.

2. **The researcher asks questions.**   My first questions were general rather than specific. However, as I gained more knowledge, the questions became more sharply focused. No matter what your research assignment, you need to begin by articulating questions, finding out where the answers lead, and then asking still more questions.

3. **The researcher seeks answers from people.**   I talked to both friends and strangers who knew about motorcycles. The people to whom I listened most closely were specialists with expert knowledge. All research projects profit when you ask knowledgeable people to help you answer questions or point you in directions where answers may be found. College communities abound with professors, researchers, working professionals, and nonacademic staff who can help out with research projects.

4. **The researcher conducts field research.**   I went to dealerships and a motorcycle club, not only to ask questions of experts but to observe and experience first hand. No matter how much other people told me, my knowledge increased when I made personal

observations. In many forms of academic research, field research is as important as library research.

5. **The researcher examines texts.**   I read motorcycle magazines, brochures, visited the library, and searched the Internet. While printed texts are helpful in practical research, they are crucial in academic research.

6. **The researcher evaluates sources.**   As the research progressed, I double-checked information to see if it could be confirmed by more than one source. In practical research, the researcher must evaluate sources to ensure that the final decision is satisfactory. Similarly, in academic research, you must evaluate sources to ensure that your final paper is convincing.

7. **The researcher writes.**   I made notes both in the field and in the library as well as wrote in my journal—all to help the research turn out just right for me. In practical research, writing helps the researcher find, remember, and explore information. In academic research, writing is even more important, since the results must eventually be reported in writing.

8. **The researcher tests and experiments.**   In my practical research, testing was simple and fairly subjective—riding different motorcycles to compare the qualities of each, in this case, eliminating those ridden as not quite right. Testing and experimentation are also regular parts of many research projects.

9. **The researcher combines and synthesizes information to arrive at new conclusions.**   My accumulated and sorted-out information led to a decision to purchase one motorcycle rather than another. In academic research, your synthesis of information leads not to a purchase, but to a well-supported thesis that will convince a skeptical audience that your research findings are correct.

What this researcher did not do, of course, is report the results in a research paper. I bought a motorcycle but did not write a paper about it. The greatest difference between practical and academic research is that the former leads to practical knowledge on which to act (the buying of a motorcycle), the latter to theoretical knowledge written for others to read (a research report or essay). So, for academic research, writing becomes a crucial final step in the process.

10. **The researcher presents the research findings in an interesting, focused, and well-documented paper.**   The remainder of this chapter explains how to select, investigate, and write about academic research topics.

◆ WRITING 2

Explain how any of the research activities described in this section were part of an investigation you once conducted, in school or out. How might you use computer-based research activities to facilitate any research project you do today—practical or academic?

RESEARCH TOPICS

Research projects usually occupy several weeks or months and are often the most important papers you write during a semester, so study the assignment carefully, begin work immediately, and allow sufficient time for the many different activities involved.

EXAMINE THE ASSIGNMENT.   First, think about the aims of the course in which the research project is assigned. What themes has the instructor emphasized? What research questions contribute to the goals of this course? In other words, before selecting a topic, assess the instructor's probable reasons for making the assignment in the first place.

Examine both the subject words and the direction words. **Subject words** (*historical, geographical, social,* etc.) specify the area of the investigation. **Direction words** (*propose* or *explain*) specify your purpose for writing—whether you should argue or report or do something else.

ASK GOOD QUESTIONS.   To begin with, make a list of all the ways your personal interests dovetail with the content of the course. What subjects have you enjoyed most? What discussions, lectures, or labs were most engaging? What recent news both interests you and relates to the course material? After each item, list the questions that might lead you to interesting research, then select the one that meets the following conditions:

- It's a question to which you don't already know the answer.
- It requires more than a yes or no answer.
- It's a question that you have a reasonable chance of answering.

In the following example, a general subject is turned into a specific question.

GENERAL SUBJECT   *What's the health of the environment in the state of Vermont?* (too broad, not sure where to begin).

GENERAL TOPIC   *How governmental and corporate policies in the state of Vermont protect the environment.* (narrower, but this could be a book).

FOCUSED TOPIC   *Which corporations in Vermont have policies that protect the environment?* (more specific, but the "which" question would generate a list rather than a full-fledged examination of an issue).

FINAL TOPIC   *How does Ben and Jerry's Ice Cream company make a profit and protect the environment at the same time?* (specific place to read about, visit, and find people to interview).

WRITE WITH AUTHORITY.   Whenever you undertake research, you join an ongoing conversation among a select community of people who are knowledgeable about the subject. As you collect information, you also begin to be knowledgeable and gain an authoritative voice. Your goal should be to become enough of an expert on your topic that you can teach your classmates and instructor something they didn't already know about your topic. One good way to write like an expert is to translate all the crucial information about your topic into your own words. Do this on note cards, in journal entries, and throughout paper drafts so your final draft will be written in your own strong voice.

KEEP AN OPEN MIND.   Don't be surprised if, once you begin researching, questions and answers multiply and change. For example, suppose you start out researching local recycling efforts, but you stumble upon the problem of finding buyers for recycled material. One source raises the question of processing recycled materials, another on manufacturing difficulties with recycled material, while another source turns the whole question back to consumer education. All of these concerns are related, but if you attempt to study them all with equal intensity, your paper will be either very long or very superficial. Chances are one of these more limited topics may interest you more than the first question you started with—which is as it should be. Follow your strongest interests, and you'll go deeper with more satisfaction and write a better paper in the bargain.

THESIS-BASED RESEARCH

When an answer to your research question starts to take shape, form a *working thesis,* which will be a preliminary or tentative answer to your initial question. As you investigate further, you will look for information that substantiates, refutes, or modifies this thesis. When additional research leads you in a different direction, be ready to redirect your investigation and revise your thesis.

Whether or not you already have a working thesis will determine what type of research you undertake. **Informational research** is conducted when you don't know the answer to the question or don't have a firm opinion about the topic. You enter this kind of investigation with an open mind, focusing on the question, not on a predetermined answer. As you become more knowledgeable, your information will begin to answer the question you started with—at which point you'll begin shaping the main point of your paper. Such research might be characterized as thesis-finding.

Persuasive research, however, is conducted to prove a point you already believe in. You enter such projects having already formulated a working thesis—the tentative answer to your question, the side of a debate or argument you want to support. For example, even as you began research on the environmental policies of Ben and Jerry's Ice Cream Company, local and national media publicity had led you to believe this company was environmentally friendly; in other words, you began with a belief to verify, so you'd be surprised if further research disproved your initial hunch. However, you might find out that publicity about a company was one thing, but getting the scoop from employees was something else, causing you to revise your first thesis. The best papers will be those that most honestly report what's closest to the truth, even if a different truth than you started with (for more detailed information on working with theses, see Chapters 10 and 11.)

◆ WRITING 3

Select a topic that interests you and that is compatible with the research assignment. List ten questions about this topic. Select the question that most interests you and freewrite a possible answer for ten or more minutes. Why does it interest you? Where would you start looking to pursue answers further?

A RESEARCH LOG

A **research log** can help you keep track of the scope, purpose, and possibilities of any research project. Such a log is essentially a journal kept in paper notebook or on a notebook computer in which you write to yourself about the process of doing research by asking questions and monitoring the results. Questions you might ask include the following:

- What subject do I want to research?
- What information have I found so far?
- What do I still need to find?
- Where am I most likely to find it?
- What evidence best supports my working thesis?
- What evidence challenges my working thesis?
- How is my thesis changing from where it started?

Writing out answers to these questions in your log clarifies your tasks as you go along, forcing you to articulate ideas and examine supporting evidence critically. Novice researchers often waste time tracking down sources that are not really useful. But posing and answering questions in writing as you investigate will make research more efficient. When you keep notes in log form, record them by date found and allow room to add cross-referencing notes to other entries. The following entries are from a first-year student's handwritten research log:

> 11/12 With over a hundred thousand of hits on Google (!), I decided to limit my research by going to the library. In checking the subject headings, I couldn't seem to find any books specifically on ozone depletion. But the reference librarian suggested I check periodicals because it takes so long for books to come out on new science subjects. In the General Science Index I found a dozen articles that pointed me in the right direction—now all I need to do is actually start reading them.

> 11/17 Conference today with Lawrence about the ozone hole thesis—said I don't really have so much a thesis as a lot of information aiming in the same direction—whatever that means. Suggested I look at what I've found already and then back up to see what question it answers—that will probably point to my thesis.

◆ WRITING 4

Keep a research log for the duration of one research project. Write in it as often as you think or research about your subject. When your project is finished, review your log and assess how it helped you and determine whether you'll keep one for your next project.

A RESEARCH PLAN

Research writing benefits from the multistage process of planning, composing, revising, and editing. In research writing, however, managing information and incorporating sources present special problems. The steps outlined below should serve you well in writing a research paper.

1. **Make a schedule.**   After developing some sense of the range and amount of information available, write out a schedule of when you will do what in either your research

log or daily calendar. For example, block out specific time to begin an Internet search. Write in a day for a first library visit. Arrange interview appointments well in advance, with time to reschedule in case a meeting has to be postponed. And allow enough time not only for writing but for revising and editing.

2. **Include primary and secondary sources.** To conduct any kind of research, you need to identify appropriate sources of information, consult and evaluate these sources, and take good notes recording the information you collect. You also need to understand how each source works as evidence.

Primary sources consist of original documents and accounts by participants or eyewitnesses, as opposed to descriptions or interpretations by other researchers. **Secondary sources** are articles, books, chapters, Web pages, and people whose information is obtained from other sources rather than first-hand experience, who have their own opinions about your research subject.

For example, if you were exploring the development of a novelist's style, primary sources would include the novels themselves, as well as, for example, the novelist's manuscripts and correspondence or contemporary interviewer's account of the novelist's views on writing. Other people's reviews and critical interpretations of the novels would be secondary sources. If you were researching the Ben and Jerry's Ice Cream Company, plant visits, employee interviews, and published financial documents would be primary sources from which to shape your own opinions, while articles *about* the company by journalists would be secondary sources.

What constitutes a primary source will differ according to the field and your research question. For example, the novel *Moby Dick* is a primary source if you are studying it as literature. However, information in *Moby Dick* is a secondary source if you are investigating nineteenth-century whaling and referring to its descriptions of harpooning.

Most research essays use both primary and secondary sources. Primary sources ground the essay in first-hand knowledge and verifiable facts; secondary sources supply the authoritative context for your discussion and provide support for your own interpretation or argument. Most research essays are based on library and Internet sources. However, some of the most interesting research essays are also based on **field research**, which derives from site visits and firsthand interviews with people who have expert knowledge of your subject. In other words, you conduct field research simply by going places, observing carefully, and reporting what you find.

◆ WRITING 5

On one page of your research log, design a research plan that includes library, Internet, and field investigations. In this plan, list sources you have already found as well as those you hope to find.

3. **Chose your approach.** Written research can be reported in one of two distinctly different ways: **thesis first** as in conventional academic papers, or **delayed thesis** as in journalism and popular nonfiction. Academic research papers usually are written *thesis first,* where the writer reports the answer to the research question early in the paper and substantiates the answer in the balance of the paper. Such papers written in the sciences and social sciences commonly begin with a paragraph-length abstract that summarizes the findings of the whole paper before the reader even reads the paper. The purpose of this form is to present information in the most rapid and economical way possible in order to be most useful to subsequent researchers.

A clear thesis-driven paper not only helps readers quickly understand what your research turned up, it also helps you, the writer, organize your thoughts and energies when writing. To write your thesis-first paper in academic style, you might address the following questions:

- *Is it interesting?* An informational thesis should answer a question that is worth asking: *Why is the cartoon show, The Smurfs,* thought to be communist propaganda? A persuasive thesis should take a position on a debatable issue and include a proposal for change: *Mountain bikes should be allowed on wilderness trails.*
- *Is it precise and specific?* Instead of arguing in favor of less pollution in the lake, explain how to stop the zebra mussel infestation.
- *Is it manageable?* Try to split the difference between having too much information and not enough.
- *Does it adequately reflect my research and the expected shape of my paper?* Your thesis should state the major point of your paper.

(To read a thesis-first academic paper, read Andrew Turner's "The Two Freedoms of Henry David Thoreau," Chapter 30.)

In contrast to academic papers, research writing in popular nonfiction such as you find in the newspaper feature articles and *The New Yorker* magazine is usually presented with a *delayed thesis,* so that readers follow along with the writer on his or her search for an answer. (Sometimes, in fact, such a paper might end with more questions than a specific answer.) While it takes longer for readers to find the results of the research, the paper is usually more exciting to read as readers become progressively more curious about the answer to the question which began the paper but won't be revealed until the end.

To write your research in the style of popular nonfiction, consider asking the following questions in your paper:

- Where did I look first to answer my question? What did I find out? What did I not find out?

- When I checked the World Wide Web, how many sources did I find? How many useful sources did I find? What made a source useful? What didn't I find?
- What places did I visit physically? What did each look like? What did I find out there? What was missing?
- What person or people did I talk to? Who granted me an interview? When, where? What did each person look like? What did the setting look like? What did I learn there? What other leads did I find?
- What further questions have occurred as I've tried to answer the first question?
- When did I turn to the library? Where did I look—books, periodicals, data bases, other sources? How many of what kind did I find? How many did I read? What did I learn?
- Where and when did one source contradict another? How did I decide which to believe?
- How did I conclude my search? How satisfied am I now? Did I find one answer to my question? More than one answer? No answer?
- What related questions would I pursue, had I more time? Another life?

(For an academic paper with a delayed thesis approach, read see Katie Moll's "The Smurfs as Communist Propaganda" at the end of Chapter 10.)

4. **Revise, revise, revise.**   When drafting, you must follow your strongest research interests and try to answer the question you most care about. However, sometimes what began as informational research may become argument as the process of drafting the paper tips your original neutrality one way or another. Or a research investigation that starts out to prove a thesis may, as you draft, become a more neutral, informative paper of various perspectives, especially when multiple causes or complications surface in what had seemed a straightforward case.

Be ready to spend a great deal of time revising your draft, adding new research information, and incorporating sources smoothly into your prose. Such work takes a great deal of thought, and you'll want to revise your paper several times. (Consult Part Three for helpful strategies on revising your draft.)

5. **Edit and proofread.**   Editing a research paper requires extra time. Not only should you check your own writing, but you should also pay special attention to where and how you use sources (see Chapter 27) and use the correct documentation style (Research References 1 and 2). The editing stage is also a good time to assess your use of quotations, paraphrase, and summary to make sure you have not misquoted or used a source without crediting it.

◆ SUGGESTIONS FOR WRITING AND RESEARCH

Individual

1. Select a research topic that interests you and write an exploratory draft about it. First, write out everything you already know about the topic. Second, write out everything you want to know about the topic. Third, identify experts you can contact. Finally, make a list of questions you need answered. Plan to put this paper through a process that includes not only planning, drafting, revising, and editing but locating, evaluating, and using sources.

2. Keeping in mind the research topic you developed in assignment 1, visit the library and conduct a search of available resources. What do you find? Where do you find it? Show your questions to a reference librarian and ask what additional electronic databases he or she would suggest. Finally, don't forget the Internet, an ever-expanding source of information on virtually any topic you can think of.

3. After completing assignments 1 and 2, find a person who knows something about your topic and ask him or her for leads about doing further research: Who else would this person recommend you speak with? What books or articles would he or she recommend? What's the first thing this expert would do to find out information? Finally, look for a "virtual" person, someone available through an e-mail listserv or on the Internet with whom you might chat to expand your knowledge.

Collaborative

1. Join with a classmate or classmates to write a collaborative research essay. Develop plans for dividing tasks among members of the group.

2. After completing a collaborative research essay, write a short report in which you explain the collaborative strategies your group used and evaluate their usefulness.

CHAPTER TWENTY-FOUR

Conducting Library Research

I'm beginning to understand the importance of feeling safe in order to be creative and productive. Here, in the library, I feel secure, protected from real violence, and isolated from everyday distractions. There are just enough people for security's sake, but not so many that I feel crowded. And besides, I'm surrounded by all these books, all these great minds who dwell in this hallowed space! I am comfortable, safe, and beginning to get an idea for my paper.

JUDITH

What is it like today, researching in a modern college library? When our first-year students finished a major research project, we asked them to describe their library research experience, and here are some of their comments:

> *Frances:* "I could find all the library sources from just one computer search instead of looking one place for books, another for periodicals, and still another for films and CDs. It was awesome!"

> *David:* "The quality of my research was much better when I went to the library . . . the sources were more informative and more trustworthy."

> *Elena:* "Researching in the library puts you in a scholarly mood—you look harder and goof off less."

> *Tammy:* "The library lady helped me when I was stuck. When you research at the library, you never feel alone."

Some topics might favor Internet research while other topics might favor local field research. But the most comprehensive collection of *reliable* information for college research assignments remains the library. Unlike information from the Internet and field, library sources are screened by experts and critics before being catalogued and shelved. Just because it's cataloged, of course, doesn't certify it's accurate, true, or the last word, but expert screening increases the odds that the information is trustworthy. In addition, the reference librarian is on your team and can usually guide you to the right places.

LEARNING YOUR LIBRARY

To learn about the library, go there, walk slowly through it, read the signs, poke your nose into nooks and crannies, and browse through a few books or magazines. If there is an introductory video, pause to see it. If there is a self-paced or guided tour, take it. Read informational handouts and pamphlets. By the time you leave, know how to find the following:

The **online catalog**, a computerize database that tells you which books and other sources your library owns and where they are located.

The **stacks**, where books and periodicals are stored.

The **circulation desk**, where you check out and reserve books and get information on procedures and resources.

The **periodical room**, which houses current issues of magazines, journals, and newspapers.

The **reference room**, which contains general reference works, such as dictionaries and encyclopedias, along with guides and indexes to more specific sources information.

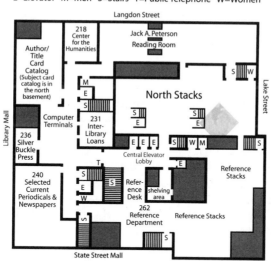

Floor 2 Memorial Library
E=Elevator M=Men S=Stairs T=Public Telephone W=Women

To take full advantage of library resources, keep the following suggestions in mind:

- *Visit early and often.*   As soon as you receive a research assignment, visit the library to find out what resources are available for your project. Even if your initial research indicates a wealth of material, you may not be able to find everything the first time, as a book may be checked out, or your library may not subscribe to a certain periodical, or there are still resources you haven't learned about.

- *Take notes.*   Even in this computerized world it helps to bring index cards to the library—3 × 5 cards for bibliographical information and 4 × 6 cards for

notes—from your first visit on. Good substitutes, of course, include your laptop computer or research log notebook.

- *Check general sources first.*   Look at dictionaries, encyclopedias, atlases, and
yearbooks for background information about your topic. An hour spent with
these general sources will give you a quick overview of the scope and range of
your topic and will lead you to more specific information.
- *Ask for help.*   Talk to librarians. At first you might show them your assignment
and describe your topic and your research plans; later you might ask them for
help in finding a particular source or ask whether they know of any sources
that you have not checked yet. Librarians are professional information experts,
so use them.

FINDING INFORMATION

Most of the information you need to find will be contained in reference books, in other
books, and in periodicals (journals, magazines, and newspapers). To locate these sources,
you'll need a variety of tools including the *online catalog* and *databases,* as well as *periodical
indexes.* To use these resources efficiently, use the following four-step process:

1. Consult *general reference works* to gain background information and basic facts.
2. Consult *specialized reference works* to find relevant articles on all topics.
3. Consult the *online catalog* to identify library books on your topic.
4. Consult *other sources* as needed.

Consult General Reference Works

Use **databases** (also called indexes) at your college or university library to locate general reference sources. Databases are guides to the material published within works, sometimes
within books but more often within periodicals (magazines, journals, newspapers), which
are published at set periods throughout the year. They focus on particular areas of interest,
and their information is more current than that found in books. Because so many periodical issues are published each year and because every issue can contain dozens of articles on
various topics, using a periodical index or database is essential to finding the article you need.
Each index or database covers a particular group of periodicals. Make sure that the index
you select contains the journals, magazines, and newspapers that you want to use as sources.

General reference works provide background information and basic facts about a topic.
The summaries, overviews, and definitions in these sources can help you decide whether to
pursue a topic further and where to turn next for information. The information in these
sources is necessarily general and will not be sufficient by itself as the basis for most research
projects—in fact, general reference works are not strong sources to cite in research papers.

Many indexes, called **full-text databases,** allow you to print out the full text of an article you find, thus simplifying your search process. But beware: Some texts are abbreviated
when they are stored on the computer, and others omit accompanying information such as
sidebars or graphics. In some cases, you may have to pay to retrieve the full text of an article. If an article looks important but is not retrievable in full text form, be sure seek out the
periodical (paper or electronic version), and read the article.

Whichever search tool you use, there is nothing magic about information transferred over a computer. You will need the same critical skills you use to evaluate printed materials, although the clues may be harder to understand when you find documents online. Is the author identified? Is that person a professional in the field or an interested amateur? What are his or her biases likely to be? Does the document you have located represent an individual's opinion or peer-reviewed research?

Following are some of the most useful general reference works to provide context and background information for research projects:

Almanacs and yearbooks. Almanacs and yearbooks provide up-to-date information, including many statistics, on politics, agriculture, economics, and population. See especially *Facts on File: News Digest* (1940–present), an index to current events reported in newspapers worldwide. (Also CD-ROM, 1980–present) and *World Almanac and Book of Facts* (1868–present), which reviews important events of the past year as well as data on a wide variety of topics, including sports, government, science, business, and education.

Atlases. Atlases such as the *Hammond Atlas of the World,* the *National Geographic Atlas of the World,* and the *Times Atlas of the World* can help you identify places anywhere in the world and provide information on population, climate, and industry.

Biographical dictionaries. Biographical dictionaries contain information on people who have made some mark on history in many different fields. Consult the following: *Contemporary Authors* (1962–present), containing short biographies of authors who have published during the year; *Current Biography* (1940–present), containing articles and photographs of people in the news; and *Who's Who in America* (1899–present), the standard biographical reference for living Americans.

Dictionaries. Dictionaries contain definitions and histories of words along with information on their correct usage.

Encyclopedias. Encyclopedias provide elementary information, explanations, and definitions of virtually every topic, concept, country, institution, historical person or movement, and cultural artifact imaginable. One-volume works such as the *Random House Encyclopedia* and *The Columbia Encyclopedia* give brief overviews. Larger works such as *Collier's Encyclopedia* (24 volumes) and the *New Encyclopedia Britannica* (32 volumes, also online) contain more detailed information.

The best way to locate and search for general reference works is to use the **databases** available online at most university libraries. Access is usually restricted, so check to see which of the following databases your university subscribes to:

Academic Search Premier. Indexes over 3,400 scholarly publications, including humanities, sciences, social sciences, education, engineering, languages, and literature in full-text access.

ArticleFirst. Indexes over 15,000 journals in business, humanities, medicine, science, and social science.

Expanded Academic ASAP. Indexes over 2,000 periodical in the arts, humanities, sciences, and social sciences, and many newspapers.

Factiva. Full-text access to major newspapers, business journals, and stock market reports.

LexusNexus Academic. Indexes a wide range of magazines, newspapers, and government documents, all available full-text.

◆ WRITING 1

Look up background information on your research topic, using at least three databases and three general reference works described in this section.

Consult Specialized Reference Works

Also plan to use university online **databases** to search for *specialized reference works* that contain detailed and technical information in a particular field or discipline. They often contain articles by well-known authorities and sometimes have bibliographies and cross-references that can lead to other sources. Access is usually restricted, so check to see which databases your university subscribes to.

A major online system commonly found in college libraries is *Dialog,* which offers more than 400 specialized databases. Some of the most commonly used databases (content identified by title) within *Dialog* include, Arts and Humanities Search (1980–present), ERIC (Educational Resources Information Center, 1966–present), MLA International Bibliography (1963–present); PsycINFO (1967–present), Scisearch (1974–present), and Social Scisearch (1972–present).

To use *Dialog,* you usually need the assistance of a reference librarian. The library is charged a fee for each search, calculated according to the time spent and the number of entries retrieved. Some libraries have the person requesting the search pay the fee; others limit the time allotted for each search. Be sure to ask what your library's policy is.

Consult the Online Catalog

All catalogs provide the same basic information. They list items by author, title, and subject; describe their physical format and content; and tell where in the library to find them. Consult the online catalog to find all books, journals, newspapers, and audiovisual material the library owns. Most online catalogs can be accessed from locations outside the library.

Plan to use the library catalog in several ways. If you already know the title of a work, the catalog confirms your library owns it and tells where it's located. You can also browse the catalog for works relevant to your topic. And you can also search the online catalogs of other libraries via the World Wide Web. Many libraries can obtain a work owned by another library through an interlibrary loan, a process that may take anywhere from a few days to a few weeks.

Note: You will not find individual journal articles listed in the catalog; to find those you will need to consult the periodical indexes.

Online catalog systems vary slightly from library to library, though all systems follow the same general principles. Most online catalogs allow you to search with partial

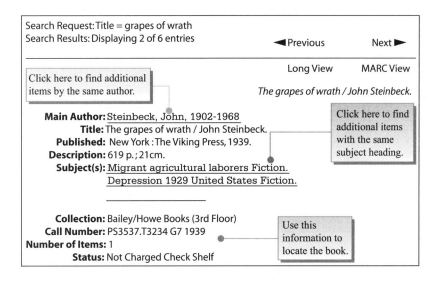

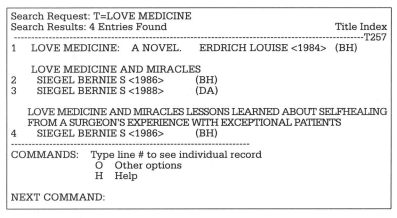

Results of a title search in an online catalog

information. For example, if you know that the title of a novel begins with the words *Love Medicine* but you can't remember the rest of it, you can ask the catalog computer to search for the title *Love Medicine*. It will present you with a list of all works that begin with those words.

Most online catalogs also allow you to perform keyword searches, allowing the computer to search different parts of the record at once. To perform a keyword search, use the words you've identified as describing your topic, linked by *and* or *or* as appropriate. For example, if you're trying to research fictional accounts of Dakota Indians, you can search for *"Dakota Indians" and "fiction."* The computer will present you with a list of works that fit that description.

```
Search Request: T=LOVE MEDICINE
BOOK - Record 1 of 5 Entries Found                          Long View
------------------------------Screen-1-of-1-------------------------------------------T259
Author:          Erdrich, Louise.
Title:           Love medicine : a novel
Edition:         1st ed.
Published:       New York : Holt, Rinehart, and Winston, c1984.
Description:     viii, 275 p. ; 22cm.
Subjects(LC):    Indians of North America--North Dakota--Fiction.
-------------------------------------------------------------------------------------
   LOCATION;            CALL NUMBER             STATUS
1 Halley Stacks         PS3555.R42 L6 1984      Not checked out

   COMMANDS:     P  Previous screen
                 O  Other options
                 H  Help

NEXT COMMAND:
```

Full information on a book in an online catalog

How to Use Call Numbers

To find books your library owns, use the book's call number to locate it in the stacks. Most academic libraries use the Library of Congress system, whose call numbers begin with letters. Some libraries still use the older Dewey Decimal system, whose call numbers consist entirely of numbers. In either case, the first letters or numbers indicate the general subject area. Because libraries shelve all books for a general subject area together, this portion of the call number tells you where in the library to find the book you want. Be sure to copy a book's call number exactly as it appears in the catalog. When you have located your book in the stacks, look at other books in the areas to see if any of those might also be useful.

Other Sources of Information

Government documents. The U.S. government publishes numerous reports, pamphlets, catalogs, and newsletters on most issues of national concern. Consult the *Monthly Catalogue of United States Government Publications* and the *United States Government Publications Index,* both available electronically.

Nonprint media. Records, CDs, audiocassettes, videotapes, slides, photographs, and other media may also be located through the library catalog.

Pamphlets. Pamphlets and brochures published by government agencies and private organizations are generally stored in a library's vertical file. The *Vertical File Index: A Subject and Title Index to Selected Pamphlet Material* (1932/35–present) lists many of the available titles. Many are also available via the World Wide Web.

Special collections. Rare books, manuscripts, and items of local interest are commonly found in a special room or section of the library.

Maps and geographic information systems (GIS). Maps and atlases depict much more than roads and state boundaries, including information on population density, language patterns, soil types, and much more.

◆ WRITING 2

Identify three distinct kinds of information in your library's holdings (book periodical, other), locate these, and take notes on both their usefulness and the process you used to obtain each.

TAKING NOTES

Taking good notes will make the whole research process easier, enabling you to locate and remember sources and helping you use them effectively in your writing. For short research projects requiring only a few sources, it is easy to take careful notes in a research log or class notebook and refer to them as needed when writing your paper. Or you can photocopy or print out whole articles or chapters and take them home for further study. However, for any research project requiring more than a few sources, use either a card-based system or laptop computer to record and sort sources and information.

PE
1405
.U6
M55
1991

Miller, Susan, <u>Textual Carnivals</u>.
Carbondale: Southern Illinois UP, 1991.

Bibliographic card for a book using MLA documentation style

Make Bibliographic Notes

A bibliographic note identifies the source, not what's in it. When you locate a useful source, write all the information necessary to find that source again on a 3 × 5 index card or computer equivalent, using a separate "card" for each work. Do this as you find each source, even before even taking notes from the source. If you create *bibliographic notes* as you go along, then at the end you can easily arrange them in alphabetical order to prepare the reference list required at the end of formal academic papers. (For more complete information on citing bibliographic sources see Research References 1 and 2.)

Make Information Notes

Make paper or electronic notes to record the relevant information found in your sources. To write a research essay, you'll work from these note cards, so be sure they contain all the information you need from every source you intend to use. Also try to focus them on your research question, so that their relevance is clear when you read them later. If using paper cards, use 4 × 6 index cards for information and 3 × 5 for bibliographic sources. These different sizes will also help keep the two sets separate. A typical note card should contain only one piece of information or one idea to allow you to arrange and rearrange the information in different ways as you write. At the top of each note card, identify the source through brief bibliographic identification (author and title), and note the page numbers on which the information appears. Personal notes, including ideas for possible use of the information or cross-references to other information, should be clearly distinguished from material that comes from the source; they might be put at the bottom in parentheses.

Lewis, <u>Green Delusions</u>, p. 230
Reasons for overpopulation in poor countries

Some experts believe that birth rates are linked to the "economic value" of children to their parents. Poor countries have higher birth rates because parents there rely on children to work for the family and to take care of them in old age. The more children, particularly sons, the better off the family is financially. In wealthier countries parents have fewer children because they cost more in terms of education and they contribute less.

(Based on Caldwell and Cain—check these further?)

Note card containing a paraphrase

Quote, Paraphrase, or Summarize as Needed

When recording information, you must take steps to avoid **plagiarism** (see Chapter 27). Do this by making distinctions among quoting directly, paraphrasing, and summarizing. A **direct quotation** is an exact duplication of the author's words in the original source. Put quotation marks around direct quotations on your note cards so that you will know later that these words are the author's, not yours. A **paraphrase** is a restatement of the author's words in your own words. Paraphrase to simplify or clarify the original author's point. A paraphrase must restate the original facts or ideas fully and correctly. A **summary** is a brief condensation or distillation of the main point of the original source. Like a paraphrase, a summary should be in your own words, and all facts and ideas should be accurately represented. (See Chapter 27 for more information quotes, paraphrases, and summaries.)

The major advantage of copying exact *quotations* is that it allows you to decide later, while writing the paper, whether to include a quotation or to paraphrase or summarize. In general, copy direct quotations only when the author's words are particularly lively or persuasive. Photocopying machines and computer printers make it easy to collect direct quo-

---

INFORMATION TO BE RECORDED ON BIBLIOGRAPHIC CARDS

For Books

1. Call number or other location information
2. Full name(s) of author(s)
3. Full title and subtitle
4. Edition or volume number
5. Editor or translator
6. Place of publication
7. Publisher and date of publication
8. Inclusive page numbers for relevant sections in longer works

For Periodicals

1. Full name(s) of author(s)
2. Full title and subtitle of articles
3. Periodical title
4. Periodical volume and number
5. Periodical date
6. Inclusive page numbers of article
7. Library call number or other location information

---

tations, but be sure to highlight the pertinent material or make notes to yourself on the copy so you can remember later what you wanted to quote and why. For ease of organizing notes, many researchers cut out the pertinent quotation and paste it to a note card.

A good *paraphrase* can help clarify a difficult passage by simplifying complex sentence structure and vocabulary into language with which you are more comfortable. Be careful not to distort the author's ideas. Use paraphrases when you need to record details but not exact words.

Because a *summary* boils a source down to its essentials, it is particularly useful when specific details in the source are unimportant or irrelevant to your research question. You may often find that you can summarize several paragraphs or even an entire article or chapter in just a few sentences without losing any useful information. It is a good idea to note when a particular card contains a summary so you'll remember later that it leaves out detailed supporting information.

◆ WRITING 3

Describe the most important, useful, or surprising thing you have learned about the library since exploring it as part of your research project. Share your discovery with classmates, and listen to theirs. Are you comfortable in the library? Why or why not? How does technology help or hinder the research process? Explain in an online journal entry and share this with the class.

CRITICAL USE TEST FOR TEXTUAL SOURCES

Ask the following questions of each source you read before deciding to use it.

- Subject. Is the subject *directly related* to my research question? Does it provide information that supports my view? Does it provide helpful context or background information? Does it contain quotations or facts that I will want to quote in my paper?
- Author. What do I really know about the author's reputation? Does the book or periodical provide any biographical information? Is this author cited by other sources? Am I aware of any biases that might limit the author's credibility?
- Date. When was this source published? Is it sufficiently up to date to suit my purpose? Does it represent common, widely accepted views, or does it introduce a new perspective or discovery?
- Publisher. Who published this source? Is it a major publisher, a university press, or a scholarly organization that would subject material to a rigorous review procedure?
- Counterauthority. Does the source address or present counterarguments on issues I intend to discuss ? Each point of view is essential for examining an issue completely.

EVALUATING LIBRARY SOURCES

Many of the books, periodicals, and documents in special collections have been recommended for library acquisition by scholars and librarians with special expertise in each of the many subject areas the library catalogs. While the Internet now provides additional and more easily accessed sources on every imaginable topic, these sources are not subject to the same screening and cataloging process as library sources and need additional critical appraisal. Regardless of origin, all information sources need to be questioned by your critical intelligence for credibility and usefulness. Though the library remains the main repository of knowledge on a college campus, you cannot use even library sources without subjecting each source to careful scrutiny. Two of the main reasons for questioning a source found in the library have to do with *time* (when was it judged true?) and *perspective* (who said it was true and for what reason?).

Locate date. Most library documents, especially those created since the advent of copyright laws at the end of the nineteenth century, include their date of publication on or inside the cover of the document itself, in most cases a fact that you can rely on. In some cases, such as articles first published in one place then reprinted in another, you may have to dig harder for the original date, but if you check the permissions page, you'll find it.

However, one of the main reasons library sources lose reliability, and hence credibility, is the simple passage of time. Sources become outdated and, therefore, unreliable. For example, compare any fifty-year-old atlas or encyclopedia entry about African, Asian, or European nations with the latest edition of the same work, and you'll find changes so striking as to make the older source completely outdated. Geographical, political, or statistical information valid in 1955 has inevitably changed by 2005—in many cases, radically so. Pay attention to the date a source was created, and reflect on what may have happened since then.

At the same time, dated information may still be highly useful—which is why old texts remain in the library. Once you know the source date, you can decide whether or not it will still help your paper. If you are studying change over time, for example, old statistical information would be useful baseline data to demonstrate what has changed since. But if you are studying current culture, the dated information may actually be misleading. In other words, when evaluating whether a dated source serves your purpose, know what that purpose is.

Identify perspective. The second critical question to ask of any source is what point of view or perspective it represents. *Who* created the source and for *what purpose?* This second critical question is more difficult to answer quickly because the author's point of view is seldom seldom identified or summarized on the source itself. And when it is, this information, being a creation of the author, cannot always be believed.

To trust a source, you need to learn to analyze its assumptions, evidence, biases, and reasoning—which together constitute the author's perspective. In essence, you need to ask:

- What is this writer's purpose—scholarly analysis, political advocacy, entertainment, or something else?
- Will a quick perusal of the Introduction or first chapter reveal what the writer assumes about the subject or audience?
- Can you tell which statements are facts, which are inferences drawn from facts, and which are strictly matters of opinion?
- Does a first reading of the evidence persuade you?
- Is the logic of the position apparent and/or credible?
- Are there relevant points the writer *doesn't* mention?
- Do the answers to these questions make you more or less willing to accept the author's conclusions?

Although at first it may seem daunting or even futile to try to answer all these questions about every source, have patience and give the research process the time it needs. At the beginning of a research project, when you're still trying to gain context and overview and you've looked at only one source, it's difficult to recognize an author's purpose and viewpoint. However, as you read further and begin to compare one source to another, differences will emerge, especially if you read extensively and take notes. The more differences you note, the more critically aware you become and the more you know why, how, and where a source might help you. *Remember, the more you learn, the more you learn.* Will it be useful?

Critically review. To review a library source with a critical eye, reread Chapter 2 and plan to ask both first and second questions of the text (see pp. 13–14). In short, the answers to first questions are generally factual, the result of probing the text (identifying the title, table of contents, chapter headings, index, and so on). The answers to second questions are more inferential, the result of analyzing the assertions, evidence, and language of the text (identifying the perspective of author and sources).To gain a larger perspective on an especially interesting source, ask the following questions:

- *Publication date.*   What is the significance of the publication date for your purposes? Consult the *Book Review Index* or *Book Review Digest* to locate reviews of the book sources at the time of publication to help you evaluate their credibility. For articles in general-interest magazines and scholarly or professional journals, you can often find useful commentary in letters to the editor of subsequent issues.
- *Author perspective.*   In each source, what are the author's point of view and purpose? Are the claims made in the text reasonable? Is the evidence based on

fact, inference, or opinion? Is the language careful or careless, neutral or biased, calm or strident? Does the author take other perspectives into account?

- *External reviews.*   Does the information in one source support or contradict that in other sources? Do a subject search of the author in the library catalog, in a general periodical index, or on the World Wide Web to find out how the author is viewed by other experts and how your source fits in with the author's other works.

◆ SUGGESTIONS FOR LIBRARY RESEARCH PROJECTS

Individual

Find any text applicable to your current research that advocates a position or makes an argument. Look at the *copyright date*. Read the *Introduction*. Review the *Table of Contents*. Skim the *first chapter*. What can you infer about the author's purpose, assumptions, and point of view? How persuasive is the argument? Finally, check your own analysis against a source review you find in *Book Review Digest* or on the Internet.

Collaborative

Your school experience of a dozen or more years already tells you that library research can find information about an unlimited number of topics. For the sake of exercise, see what type of library information you can locate to supplement the research you conducted at the end of Chapter 23, either individually or as a collaborative project.

CHAPTER TWENTY-FIVE

Conducting Internet Research

The idea of research has really changed for me since I've been using my computer for Web searches. Finding sources and adding new information to a paper seems to be almost a natural part of writing papers and not such a big deal, not something separate from the writing itself.

AMY

The Internet provides a wide variety of information unavailable either in the library or in the field. Many Web sites now provide both primary and secondary research sources. Much of the delight—as well as the difficulty—of the Internet stems from the fact that no single agency or company is responsible for organizing or policing it. No one knows exactly what is on it, nor is there a central card catalog or index showing what's available, from whom, or where it's located. While even a casual query with a good descriptive key word on Google or Yahoo! will get you many sources of information, only some will prove useful; the vast majority will prove to be either too commercial, superficial, or of questionable authenticity. Because of the uneven and unscreened nature of Internet information, it's important that for academic research projects you also consult the library and, where appropriate, the field for further information.

To use the Internet for academic research projects, treat the searches and sources you find there with the same formal seriousness you do with library sources—which means keeping careful records of where you search, how you search, and what you find. Following are suggestions for academic researching on the Internet.

USING MULTIPLE SEARCH ENGINES

While it's especially easy to search the most popular search engines, Yahoo! and Google, with descriptive words and locate an extensive list of potential sources, be aware that even if you use the same key words, each of these engines will locate different material organized in different ways. For example, the Yahoo! page shows nearly 5,000,000 sites, with seven of the nine sites being commercial manufacturers. In contrast, the Google site lists about 2,000,000 sites, with each of the first eight sites listing a different category of mountain bike information (products, magazines, manufacturers, dealers, racing). Only one common URL showed up in the first page listing.

Comparing these two pages tells you three important things: First, each search engine will, in fact, turn up far *more information* than you could possibly look at—millions of sites. Second, each will turn up *different information*. And third, each *organizes information* differently—though these differences are disappearing. Now, even Yahoo!, once known for cataloguing information by topic in human-created directories library style (as *Britannica,* and *LookSmart* continue to do), now includes crawler-based technology similar to Google, Alta Vista, Hotbot, Lycos, and Teoma, which automatically compile listings based on key word

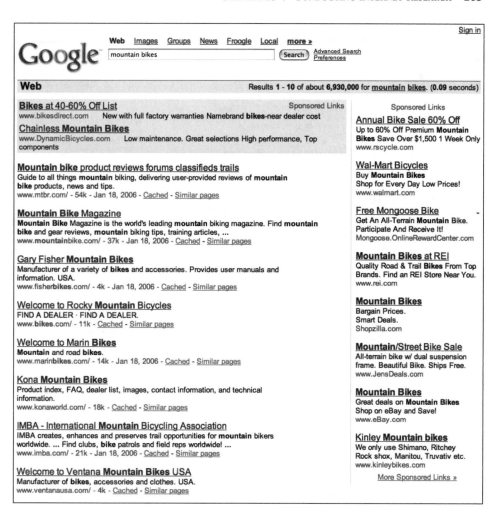

frequency. To learn more about search engine operation, ratings, and news, visit the user-friendly Web site *Search Engine Watch* <www.searchenginewatch.com>.

NARROWING YOUR WEB SEARCH

It's obvious that typing in key words on popular search engines such as Google and Yahoo! gets you both more information than you can use and not enough that's specifically useful. Following are three simple tips from Danny Sullivan of *Search Engine Watch* to get the most useful information in the shortest amount of time from virtually any search engine—*add, subtract,* and *multiply:*

- *Add* as many key terms as you can think of to limit the number of sites to those with the most useful information. For example, to find more particular information about *mountain bikes,* add further words that describe your interest—*on wilderness trails in New York,* for instance—and connect these key words with

Sign in

Google

Web   Images   Groups   News   Froogle   Local   **more »**

mountain bikes +wilderness trails +New York –racing   [Search]   Advanced Search   Preferences

Web   Results **1 - 10** of about **215,000** for mountain bikes +wilderness trails +New York -racing. (0.12 seconds)

IMBA - International **Mountain** Bicycling Association
IMBA creates, enhances and preserves **trail** opportunities for **mountain** bikers ... Nevada,
New Hampshire, **New** Jersey, **New** Mexico, **New York**, North Carolina ...
www.imba.com/ - 21k - Jan 18, 2006 - Cached - Similar pages

GORP - Adirondack Forest Preserve - Nordic Skiing in **New York**
This **wilderness** area contains a network of **trails** that connect 22 small and ... For complete
information, refer to "Horse **Trails** in **New York** State" and ...
gorp.away.com/gorp/location/ny/ski_adir.htm - 120k - Cached - Similar pages

Western **New York Mountain** Bicycling Association :: View topic ...
Western **New York Mountain** Bicycling Association Forum Index, Western **New York**
Mountain ... Author, Discussion on **trails** conditions or **Wilderness** designation ...
www.wnymba.org/viewtopic.php?t=1548 - 37k - Cached - Similar pages

Western **New York Mountain** Bicycling Association :: **Trail** Guide
Western **New York Mountain** Bicycling Association Forum Index ... Designated **mountain**
bike trails available **Trails** open to hiking Designated equestrian **trails** ...
www.wnymba.org/trails.php?trail=6 - 26k - Cached - Similar pages

Mountain Bike Trails New York : Free NY recreational **bike** ride ...
Bikekinetix is a **mountain bike trails** guide to **bike** rides in **New York** that provide a scenic,
wilderness, historical or romantic experience for both the ...
www.bikekinetix.com/main_ny.php - 29k - Cached - Similar pages

NYNJTC: Where to Ride Your **Mountain Bike**
The **New York-New** Jersey **Trail** Conference maintains over 1600 miles of **trails** in ...
Mountain Bike Issues. **Trail** Use Policy NY-NJ **Trail** Conference; ATC **Trail** ...
www.nynjtc.org/trails/bikes.html - 16k - Cached - Similar pages

Adventure Camp - 13 Day Sessions
New England **Mountain Bike** Ages 12-14 | **New** England. Master your **trail** riding skills on ...
Mountains of **New York** State on this 8-day **wilderness** adventure. ...
www.bu.edu/outdoor/adventure/13_day/ - 34k - Jan 19, 2006 - Cached - Similar pages

Trail results for Lake Placid **New York**
Peninsula **Trails** ... an excellent **mountain bike** warm-up if you are ... **New York Trails**; Best
Trails of **New York**; Best **Mountain** Biking Destinations; Best . ...
www.trails.com/AdvancedFind. asp?Keyword=Lake+Placid&state=NY - 45k -
Cached - Similar pages

Sponsored Links

WTB Cycling Components
Save on WTB (**Wilderness** Trail
Bikes) gear at JensonUSA.com
www.JensonUSA.com

Bikes at 40-60% Off List
New with full factory warranties
Namebrand **bikes**-near dealer cost
www.bikesdirect.com

Mountain Bikes at REI
Quality Road & Trail **Bikes** From Top
Brands. Find an REI Store Near You.
www.rei.com

NYC's favorite Bike store
Featuring Bicycles by Trek, Marin
Specialized, Dahon plus more
www.bicyclehabitat.com
New York

Trails Bikes
Quality **new** and used items.
Find **trails bikes** now!
www.ebay.com

singletracks.com
Hundreds of **mountain** bike trail
listings, discover a ride near you!
www.singletracks.com

Mountain Bikes
Find Nearby **Mountain Bikes** Here.
New York City's Local Search.
NewYorkCity.Local.Com
New York, NY

plus signs (+): *mountain bikes + wilderness trails + New York.* Samples below show
the more specific information Google now provides:

- *Subtract.*   If you wanted to look specifically at mountain bike wilderness trails in
  New York, but omit sites that included *racing,* include a minus sign (no space) next
  to the word you want to exclude: *mountain bikes + wilderness trails + New York
  – racing.* The resulting search now drops out sites such as the first one above.

- *Multiply.*   If you want to find very specific information on the Web and you know
  the title or phrase that describes this information, put quotation marks
  (" ") around those word to conduct what's called a "phrase search." Quotation
  marks placed around precise language multiply the chances of finding exactly
  what you are looking for. To reverse the above example, if we put quotation marks
  around the phrase *"mountain bike racing"* on Google, Yahoo!, Teoma, Alta Vista
  and most of the other search engines, we would find very specific information that
  might be useful in serious research (see below for an example from Google):

And, as you've no doubt already learned from you own Web searching, the Internet
is a very friendly place for trial and error experiments. In fact, my own first few tries with

the minus symbol (–) failed because I put a space after the sign which kept including *racing* in the *mountain bike* category; once I dropped the space after the sign, the term *racing* was excluded as I intended.

◆ WRITING 1

Search for a topic of special interest using three different search engines and/or directories from the list above. Compare the results and note both similarities and differences in the information each searching tool provides. Explain why, in future searches, one engine or directory *would* or *would not* provide you with adequate information.

KEEPING A RESEARCH LOG

To increase the seriousness of your Web exploration, document all aspects of your Web search—as you would library and field searches—in a chronological research notebook that itemizes the key words used, the URLs of sites visited, and the dates on which you visited these sites. I'd especially recommend an 8-1/2 × 11 inch loose-leaf notebook in which you could interleave and cross-reference useful related notes, illustrations, and printed Web pages.

PRINTING HARD COPY OF WEB PAGES

Whether in the library, computer lab, or on your own computer, get in the habit of printing hard copies of useful source pages that include each page's URL. Integrate these pages with research log notes.

BOOKMARKING FAVORITE SITES

On your own computer, you can also save especially useful locations as bookmarks or favorites to which you can easily return for additional searches—see criteria for bookmarking a site later in this chapter.

INVESTIGATING NONPROFIT SITES

To locate information on ideas, issues, statistics, and institutions with little or no commercial or political bias, search the relevant following sites:

- *Amazon.com*   <http://www.amazon.com/>: While not a nonprofit, this company lists both in-print and out-of-print book titles, including publication data, readers' reviews, and related titles.
- *Bartleby.com*   <http://www.bartleby.com>: Offers searchable literary texts including poetry, fiction, drama, and criticism.
- *Biographical dictionary*   <http://www.s9.com/biography>: Includes over 28,000 notable men and women, located by birth years, death years, positions held, professions, literary and artistic works, achievements, and other keywords.
- *Chronology of U.S. Historical Documents*   <www.law.ou.edu/hist>: Primary historical sources arranged in chronological order, maintained by the University of Oklahoma, College of Law.
- *Information Please*   <http://www.infoplease.com>: An online almanac with topics from architecture to biography to historical statistics to weather.
- *Internet Public Library*   <http://www.ipl.org/>: The University of Michigan School of Information maintains this site.
- *Invisible Web*   <www.invisible-web.com/>: A directory of academic and government search tools.
- *Learn the Net Inc.*   http://www.learnthenet.com/english/index: Web tours and training.
- *Library of Congress Online Catalog*   <http://catalog.loc.gov/>. A wealth of government-sponsored documents available.
- *RefDesk.com*   <http://www.refdesk.com/>: A site dedicated to research of all kinds.
- *Reference.com*   <http://www.reference.com>: Dictionaries, thesauri, encyclopedias, atlases, and more.

- *University of Michigan Documents Center*   <www.lib.umich.edu/govdocs>: A collection of local, regional, state, federal, and foreign government information.
- *University of Wisconsin Internet Scout*   <http://scout.wisc.edu/>: Academic resources on the Internet.
- *U.S. Census Bureau*   <http://www.census.gov>: A primary source for government demographic and economic data.

USING E-MAIL TO CONDUCT LONG-DISTANCE INTERVIEWS

Electronic mail has become an easy and accepted method of conducting interviews with authors, artists, experts, university faculty, government officials, and anyone else whose e-mail address you have access to. E-mail addresses are commonly found on personal, agency, commercial, or institutional Web sites, and are posted so that people can contact them. Many people prefer to be contacted by e-mail rather than telephone because they can respond on their own time after thinking about your request. Be sure to identify yourself, be specific about the information you request, and be polite. Also feel free to ask about other people and resources to contact.

◆ WRITING 2

Investigate a topic of your choice using any two of the nonprofit sites listed above and print out useful pages, complete with URLs. In addition, contact at least one source by e-mail and ask specific questions, Keep track of all you find in a notebook you now call a research log.

EVALUATING WEB SOURCES

The Internet contains a dizzying wealth of potential research material, but many of the sources are commercial—someone is trying to sell you something—and many sources are biased personal opinion—not necessarily by experts—because virtually anybody can post ideas on a Web site. At the same time, many other Internet sources contain first-rate and one-of-a-kind material that meets the same high standards of objectivity, fairness, and accuracy as material cataloged in a library or published in major periodicals such as *The New York Times* or *Washington Post*. In other words, the Internet is a valuable resource that you need to search with a mixture of skepticism and skill. The following guidelines will help you evaluate the usefulness of most Internet sources.

Scan site summaries. Read the one- or two-line description of each site carefully to see how closely the site matches your research needs. Key-word searches, in particular, turn up sites simply on the basis of the frequency of the the words, but do not distinguish among the multiple meanings words may have. (Once when remodeling our house, I searched the Internet for doors and found as many hits to the legendary rock band, *The Doors,* as for the kind with hinges that open and shut.) Notice, too, if the key words (which appear in bold face) are in close proximity to each other or spread throughout the entry—the closer the words, the greater likelihood it's the meaning you want. Remember, if you can identify what you are looking for by using a commonly phrase ("mountain bike racing" or "screen doors"), place quotation marks around the phrase to limit the search even further.

Identify domain names. Look next at the suffixes attached to the URL (Universal Resource Locator, the Internet address) of every Web site. The end extension, following a dot, identifies the type of organization that published the site. This extension, called a domain name, suggests the general nature of the site and will be your next indicator of what individual or organization sponsored the site:

- Sites with **.com** (commercial) and **.biz** (business) represent companies advertising their goods or services. Each will speak with a sales bias, yet many will also include at least a limited amount of information pertinent to solving problems—limited because few .com sites will make readers aware of competing products or points of view. *To use information gleaned from these sites, always check as many such sites as you can to see the full range of information available.*

- Sites with **.gov** (government) and **.mil** (military) present official information from the governmental sponsoring agencies that is authentic, in that a government or military agency stands behind it, but may also include the political bias of the specific agency or individual who created the site. *To use information gleaned from these sites, check to see what nongovernmental sites (.net, .org, .edu) have to say about the same subject.*

- Sites with **.org** (nonprofit organization) represent organizations and media outlets that are more likely marketing ideas instead of products. Compare, for example, nonprofit sites by *Pro-Choice America* <www.naral.org/> versus the *National Right to Life* site <www.nrlc.org> to see nonprofit groups with radically differing points of view on the subject of abortion. *To use information gleaned from these sites, it's helpful to check more than one site with the same bias as well as consult sites with an opposing point of view.*

- Sites with.**edu** (education) indicate school, college, or university sites, and thus come with high initial credibility. At the same time, such sites may be created for many reasons (sharing research, marketing programs) and by many authors (professors, students, administrators, PR departments), so that credibility should not be automatic. *To use information gleaned from these sites, also gather comparative information from other sites.*

- Sites with **.name** or a tilde (~) in the URL present one person's point of view. *To use information gleaned from these sites, learn as much as you can about the individual whose view are represented, so it pays to do a Google or Yahoo! search of the site's author as well as check other subject sites.*

- Sites with **.museum** (museum), **.net** (networks and news agencies), and **.inf** present information that might be expected to be objective in nature. At the same time, these domain names are not used as often as the other names discussed here. *To use information gleaned from these sites, follow the general rule of looking for source information in as many sites as possible.*

In the event you want to identify the ownership of a domain name—who actually paid to have this site created—journalist Alan Hayakawa suggests using an ownership locator called *WHOIS*. Log onto Network Solutions, <http://www.netsol. com>, and click on the link called *WHOIS*. Enter only the second-level and top-level domain name (google.com, not <www.google.com>), and *WHOIS* returns the owner's name, address, and contact information (often including an e-mail address).

Question each Web site. As in all research sources where more than one perspective, opinion, or solution is available, at some point you need to decide which sources are most useful—credible, reliable, objective, accurate, timely. Perhaps the best way to test a questionable Internet source is to query it with **reporter's questions** (*who, what, when, where, why*) and see if it remains useful. If you are able to answer most of the following questions about a source positively, you should be able to use it in your research writing.

WHO IS THE AUTHOR OF THE SITE?

- Is a site author identified? (*It's simple: Anonymous sources are less credible.*)
- Is the author authoritative, by virtue of credentials, experience, or displayed knowledge?
- Does the author cite credentials? (*What kind? Where from?*)
- Does the author speak in an official capacity for an organization, institution, or government agency? (*Check for neutral and objective language vs. individual opinion and first-person pronouns.*)
- If no individual is named, is there a sponsoring organization ? (*What can you find out about the organization by searching the Web or library?*)
- Does the site provide a link to the organization's or author's home page? (*A good sign, check it out.*)
- Is there a way to contact the author or organization, by mail, telephone, or e-mail? (*If so, consider an e-mail query.*)
- If you cannot identify the author or sponsor of the site, how does that affect your estimate of its credibility? How will it affect your readers?

WHAT IDEAS OR INFORMATION IS PRESENTED?

- Do you understand the ideas and the terms? (*If not, pause here for homework or drop the site.*)
- Can you summarize the central ideas or claims in your own words? (*Very useful now as well as when you write.*)
- Would you judge the information to be substantial or superficial? (*How do you know? Look for details, facts, statistics vs. absence of clichés and limited generalities.*)
- Is information documented by reliable citations? (*The more known or respected the publication sources, the higher the credibility.*)
- Does the site contain facts, inference, analysis, opinion, speculation? (*If the author distinguishes among these types of information, points are gained; if not, points are lost.*)
- Is the information balanced or one-sided? Are other points of view respectfully addressed, dismissed, or ignored? (*Be cautious if opposing viewpoints are ignored or savaged.*)
- Does the site contain advertising? (*Note how intense and if clearly identified.*)
- What information is missing? (*To find out, check similar subject sites.*)

WHERE DOES THE INFORMATION COME FROM?

- **What does the** domain name—**com, .edu, .gov, .org,** etc.—tell you about sponsorship?
- Does the author identify the source of the information or describe how it was generated? *(If not, be careful about using it.)*
- Has the information appeared previously in print? *(If the print source is reputable or peer-reviewed, it gains credibility.)*

WHEN WAS THE SITE CREATED?

- How recently was the site updated, or when was the information posted? *(The more recent, the more updated, the better.)*
- How does a missing date affect the information's credibility? *(The fewer creation markers, the lower the credibility.)*
- Is the site complete or under construction? *(If not complete, include that information in your citation.)*
- Does the site appear to change frequently? *(Make a printout including the date and URL so that if the site is revised, you have an authoritative record of what it said.)*

WHY IS THE INFORMATION PRESENTED?

- Does the purpose seem to be to inform, persuade, entertain, sell? *(Check domain name, look for value judgment words, see what it's selling, and see whether or not you laugh.)*
- Is the graphic presentation effective and unobtrusive? Does sound or animation contribute or detract? *(If either visual images or sound are important, how would/could you represent these in your paper?)*
- Are there links to other sites? Are the links current? Are the linked sites authoritative? *(Positive answers to these questions help; negative ones do not.)*

TESTING A WEB SITE

While the list of possible evaluative questions—*who, what, where, when, why*—along with the many subquestions seems long and rather complicated, in truth, serious researchers quickly internalize them. Once a given site is examined with these questions in mind, it quickly gives up its value and usefulness.

For example, suppose I want to do a research project on hybrid automobiles, and am specifically interested to see what, if any, incentives are currently available to consumers to purchase hybrids. A Yahoo! search turned up 65,100 possible sites using the key words "hybrid automobiles + incentives." Looking only at the first page of entries, I see a wide variety of sites that look interesting, including URLs with five different domain names (.gov, .com, .edu, .org, and .net)—which means a lot of different organizations offer information about incentives for buying hybrid automobiles (see below).

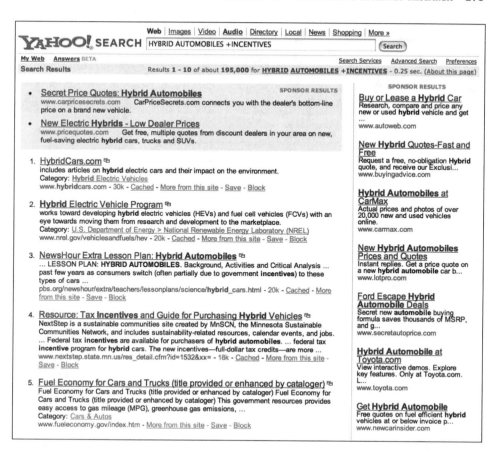

I'd like to bookmark the most useful sites for more serious investigation later on, so I review each site summary to see how closely it matches my interest—what the domain name tells me about sponsorship and purpose. Then I click on interesting sites to use to peruse the information more critically; sometimes I can tell its usefulness and credibility at a glance, while other times I need to ask the *who, what, where, when, why* questions.

The first site is a government site (**.gov**) so I expect truthful public information to be presented in unbiased language. A quick glance reveals information about current government programs, projects, and policies related to hybrid transportation. The site is sponsored by the National Renewable Energy Laboratory (sounds official, but I don't know much about it so that may require further investigation), includes links to the Hybrid Electric Fuel Cell project, R&D, and Publications. In other words, this source contains a wealth of material that I'll download later for more careful study—I bookmark the page and move on.

Next I investigate the nonprofit site sponsored by PBS (**.org**). The site is sponsored by MacNeil-Lehrer Productions—a highly respected public television news show and dated 2005, so I expect the site to be serious and informative rather than commercial. What I find is: A two-page high-school lesson plan by a physics teacher, a "retired nuclear submarine commander" who intends to examine How a Series Hybrid Car Works, How a Parallel Hybrid Car Works, Typical Fuel Savings of Hybrid Cars vs. Conventional Cars, and Exhaust

Emission Results of Hybrid vs. Conventional Cars. The site has useful background information, links to other informative sites, and high credibility. I bookmark it.

I look at one more site that sounds interesting, "States Engaging Citizens to Consider Green Cars," but because it's a commercial site (**.com**) I'm not sure whether I'll find useful information or a sales pitch—a good site to query with critical questions.

WHO?   The Auto Channel <www.theautochannel.com> sponsors this Web site full of a variety of information about hybrid automobiles. While no individual name appears on the site, the site clearly invites communication: "**Send your** questions, comments, and suggestions to Editor-in-Chief@theautochannel.com."

WHAT?   The site features a brief but documented article about states that offer incentives for buying hybrid cars. It includes first-page links for comparing different brands of hybrids (Toyota, Honda) as well as looking up prices on any car brand (PriceQuotes.com). The second page features fifteen links to documented and dated news stories about such subjects as "Automobile Dealers," "Vehicles and the Environment," "Teens and Cars," and so on, each of which features links to ever more specialized auto industry information.

WHERE?   Information in the feature story comes from named sources, including Web sites (AIADA.org) along with several named state officials (Oregon, California) as well as *USA Today* and R. L. Polk & company. Links provide information about products world wide

PBS HOME   PROGRAMS A-Z   TV SCHEDULES   SUPPORT PBS   SHOP PBS   SEARCH PBS

NEWSHOUR   A NewsHour with Jim Lehrer special for students

EXTRA

LESSON PLAN: HYBRID AUTOMOBILES
Background, Activities and Critical Analysis
By Ed Linz, a Physics teacher at West Springfield High School in Springfield, VA

Subject(s): Physics, Engineering, Environmental Science, Social Studies

Time: 2 class periods

Lesson Objectives: Students will:

- Understand the basic principles of gasoline engines as propulsion for vehicles
- Be able to list pro's and con's associated with gasoline engines
- Cite reasons why alternatives for gasoline engines are being considered
- Understand differences between a motor and an engine
- Understand relationship between a motor and a generator
- Understand basic principles of operation of hybrid vehicles
- Be able to discuss different types of hybrid vehicles
- Understand pros and cons associated with hybrid vehicles

Overview:
Hybrid automobiles have been increasingly in the news as state and federal governments struggle to find ways to reduce consumption of fossil fuels and to lessen exhaust pollutants into the atmosphere. One method of accomplishing both objectives is to produce vehicles that use electricity for propulsion because no fossil fuels are directly involved and there are essentially no emissions. However, purely electric vehicles have met with little success in the marketplace due to lack of a national network for re-charging automobile batteries and the relatively limited range which these electric vehicles can achieve without recharging As a result of these shortcomings, automobile manufacturers began to develop "hybrid" vehicles, that is, automobiles that retain the range and re-fueling advantages of internal combustion engines with the environmentally desirable characteristics of electric motors. Sales of such hybrid vehicles have been rising almost geometrically in the past few years as consumers switch (often partially due to government incentives) to these types of cars. But is this good science, or is it simply an interim measure to delay the inevitable exhaustion of fossil fuel resources? And to what extent do hybrid vehicles improve the environment?

(Korea, Japan, Germany, China, Mexico, to name a few), many in the form of printed press releases from automobile companies and automotive newsletters, all of which include dates. Most include named spokespeople. The published e-mail address of the editor may be a lead to contacting other names and addresses associated with the link.

WHEN?   The site includes the date it was created (5/25/05); the printout includes the date I visited the site (7/19/05), and all linked stories associated with the site are dated as well.

WHY?   The site appears to be a clearing house for the latest news regarding hybrid automobile manufacturers, developments, and trends. A note at the bottom solicits hybrid news: "Submit press releases or news stories to <u>submit@theautochannel.com</u>." It's also a commercial site promoting the buying of hybrid automobiles both in promotional press releases and overt advertising, but it doesn't obviously favor one brand over another. At the same time, I would not expect to find much material critical of hybrids in general or any brands in particular.

After critically testing this Auto Channel site, I believe it will be an avenue to many sources of late-breaking news regarding hybrids, useful for either an academic research paper or a consumer purchase. I bookmark it.

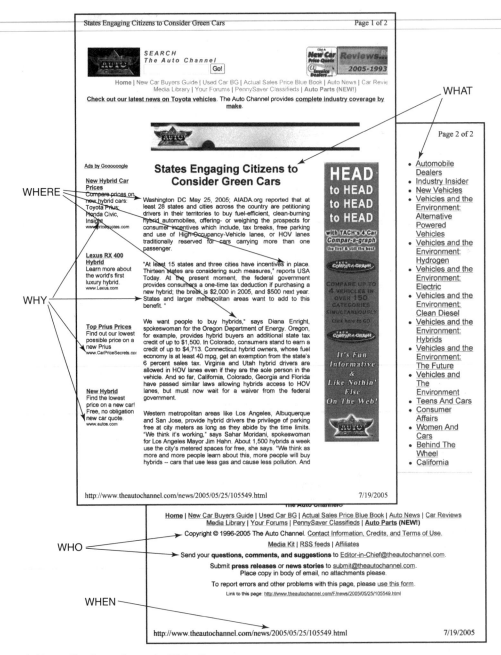

Asking critical questions of a Web site.

◆ SUGGESTIONS FOR INTERNET RESEARCH PROJECTS

Individual and/or Collaborative
Investigate, alone or with a partner, any complex institution or organization frequently mentioned on the news or in the newspaper. Plan to write a feature story for your classroom audience that profiles this subject using a variety of Internet sources: Use more than one search engine; include a variety of domain sources; e-mail interview people associated with this organization; test all sources for accuracy, timeliness, and credibility; and document them appropriately.

CHAPTER TWENTY-SIX

Conducting Field Research

Talking to the author was a lot different from reading her book. She was actually there, friendly, smiling sometimes, thinking out loud, telling me inside stories and trade secrets, and when she didn't know an answer, she didn't pretend that she did. Her stories really make my paper come alive.

MARY

Research is an active and unpredictable process requiring serious investigators to find answers, wherever those happen to be. Depending on your research question, you may need to seek answers by visiting museums, attending concerts, interviewing politicians, observing classrooms, or following leads down some wooded trail. Investigations that take place outside the library are commonly called **field research.**

After our first-year students completed a writing project in which field research played a central part, we asked them what they thought of this kind of research. Here is what they told us:

John: "Without question, it was interviews that gave me the most current and interesting information for my forestry paper. I could ask my own questions and not have to dig through useless information to get the answer."

Angel: "When I quoted Congressman Sanders' personal views on gun control, his voice made my voice stronger and more believable."

Jose: "Field research was very frustrating to me. No one would ever return my phone calls or answer my questions directly."

Kate: "I enjoy field research because I'm more personally involved in it. It's harder than library or Web research—calling and making appointments and going places—but it is more entertaining."

Field research adds liveliness, immediacy, and credibility to a research paper, especially when used in conjunction with library and Internet research. In fact, it's always a good idea to learn as much as you can about the subject of your research via a library or Web search before conducting an interview; the people you talk to will see that you're informed and will give you more detailed information. At the same time, good field research often takes more time and preparation than browsing the Web or an online catalog, so it can also be frustrating.

Field researchers collect primary source information not yet recorded or assessed by somebody else, and so they have the chance to uncover new facts and develop original interpretations. To

conduct such research, you first need to determine which people, places, things, or events can give you the information you need. Then you must go out in the field and either **observe** by watching carefully or **interview** by asking questions of a particular person.

PLANNING FIELD RESEARCH

Unlike a library, which bundles millions of bits of every kind of information in a single location, "fields" are everywhere, including on campus (academic departments, administrative offices, labs, libraries, dining and sports facilities, and dormitories) as well as the neighborhood beyond the campus (theaters, malls, parks, playgrounds, farms, factories, and so on). Field information is not cataloged, organized, indexed, or shelved for your convenience. Obtaining it requires diligence, energy, and careful planning.

- *Consider your research question as it now stands.* What field sources that would bolster your argument or add to your report?
- *Select your contacts and sites.* Find the person, place, thing, or event

most helpful to you. Decide whether you will collect observations, conduct interviews, or do both.

- *Schedule research in advance.*   Interviews, trips, and events don't always work according to plan. Allow time for glitches, such as having to reschedule an interview or return for more information.
- *Do your homework.*   Visit the library or conduct a Google search before conducting extensive field research. No matter from whom, where, or what you intend to collect information, there's background information that can help you make more insightful observations or formulate better interview questions.
- *Log what you find.*   Record visits, questions, phone calls, and conversations in a research log. Write from the very beginning about topics, questions, methods, and answers. Record even dead-end searches, to remind yourself that you tried them.

◆ WRITING 1: APPLICATION

Begin a field research log by speculating on the feasibility of using field research information to help answer your question. Identify two sites you might visit and three subjects you might interview.

INTERVIEWING

If you are comfortable talking to strangers, then you have a head start on being a good interviewer. In many respects, a good interview is simply a good conversation. If you consider yourself shy, don't worry, for you can still learn how to ask good interview questions that will elicit useful answers. Your chances of obtaining good interview material increase radically when you've thought about what questions you want to pose ahead of time. The following guidelines should help you conduct good interviews:

Select the right person. People differ in both the amount and kind of knowledge they have. Not everyone who knows something about your research topic will be able to give you the information you need. Ask yourself (1) exactly what information you need, (2) why you need it, (3) who is likely to have it, and (4) how you might gain it.

Most research projects benefit from more than one perspective, so plan on more than one interview. For example, to research Lake Erie pollution, you could interview someone who lives on the shore, a chemist who knows about pesticide decomposition, a vice president of a nearby paper company, and people who frequent the waterfront.

Know your subject. Before you talk to an expert about your topic, make sure you know something about it yourself. Be able to define or describe your interest in it, know the general issues, and learn what your interview subject has already said about it in books, articles, or interviews. In this way, you will ask sharper questions, get to the point faster, and be more interesting for your subject to talk with. Plan appropriate questions.

Create a working script. A good interview doesn't follow a script, but it usually starts with one. Before you begin an interview, write out the questions you plan to ask and arrange them so that they build on each other—general questions first, specific ones later. If you or your subject digresses, your questions can remind you to get back on track.

Ask both open and closed questions. Different kinds of questions elicit different kinds of information. Open questions place few limits on the answers given: Why did you decide to major in business? What are your plans for the future? Closed questions specify the information you want and usually elicit brief responses: When did you receive your degree? From what college? Open questions usually provide general information, while closed questions supply details.

Ask follow-up questions. Listen closely to the answers you receive. When the information is incomplete or confusing, ask follow-up questions requesting clarification. Such questions are seldom scripted, so plan on using your wits to direct your subject toward the information you consider most important.

Use silence. If you don't get an immediate response to a question, wait a bit before asking another one. In some cases, your question may not have been clear and you will need to rephrase it. But in many cases your interview subject is simply collecting his or her thoughts, not ignoring you. After a slight pause, you may hear thoughtful answers worth waiting for.

Read body language. Be aware of what your subject is doing while answering the questions. Does he or she look you in the eye? fidget and squirm? look distracted or bored? smile? From these visual cues you may be able to infer when your subject is speaking most frankly, doesn't want to give more information, or is tired of answering questions.

Take content notes. Many interviewers take notes on a pad that is spiral-bound on top, which allows for quick page flipping. Don't try to write down everything, just major ideas and telling statements in the subject's own words that you might want to use as quotations in your paper. Omitting small words, focusing on the most distinctive and precise language, and using common abbreviations make note taking more efficient.

Take context notes. Note your subject's physical appearance, facial expressions, and clothing, as well as the interview setting itself. These details will be useful later when you reconstruct the interview, helping you represent it more vividly in your paper.

Tape-record with permission only. If you plan to use a tape recorder, ask for permission in advance. The advantage of tape recording is that you have a complete record of the conversation. Sometimes on hearing the person a second time, you notice important things you missed earlier. However, sometimes tape recorders make subjects nervous. Be aware that transcribing a tape is time consuming. It's a good idea to have pen in hand to catch highlights or jot down additional questions.

Confirm important assertions. When your subject says something especially important or controversial, read back your notes aloud to check for accuracy and to allow your subject to elaborate. Some interviewers do this during the interview, others at the end.

Review your notes. Notes taken during an interview are brief reminders of what your subject said, not complete quotations. You need to write out the complete information they represent as soon after the interview as you can, certainly within twenty-four hours. Supplement the notes with other remembered details while they're still fresh, recording them on note cards or directly into a computer file that you can refer to as you write your paper.

Interview electronically. It is possible, and useful, to contact individuals via telephone, electronic mail, or the Internet. Phone interviews are quick and obvious ways of finding out information on short notice. If your interviewee has an e-mail address, asking questions via this medium is even less intrusive than telephoning, as your subject can answer when doing so is convenient—quickly, specifically, and in writing.

◆ WRITING 2: EXPLORATION

Describe any experience you have had as either interviewer or interviewee. Drawing on your own experience, what additional advice would you give to researchers setting out to interview a subject?

THINKING CRITICALLY ABOUT FIELD SOURCES

When using field sources on or off campus in writing classes or across the curriculum, analyze each source's underlying assumptions, determine the reliability and credibility of the source, and develop an interpretation of your source's information that helps you answer your research question. To assess the value of field resources, ask yourself the following questions:

- *What is the most important point this source makes?*   How does it address my research question? How might this point fit into my paper and how should I articulate it?
- *What evidence did the source provide that supports this point?*   Is it strong or weak? Can I use it and build on it? Should I question or refute it?
- *Does the information support my working thesis?*   If so, how? How can I express the support in writing?
- *Does the information challenge my working thesis?*   If so, how? Can I refute the information or contradiction? Or should I revise my thesis to take the new information into account?
- *Does the information support or contradict information collected from other sources?*   How so? How can I resolve any contradictions? Do I need to seek other sources for confirmation?
- *Is the source reliable?*   Does any of the information from this source seem illogical or not credible? Has any of the information been contradicted by a more authoritative source?
- *Is the source biased?*   Does the interview subject have a reason to be biased in any way? Would the selection of a different site have produced different information?

CONDUCTING SURVEYS

Surveys are commonly used in the social sciences to collect data from more than one person. A survey is a structured interview in which respondents are all asked the same questions and their answers tabulated and interpreted. Researchers usually conduct surveys to discover attitudes, beliefs, or habits of the general public or segments of the population. They may try to predict how soccer moms will vote in an election, determine the popularity of a new movie with teenage audiences, compare the eating habits of students who live off campus to those of students who eat in college dining halls, and so on.

For research purposes, respondents to surveys can be treated like experts because they are being asked for opinions or information about their own behavior. However, to get useful answers, you must ask your questions skillfully. Wording that suggests a right or wrong answer reveals the researcher's biases and preconceived ideas more than the subject's candid responses. Furthermore, the questions should be easy to understand and answer, and they should be reviewed to make sure they are relevant to the research topic or hypothesis. The format for questioning and the way the research is conducted also have an influence on responses. For example, to get complete and honest answers about a sensitive or highly personal issue, the researcher would probably use anonymous written surveys to ensure confidentiality. Other survey techniques involve oral interviews in which the researcher records each subject's responses on a written form.

Surveys are usually brief, to gain the cooperation of a sufficiently large number of respondents. And to enable the researcher to compare answers, the questions are usually closed, although open-ended questions may be used to gain additional information or insights. Surveys are treated briefly here because, in truth, the designing of good survey questions, distributing of surveys, and assessment of the results is a highly complex and sophisticated business. To get some idea of the steps involved in formulating an effective survey, consult either of the following helpful Internet sources:

- *Questionnaires and Surveys: A Free Tutorial* <http://www.statpac.com/surveys/>
- *Creative Systems Research, The Survey System* <http://www.surveysystem.com/sdesign.htm>

A further complication arises if the survey you are considering requests sensitive information (such as personal experience with drugs, alcohol, or sex) from identifiable subjects. All colleges and universities have "human subject" boards or committees, which need to approve any research that could compromise the privacy of students, staff, or faculty. Consequently, consult your instructor before launching any survey on or off campus.

However, the simple, informal polling of people to request opinions takes place quite often in daily college life, such as every time a class takes a vote or a professor asks the class for opinions or interpretations of texts. In one case, a student who was writing a self-profile wanted to find out how she was perceived by others. First, Anna made a list of ten people who knew her in different ways—her mother, father, older sister, roommate, best friend, favorite teacher, and so on. Next, she invited each to make a list of five words that best characterized her. Finally, she asked each to call her answering machine on a day when she knew she would not be home and name these five words. In this way, she was able to collect original outside opinion (field research) in a nonthreatening manner that she then wove into her profile paper, combining others' opinions with her own self-assessments. The external points of view added an interesting (and sometimes surprising) view of herself as well as other voices to her paper.

◆ WRITING 3: APPLICATION

Invent a simple survey (no more than five questions) to generate external information about any paper topic you are working on. To implement the survey, plan to use a one-page paper handout, a brief e-mail message, or the telephone to collect responses. Perhaps the easiest way to do this is to try it out on your classmates first.

◆ OBSERVING

Another kind of field research calls for closely observing people, places, things, or events and then describing them accurately to show readers what you saw and experienced. While the term *observation* literally denotes visual perception, it also applies to information collected on site through other senses. The following suggestions may help you conduct field observations:

Select a good site. Like interviewing, observing requires that you know where to go and what to look for. Have your research question in mind and identify places where observation might yield useful information. For example, historical research on a small town might be enhanced by visits to the county courthouse, the town clerk, or the local cemetery.

Do your homework. To observe well, you need to know what you are looking for and what you are looking at. If you are observing a political speech, know the issues and the players; if you visit an industrial complex, know what is manufactured there. Researching background information at the library or elsewhere will allow you to use your site time more efficiently.

Plan your visit. Learn not only where the place is located on a map but how to gain access; call ahead to ask directions. Find out where you should go when you first arrive. If relevant, ask which places are open to you, which are off limits, and which you could visit with permission. Find out about visiting hours; if you want to visit at odd hours, you may need special permission. Depending on the place, after-hours visits can provide detailed information not available to the general public.

Take good notes. At any site there's a lot going on that casual observers take for granted. As a researcher you should take nothing for granted. Keep in mind that without notes, as soon as you leave a site you forget more than half of what was there. Review and rewrite your observation notes as soon after your site visit as possible. Make your notes as precise as possible, indicating the color, shape, size, texture, and arrangement of everything you can.

Taking field notes is a lot easier in a notebook with a stiff cover so you can write standing, sitting, or squatting; a table may not be available. Double-entry notebooks are useful for site visits because they allow you to record facts in one column and interpretations of those facts in the other. Unless you're a very skilled typist, a laptop computer may be more trouble than it's worth.

Visual images also provide excellent memory aids, so consider sketching, photographing, or videotaping the site you visit. If you speak your notes into a tape recorder, you will also pick up the characteristic sounds of the site.

EVALUATING FIELD SOURCES

Everything said about critically questioning library sources would hold true for field sources if people and places were as carefully documented, reviewed, and catalogued. Evaluating the credibility of an interview subject or usefulness of a site visit is just as important as a print or electronic source, but more more problematic, as one doesn't stay put and the other is not very articulate.

INTERVIEWS

An interview is usually a one-time event. The subject may no longer be available for cross-checking or may change his or her mind. Be careful to find out whether an individual speaks for an organization or for him- or herself alone. Get permission in advance from the interviewee if you plan to tape-record. Then after the interview subject agrees to be recorded, start the recorder, and ask again for permission to record so you have confirming evidence of that agreement. Basically, what you will be doing is "freezing" the interview, but take copious notes anyway. Then transcribe the whole session to allow you to quote exactly what was said, but to pick and choose from a variety of accurate statements.

Once an interview is taped, you can apply to it all the critical and analytical questions you would to a written source, asking for other opinions to verify certain statements or, if your interviewee is a public figure, looking up his or her record in a newspaper index or biographical review. If you cannot tape-record, take notes as carefully as possible; review main points with your subject before the interview ends, and then, at your leisure, apply as many as possible of the same analytical procedures to your notes as you would to a cat-alogued text.

For example, in writing a paper about local lake pollution, you might interview a bi-ology professor who teaches a college course on lake pollution. In her office, she tells you that the most severe pollution is caused not by paper mills but by farm fertilizer—which sur-prises you. After transcribing your tape (or reviewing your notes), you cross-check her assertion by talking to other experts in the state department of natural resources and by re-viewing text sources found in the library or on the World Web. Note how you've been crit-ical in two ways: First, you sought out an expert whose credentials gave her advance credibility; second, you sought to verify her statements by confirming them with other reli-able sources.

SITE VISITS

Any research essay written about a topic with local dimensions gains credibility when it shows evidence the writer has investigated it firsthand, whether it's electric automobiles or local graveyards. For example, a recent first-year research paper focused on the practical in-troduction of electric automobiles into America's car culture. Adam visited the local organ-ization promoting these cars, interviewed the manager, and test-drove one of the electric vehicles. While his paper also included conventional sources from periodicals, it gained extra credibility from his personal account, his interview quotations, statements from brochures, and photographs of the vehicle he took for a test ride.

When you visit a place to locate evidence to support the claims you make in a paper, make photographic or video records of what it looks like and what you find. Take copious notes about time, sensory details, location, size, shape, color, number, and so forth. Pic-tures and careful verbal descriptions essentially freeze your visit and will help you in writ-ing the paper in several ways. First, in writing your paper, you may include the photographs as well as specific details that would be difficult to invent had you not been present—both of which add credibility for original research. Second, even if you do not include photos or directly quote your notes, they will still jog your memory about what, exactly, you found and thus help you write more accurately. Finally, these recordings—assuming they are rel-atively objective in perspective and language—will help you maintain a neutral rather than a biased perspective.

On the one hand, evaluating the usefulness of an interview or site visit is simple: Ask yourself whether the details gathered on your visit to the site support the assertions made by your paper. In his electric car essay, for instance, Adam was able to testify positively to the automobile's quietness and ample acceleration as well as negatively, noting his fear the battery would run down before he returned to a charging station.

On the other hand, evaluating any field source becomes more complicated when you realize that you are both the creator and evaluator of the material at the same time. In site visits, the material is out there, and in and of itself, it has no meaning or value until you, the recorder, assign it. This material has not been filtered through the lens of another writer. *You* are the interpreter of what you witness, and when you introduce field evidence, it's your own bias that will show up in the way you use language; you will lead your reader one way or another depending on whether you describe the lake water as *cloudy, murky,* or *filthy* or label the electric car as *slow, hesitant,* or *a dog.* In other words, you assign a value to (evalu-ate) your field evidence by the way you present it in your paper.

◆ WRITING 4

List two field sources for a current research paper. Examine each for evidence of your role in creating it and for evidence of your bias. Which source did you find more trustworthy? Which one helped your paper more? Why? Looking back, what would you have done differently during your interview or site visit? How do you plan to make up for any limitations of your field research?

◆ SUGGESTIONS FOR WRITING AND RESEARCH

Individual

1. Plan a research project that focuses on a local place (park, playground, street, building, business, or institution) and make a research plan that includes going there, describing what you find, and interviewing somebody. Make a similar plan for at least one electronic source. Conduct the research.
2. Plan a research project that begins with an issue of some concern to you. Identify a local manifestation of this issue that would profit from field research. Also consult the library or World Wide Web to place your issue in a larger context. Conduct the research, using field techniques appropriate to your topic.

Collaborative

Create a team of two to four classmates who would like to join you in researching the project you planned for individual assignment 1 or 2 above. Plan the necessary activities to make this project work. Divide the labor so that each of you brings some information to the group by next week's class meeting. Make a copy of your research information for each group member, including typed transcripts of interviews, copies of e-mail interviews, and photocopies of visual information. You may each write an individual paper based on your collective research, or you may team up and write a collaborative paper.

CHAPTER TWENTY-SEVEN

Working with Sources

I really don't mind doing the research. The library, once you get to know it, is a very friendly place. But when I go to write the paper I keep forgetting all the rules about what to quote, and what not to quote, and how to introduce quotations and not make them too long or too short. It seems like that part could be less confusing.

JASON

Locating potential sources for a research project is one thing; deciding which ones to include, where to use them, and how to incorporate them is something else. Some writers begin making use of their sources in early exploratory drafts, perhaps by trying out a pithy quotation to see how it brings a paragraph into focus. Others prefer to sift and arrange their note cards in neat stacks before making any decisions about what to include in their essays. No matter how you begin writing with sources, there comes a time when you will need to incorporate them finally, smoothly, effectively, and correctly into your paper.

CONTROLLING SOURCES

Once you've researched and begin composing your essay, you need to decide which sources to use, how and where. You can't make this decision on the basis of how much time you spent finding each source, but rather on how useful it is in answering your research question.

Serious research is vital and dynamic, which means it's always changing. Just as you can't expect your first working thesis to be your final thesis, you can't expect to know in advance which sources are going to prove most fruitful. And don't think that you can't collect more information once you've begun drafting. At each step in the process you see your research question more clearly and know better what sources you need to answer it. Similarly, and perhaps especially when engaging in field research, writers of research essays often gain an increased sense of audience as their research progresses, which pays off in increasingly reader-oriented writing.

Organizing and Synthesizing Sources

You need to control your sources rather than letting them control you, so somtime after you've begun collecting information, generate a **working outline** of your major ideas— "working," because it's important that outlines change as ideas evolve. It's more helpful to compose an outline separate from your research notes than to compose one from your notes. The former will have the logic of a coherent set of thoughts while the latter will only have the logic formed by what sources you've found so far. Outline first and you won't be tempted to find a place for every note and to gloss over areas where you haven't done enough research.

Once you have outlined or begun drafting and have a good sense of the shape and direction of your paper, arrange the note cards so that they correspond to your outline, and put bibliographic cards in alphabetical order by the author's last name. Integrate field research notes as best you can, depending on their format. Finally, go back to your outline and annotate it according to which source goes where, and which points as yet have no sources to back them up. By doing this, you can see whether there are any ideas that need more research. In addition, look for connections between one source and subsequent sources.

Next, decide upon some balance among your sources so you remain the director of the research production, your ideas on center stage, and your sources the supporting cast. Keep in mind that referring too often to a single source—unless it is itself the focus of your paper, as in frequent references to the text *Moby Dick* because it's the text you are interpreting—suggests over-reliance on a single point of view. If you find yourself referring largely to one source—and therefore one point of view—make sure that you have sufficient references to add other points of view to your paper.

◆ WRITING 1

Draft a tentative thesis and working outline for your research paper. Then arrange your note cards according to that outline. Look for too many references to a single source as well as places where you've no external sources to support you. This procedure is equally easy with card or computer notes. Plan on rearranging this initial plan as many times as needed as ideas evolve.

Integrating Information

The notes you made during your research may be in many forms. For some sources, you will have copied down direct quotations; for others, you will have paraphrased or summarized important information. For some field sources, you may have made extensive notes on background information, such as your interview subject's appearance. Simply because you've quoted or paraphrased a particular source in your notes, however, doesn't mean you have to use a quotation or paraphrase from this source in your paper. Make decisions about how to use sources based on your goals, not on the format of your research notes.

If you've taken source notes in your own words to help with paraphrasing and summarizing an expert's ideas, and carefully set off quotations with quotation marks, you're in good shape to integrate them smoothly into your own textual ideas. Different disciplines have different conventions for documentation. The examples in this chapter use the documentation style of the Modern Language Association (MLA), the style preferred in English and foreign language departments. (For MLA and APA documentation styles, see References 1 and 2.)

Integrating Quotations

Direct quotations will be most effective when you integrate them smoothly into the flow of your paper. You can do this by introducing the source and reason for the quotation in a phrase or sentence. Readers should be able to follow your meaning easily and to see the relevance of the quotation immediately.

INTRODUCE QUOTATIONS.   Readers need to know who is speaking, so introduce quoted material with a **signal phrase** (sometimes called a **attributory phrase**) so the reader knows the source and purpose of quotation.

If the source is well known, name alone will be enough.

> Henry David Thoreau asserts in *Walden,* "The mass of men lead lives of quiet desperation" (5).

If your paper focuses on the published work itself, introduce a quotation with the work's title rather than the author's name, as long as the reference is clear.

> *Walden* sets forth one individual's antidote against the "lives of quiet desperation" led by the working class in mid-nineteenth-century America (Thoreau 5).

If either author or source is not well known, introduce the quotation with a brief explanation to give your readers enough context to understand the quotation.

> Mary Catherine Bateson, daughter of anthropologist Margaret Mead, has become, in her own right, a student of modern civilization. In *Composing a Life* she writes, "The twentieth century has been called the century of the refugee because of the vast numbers of people uprooted by war and politics from their homes" (8).

> A strong argument in favor of outlining sometime during the writing process is found in *The Handbook of Technical Writing:* "Outlining provides structure to your writing by assuring that it has a beginning (introduction), a middle (main body), and an end (conclusion)" (Brusaw, Alred, and Oliu, 426).

SELECT THE RIGHT SIGNAL PHRASE.   There are certain *signal phrases* to tell the reader that the words or ideas that follow come from another source. A signal phrase is a verb that indicates the tone or intention of the author. To avoid monotony, vary the placement and words of the signal phrases you use. Note the differences, both slight and significant, in the following signal phrases:

acknowledges	denies	points out
admits	emphasizes	refutes

agrees	endorses	reports
argues	finds	reveals
asserts	grants	says
believes	illustrates	shows
claims	implies	states
comments	insists	suggests
concedes	maintains	thinks
concludes	notes	writes
declares	observes	

QUOTE SMOOTHLY AND CORRECTLY.   To use a *direct quotation* you must use an author's or speaker's exact words. Slight changes in wording are permitted, but these changes must be clearly marked. Although you can't change what a source says, you do have control over how much of it you use. Too much quotation can imply that you have little to say for yourself. Use only as long a quotation as you need to make your point. Remember that quotations should be used to support your points, not to say them for you.

To *shorten* a quotation, so that only the most important information is included, integrate it smoothly and correctly in the body of your paragraph to provide minimal disruption for your reader. Unless the source quoted is itself the topic of the paper (as in a literary interpretation), limit brief quotations to no more than two per page and long quotations to no more than one every three pages. The following examples illustrate both correct and incorrect use of quoted material.

ORIGINAL PASSAGE

The dialogue throughout the movie is once again its weakest point: The characters talk in what sounds like Basic English, without color, wit or verbal delight, as if they were channeling Berlitz. The exceptions are Palpatine and of course Yoda, whose speech (voiced by Frank Oz) reminds me of Wolcott Gibbs' famous line about the early style of *Time* magazine: "Backward ran sentences until reeled the mind." *Roger Ebert review of* Star Wars Episode III: Revenge of the Siths, *Roger Ebert.com*

DISTORTED QUOTATION

According to film critic, Roger Ebert, all the characters in *Star Wars Episode III: Revenge of the Siths* "talk in what sounds like Basic English, without color, wit or verbal delight, as if they were channeling Berlitz."

The exceptions noted by Ebert in the original passage are missing.

ACCURATE QUOTATION

According to film critic, Roger Ebert, all the characters, with the exceptions of Yoda and Palpatine, "talk in what sounds like Basic English, without color, wit or verbal delight, as if they were channeling Berlitz."

OMIT OR SUBSTITUTE WORDS JUDICIOUSLY.   Cutting out words for the sake of brevity is often useful, but do not distort meaning. Indicate omitted words by using **ellipsis points** (three dots within a sentence, four to indicate a second sentence). Indicate any changes or additions with brackets.

DISTORTED QUOTATION

In reviewing the last episode of the *Star Wars* saga, film critic Roger Ebert claims that, "The dialogue throughout the [*Revenge of the Siths*] . . . sounds like Basic English, without color, wit or verbal delight, as if they were channeling Berlitz."

While use of the ellipsis and bracket are technically correct, the missing words indicated by the ellipsis leave out Ebert's exceptions and again distort the meaning of the original passage.

USE BLOCK FORMAT FOR LONG QUOTATIONS.   Brief quotations should be embedded in the main body of your paper and enclosed in quotation marks. All of the previous examples are brief and would be embedded within paragraphs as normal sentences. According to MLA style guidelines, a brief quotation consists of four or fewer typed lines.

However, longer quotations (more than five lines) should be set off in block format, indented, but spaced the same as the normal text.

- Introduce the quotation in the last line of normal text with a sentence that ends with a colon.
- Indent ten spaces, then begin the quote.
- Do not use quotation marks, as the indentation signals direct quotation.
- Include page number after end punctuation in parentheses.

In *The Magical Classroom* Michael Strauss says:

> If they were candid, most magicians would say they are trying to entertain us by hiding the truth. They challenge us to discover what they

have hidden. And we respond by trying to figure out the underlying causes of the magical effects and illusions we see. Like scientists, we search for the truth, for what might be hidden from our senses. (2)

EXPLAIN AND CLARIFY QUOTATIONS.   Sometimes you will need to explain a quotation in order to clarify why it's relevant and what it means in the context of your discussion.

In *A Sand County Almanac,* Aldo Leopold invites modern urban readers to confront what they lose by living in the city: "There are two spiritual dangers in not owning a farm. One is the danger of supposing that breakfast comes from the grocery, and the other that heat comes from the furnace" (6). Leopold sees city-dwellers as self-centered children, blissfully but dangerously unaware of how their basic needs are met.

You may also need to clarify what a word or reference means. Do this by using square brackets.

ADJUST GRAMMAR FOR CLARITY.   A passage containing a quotation must follow all the rules of grammatical sentence structure: Tenses should be consistent, verbs and subjects should agree, and so on. If the form of the quotation doesn't quite fit the grammar of your own sentences, you can either quote less of the original source, change your sentences, or make a slight alteration in the quotation. Use this last option sparingly, and always indicate any changes with brackets.

UNCLEAR

In *A Sand County Almanac,* Aldo Leopold follows various animals, including a skunk and a rabbit, through fresh snow. He wonders, "What got him out of bed?" (5).

It is not clear whether "him" refers to the skunk or the rabbit.

CLEAR

In *A Sand County Almanac,* Aldo Leopold follows various animals, including a skunk and a rabbit, through fresh snow. He wonders, "What got [the skunk] out of bed?" (5).

GRAMMATICALLY INCOMPATIBLE

In *A Sand County Almanac,* Aldo Leopold said that living in the city is a "spiritual danger" if people "supposing that breakfast comes from the grocery."

To be grammatically correct, the writer needs to change supposing from a gerund (-ing word) to the verb form suppose. One way is to make the change inside the quotation marks with brackets.

GRAMMATICALLY COMPATIBLE

In *A Sand County Almanac,* Aldo Leopold said that living in the city is a "spiritual danger" if people "[suppose] that breakfast comes from the grocery."

Another option is to start the quotation one word later.

GRAMMATICALLY COMPATIBLE

In *A Sand County Almanac*, Aldo Leopold said that living in the city is a "spiritual danger" if people assume "that breakfast comes from the grocery."

Still another option is to recast the sentence completely.

GRAMMATICALLY COMPATIBLE

According to Aldo Leopold, city dwellers who assume "that breakfast comes from the grocery" are out of tune with the world of nature (*A Sand County Almanac* 6).

WHEN TO QUOTE

Direct quotation should be reserved for cases in which you cannot express the ideas better yourself. Use quotations when the original words are especially precise, clear, powerful, or vivid.

- *Precise.* Use quotations when the words are important in themselves or when the author makes fine but important distinctions.

    Government, even in its best state, is but a necessary evil; in it worst state, an intolerable one. *Thomas Paine*

- *Clear.* Use quotation when the author's ideas are complex and difficult to paraphrase.

    Paragraphs tell readers how writers want to be read. *William Blake*

- *Powerful.* Use quotation when the words are especially authoritative and memorable.

    You shall know the truth, and the truth shall make you free. *The King James Bible*

- *Vivid.* Use quotation when the language is lively and colorful, when it reveals something of the author's or speaker's character.

    Writing, I'm more involved in it, but not as attached. *Karen, student*

◆ WRITING 2

Read through your research materials, highlighting any quotations you might want to incorporate into your paper. Use your research log to explore why you think these words should be quoted directly. Also note where in your essay a quotation would add clarity, color, or life; then see if you can find one to serve that purpose.

PARAPHRASING AND SUMMARIZING

Taking notes is often a combination of quoting directly, paraphrasing, and summarizing. On one hand, it's important to have direct quotes to incorporate judiciously into your text; on the other hand, it helps to write as many research notes as possible in your own words to make sure you understand them—which is where the skills of paraphrasing and summarizing become important. Remember that another author's ideas, even restated in your own words, need to be documented and attributed.

Paraphrase

When you *paraphrase,* you restate a source's ideas in your own words. The point of paraphrasing is to make the ideas clearer by simplifying and explaining the author's original language to your readers and to yourself, and to express the ideas in the way that best suits your purpose. In paraphrasing, attempt to preserve the intent of the original statement and to fit the paraphrased statement smoothly into the immediate context of your essay.

The best way to make an accurate paraphrase is to stay close to the order and structure of the original passage, to reproduce its emphasis and details. However, don't use the same sentence patterns or vocabulary or you risk inadvertently plagiarizing the source.

If the original source has used a well-established or technical term for a concept, you do not need to find a synonym for it. If you believe that the original source's exact words are the best possible expressions of some points, you may use brief direct quotations within your paraphrase, as long as you indicate these with quotation marks.

Keep in mind why you are including this source; doing so will help you to decide how to phrase the ideas. Be careful, though, not to introduce your own comments or reflections in the middle of a paraphrase unless you make it very clear that these are your thoughts, not the original author's or speaker's.

ORIGINAL PASSAGE

The affluent, educated, liberated women of the First World, who can enjoy freedom unavailable to any woman ever before, do not feel as free as they want to. And they can no longer restrict to the subconscious their sense that this lack of freedom has something to do with—with apparently frivolous issues, things that really should not matter. Many are ashamed to admit that such trivial concerns—to do with physical appearance, bodies, faces, hair, clothes—matter so much.

NAOMI WOLF, *THE BEAUTY MYTH* (9)

INACCURATE PARAPHRASE

In *The Beauty Myth,* Naomi Wolf argues that First World women, who still have less freedom than they would like to have, restrict to their subconscious those matters having to do with physical appearance—things that are not really important to them (9).

ACCURATE PARAPHRASE

In *The Beauty Myth,* Naomi Wolf asserts that First World women, despite their affluence, education, and liberation, still do not feel very free. Moreover, many of these women are aware that this lack of freedom is influenced by superficial things having primarily to do with their physical appearance—things that should not matter so much (9).

WHEN TO PARAPHRASE

Paraphrases generally re-create the original source's order, structure, and emphasis and include most of its details.

- *Clarity.* Use paraphrase to make complex ideas clear to your readers.
- *Details.* Use paraphrase to tailor the presentation of details that an author or speaker has described at great length to the goals of your paper.
- *Emphasis.* Use paraphrase when including an author's or speaker's point suits the emphasis you want to make in your paper.

◆ WRITING 3

Read through your note cards for any passages you quoted directly from an original source. Find source quotes that now seem wordy, unclear, or longer than necessary. Paraphrase notes that you expect to use in your paper. Exchange your paraphrases and the originals with a classmate, and assess each other's work.

Summarize

To distill a source's words down to the main ideas and state these in your own words is to *summarize.* A summary includes only the essentials of the original source, not the supporting details, and is consequently shorter than the original.

Keep in mind that summaries are generalizations and that too many generalizations can make your writing vague and tedious. You should occasionally supplement summaries with brief direct quotations or evocative details collected through observation to keep readers in touch with the original source.

Summaries vary in length, and the length of the original source is not necessarily related to the length of the summary you write. Depending on the focus of your paper, you may need to summarize an entire novel in a sentence or two, or you may need to summarize a brief journal article in two or three paragraphs. Remember that the more material you attempt to summarize in a short space, the more you will necessarily generalize and abstract it. Reduce a text as far as you can while still providing all the information your readers need to know. Be careful, though, not to distort the original's meaning.

ORIGINAL PASSAGE

For a long time I never liked to look a chimpanzee straight in the eye—I assumed that, as is the case with most primates, this would be interpreted as a threat or at least as a breach of good manners. Not so. As long as one looks with gentleness, without arrogance, a chimpanzee will understand and may even return the look.

JANE GOODALL, *Through a Window* (12)

INACCURATE SUMMARY

Goodall learned from her experiences with chimpanzees that they react positively to direct looks from humans (12).

ACCURATE SUMMARY

Goodall reports that when humans look directly but gently into chimpanzees' eyes, the chimps are not threatened and may even return the look (12).

WHEN TO SUMMARIZE

As you draft, summarize often so that your paper doesn't turn into a string of undigested quotations.

- *Main points.* Use summary when your readers need to know the main point the original source makes but not the supporting details.
- *Overviews.* Sometimes you may want to devise a few sentences that will effectively support your discussion without going on and on. Use summary to provide an overview or an interesting aside without digressing too far from your paper's focus.
- *Condensation.* You may have taken extensive notes on a particular article or observation, only to discover in the course of drafting that you do not need all that detail. Use summary to condense lengthy or rambling notes into a few effective sentences.

◆ WRITING 4

Review any sources on which you have taken particularly extensive notes. Would it be possible to condense these notes into a briefer summary of the entire work? Would it serve your purpose to do so? Why or why not?

Identify Internet Sources in Signal Phrases

When you quote, paraphrase, or summarize *authoritative* sources from the World Wide Web—and there are many such sources on the Web—you need to be sure to emphasize the nature of that authority when you introduce the source. Although library and field sources also need to be introduced carefully, readers don't regard them with quite the skepticism and distrust they've learned while surfing the Net.

For example, in looking for information about the zebra mussel infestation in Lake Champlain, a team of students located the following sources on the Internet, noting that the first two, a university site (**.edu**) and a nonprofit site (**.org**) were more likely to be impartial than the third commercial site (**.com**). However, the student researchers were able to use both the educational and the commercial information by carefully specifying what was to be learned by each source in careful signal phrases introducing block quotations.

Zebra Mussels and Other Nonindigenous Species
... **Zebra mussels** also had colonized New York's Finger **Lakes**, **Lake Champlain**, Wisconsin's **Lake** Winnebago, Kentucky **Lake**, and nearly 100 smaller inland **lakes** ...
www.seagrant.wisc.edu/communications/greatlakes/GLnetwork/exotics.html - 23k - Cached - Similar pages

Invasive Species Lake Champlain
... **Zebra Mussel** Monitoring Program - Excellent explanation of the **Lake Champlain** Basin Program's **Zebra Mussel** Monitoring program. ...
www.lclt.org/invasive.htm - 47k - Cached - Similar pages]

Zebra Mussel filters by ZeeStop Filter designed to stop **Zebra Mussels**
... your **lake** water line from sand, silt and the ever present **Zebra Mussel**. ...
Lake Champlain, Mississippi River, Erie Canal, Hudson River and most **lakes** ...
www.zeestop.com/

Information supplied by The University of Wisconsin, Sea Grant Institute details the destructive nature of the zebra mussel in fresh water lakes:

> The prolific mollusk tends to biofoul and restrict the flow of water through intake pipes, disrupting supplies of drinking, cooling, processing and irrigating water to the nation's domestic infrastructure. The mussel also attaches to boat hulls, docks, locks, breakwaters and navigation aids, increasing maintenance costs and impeding waterborne transport.

The pesky zebra mussel had given rise to new commercial enterprises to help lakefront homeowners cope with the destructive mollusks. For example, Zee Stop. Com promises:

> The use of a Zeestop Filter should prolong the life of your entire plumbing system. Valve seats and washers should last longer without the grit that shortens their life expectance. Hot water tanks should not accumulate sediment brought in with the water, leading to longer element life. Other water filters such as carbon filters should not need to be replaced as often.

AVOIDING PLAGIARISM

The rule is simple: When you use other people's ideas or language in writing a paper, you should give credit to those people whose ideas and words you have used. If you don't, you have stolen their ideas or words and are guilty of plagiarism. In Western culture, plagiarism is a serious offense, one that has cost writers, reporters, artists, musicians, and scientists their reputations, jobs, and enormous amounts of money. Plagiarism is especially serious within academic communities, where the generation of original research, ideas, and words is the central mission of the institution.

The Internet has made the copying of sources especially easy, which saves researchers an enormous amount of time. However, easy Internet copying has also made it both intentional and unintentional plagiarism easy. To avoid plagiarizing, you need to know exactly *what it is* and *how to avoid committing it.*

What Plagiarism Is

Plagiarism is putting one's name on a paper written by a friend and passing it in. Plagiarism is buying a term paper from an Internet term-paper factory and pretending to have written it. Plagiarism is downloading a report from the Internet and pretending to have written it. And plagiarism is pasting in a phrase, sentence, paragraph, passage, or portion of anybody else's work in any paper and not giving that author credit. In any of these flagrant examples, the intent to plagiarize is deliberate and obvious, something that serious and honorable students would never do.

However, plagiarism also occurs when well-meaning students get careless in taking notes from library or Internet sources or in copying those notes into paper drafts. Following are three examples of *unintentional* plagiarism: (1) A student copies a passage word for word from an Internet site and pastes it word for word into a paper, but forgets to include quotation marks or author attribution. (2) A student summarizes, but does not directly quote, a published author's idea and omits both author name and source title. (3) A student credits an author's idea in a signal phrase (According to John Smith . . .) but omits quotation marks around the author's exact phrases. None of these may be intentional, but each is an act of plagiarism, and each could be easily avoided by clearer knowledge and more careful research and writing practice.

What Plagiarism Is Not

Writers don't need to attribute everything they write or say to specific sources. For example, what we call *common knowledge* does not need documentation. You do not need to credit common historical, cultural, or geographical information that an educated adult American person can be expected to know. Nor do you need to attribute to specific authorities the factual information that appears in multiple sources, such as the dates of historical events (the sacking of Rome in 410 A.D., the Declaration of Independence in 1776), the names and locations of states and cities, the general laws of science (gravity, motion), statements of well-known theories (feminism, liberalism, evolution).

You don't need to document phrases in widespread use in your own culture (global warming, cloning, urban sprawl). Nor do you need to document what is well known in the field in which you are writing that can be found in textbooks and lectures. For example, in a paper written about Sigmund Freud for a psychology professor, don't document the terms *libido* or *superego*. In a paper written for English, history, art, or philosophy, don't document *Victorian, the Roaring Twenties, modern,* or *postmodern.* In other words, within a given interpretative community, basic ideas and knowledge can be assumed to be the common property of all members of that community. However, specific positions or interpretations within a community do need specifically to be identified: How fellow psychotherapists Jung and Adler viewed Freud; how one specific critic viewed Victorian manners compared to another critic, and so on.

Recognizing and Avoiding Plagiarism

If the author of an article, book, or Web site offers unique opinions or interpretations about any type of common knowledge (see earlier examples), these should be credited using the proper documentation style. For example, in writing a paper for an English or film professor about comic book heroes portrayed in the movies, you decide to use this passage in Roger Ebert's review of *Spider-Man* for *Chicago Sun Times,* May 3, 2002:

> **Remember the first time you saw the characters defy gravity in *Crouching Tiger, Hidden Dragon*? They transcended gravity, but they didn't dismiss it: They seemed to possess weight, dimension and presence. Spider-Man as he leaps across the rooftops is landing too lightly, rebounding too much like a bouncing ball. He looks like a video game figure, not like a person having an amazing experience.**

Now, Ebert's whole review is readily available on the Internet, easily accessed via the Internet Movie Database http://www.imdb.com/, so that it's easy to block and copy parts of it to paste directly into the paper you are writing. (In an academic paper, the citation would appear on a "Works Cited" (MLA) or "Reference" (APA) page; if academic style is not required, including author and title in a signal phrase would give proper credit.) If the research writer does not follow proper citation guidelines, he or she might inadvertently plagiarize, as the following examples illustrate.

- It is plagiarism if the student cut and pasted the *Spider-Man* passage above directly into the paper without acknowledging that it was written by Roger Ebert.

  - To fix, credit in a signal phrase (According to Roger Ebert . . .), put the passage in quotation marks and in an academic paper, identify where the passage came from and when it was published on a works cited page (MLA) or reference page (APA). (See Research References 1 & 2.)

- It is plagiarism if the student wrote: *The problem with* Spider-Man *is the video-game quality of the characters who bound from roof to roof and don't seem to be affected by gravity—unlike the more realistic figures in the movie* Crouching Tiger, Hidden Dragon. In this case the student lifts Ebert's idea in clearly identifiable ways, but does not quote Ebert directly.

  - To fix, credit in a signal phrase *Roger Ebert claims the problem with* Spider-Man *is the video-game quality . . .*) and, if an academic paper, identify where the passage came from and when it was published in the appropriate academic convention.

- It is plagiarism if the student lifted key portions of Ebert's exact language from the passage without using quotation marks: *Roger Ebert claims that the characters in* Crouching Tiger, Hidden Dragon *transcended gravity, but they didn't dismiss it.* Though Ebert is credited with the idea, he is not credited with the language.

  - To fix, put quotation marks around the words borrowed: *Roger Ebert claims that the characters in* Crouching Tiger, Hidden Dragon *"transcended gravity, but they didn't dismiss it."* Again, if this is an academic paper, identify where the passage came from and when it was published on the appropriate reference page.

GUIDELINES FOR AVOIDING PLAGIARISM

Plagiarism is a serious offense in every field and department across the curriculum. In simplest terms, it's the act of copying somebody else's work and passing it off as your own. In addition to the many obvious cases described in this chapter, it's also plagiarism to copy the results of a neighbor's biology experiment in your lab report; it's plagiarism to copy a chart or graph from an economics textbook and not attribute it; and it's a form of plagiarism to hand in somebody else's field notes and claim them as yours. Below are simple guidelines for avoiding plagiarism:

- For all copied sources, note *who said what, where,* and*when.*
- When using quoted material, do not distort or intentionally modify an author's meaning.
- Print out and save at least the first page of all online material, making sure it contains the Internet address and date.
- Hand copy identifying information (name, title, date, place of publication) on all photocopied or printed source pages.
- In using direct quotation, place all exactly copied language quotation marks.
- In writing a paraphrase or summary, credit the author *and* recast the original material into your own language.
- Identify all borrowed ideas and language with appropriate references using the appropriate documentation system (MLA, APA, etc.).

◆ SUGGESTIONS FOR WRITING AND RESEARCH

Individual and Collaborative
Review the guidelines throughout this chapter on using sources correctly, especially *integrating and introducing quotations, paraphrasing, summarizing, using visual images,* and *avoiding plagiarism.* Then reflect, in an informal freewrite, on previous research papers you have written, recalling which guidelines you generally followed and which ones you did not. Exchange freewrites with a partner, read each other's confessions, and tell each other which guidelines you will follow more carefully in the future.

CHAPTER TWENTY-EIGHT

Writing for the World at Large

I feel pretty good about the writing I've done over the past four years. I mean, I can see how much I learned and how much better my papers are this year than when I started as a freshman. But I'm a little worried about the kind of writing I'll have to if and when I get a job. Any suggestions?

JESSE

How important will writing be in the world of work beyond college? In many cases, the answer is "very." At the same time, if you took college writing seriously, you've already learned the basic skills needed for writing as a professional (law, medicine, education, social work, engineering) or in a business, corporation, government, or nonprofit agency. What are these basics, you ask? First, knowing how to shape your language with a clear purpose toward a specific audience in a readable style. Second, being familiar with the conventions of standard written English (spelling, punctuation, grammar). And if you've read the preceding chapters I'm betting you already understand these basics.

The remainder of this chapter outlines a core of writing tasks commonly found in the world of writing outside of college: *applying for jobs; writing business letters, memos,* and *e-mail; sending letters to editors; writing reports,* and *composing newsletters, pamphlets,* and *brochures.* In most cases, you won't know your audience or where your writing will travel once it leaves your desk—which means it had better stand pretty well on its own and represent clearly what you intend. I'll try to steer you to more specialized resources than this short volume can provide to help you master the details of any of these forms.

WRITING ON THE JOB

Like writing in the social and physical sciences, writing in business, government, and the professions puts a premium on presenting information clearly; like writing in the humanities, it is highly influenced by the relation between writer and reader. The guiding objectives in most workaday writing are efficiency, accuracy, and responsibility: Procedures are designed for minimal waste of time and energy, care is taken to avoid errors, and transactions are conducted fairly. Such writing is primarily practical and instrumental, because its goal is to get things done. For efficiency, it should be simple, direct, and brief; for accuracy, it should convey correct information and conform to standard conventions; and for responsibility, it should be honest and courteous.

On-the-job writing is always about audience. To whom is the communication being written? What information do audience members already have? What else do they need to know? And what, if any, secondary audience may end up reading this?

First Things First

Because most on-the-job writing is highly purposeful, the language should be simple, direct, economical, and conventional. If you don't know the audience personally, prefer a formal, but friendly tone. If you know the audience, a more personal, informal tone may be appropriate—a matter mostly of good judgment. The following guidelines should help:

- *Start fast.*   State the main point immediately, and avoid digression or repetition unless highly purposeful. Your reader's time—as well as your own—is valuable.
- *Write in a simple, direct style.*   Keep your sentences as straightforward and readable as possible. Test this by reading your writing out loud to yourself.
- *Choose the active voice*   (*state the main point*) rather than the passive voice (*the main point should be stated*) because it's more direct, clear, and economical.
- *Use jargon sparingly.*   Write out complete names of companies, products, and titles. Explain any terms that could be misunderstood by an outside audience.
- *Avoid emotional and biased language.*   Write respectfully to your audience and treat them fairly, whether making a proposal or lodging a complaint.
- *Use numbers, bullets, or subheadings*   to help readers locate information quickly.
- *Use graphs, charts, and other illustrations*   when they convey information more clearly than verbal language.

WRITING BUSINESS LETTERS

Business letters commonly are written to request, inform, apply, or complain to an audience who is, in many cases, unknown to the letter writer. Successful letters state their purpose clearly and provide all information needed to make both understanding and responding easy for the reader. Traditional business letters contain the elements that follow (see Figure 28.1).

Block Paragraphs

Type your letter on 8½ × 11″ paper, one side only, using a block format, in which every element of the letter is typed flush with the left margin and paragraphs are not indented. When using this format, note that each paragraph should have its own clear and distinct topic or focus; the white space between paragraphs makes each stand out distinctly for easy reading.

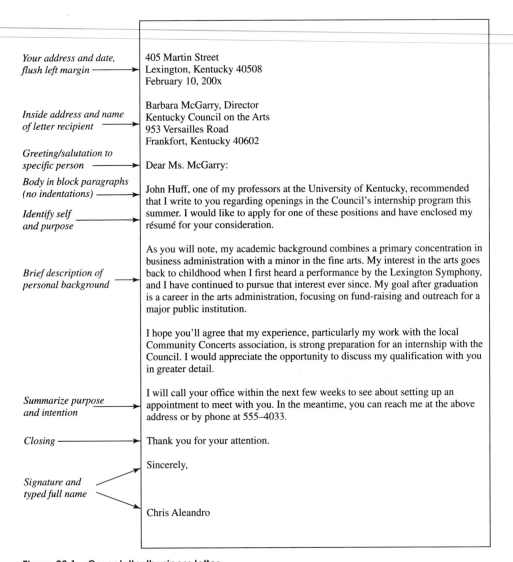

Your address and date,
flush left margin ——————▶   405 Martin Street
Lexington, Kentucky 40508
February 10, 200x

Inside address and name
of letter recipient ——————▶   Barbara McGarry, Director
Kentucky Council on the Arts
953 Versailles Road
Frankfort, Kentucky 40602

Greeting/salutation to
specific person ——————▶   Dear Ms. McGarry:

Body in block paragraphs
(no indentations) ——————▶   John Huff, one of my professors at the University of Kentucky, recommended
that I write to you regarding openings in the Council's internship program this
Identify self
and purpose ——————▶   summer. I would like to apply for one of these positions and have enclosed my
résumé for your consideration.

As you will note, my academic background combines a primary concentration in
business administration with a minor in the fine arts. My interest in the arts goes
Brief description of ——————▶   back to childhood when I first heard a performance by the Lexington Symphony,
personal background   and I have continued to pursue that interest ever since. My goal after graduation
is a career in the arts administration, focusing on fund-raising and outreach for a
major public institution.

I hope you'll agree that my experience, particularly my work with the local
Community Concerts association, is strong preparation for an internship with the
Council. I would appreciate the opportunity to discuss my qualification with you
in greater detail.

Summarize purpose
and intention ——————▶   I will call your office within the next few weeks to see about setting up an
appointment to meet with you. In the meantime, you can reach me at the above
address or by phone at 555–4033.

Closing ——————▶   Thank you for your attention.

Sincerely,

Signature and
typed full name

Chris Aleandro

Figure 28.1   Cover letter/business letter

Heading

Type your own address (but not name) and the date, single-spaced, approximately one inch
from the top at the top right corner of the first page of the letter. Spell out all street and town
names and months in full; abbreviate state names using the standard postal abbreviations;
include the zip code. If you are using letterhead stationery, type the date two lines below the
letterhead address.

Inside Address

Type the recipient's address two or more lines below the heading (depending on how much space is needed to center the letter on the page) flush with the left margin. Include the person's full name (and a courtesy title, if appropriate), followed by his or her position (if needed), the name of the division within the company, the company name, and the full street, city, and state address.

When writing to an unknown person, always try to find out the name, perhaps by calling the company switchboard. If doing this is impossible, use an appropriate title (*Personnel Director* or *Claims Manager,* for example) in place of a name.

Greeting

Type the opening salutation two lines below the inside address (*Dear Dr. Jones, Dear James Wong, Dear Ms. McGarry*) followed by a colon. If you and the recipient are on a first-name basis, it is appropriate to use only the first name. If you do not know the recipient's name, use *To Whom It May Concern* or some variation of *Dear Claims Manager* or *Attention: Director of Marketing* (the latter without a second colon). Avoid the old-fashioned *Dear Sir* or *Dear Sir or Madam.*

Body

Begin the main section of the letter double-spaced below the greeting. Single-space within paragraphs; double-space between paragraphs. If your reason for writing is clear and simple, state it directly in the first paragraph. If it is absolutely necessary to detail a situation, to provide background, or to supply context, do so in the first paragraph or two, and then move on to describe your purpose in writing. Remember, briefer is better.

If your letter is more than one page long, type the addressee's last name, the date, and the page number flush with the right margin of each subsequent page.

Closing

Type the complimentary closing two lines below the last line of the body of the letter. The most common closings are *Sincerely, Cordially, Yours truly, Respectfully yours* (formal), and *Best regards* (informal). Capitalize only the first word of the closing; follow it with a comma.

Signature

Type your full name, including any title, four lines below the closing. Sign the letter in blue or black ink in the space above your typed name; use your full name if you do not know the person well; you may use only your first name if you have addressed the recipient by first name.

Additional Information

You may provide additional brief information below your signature, flush with the left margin. Such information may include recipients of copies of the letter (*cc: Jennifer Rodriguez*); the word *Enclosure* (or the abbreviation *enc.*) to indicate you are also enclosing additional material mentioned in the letter; and, if the letter was typed by someone other than the writer, both the writer's and the typist's initials (*TF/jlw*).

Use common sense when you write business letters; write on good-quality paper; proofread with your computer and with your own eye; correct all errors on screen before printing out; save a copy in a file that's easy to find. See Chris Aleandro's cover letter for a good example of a business letter (Figure 28.1).

For more information on writing business letters and resume cover letters, consult the following online sites:

- *Business letter writing:* businessletterpunch.com—an interactive online **business letter writing** tutorial *<www.businessletterpunch.com>*
- *Business letter format:* *<www.wisc.edu/writing/Handbook/BusinessLetter.htm>*

WRITING RÉSUMÉS

A résumé is a brief summary of an applicant's qualifications for employment. It outlines education, work experience, and other activities and interests so a prospective employer can decide quickly whether or not an applicant is a good prospect for a particular job. Try to tailor your résumé for the position you are seeking by emphasizing experience that is most relevant to the position. Preparing a résumé on a computer lets you revise it easily and quickly.

Résumés should be brief and to the point, preferably no more than a page long (if relevant experience is extensive, more than one page is acceptable). Résumé formats vary in minor ways, but most include the following information.

Personal Information

Résumés begin with the applicant's name, address, and phone number, as well as e-mail and fax address if available. Center these at the top of the page, using one-inch margins (see Figures 28.2 and 28.3).

Objective

Some college résumés include a line summarizing the applicant's objective, either naming the specific job sought or describing a larger career goal (Figure 28.3); others provide this information in the cover letter, keeping the résumé itself more general (Figure 28.2).

Education

Most first-time job applicants list their educational background first, since their employment history is likely to be fairly limited. Name the last two or three schools attended (including dates of attendance and degrees), always listing the most recent school attended first. Indi-

Chris Aleandro

405 Martin Street
Lexington, KY 40508
caleandr@magic.uk.edu

Education	B.A., University of Kentucky (expected May 2006) Major: Business Minor: Art history Grade point average: 3.87 Honors Thesis: "The Art of Business" Graduate, Henry Clay High School (Lexington, KY) 1998–2002
Awards, Honors	Martin Perry Scholarship for Outstanding Business Major Honors, School of Business
Employment	2004–2005 Habitat for Humanity: Co-chaired campus fund-raising drive that raised $55,000. 2003–2004 Community Concerts, Inc.: Part-time promotion assistant; assist with scheduling, publicity, subscription procedures, and fund-raising. 2002–2003 Art in the Schools Program Volunteer, through the Education Division, Lexington Center for the Arts: Trained to conduct art appreciation presentations in school classrooms, visiting one school a month. 2001–2003 Record City (part time and summers): Sales clerk and assistant manager in a music store.
Special Skills	*Word 2000, PowerPoint, Excel,* Web page design.
Special Interests	Journalism, watercolor painting, pottery, digital photography, cross-country skiing.
References	Available on request.

Figure 28.2   Chronological résumé

cate major areas of study, and highlight any relevant courses. Also consider including grade point average, awards, and anything else that shows you in a good light. When the employment history is more detailed, educational background is often placed at the end of the résumé. If you've written a senior or master's thesis, include its title and the name of your thesis director.

Susan Anderson

CURRENT ADDRESS   222 Summit Street, Burlington, VT 05401
TELEPHONE AND E-MAIL   (802) 864-XXXX; susan.anderson@XXX.XXX

OBJECTIVE: Researcher/writer for nonprofit environmental organization.

EDUCATION

    University of Vermont. School of Natural Resources, Geology and English
        double major. GPA: 3.6. Expected graduation, May 2006.
    Fairfield High School. Fairfield, OH. 1998–2002. Activities included debate
        team, Spanish club, student newspaper, field hockey, swimming.

SKILLS

    Field research. Extensive experience analyzing natural plant communities,
        quantifying data, surveying field sites, and drawing topographical site maps.
    Newsletter publication. Familiar with all aspects of editorial and feature writing,
        layout, production, and fund-raising for nonprofit newsletters.
    Computer literacy. Fluent in *MS Word, Excel, PowerPoint, Adobe Premier,*
        Sigmaplot, INFORM, Quark Xpress.
    Oral communication. Confident public speaker to large and small audiences
        after three years on the university debate team.
    Spanish. Fluent after four years of secondary and college study, including
        AFS summer abroad in Quito, Ecuador.

RELEVANT ENVIROMENTAL COURSEWORK

    Field Ecology Methods
    Landscape and Ecosystem Ecology
    Fundamentals of Field Science
    Landscape Inventory and Assessment

RESEARCH EXPERIENCE

    Southwest Earth Studies, June–August 2005. Internship to research public policy
        of acid mine drainage in the San Juan mountains, National Science Foundation.
    Field Research of the Newark Rift Basin, June 2004. Internship to study water
        flow in the Newark rift basin, Newark Environmental Foundation program.

COMMUNICATION EXPERIENCE

    Teaching Fellow, School of Natural Resources, University of Vermont, January
        2005–present. Teach lab for a course, Environmental Problem Solving.
    Editorial Assistant, *Wild Gulf Journal,* The Chewonki Foundation, January 2004
        –December 2005. Edited a quarterly journal of environmental education.
    Tutor, Writing Center, University of Vermont, September 2003–December,
        2004. Counseled students in writing undergraduate papers in introductory
        and intermediate geology courses.

LEADERSHIP EXPERIENCE

    English Majors' Student Representative, University of Vermont, September
        2003–May 2004. Elected to represent 200 English majors and participate as
        a voting member at faculty meetings and curriculum revision committee
    Local Foods Coordinator, Onion River Coop. Burlington, VT. January 2001–May 2002.
        Ordered and coordinated pick-ups from local farms.

REFERENCES: Available upon request.

Figure 28.3   Skills–based résumé

Work Experience

Starting with the most recent, list all relevant jobs, including company name, dates of employment, and a brief job description. Use your judgment about listing jobs where you had difficulties with your employer.

Special Skills or Interests

It is often useful to mention special skills, interests, or activities that provide additional clues about your abilities and personality.

References

Provide the names, addresses, and phone numbers of two or three people—teachers, supervisors, employers—who you trust to give a good reference for you. (Make sure you get their permission first.) Alternatively, you may want to conclude with the line "References available on request."

For more information on writing resumes as well as other samples and styles to look at, consult the following online sources:

- *How to Write a Masterpiece of a Resume:* <*www.rockportinstitute.com/resumes .html*>
- *How to Write a Resume—Career Services at Capital University:* <*www.capital.edu/ cc/car/csresumea.html*>

WRITING COVER LETTERS

While not part of the résumé itself, a cover letter is a standard accompaniment to a résumé. Like all business letters, keep this letter as brief as possible, especially when you suspect your audience may be reading many such letters. At the same time, a cover letter may convey something of your voice, including tone, style, values, and personality. Be clear and direct; avoid being too cute or pretentious. Again, use good judgment here; the cover letter introduces you to your audience, and first impressions are important (see Figure 28.1).

WRITING MEMOS

Memo is short for *memorandum,* which is defined as a short note or reminder to someone to do something. Memos are used in business and college offices to suggest that actions be taken or to alert one or more people about a change in policy or an upcoming meeting. Part of the value of the memo is that the memo writer retains a record (a memory) that something was communicated to certain people on such and such a date.

Memo format is simple and direct. Names of both receiver and sender, along with the date and subject, are included at the top of the page so that the receiver knows instantly what this message is about. The simple standard format has the following parts:

To: Name of person or persons to whom it will be sent (flush left)
From: Name of memo sender
Re: Regarding what subject
Date (at right margin)

Following is a typical memo:

To: Paul, Sue, Tony, and Jean

From: Toby

Re: Curriculum Committee meeting

Date: December 6 200X

Our last meeting of the semester will be Tuesday (1/30) at 3:30 P.M. in Old Mill, room 104. The agenda is to plan discussion items for the spring semester and explore the possibility of a holiday party. Sue will provide refreshments.

For more detailed information on writing effective memos, consult either of the following Web sites:

- Memo writing: <owl.english.purdue.edu/handouts/pw/p_memo.html>
- How to write a memo: <www.suite101.com/article.cfm/5381/34825>

THE CONVENTIONS OF E-MAIL

In terms of formality, memos and electronic mail (e-mail) used in work settings exist somewhere in the middle of a continuum with formal letters at one end and casual telephone conversation at the other end. Like formal letters, writing conventions count. Like telephone conversation, many informal exchanges can take place in a short time. And like memos, a simple fixed format (To, Cc, Subject) gets you started quickly.

Formal letters—memos—e-mail—telephone talk

While writing an e-mail message to a friend can be about anything at all and take any form you're both comfortable with (no capital letters, casual punctuation, frequent emoticons, etc.), writing to conduct business is another matter altogether. When communicating with people you don't know well, especially if something important is at stake (applying for a job, sending a letter to an editor, closing a deal), it's best to follow the accepted conventions of the medium—and the conventions of e-mail, like the medium itself, fall somewhere between the formality of business letters and the informality of telephone talk. The following guidelines may help:

- *Be brief.* People are impatient about reading long messages on computer monitors; the longer the text, the more likely people will skim.

- *Be informal.*   Even in business communications, people expect e-mail to be informal and friendly—*I* and *you* and contractions are acceptable—but people also expect to see full sentences and normal capitalization and punctuation.
- *Read your audience.*   Think about your audience before you write, and be especially careful, correct, and courteous if you don't know your audience.
- *Get to the point.*   E-mail should be purposeful, direct, and to the point. Use the message line, as you would in a memo, to indicate your subject.
- *Focus.*   E-mails that make a single point or ask a particular question receive the quickest and most direct responses. Your respondent may miss something important if you include too many items.
- *Number items.*   If it's important to address several issues or questions in a single e-mail, number them so the points are clear and don't get lost at the receiving end.
- *Check often.*   E-mail is fast and efficient only if it's checked regularly; if e-mail is an expected mode of communication, check it daily.
- *Reply promptly.*   E-mail has caught on quickly in our culture because it's so much faster than conventional mail. Replies are best made the same or the following day.
- *Reread all outgoing messages.*   Because e-mail is fast, people don't spend a lot of time revising it. However, you'll save yourself some embarrassment by proofreading both message and audience address before sending it.
- *Be courteous.*   Address people by name (*Dr. Smith; Hi, Robyn*); end with a salutation (*Thanks for your help*); and don't "flame" with angry, insulting messages you'll regret later.
- *Respect privacy and copyright.*   Don't forward messages or publish copyrighted material without permission.

For more information about the conventions and "netiquette" of e-mail writing consult

- *Beginner's Guide to Effective Email* <www.webfoot.com/advice/**email**.top.html>

LETTERS TO THE EDITOR

As either concerned citizen or expert professional, you may be moved to comment on, correct, rebut, or celebrate an item you read in the newspaper or hear on the news. Such Letters to the Editor are the most common ways for people to express opinions to a wide public audience. While there are no rules that govern the writing of such letters, the following strategies will make your letter more likely to be published, read, and have an influence than not:

- *Address "Letter to the Editor."*   Include the full and correct name of the medium you hope will print your letter.
- *Identify yourself.*   Include your full name, address, phone number and e-mail address. Other than your name, editors will not publish this information but may want to verify that you are who you say you are.
- *Keep it short.*   Brief letters are more likely to be published and read than long ones, so keep it under 200 words.

- *Summarize the issue.*   Briefly review the issue or concern that triggered your letter before expressing your own concern. Include the headline of the article and date it was published.
- *Be timely.*   Respond to issues while they are still newsworthy.
- *Focus on one issue per letter.*   To keep reader attention, write about a single concern per letter to keep editor and reader attention.
- *Organize your response.*   Summarize the issue, state your opinion, present your evidence, and get out fast.
- *Cite authority.*   Quote expert opinion and use facts to back up your opinion.
- *Be fair.*   If you want a fair hearing from an editor and from readers, be fair, polite, and reasonable; limit biased language; and don't indulge in name calling.
- *Write in a simple style.*   Prefer short words, simple sentences, and active voice, so the broadest possible audience will understand you.
- *Don't presume reader knowledge.*   Provide context and explain any technical terminology and all acronyms.
- *Print your message carefully.*   Whether you use e-mail, U.S. Mail, or fax, compose in conventional sentences and paragraphs, and use a font that is clear and easy to read (10–12 pt.).
- *Send e-mail.*   If the newspaper encourages e-mail, use it, because it's quicker and simpler to reprint, but do not include attachments, as they won't be opened for fear of viruses.
- *Proofread carefully for errors in spelling, punctuation and grammar.*   Editors usually publish exactly what you send, so don't risk public embarrassment because of silly error.

For additional online help in writing letters of advocacy and protest consult:

- *Tips on Writing Letters to the Editor* <www.hsus.org/legislation_laws/citizen_ lobbyist_center/ lobbying_101/tips_on_**writing_letters**_to_ the_**editor**.html>

WRITING REPORTS

Research reports of one kind or another are the formal documents that support decision making in business, government, industry, medicine, education, and a host of nonprofit agencies. Written reports are the end product of methodical information gathering and data collection, of lab and field experimentation, as well as the back-and-forth discussions of committees. Written reports inform presidents, congressmen, senators, CEO's, managers, editors, broadcasters, and nearly every individual or agency wishing to make informed decisions about policies, products, and actions. In other words, written reports back up decision making throughout the working world and, sooner or later, if you're gainfully employed, you're going to contribute to or author one yourself.

Report formats, styles, and lengths vary widely, but all reports have a similar objective: to convey information clearly, correctly, economically, and predictably. If you are working for a specific organization, chances are it has a ready-made format for you to follow. If not, the following guidelines may help.

Report Format

Not all reports need all the following information, so it's a good idea to assess the size and formality of the report you are working on and decide which of the following components best suits your task and audience. A major formal report may, in fact, have all the following components:

- *Letter of transmittal.*   When a report is submitted, it is usually accompanied by a letter addressed to the recipient explaining the nature of the report and signed by those responsible for writing it.
- *Title page.*   A cover that includes the title of the report, who has written it, and the date it was written/submitted. The report title should describe the project simply, directly, and clearly and not try to be too clever (prefer *The Faculty Writing Project: A Two-Year Report,* not *Write on Faculty!*).
- *Acknowledgments.*   A page or paragraph thanking people or organizations who have helped compile the report.
- *Table of Contents.*   For long reports (ten pages or more), create a table of contents (TOC) listing the subhead titles within the report and identifying the page numbers on which they will be found. A TOC will help readers navigate easily.
- *Executive summary or abstract.*   In many instances, this will be the most important (because most widely read) part of the report. A summary or abstract advertises up front, what the report concludes and recommends. Write this section last, in neutral descriptive language when you are sure of the results.
- *Introduction/background.*   Summarizes the history or background of the project to familiarize any audience with the context for the information about to be provided and briefly explains what information the report will provide.
- *Method or procedure.*   Some reports, especially those in technical fields, will want a separate step-by-step description of how the information in the report was arrived at. This section outlines how you gathered information, where from, and how much—via interviews? surveys? experiments? library research? and so on.
- *Body of report.*   The major part of the report contains the main topics of the report presented in some reasonable, logical order, each identified by subheads and often numbered. It should contain sufficient information to justify the conclusions and recommendations which follow. It goes without saying that appropriate information should be included, irrelevant information omitted.
- *Conclusion.*   Explains what the project concluded and why it is credible and important. No new information should be presented here. Sets up the final important section of the report.
- *Recommendations.*   Informs readers what you believe should be done in light of the report's findings. Should follow directly from the information in the body and the conclusion; the more specific, the better.
- *References/bibliography.*   As in academic papers, readers want to know what sources you consulted and what experts you talked with. (References are items referred to in the report, while a bibliography contains additional material not specifically referred to, but which readers may want to follow up.)
- *Appendices.*   An appendix includes documents that are related to the report or from which information has been culled, but which are not deemed central to

understanding the main thrust of the report. Cross-reference in the text and, if more than one, number or alphabetize.

Report Style

Follow the general stylistic advice for most on-the-job writing as described throughout this chapter. Write your report in language that is clear, simple, direct, economical, and conventional. Use subheadings to organize information into manageable chunks by providing bold face headings for the different parts or categories within the report. Use plenty of white space so sections and subtitles are easy to locate. Use bullets or numbers to highlight specific items (as I've done throughout this chapter.) Use tables, charts, graphs, and illustrations where such visual images aid in comprehension. Write in third-person objective language free of value judgments and emotional responses, except where a clearly identified first-person aside is necessary.

For more detailed, step-by-step directions for writing reports in a variety of work settings, consult either of the following Web sites:

- *Report Writing:* Purpose of Business Reports <planet.tvi.cc.nm.us/ba122/Reports/ Report Writing.htm>
- *UniS Skills Project Pilot Pack:* Communications—Report Writing <www .surrey.ac.uk/Skills/pack/report.html>

COMPOSING NEWSLETTERS

Newsletters are as varied in format, style, and size as the organizations that publish them. Sometimes they exist solely as printed text, sometimes as electronic text, sometimes both; sometimes they include graphics, other times text alone. If you need to design and edit a major newsletter yourself, you will want to study as many models as possible, as well as consult more detailed professional writing guidelines such as the two excellent Web sites listed at the end of this section. However, the following guidelines will get you started:

- *Know your audience.*   Who are they? What is relevant to them? What will catch their interest?
- *Know your purpose.*   Who or what in your organization are you speaking for? What do you want the newsletter to accomplish: the dispensing of information? increased attendance at meetings or events? some other kind of action?
- *Develop a publication plan.*   Plan and make known in advance when each newsletter will "hit the stands" and back up from that date to make sure to keep your publication schedule.
- *Establish a friendly, convenient format.*   Newsletter sections may be as simple as subheadings announcing *Current News; Feature Stories; Notes from Last Meeting; Agenda for Next Meeting; Upcoming Events,* and so on. (If your newsletter is published on the Web, these categories will become links for viewers to read.)
- *Establish an identifiable masthead.*   Each issue should feature a bold heading (logo, memorable image or text), called a masthead, at the top of the first

newsletter page to clearly identify the document, regardless of content which will change with each publication—a masthead may include a dominant image (Capitol building) or simply attractive lettering (**synergy**).

- *Keep the paper and the articles within it short and to the point.*   Use informational subheadings, bullets, and relevant graphics to hold reader attention.

- *Solicit contributions.*   Request submissions or assign topics to writers you trust, but don't do all the writing yourself.

- *Set deadlines*   for yourself and contributors, and keep them.

- *Be an editor.*   Edit contributions for style, clarity, economy, and correctness so that all pieces you publish are substantial and hit the target audience.

- *Use headlines and lead with best stories.*   Like published newspapers, try to engage readers early on with interesting stories.

- *Learn the difference between a story and news updates.*   In addition to news and information, a "story" will include human interest, which is most easily accomplished by including quotations from real people in their own colorful language and show that something happened with a clear beginning, middle, and ending.

- *Use graphics judiciously.*   Good images well placed improve the look of your newsletter as well as carry selected information more powerfully than print. However, pretty graphics won't make up for weak writing.

- *Publish electronic newsletters in plain text.*   Be concise and include graphics only if you know all subscribers can open them (solicit feedback from e-mail recipients to find out how your text comes across).

- *Solicit reader responses.*   Find out how your newsletter is being received by looking for feedback: ask readers what they think; notice whether it gets talked about in the halls, lunchroom, or by the water cooler.

For additional online help designing newsletters, consult either of the following Web sites:

- *Newsletters: 15 Tips on Writing, Editing* <www.topstory.ca/newsletters.html>.
- *Portland State University—Office of Publications. Newsletter Writing Tips: Publications Office Style Guide* <www.publications.pdx.edu/tips.html>.

COMPOSING BROCHURES, PAMPHLETS, POSTERS, AND FLYERS

Brochures and pamphlets are small booklets you might design and write to publicize an issue, event, product, or organization. A *pamphlet* usually focuses on a current issue, such as the twelve-page booklet promoting healthy living that you might pick up in a doctor's office published by the National Institute of Health. A *brochure* is even shorter than a pamphlet—often just a single paper folded once (creates four "pages") or twice (creates six "pages") to fit in an envelope or be stapled and mailed—that provides information about or advertises a specific subject, such as the promotional brochure I created to advertise an upcoming faculty writing workshop (right). *Flyers* and *posters* which advertise upcoming events are typically one-sided and meant to be displayed fully open. They can be mailed or attached to bulletin boards or other empty wall space.

All of these forms are meant to catch viewer attention by a combination of bold text and attractive images. The following guidelines focus on designing a simple four-panel booklet (one sheet 8½ × 11 or 14″ paper, folded once (the example here is 14, which makes four pages 8½ × 7 to work with); however, the design principles apply equally to all of these forms, whether one page or six—the main difference that applies to flyers and posters will be the enlarging of images and text to fit the larger single-page displays of these media.

- *Front brochure cover.*   Make it visually appealing with an attractive graphic, logo, or title that invites the reader to open up and read further. But keep it clean, without too much information—that's what the space inside is for.
- *Inside, second page.*   The inside of front cover (p. 2 as shown) is the most important

Page 1   Front Cover

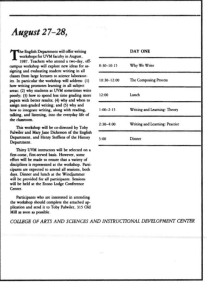

Page 2   Inside

space, so put your most important message here. Use headings and subheadings to call attention to different aspects of the event, product, or issue involved.

- *Inside third page.*   This page (page 3) faces the second page and provides space to complete your explanation or agenda. If the event is a workshop or conference, this is an excellent place for a chart outlining the titles and times of scheduled events. (In the accompanying example, the third page is split in two, making an application tearsheet the respondent can send back to register for the workshop.)
- *Back cover.*   Provide contact information only, since this is the space least likely to be read. If document is to be mailed, consider an additional fold (p. 4 right) and add reader address here (p. 4 left of fold).
- *Style suggestions.*   Write economically, so readers find information quickly without wading through unnecessary or digressive language. Choose simple language: short words rather than long, simple rather than complex sentences; avoid or explain all technical terms and acronyms. This advice goes double for posters and flyers, which have only one page on which to present their case.
- *Point of view.*   Third person neutral language is appropriate for dispensing information. Second person, or direct address to reader, suits an invitation to an event or purchase of a product.
- *Graphics.*   Brochures, pamphlets, posters, and flyers are more attractive with relevant graphics; however, be aware that space is limited, so graphics need to convey important information and be modest in size.

For additional online help with more detailed information designing brochures and flyers, consult:

- *Brochure Design Tip* <www.tips-strategies-and-solutions.com/1/brochures-design-tip.html>
- *Community Toolbox—Consensus Building* <www.nps.gov/phso/rtcatoolbox/writcom_brochures.html>

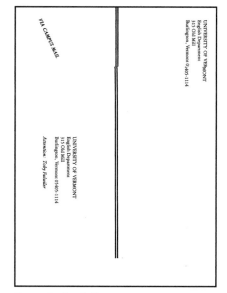

Page 3   Inside

Page 4   Back Cover

◆ SUGGESTIONS FOR WRITING AND RESEARCH

Individual or Collaborative

Following is an excellent collaborative project to be done by a class, though a small group or individual alone could also accomplish it. Fan out and collect as many samples of on-the-job writing as you in your local community: Collect material from display racks at offices, stores, and businesses; find published information on bulletin boards; visit the university public relations department to gather brochures, flyers, and newsletters created by your own school. Assemble and categorize these samples to create a class library of on-the-job writing, following the categories outlined in this chapter and adding new ones not covered here. Post this catalog on a class Web site for future writer reference.

Documenting Sources: MLA

Papers in language and literature use the documentation system of the *Modern Language Association (MLA)*. Language and literature courses are concerned with reading and writing about texts such as poems, novels, plays, and essays written by published authors as well as by students. (The term *text* is defined here broadly to include films, visual arts, advertisements—anything that can be read and interpreted.) What sets literary studies apart from most other disciplines is the attention devoted to all elements of written language. In these courses, writing is not only the means of study but often the object of study as well: Works are examined for their *form* and *style* as well as their *content*. Texts are read, listened to, discussed, and written about so students can discover what these texts are, how they work, what they mean, and what makes them exceptional or flawed. Moreover, literary studies often draw on ideas from other disciplines. For instance, reading a single novel such as Charles Dickens' *David Copperfield* can teach readers a little about sociology, psychology, history, geography, architecture, political science, and economics as well as the esthetics of novel writing.

In other words, when writing about texts, research in one direction or another can greatly expand your knowldege and understanding of any text. Research assignments commonly require you to read, analyze, synthesize, and assess what other critics have said about a work you are studying. In most cases, you will be expected to develop your own ideas based on your close reading of the *primary sources* (the work itself plus original documents such as letters, journals, and interviews), and to introduce *secondary sources* (other published views of the work) as a way of supporting, expanding, or contrasting your initial views.

317

THE ROLE OF DOCUMENTATION IN TEXTUAL STUDY

When you research and write in disciplines such as English, foreign languages, and art history, you can focus on a text's ideas, author, formal qualities, themes, or historical and cultural context. For such essays, you need to document **primary sources,** the text itself (which in addition to printed texts, may include art, music, and other human-made objects) and perhaps other primary works to which you may compare it. In addition, you can expand your knowledge of any text by referring to **secondary sources,** what others have said about the primary. Your text-based assignment may include any of the following directions, and each one can be enhanced and made stronger by careful citation of the primary source and additional consultation with secondary sources.

- *Appreciating texts.*   You write about the text's features that most move or engage you—the beauty or strangeness of the setting, the character with whom you most identify, the plot as it winds from beginning to end, or the turns and rhythms of the language. One strategy for using research sources would be first to document the passages and pages of the primary text that most move you; next to document secondary sources to confirm (or question) your own first assessment; then to conclude by affirming or modifying your own first assessment.
- *Analyzing texts.*   You ask questions such as *How is it put together?* or *How does it work?* Analysis involves looking at a text's component parts (chapters, for example) and the system that makes it work as a whole (such as the plot), defining what they are, describing what they are like, and explaining how they function. This analytic activity is sometimes required by itself, but more commonly as part of a larger interpretive or evaluative activity (see following). A good analytical research strategy would be to document the pattern of passages in the *primary text* that support your own first analysis; then to document how close readers in *secondary sources* expand or raise questions about your own initial reading.
- *Interpreting texts.*   You ask, *What does it mean? How do I know what it means?* and *Why was it made?* Interpretations often vary widely from reader to reader and may provoke quite a bit of disagreement, as each reader analyzes a text in different ways. A good argumentative research strategy might be to document the passages in the primary text that support your own first interpretation; next to document interpretations you find in secondary sources at odds with your own; finally to document the secondary sources that support your interpretation.
- *Evaluating texts.*   *How good is it? What makes it worth reading?* These are questions of judgment, based on criteria that might differ considerably from person to person. For example, a book reviewer will commonly summarize, analyze, and briefly interpret a text on the way to recommending it as an important text to read (or not). One research strategy would be to document a range of secondary sources that reveal multiple reading recommendations. For instance, one reviewer judges a poem good because its rhythm and imagery are pleasing (esthetic criteria), another praises the poem's subversive qualities (political criteria), and a third (secondary) looks for underlying assumptions or values (philosophical criteria). Conclude with your own personal assessment by reviewing the reviewers.

- *Inferring cultural values.*   You can also use literary and other texts to study culture by asking, *What are the values of the people depicted in the text?* and *How do the scenes, settings, and characters reveal the character of the broader culture?* To find answers to these and other questions, it is common to compare the text with other texts produced at the same or different times. To raise cultural questions, document the passage in the primary text that describes a historical event or scene, then in secondary sources, locate and document similar scenes from different eras or contrasting scenes from the same era.

DOCUMENTING SOURCES: MLA STYLE

The Modern Language Association (MLA) system is the preferred form for documenting research sources when you write about literature or language.

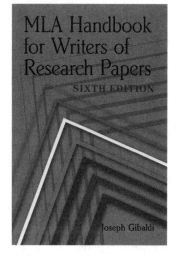

- All sources are briefly documented in the text by an identifying name and page number (generally in parentheses).
- A Works Cited section at the end of the paper lists full publication data for each source cited.
- Additional explanatory information provided by the writer of the paper (but not from external sources) goes either in footnotes at the foot of the page or in a Notes section after the close of the paper.

The MLA system is explained in more detail in the *MLA Handbook for Writers of Research Papers,* 6th ed. (New York: MLA, 2003) aimed specifically at undergraduate writers, as well as *The MLA Style Manual and Guide to Scholarly Publishing,* second edition (1998) aimed at graduate students and faculty.

The MLA system provides a simple, concise, and thorough way for writers to acknowledge their research sources. In the MLA system, authors use footnotes and/or endnotes to provide additional, explanatory information, but not to cite information provided by external sources. Whenever possible, the MLA system includes explanatory information in the text itself and limits the use of footnotes or endnotes. Pay careful attention to the practical mechanics of documentation so that readers can readily identify, understand, and locate your sources.

CONVENTIONS FOR IN-TEXT CITATIONS

In-text citations identify ideas and information borrowed from other writers and refer readers to the Works Cited list at the end of the paper, where they can find complete publication information about each source. The disciplines of languages and literature are less concerned with the date at which something was written than with the internal qualities of texts. Therefore, the brief MLA citations in the text feature *author names, text titles,* and *page numbers,* while other disciplines in which currency is most important (the sciences and social sciences) feature dates instead of titles within the text. MLA style is economical, providing only as much in-text information as readers need in order to locate more complete information in the Works Cited list. Following are brief examples of how in-text citation works, while the balance of the chapter includes sample entries formatted for the Works Cited page. A sample paper using MLA documentation concludes the chapter.

1. **Single work by one or more authors**

When you quote, paraphrase, or summarize a source, include the last name of the source's author, if known, and, in parentheses, the page or pages on which the original information appeared. Do not include the word *page* or the abbreviation *p.* or *pp.* You may mention the author's name in the sentence or put it in parentheses preceding the page number(s).

> Carol Lea Clark explains the basic necessities for the creation of a page on the World Wide Web (77).

> Provided one has certain "basic ingredients," the Web offers potential worldwide publication to individuals (Clark 77).

Note that a parenthetical reference at the end of a sentence comes before the period. No punctuation is used between the author's last name and the page number(s).

If you cite a work with two or three authors, your in-text parenthetical citation must include all authors' names: (Rombauer and Becker 715), (Child, Bertholle, and Beck 215). For works with more than three authors, you may list all the authors or, to avoid awkwardness, use the first author's name and add *et al.* (Latin, "and others") without a comma: (*Britton et al. 395*).

2. **Two or more works by the same author**

If your paper has references to two or more works by the same author, either mention the title of the specific work in the text or include a shortened version of the title (usually the first one or two important words) in the parenthetical citation.

> According to Lewis Thomas in <u>Lives of a Cell</u>, many bacteria become dangerous only if they manufacture exotoxins (76).

> According to Lewis Thomas, many bacteria become dangerous only if they manufacture exotoxins (<u>Lives</u> 76).

> Many bacteria become dangerous only if they manufacture exotoxins (Thomas, <u>Lives</u> 76).

If both the author's name and a shortened version of the title are in a parenthetical citation, a comma separates them, but there is no comma before the page number.

3. **Unknown author**

When the author of a work is unknown, use either the complete title in the text or a shortened version of it in the parenthetical citation, along with the page number.

> According to <u>Statistical Abstracts</u>, the literacy rate for Mexico stood at 75 percent in 1990, up 4 percent from census figures ten years earlier (374).

> The literacy rate for Mexico stood at 75 percent in 1990, up 4 percent from census figures ten years earlier (<u>Statistical</u> 374).

4. Corporate or organizational author

When no author is listed for a work published by a corporation, organization, or association, indicate the group's full name in any parenthetical reference: (*Florida League of Women Voters* 3). If the name is long, cite it in the sentence and put only the page number in parentheses.

5. Authors with the same last name

When you cite works by two or more authors with the same last name, include the first initial of each author's name in the parenthetical citation: (*C. Miller 63; S. Miller 101–04*).

6. Works in more than one volume

When your sources are in more than one volume of a multivolume work, indicate the volume number for each citation before the page number, and follow it with a colon and one space: (*Hill 2: 70*). If your source is in only one volume of a multivolume work, don't include the volume number in the text, but do on the Works Cited list.

7. One-page works

When you refer to a work that is one page long, do not include the page number in your citation.

8. Quotation from an indirect source

When a quotation or any information in your source is originally from another source, use the abbreviation *qtd. in.*

> Lester Brown of Worldwatch believes that international agricultural production has reached its limit and that "we're going to be in trouble on the food front before this decade is out" (qtd. in Mann 51).

9. Literary works

In citing literary prose works available in various editions, provide additional information (such as chapter number or scene number) for readers who may be consulting a different edition. Use a semicolon to separate the page number from this additional information: (*331; bk. 10, ch. 5*). In citing poems, provide only line numbers for reference; include the word *line* or *lines* in the first such reference. Providing this information will help your audience find the passages *in any source where those works are reprinted.*

> In "The Mother," Gwendolyn Brooks remembers "[. . .] the children you got that you did not get" (line 1); children that "never giggled or planned or cried" (30).

Cite verse plays using act, scene, and line numbers, separated by periods: (*Hamlet 4.4.31–39*).

10. More than one work in a citation

To cite more than one work in a parenthetical reference, separate them with semicolons: (*Aronson, Golden Shore 177; Didion 49–50*).

11. Long quotation set off from text

Set off quotations of <u>four or more lines</u> by indentation. Indent the quotation one inch or ten spaces from the left margin of the text (not from the paper's edge), double-space, and omit quotation marks. The parenthetical citation follows end punctuation (unlike shorter, integrated quotes) and is not followed by a period.

> Fellow author W. Somerset Maugham, admiring Austen, but not blindly, had this to say about her dialogue:
>
>> No one has ever looked upon Jane Austen as a great stylist. Her spelling was peculiar and her grammar often shaky, but she had a good ear. Her dialogue is probably as natural as dialogue can ever be. To set down on paper speech as it is spoken would be very tedious, and some arrangement of it is necessary (434).

CONVENTIONS FOR ENDNOTES AND FOOTNOTES

MLA notes are used primarily to offer comments, explanations, or additional information (especially source-related information) that cannot be smoothly or easily accommodated in the text of the paper. Use notes also to cite several sources within a single context if a series of *in-text* references might detract from the readability of the text. In general, however, omit additional information, outside the "mainstream" of your text, unless it is necessary for clarification or justification.

If a note is necessary, insert a raised (superscript) numeral at the reference point in the text; introduce the note itself with a corresponding raised numeral, and indent it.

TEXT WITH SUPERSCRIPT

The standard ingredients for guacamole include avocados, lemon juice, onion, tomatoes, coriander, salt, and pepper.[1] Hurtado's poem, however, gives this traditional dish a whole new twist (lines 10–17).

NOTE

[1]For variations see Beard 314, Egerton 197, Eckhardt 92, and Kafka 26. Beard's version, which includes olives and green peppers, is the most unusual.

The references listed in the notes should appear in the Works Cited list.

Notes may be placed either at the bottom of the page on which the text reference appears (*footnotes*) or be included double-spaced, on a separate page at the end of your paper (*endnotes*). Endnote pages should be placed between the text of the paper and the Works Cited, with the title "Note" or "Notes."

CONVENTIONS FOR LIST OF WORKS CITED

All sources mentioned in academic or professional writing should be identified on a concluding list of *works cited*. These entries are formatted in specific ways so that the reader can readily find information.

Format. After the final page, title a separate page "Works Cited," one inch from the top, centered, but not underlined or in quotation marks.

Exception: If you are required to list all the works you have read in researching the topic—not just those to which you have actually referred in your text or notes—you should title this list "Works Consulted" rather than "Works Cited."

Double-space between the Works Cited title and your first entry. Begin each entry at the left margin, indenting the second and all subsequent lines of each entry five spaces. Double-space both between and within entries. If the list runs to more than one page, continue numbering pages in sequence but do not repeat the title.

Order of entries. Alphabetize the entries according to authors' last names. If two or more authors have the same last name, alphabetize by first name or initial. For entries by an unknown author, alphabetize according to the first word of the title, excluding an initial *A, An,* or *The.*

1. Book by one author

Benjamin, Jessica. <u>The Bonds of Love: Psychoanalysis, Feminism, and the Problem of Domination</u>. New York: Prometheus, 1988.

2. Book by two or three authors

Zweigenhaft, Richard L., and G. William Domhoff. <u>Blacks in the White Establishment</u>. New Haven: Yale UP, 1991.

Author names after the first are identified first name first, and the final author's name is preceded by *and.*

3. Book by more than three authors

Belenky, Mary Field, et al. <u>Women's Ways of Knowing: The Development of Self, Voice, and Mind</u>. New York: Basic, 1986.

If a work has more than three authors, you may use the Latin abbreviation *et al.* or list all the authors' names in full as they appear on the title page.

4. More than one book by the same author

Nelson, Mariah Burton. <u>Are We Winning Yet?: How Women Are Changing Sports and Sports Are Changing Women</u>. New York: Basic, 1991.

—. <u>The Stronger Women Get, The More Men Love Football: Sexism and the American Culture of Sports.</u> New York: Harcourt, 1993.

If your Works Cited list contains more than one source by the same author(s), in the second and all additional entries replace the author's name with three hyphens (no spaces) followed by a period. The hyphens represent the *exact* name of the author in the preceding entry. If a source's author is not identical to that in the preceding entry, list author names in full. Two or more works with the same author are alphabetized according to title; a work by a single author precedes works by that author and one or more collaborators.

5. Book by a corporation, association, or organization

Society of Automotive Engineers. <u>Effects of Aging on Driver Performance</u>. Warrendale, PA: Society of Automotive Engineers, 1988.

Alphabetize by the name of the organization.

6. Revised edition of a book

Peek, Stephen. <u>The Game Inventor's Handbook</u>. 2nd ed. Cincinnati: Betterway, 1993.

GENERAL FORMAT FOR BOOK CITATIONS, MLA

one space   one space   one space one space

Author(s). Book Title. Place of publication: Publisher, year of publication.

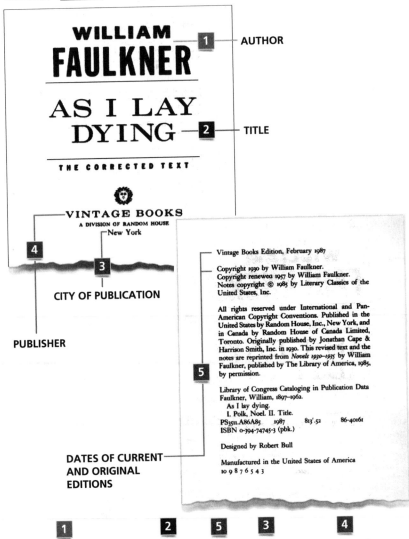

1 — AUTHOR

2 — TITLE

CITY OF PUBLICATION

PUBLISHER

DATES OF CURRENT AND ORIGINAL EDITIONS

1   **2**   **5**   **3**   **4**

Faulkner, William. As I Lay Dying. 1930. New York: Vintage-Random,

1987.

5

Title page and copyright page in front of book

1 AUTHOR OR EDITOR NAME.

Last name first, comma, and rest of the name as it appears on the publication. Period. If a work has more than one author, second and later names are listed first name first, and separated by commas (for example, *Smith, Robert, Michael Jones, and Susan Morse*). Period. If more than one work by the same author, substitute three hyphens for the author's name after the first entry:

Faulkner, William. <u>As I Lay Dying</u>. 1930. New York: Vintage-Random,

1987.

---. <u>Light in August</u>. New York: Modern Library, 1932.

2 BOOK TITLE.

List titles and subtitles fully, capitalizing them as in the original. <u>Underline</u> (or *italicize*) the titles of entire books and put quotation marks around the titles of essays, poems, and short works within larger works. Period. Do not underline the period that follows the title.

3 CITY OF PUBLICATION.

List first city of publication. If the name of a foreign city could be unfamiliar to readers, add abbreviation for the country. (See the section on abbreviations in Chapter 62.) Use a comma to separate city from country; use a colon to separate place from the publisher.

4 PUBLISHER.

Abbreviate publishers' names—for example, *Vintage* for *Vintage Books*. Omit words such as *press, publisher, inc.* Use *UP* for *University Press* (*Wisconsin UP*) or *P* (*U of Mississippi P*). If the title page indicates that a book is published under an imprint—for example, *Vintage Books* is an imprint of *Random House*—list both imprint and publisher, separated by a hyphen (*Vintage-Random*). Use a comma to separate the publisher from the publication date.

5 DATE OF PUBLICATION.

List year of publication as it appears on the copyright page. Period. If no publisher, place of publication, or date of publication is provided, use *n.p.* (for both publisher and place, to be clarified by its relation to the separating colon) or *n.d.* (for date).

For second or any subsequent editions of a book, place the appropriate numerical designation (*2nd ed., 3rd ed.,* etc.) after the name of the editor, translator, or compiler, if there is one. If not, place it after the title.

7. **Edited book**

Schaefer, Charles E., and Steven E. Reid, eds. <u>Game Play: Therapeutic Use of Childhood Games</u>. New York: Wiley, 1986.

For books with a listed editor or editors but no author, place the name of the editor(s) in the author position, followed by *ed.* or *eds.*

8. Book with an editor and an author

Hemingway, Ernest. <u>Conversations with Ernest Hemingway</u>. Ed. Matthew J. Bruccoli. Jackson: UP of Mississippi, 1986.

Books with both an editor and an author should be listed with the editor following the title, first name first, preceded by the abbreviation *Ed.*

9. Book in more than one volume

Waldrep, Tom, ed. <u>Writers on Writing</u>. 2 vols. New York: Random, 1985–88.

The total number of volumes is listed after the title. When separate volumes were published in different years, provide inclusive dates.

10. One volume of a multivolume book

Waldrep, Tom, ed. <u>Writers on Writing</u>. Vol. 2. New York: Random, 1988.

When each volume of a multivolume set has an individual title, list the volume's full publication information first, followed by series information (number of volumes, dates).

Churchill, Winston S. <u>Triumph and Tragedy</u>. Boston: Houghton, 1953. Vol. 6 of *The Second World War*. 6 vols. 1948–53.

11. Translated book

Hammarskjold, Dag. <u>Markings</u>. Trans. Leif Sjoberg and W. H. Auden. New York: Knopf, 1964.

12. Book in a series

McLeod, Susan, ed. <u>Strengthening Programs for Writing Across the Curriculum</u>. New Directions for Teaching and Learning Ser. 36. San Francisco: Jossey-Bass, 1988.

Immediately after the title, add the series information: the series name, neither underlined nor in quotation marks, and the series number, both followed by periods. Book titles within an underlined title are not underlined.

13. Reprinted book

Evans, Elizabeth E. G. <u>The Abuse of Maternity</u>. 1875. New York: Arno, 1974.

Add the original publication date after the title; then cite the current edition information.

14. Introduction, preface, foreword, or afterword

Gavorse, Joseph. Introduction. <u>The Lives of the Twelve Caesars</u>. By Suetonius. New York: Book League of America, 1937. vii–xvi.

Jacobus, Lee A. Preface. <u>Literature: An Introduction to Critical Reading</u>. By Jacobus. Upper Saddle River, NJ: Prentice, 1996. xxvii–xxxiii.

Nabokov, Vladimir. Foreword. <u>A Hero of Our Time.</u> By Mihail Lermontov. Garden City, NY: Doubleday-Anchor, 1958. v–xix.

List the author of the introduction, preface, foreword, or afterword first, followed by the title of the book. Next insert the word *By*, followed by the full name of the author of the whole work if different from the author of the piece or the last name only if the same as the author of the shorter piece.

15. Work in an anthology or chapter in an edited collection

Charen, Mona. "Much More Nasty Than They Should Be." Popular Writing in America: The Interaction of Style and Audience. 5th ed. Ed. Donald McQuade and Robert Atwan. New York: Oxford UP, 1993. 207–08.

Gay, John. The Beggar's Opera: British Dramatists from Dryden to Sheridan. Ed. George H. Nettleton and Arthur E. Case. Carbondale: Southern Illinois UP, 1975. 530–65.

Enclose the title of the work in quotation marks unless it was originally published as a book, in which case it should be underlined. The title of the anthology follows the book title and is underlined. At the end of the entry, provide inclusive page numbers for the selection. For previously published nonscholarly works, you may, as a courtesy to your reader, include the year of original publication after the title of the anthologized work. Follow this date with a period.

16. Two or more works from the same anthology or collection

Kingston, Maxine Hong. "No Name Woman." Kirszner and Mandell 46–56.

Kirszner, Laurie G., and Stephen R. Mandell, eds. The Blair Reader. 2nd ed. Ed. Laurie G. Kirszner and Stephen R. Mandell. Upper Saddle River, NJ: Prentice, 1996.

Tannen, Deborah. "Marked Women." Kirszner and Mandell 362–67.

When citing two or more selections from one anthology, list the anthology separately under the editor's name. Selection entries will then need to include only a shortened cross-reference to the anthology entry, as illustrated above.

17. Periodical article reprinted in a collection

Atwell, Nancie. "Everyone Sits at a Big Desk: Discovering Topics for Writing." English Journal 74 (1985): 35–39. Rpt. in Rhetoric and Composition: A Sourcebook for Teachers and Writers. 3rd ed. Ed. Richard Graves. Portsmouth, NH: Boynton/Cook, 1990. 76–83.

Include the full citation for the original periodical publication, followed by *Rpt. in* ("Reprinted in") and the book publication information. Provide inclusive page numbers for both sources.

18. Article in a reference book

"Behn, Aphra." The Concise Columbia Encyclopedia. 1983 ed.

"Langella, Frank." International Television and Video Almanac. 40th ed. New York: Quigley, 1995.

For signed articles in reference books, begin with the author's name. For commonly known reference works (*Concise Columbia*), you need not include full publication information or editors' names. Page and volume numbers are also unnecessary when the entries in the reference book are arranged alphabetically.

19. **Anonymous book**

The End of a Presidency. New York: Bantam, 1974.

Alphabetically arrange anonymous books (and most other sources lacking an author name) in the Works Cited list by title, excluding *A, An,* or *The*.

20. **Government document**

United States. Cong. House. Committee on Energy and Commerce. Ensuring Access to Programming for the Backyard Satellite Dish Owner. Washington: GPO, 1986.

If the author is identified, begin with that name. If not, begin with the government (country or state), followed by the agency or organization. Most U.S. government documents are printed and published by the Government Printing Office in Washington, DC. You may abbreviate this office *GPO*.

21. **Dissertation**

UNPUBLISHED

McGuire, Lisa C. "Adults' Recall and Retention of Medical Information." Diss. Bowling Green State University, 1993.

Enclose the title of an unpublished dissertation in quotation marks, followed by the abbreviation *Diss.* and the name of the university and the year.

PUBLISHED

Boothby, Daniel W. The Determinants of Earnings and Occupation for Young Women. Diss. U. of California, Berkeley, 1978. New York: Garland, 1984.

For a published dissertation, italicize or underline the title, list the university and year as for an unpublished dissertation, and then add publication information as for a book, including the order number if the publisher is University Microfilms International (UMI). The descriptive abbreviation *Diss.* still follows the title.

22. **A pamphlet**

McKay, Hughina, and Mary Brown Patton. Food Consumption of College Men. Wooster: Ohio Agricultural Experiment Station, 1943.

Cite a pamphlet just as you cite a book. Remember the abbreviations *n.p., n.d.,* and *n.pag.,* where publication information is missing. Also see item 23.

23. **A book with missing publication information**

Palka, Eugene, and Dawn M. Lake. A Bibliography of Military Geography. [New York?]: Kirby, [198-?].

The MLA practice is to provide missing publication information if possible. If the information you provide does not come from the source itself—that is, if you succeed in finding missing information through another source—you should enclose this information in brackets in the Works Cited entry [198-?]. If a date of publication can only be approximated, place a *c.* before it, the abbreviation for the Latin *circa,* or "around." You may also use the abbreviations *n.p.*—depending on placement in your entry, this abbreviation stands for either "no place" or "no publisher"—*n.d.* ("no date"), or *n.pag.* ("no pages").

24. Religious texts

Holy Bible, King James: Modern Phrased Version. New York: Oxford UP, 1980.

Use period to separate chapter from verse in in-text citation (Luke 2.12).

Quran: The Final Testament (Authorized English Version) with Arabic Text. Trans. Rashad Khalifa, Fremont: Universal Unity, 2000.

25. Article, story, or poem in a monthly or bimonthly magazine

Hawn, Matthew. "Stay on the Web: Make Your Internet Site Pay Off." Macworld Apr. 1996: 94–98.

Abbreviate all months except May, June, and July. Hyphenate months for bimonthlies, and do not list volume or issue numbers.

26. Article, story, or poem in a weekly magazine

Updike, John. "His Mother Inside Him." New Yorker 20 Apr. 1992: 34–36.

27. Article in a daily newspaper

Finn, Peter. "Death of a U-Va. Student Raises Scrutiny of Off-Campus Drinking." Washington Post 27 Sept. 1995: D1.

If an article in a newspaper is unsigned, begin with its title. Give the name of the newspaper as it appears on the masthead, excluding *A, An,* or *The.* If the city is not in the newspaper's name, it should follow the name in brackets: *Blade [Toledo, OH].* Include with the page number the letter that designates any separately numbered sections; if sections are numbered consecutively, list the section number (*sec. 2*) before the colon, preceded by a comma.

28. Article by an unknown author

"Conventionalwisdomwatch." Newsweek 13 June 2005: 5.

29. Article in a journal paginated by volume

Nelson, Jennie. "This Was an Easy Assignment: Examining How Students Interpret Academic Writing Tasks." Research in the Teaching of English 34 (1990): 362–96.

If page numbers are continuous from one issue to the next throughout the year, include only the volume number and year, not the issue or month.

30. Article in a journal paginated by issue

Tiffin, Helen. "Post-Colonialism, Post-Modernism, and the Rehabilitation of Post-Colonial History." Journal of Commonwealth Literature 23.1 (1988): 169–81.

If each issue begins with page 1, include the volume number followed by a period and the issue number. Do not include the month of publication.

31. Anonymous article

"Fraternities Sue Hamilton College over Housing Rule." Chronicle of Higher Education 41.46 (1995): A39.

GENERAL FORMAT FOR MAGAZINE AND NEWSPAPER ARTICLES, MLA

one space   one space   one space   one space

Author(s). "Article Title." Publication Title Date of publication: page numbers.

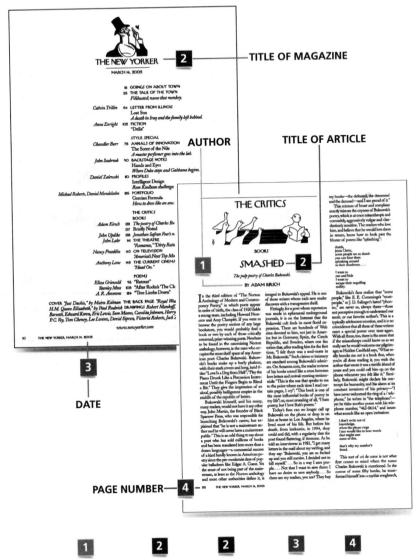

Kirsch, Adam. "Smashed." New Yorker 14 Mar. 2005: 132-36.

Magazine title page and first page of article to be referenced

1 **AUTHOR NAME.**

Last name first, comma, then rest of the name as it appears on the article. Period. If more than one author, second and later names are listed first name first, separated by commas, with *and* before last author (*Smith, Alan, Brian Jones, and Michelle Watts*). If more than one work by the same author, substitute three hyphens for the author's name after the first entry:

Kirsch, Adam. "Smashed." <u>New Yorker</u> 14 Mar. 2005: 132-36.

---. "The Lazy Gardener." <u>New York Sun</u> 28 Sept. 2005: A24.

2 **TITLES.**

List titles and subtitles fully, capitalizing as in the original. Put quotation marks around the titles of articles, poems, and short works in the periodical. Period. Underline book titles within **article titles** ("The Effect of Sunshine in Faulkner's <u>Light in August</u>"). Use single quotation marks around the titles of short works within article titles ("What's Cool in 'We Real Cool'?") *Italicize* or underline **periodical titles** and omit introductory articles (*New Yorker*, not *The New Yorker*).

3 **DATE.**

For daily, weekly, or biweekly magazines and newspapers, give day, month, and year of publication (*14 Mar. 2005*), but omit volume and issue numbers. Colon. Abbreviate all months except May, June, and July followed by a period (*Jan., Apr.*). If no date of publication, use *n.d.* in parentheses (*n.d.*).

4 **PAGE NUMBERS.**

Separate page numbers in a range with a hyphen (*42-54*). Up to 99, use all the digits for the second page numbers, and above 99 list the last two digits only (*130-38*) unless the full sequence is needed for clarity (*198-210*). If the page numbers are not consecutive (as in a newspaper), place a plus sign after the final consecutive page (39+, 52-55+). Period.

As with an anonymous book or magazine, if no author is listed for an article, begin your entry with the title and alphabetize by the first word, excluding *A*, *An*, and *The*.

32. **Microform or microfiche article**

Mayer, Caroline E. "Child-Resistant Caps to Be Made 'Adult-friendly.'" <u>Washington Post</u> 16 June 1995: A3. CD-ROM. Newsbank. (1995) CON 16: B17.

If the listing is derived from a computer-based reference source such as *Newsbank*, you may treat it exactly as you would any other periodical. To help your audience locate the source as quickly as possible, however, you should include the descriptor *CD-ROM*, the name of the service (*Newsbank*), and the available section/ grid information.

GENERAL FORMAT FOR JOURNAL ARTICLES, MLA

one space   one space   one space   one space   one space

Author(s). "Article Title." Journal Title volume number (year of publication):

page numbers.

Indent second line five spaces.

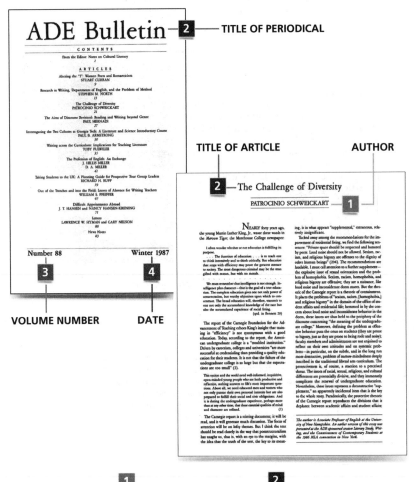

TITLE OF PERIODICAL

TITLE OF ARTICLE   AUTHOR

VOLUME NUMBER   DATE

Schweickart, Patrocinio. "The Challenge of Diversity."

ADE Bulletin 88 (1987): 21-26.

Periodical title page and first page of article to be referenced

1 AUTHOR NAME.

Last name first, comma, then rest of the name as it appears on the article. Period. If more than one author, second and later names are listed first name first, separated by commas, with *and* before last author (*Smith, Alan, Brian Jones, and Michelle Watts*). If four or more authors, you may list only first author followed by *et al.* (and others). If more than one work by the same author, substitute three hyphens for the author's name after the first entry:

> Schweickart, Patrocinio. "The Challenge of Diversity." *ADE Bulletin* 88
>
> (1987): 21-26.
>
> ---. "Reading Ourselves." *Speaking of Gender.* Ed. Elaine Showalter.
>
> New York: Routledge, 1989. 88-98.

2 TITLES.

List titles and subtitles fully, capitalizing as in the original and put quotation marks around the titles of articles, poems, and short works in the periodical. Period. Underline book titles within **article titles** ("A Reassessment of Faulkner's As I Lay Dying"). Use single quotation marks around the titles of short works within article titles ("T.S. Eliot's 'Ash Wednesday' Revisited"). *Italicize* or underline **periodical titles** (*ADE Bulletin*).

3 VOLUME, ISSUE, AND PAGE NUMBERS.

For journals paginated separately by issue (as in this example), list volume number, period, and issue number (12.2), followed by year of publication (in parentheses) and a colon: then page numbers. For journals paginated continuously, include the volume number before the year, but omit the issue number. Separate inclusive page numbers with a hyphen (*42-54*). Up to 99, use all the digits for the second page numbers, and above 99 list the last two digits only (*130-38*) unless the full sequence is needed for clarity (*198-210*). If page numbers are not consecutive, use the first page number, followed by a plus sign: 84+.

4 DATE OF PUBLICATION.

Place the year of publication for periodicals within parentheses, followed by a colon and a space to the page numbers. Never use season for a journal.

33. Editorial

"Sarajevo Reborn." Editorial. New York Times 21 Feb. 1996, natl. ed.: A18. If the editorial is signed, list the author's name first.

34. Letter to the editor and reply

Kempthorne, Charles. Letter. Kansas City Star 26 July 2002: A16.

Massing, Michael. Reply to letter of Peter Dale Scott. New York Review of Books 4 Mar. 2005: 57.

GENERAL FORMAT FOR ONLINE SOURCES, MLA

Author(s). "Article Title." Title of Site. Date of electronic publication. Page, paragraph, or section number for specific reference. Sponsoring body. Date of access <electronic address>.

Padgett, John B. "William Faulker." Mississippi Writers Page. 15 Apr. 2005. University of Mississippi English Department. 8 June 2005 <http://www.olemiss.edu/mwp/dir/faulkner_william/index. html>.

Home page, including biographical article on William Faulkner

> **1** **AUTHOR OF MATERIAL ON WEB SITE.**
> Last name first, comma, then rest of the name. Follow rules for citing books and periodicals (*Padgett, John B.*). Period. If no author is listed, begin with page title (*Mississippi Writers Page*).

> **2** **TITLE OF MATERIAL ON WEB SITE.**
> Enclose title of poem, short story, or other short work in quotation marks ("William Faulkner"). <u>Underline</u> or *italicize* the site title and subtitle. Period. If no title is obvious, use home page name as title (found in URL).

> **3** **NAME OF SPONSORING ORGANIZATION.**
> Usually found at bottom of site home page (*University of Mississippi English Department*). Period.

> **4** **PUBLICATION INFORMATION.**
> List two dates for each Internet site: first, place the date the site was created or last revised, immediately after the title (*15 Apr. 2005*). Period. Second, give the date you accessed the site (*8 June 2005*) followed directly by the URL.

> **5** **ELECTRONIC ADDRESS (URL).**
> Enclose the site address between angle brackets *(< >)* at end of the entry *<http://www.olemiss.edu/mwp/dir/faulkner_william/index.html>*. Period.

35. Review

Ross, Alex. Rev. of "Kafka's Trial" by Poul Ruders. <u>New Yorker</u> 28 Mar. 2005: 80.

"Talk to Me Now" by Jack Dahl. <u>New West News</u> 15 Jan. 2002: 24.

Works Cited entries for reviews should begin with the reviewer's name, if known, followed by the title of the review, if there is one. *Rev. of* precedes the title of the work reviewed, followed by a comma, then the word *by* and the name of the work's author. If the work of an editor, translator, etc. is being reviewed instead of an author's, an abbreviation such as *ed.* or *trans.* replaces the word *by*. If a review is unsigned and untitled, list it as *Rev. of* [title] and alphabetize it by the name of the work reviewed. If the review is unsigned but titled, begin with the title. If the review is of a performance, add pertinent descriptive information such as director, composer, or major performers.

Electronic sources include both databases—available in portable forms such as CD-ROM, diskette, or magnetic tape—and online sources accessed with a computer connected to the Internet.

DATABASES

The Works Cited entries for electronic **databases** (newsletters, journals, and conferences) should be listed like entries for articles in printed periodicals: Cite the author's name; the article or document title in quotation marks; the newsletter, journal, or conference title; the number of volume or issue; the year or date of publication (in parentheses); and the number of pages if available.

Portable databases are much like books and periodicals. Their entries in Works Cited lists are similar to those for printed material, except you must also include the following items:

- The medium of publication (*CD-ROM, diskette, magnetic tape*)
- The name of the vendor, if known (this may be different from the name of the organization that compiled the information, which must also be included)
- The date of electronic publication, in addition to the date the material originally may have been published (as for a reprinted book or article)

36. **CD-ROM database, periodically updated**

James, Caryn. "An Army as Strong as Its Weakest Link." <u>New York Times</u> 16 Sept. 1994: C8. *New York Times* Ondisc. CD-ROM. UMI-ProQuest. Oct. 1994.

If a database comes from a printed source such as a book, periodical, or collection of bibliographies or abstracts, cite this information first, followed by the title of the database (underlined), the medium of publication, the vendor name (if applicable), and the date of electronic publication. If no printed source is available, include the title of the material accessed (in quotation marks), the date of the material (if given), the underlined title of the database, the medium of publication, the vendor name, and the date of electronic publication.

37. **CD-ROM nonperiodical**

"Rhetoric." <u>The Oxford English Dictionary</u>. 2nd ed. CD-ROM. Oxford: Oxford UP, 1992.

List a nonperiodical CD-ROM as you would a book, adding the medium of publication and information about the source, if applicable. If citing only part of a work, underline the title of the selected portion or place it within quotation marks, as appropriate.

38. **Diskette or magnetic tape**

Doyle, Roddy. <u>The Woman Who Walked into Doors</u>. Magnetic tape. New York: Penguin Audiobooks, 1996.

List on the Works Cited page as you would a book, adding the medium of publication (e.g., *Diskette, magnetic tape*).

ONLINE SOURCES

Documenting information from the Internet follows the same basic guidelines as documenting other texts—who said what, where, and when. However, in citations of Internet sources, two dates are important—the date the text was created, published, or revised and the date you found the information (the access date). When both publication and access dates are available, provide them both. However, many www sources are often updated or changed, leaving no trace of the original version, so always provide the access date to show when this information was available. Thus, most electronic source entries will end with an access date immediately followed by the electronic address in angle brackets: *23 Dec. 1999* <http://www.cas.usf.edu/english>.

The following guidelines are derived from the MLA Web site at <http://www.mla.org/style_faq4>. To identify a World Wide Web source, include all the relevant items in the following order, each followed by a period except the date of access:

1. *Author*   (or editor, compiler, or translator). Give the person's full name, if known, last name first; if the name is unknown, include any alias given.
2. *Title.*   Enclose the title of a poem, short story, or article in quotation marks. Include the title of a posting to a discussion list or forum in quotation marks, followed by *Online posting.* Underline book titles.
3. *Editor, compiler, or translator.*   Include the full name, if not cited earlier, followed by the appropriate abbreviation (*Ed., Comp.,* or *Trans.*).
4. *Print source information.*   Include the same information you would give for a printed citation.
5. *Title of scholarly project, database, personal or professional site*   (underlined). If there is no title, include a description such as *Home page.* Include the name of an editor if available.
6. *Identifying number.*   For a journal, include the volume and issue numbers.
7. *Date of electronic publication.*   Include latest date of site revision if available.
8. *Discussion list information.*   Include the full name or title of the list or forum.
9. *Page, paragraph, or section numbers.*   Include only if your source includes them; do not count paragraphs or sections yourself if your source lacks numbering.
10. *Sponsorship or affiliation.*   Include the name of any organization or institution sponsoring this site.
11. *Date of access.*   Include the date you visited this site.
12. *Address.*   Enclose in angle brackets; if hyphenation is necessary, do so after angle brackets or period (see item 40).

39. **Work from an online database**

Conniff, Richard. "Approaching Walden." Yankee. 57.5 (May 1993): 84. ArticleFirst. OCLC. Bailey Howe Library, U. Vermont 2 Jun. 2005 <http://firstsearch.oclc.org>.

Give the print publication information, name the database (underlined), name of vendor, name of library, date of access, and URL.

40. **Professional site**

Yellow Wall-Paper Site. U of Texas. 1995. 4 Mar. 1998 <http://www.cwrl.utexas.edu/~daniel/amlit/wallpaper/wallpaper.html>.

41. **Government or institutional site**

"Zebra Mussels in Vermont." Home page. State of Vermont Agency of Natural Resources. 3 May 1998 <http://www.anr.state.vt.us/dec/waterq/smcap.htm>.

42. Article in a journal

Erkkila, Betsy. "The Emily Dickinson Wars." <u>The Emily Dickinson Journal</u> 5.2 (1996) 14 pars. 2 Feb. 1998 <http://www.colorado.edu/EDIS/Journal>.

43. Book

Twain, Mark. <u>The Adventures of Tom Sawyer</u>. Internet Wiretap Online Library. Carnegie Mellon U. 4 Mar. 1998 <http://www.cs.cmu.edu/Web/People/rgs/sawyr-table.html>.

44. Poem

Poe, Edgar Allan. "The Raven." <u>American Review</u>, 1845. The Poetry Archives. 4 Mar. 1998 <http://tqd.advanced.org/3247/cgibin/dispgi?poet=poe.Edgar&poem>.

45. Article in a reference database

"Jupiter." Britannica Online. Vers. 97.1.1 Mar. 1997. <u>Encyclopaedia Britannica</u>. 29 Mar. 1998 <http://www.eb.com:180>.

46. Posting to a discussion list

"New Virginia Woolf Discussion List." Online posting. 22 Feb. 1996. The Virginia Woolf Society, Ohio State U. 4 Mar. 1998 <gopher://dept.english.upenn.edu:70// OrO-1858-?Lists/20th/vwoolf>.

47. E-mail, listserv, or newsgroup (Usenet) message

Fulwiler, Toby. "A Question About Electronic Sources." E-mail to Alan Hayakawa. 23 Jan. 2004. Superman. <superman@200.uvm.edu>. "Writing Committee Meeting." Distribution list. University of Vermont. 24 Jan. 2001.

Include the author's name or Internet alias (if known, alias first, period) followed by the subject line (in quotation marks) and the date of the posting. Identify the type of communication (*Personal e-mail, Distribution list, Office communication*) before the access date. The source's e-mail address is optional, following the name in angle brackets; secure permission before including an e-mail address.

48. File transfer protocol (FTP), telnet, or gopher site

King, Jr., Martin Luther. "I Have a Dream Speech." 28 Aug. 1963. 30 Jan. 1996 <telnet://ukanaix.cc.ukans.edu>.

Substitute the abbreviation *ftp, telnet,* or *gopher* for *http* before the site address.

49. Synchronous communications (MUD, MOO, IRC)

StoneHenger. The Glass Dragon MOO. 6 Feb. 2004. Personal interview. 6 Feb. 2004 <telnet://surf.tstc.edu>.

Synchronous communications take place in real time; when they are over, an archive copy may remain, or they may simply be erased. After the posting date, include the type of discussion (e.g., *Personal interview, Group discussion*) followed by a period.

50. Home page—personal

Fulwiler, Anna. Home page. 1 Feb. 1998 <http://www.uvm.edu/~afulwile>.

51. Home page—college course or academic department

Hughes, Jeffrey. <u>Fundamentals of Field Science</u>. Course home page. Sep.-Dec. 2005. Botany department. University of Vermont, 6 May 2005 <http://www.uvm.edu/~plantbio/grad/fn>.

List instructor or department name, course or department title, the words "course" or "department" home page, for course offering add inclusive dates, department name, school, date of access, URL.

52. Online newspaper

Sandomir, Richard. "Yankees Talk Trades in Broadcast Booth." <u>New York Times on the Web</u> 4 Dec. 2001. 5 Dec. 2001 <http://www.nytimes.com/pages/business/media/index.html>.

53. Online magazine

Epperson, Sharon. "A New Way to Shop for a College." <u>Time.com</u> 4 Dec. 2001. 5 Dec. 2001 <http://www.time.com/time/education/article/0,8599,183955,00.html>.

54. Online encyclopedia

<u>Standford Encyclopedia of Philosophy</u>. Ed. Edward N. Zalta. 1995. Standford U. 5. Dec. 2001 <http://plato.stanford.edu/contents.html>.

55. Online work of art

Van Gogh, Vincent. <u>The Olive Trees</u>. 1889. Museum of Modern Art, New York. 5 Dec. 2001 <http://www.moma.org/docs/collection/paintsculpt/recent/c463.htm>.

56. Online interview

Plaxco, Jim. Interview. <u>Planetary Studies Foundation</u>. Oct. 1992. 5 Dec. 2001 <http://www.planets.org/>

57. Online film or film clip

Columbus, Chris, dir. <u>Harry Potter and the Sorcerer's Stone</u>. Trailer. Warner Brothers, 2001. 5 Dec. 2001 <http://hollywood.com>.

58. Online cartoon

Bell, Darrin. "Rudy Park." Cartoon. <u>New York Times on the Web</u> 5 Dec. 2001. 5 Dec. 2001 <http://www2.uclick.com/client/nyt/rk/>.

59. Electronic television or radio program

Chayes, Sarah. "Concorde." <u>All Things Considered</u>. Natl. Public Radio. 26 July 2000.
7 Dec. 2001 <http://www.npr.com/programs/atc/archives>.

60. Weblog entry

Rickey, Anthony. "Three Years of Hell to Become the Devil." Weblog posting. 8 June
2005. 10 June 2005 <http://www.threeyearsofhell.com/>.

Author name or pseudonym, title of site (if any) followed by the words "Weblog posting,"
date of site, date of access, and URL.

◆ DOCUMENTING OTHER SOURCES

The manner in which MLA format applies to other sources can be inferred with reasonable
accuracy from the principles for documenting books, periodicals, and online sources, the
entries beginning with *author, title, medium identification, publisher,* and *date.* Following are
specific examples of how to document other types of media.

61. Cartoon

Davis, Jim. "Garfield." Cartoon. <u>Courier</u> [Findlay, OH] 17 Feb. 1996: E4.

62. Film or videocassette

Casablanca. Dir. Michael Curtiz. Perf. Humphrey Bogart and Ingrid Bergman. Warner
Bros., *1942.*

<u>Fast Food: What's in It for You</u>. Prod. The Center for Science in the Public Interest
and Churchill Films. Videocassette. Los Angeles: Churchill, 1988.

Lewis, Joseph H., dir. *Gun Crazy.* Screenplay by Dalton Trumbo. King Bros., 1950.

Begin with the title, followed by the director, the studio, and the year released. Op-
tionally, you may include the names of lead actors, producer, and the like between the title
and the distribution information. If your essay is concerned with a particular person's work
on a film, begin with that person's name, arranging all other information accordingly.

63. Personal interview

Holden, James. Personal interview. 12 Jan. 2005.

Morser, John. Professor of Political Science, U of Wisconsin. Telephone interview.
15 June. 2001.

Begin with the interviewee's name and specify the kind of interview and the date.
Identify the interviewee's position if relevant to the purpose of the interview.

64. Published or broadcast interview

Sowell, Thomas. "Affirmative Action Programs." Interview. <u>All Things Considered</u>. NPR. WGTE, Toledo. 5 June 1990.

For published or broadcast interviews, begin with the interviewee's name. Include appropriate publication information for a periodical or book and appropriate broadcast information for a radio or television program.

65. Print advertisement

Cadillac DeVille. Advertisement. <u>New York Times</u> 21 Feb. 2004, natl. ed.: A20.

Begin with the name of the product, followed by the description *Advertisement* and normal publication information for the source.

66. Unpublished lecture, public address, or speech

Graves, Donald. "When Bad Things Happen to Good Ideas." National Council of Teachers of English Convention. St. Louis, 21 Nov. 1989.

Begin with the speaker, followed by the title (if any), the meeting (and sponsoring organization, if needed), the location, and the date. If it is untitled, use a descriptive label (such as *Speech*) with no quotation marks.

67. Personal or unpublished letter

Friedman, Paul. Letter to the author. 18 Mar. 1999.

Personal letters and e-mail messages are handled nearly identically in Works Cited entries. Begin with the name of the writer, identify the type of communication (e.g., *Letter*), and specify the audience. Include the date written if known, and the date received if not. To cite an unpublished letter from an archive or private collection, include information that locates the holding (for example, *Quinn-Adams Papers. Lexington Historical Society. Lexington, KY.*).

68. Published letter

King, Jr., Martin Luther. "Letter from Birmingham Jail." 28 Aug. 1963. <u>Civil Disobedience in Focus</u>. Ed. Hugo Adam Bedau. New York: Routledge, 1991. 68–84.

Cite published letters as you would a selection from an anthology. Specify the audience in the letter title (if known). Include the date of the letter immediately after its title. Place the page number(s) after the publisher information. If you cite more than one letter from a collection, cite the entire work in the Works Cited list, and indicate individual dates and page numbers in your text.

69. Map

Ohio River: Foster, KY, to New Martinsville, WV. Map. Huntington: U.S. Corps of Engineers, 1986.

Cite a map as you would a book by an unknown author. Underline the title, and identify the item as a map or chart.

70. Performance

Rumors. By Neil Simon. Dir. Gene Saks. Broadhurst Theater, New York. 17 Nov. 1988.

Bissex, Rachel. Folk Songs. Flynn Theater. Burlington, VT. 14 May 2000.

Identify the pertinent details, such as title, place, and date of performance. If you focus on a particular person in your essay, such as the director or conductor, lead with that person's name. For a recital or individual concert, lead with the performer's name.

71. Audio recording

Springsteen, Bruce. "Devils & Dust." Devils and Dust. New York: Sony BMG Music Entertainment, CN 93900, 2005.

Depending on the focus of your essay, begin with the artist, composer, or conductor. Enclose song titles in quotation marks, followed by the recording title, underlined. Do not underline musical compositions identified only by form, number, and key. If you are *not* citing a compact disc, specify the recording format. End with the company label, the catalog number if known, and the date of issue.

72. Television or radio broadcast

"Emissary." Star Trek: Deep Space Nine. Teleplay by Michael Pillar. Story by Rick Berman and Michael Pillar. Dir. David Carson. Fox. WFLX, West Palm Beach, FL. 9 Jan. 1993.

If the broadcast is not an episode of a series or the episode is untitled, begin with the program title. Include the network, the station and city, and the date of broadcast. The inclusion of other information—such as narrator, writer, director, or performers—depends on the purpose of your citation.

73. Work of art (photograph, painting, sculpture, etc.)

Holbein, Hans. Portrait of Erasmus. Musée du Louvre, Paris. The Louvre Museum. By Germain Bazin. New York: Abrams, n.d., 148.

Begin with the artist's name. Follow with the work's title, and conclude with the location. If your source is a book, also give pertinent publication information.

RESEARCH ESSAY: MLA STYLE

The following research essay was written by a first-year college student, Andrew Turner, in response to an assignment to write about a major American author using both primary and secondary sources in formal MLA style.

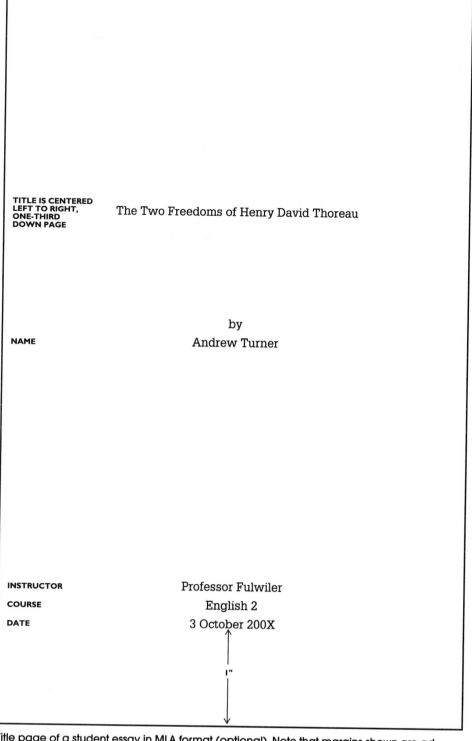

**TITLE IS CENTERED
LEFT TO RIGHT,
ONE-THIRD
DOWN PAGE**
The Two Freedoms of Henry David Thoreau

by
NAME Andrew Turner

INSTRUCTOR Professor Fulwiler

COURSE English 2

DATE 3 October 200X

I"

Title page of a student essay in MLA format (optional). Note that margins shown are adjusted to fit space limitations of this book. Follow actual dimensions shown and your instructor's directions.

DOUBLE SPACE

WRITER OPENS WITH THESIS.

WRITER IDENTIFIES TWO WORKS TO BE EXAMINED.

ABBREVIATED TITLE IS USED AFTER WORK HAS BEEN IDENTIFIED BY FULL TITLE.

WRITER'S LAST NAME AND PAGE NUMBER APPEAR ON EACH PAGE.

ONLY THE PAGE NUMBER IS NEEDED WHEN SOURCE IS INTRODUCED IN THE SENTENCE.

SHORT TITLE IS ADDED TO PAGE NUMBER BECAUSE TWO WORKS BY SAME AUTHOR APPEAR ON WORKS CITED PAGE.

PAGE NUMBER ONLY IS USED BECAUSE THE CONTEXT IDENTIFIES THE WORK.

TITLE IS REPEATED FROM THE TITLE PAGE.

The Two Freedoms of Henry David Thoreau

Henry David Thoreau led millions of people throughout the world to think about individual freedom in a new way. During his lifetime, he attempted to live free of unjust governmental constraints as well as conventional social expectations. In his 1849 essay "On the Duty of Civil Disobedience," he makes his strongest case against governmental interference in the lives of citizens. In his 1854 book <u>Walden, or, Life in the Woods</u>, he makes the case for living free from social conventions and expectations.

Thoreau opens "Civil Disobedience" with his statement that "that government is best which governs not at all" (222). He argues that a government should allow its people to be as free as possible, providing for the needs of the people without infringing on their daily lives. Thoreau explains, "The government does not concern me much, and I shall bestow the fewest possible thoughts on it. It is not for many moments that I live under a government" ("Civil" 238). In other words, in his daily life he attends to his business of eating, sleeping, and earning a living and not dealing in any noticeable way with an entity called "a government."

Because Thoreau did not want his freedom overshadowed by governmental regulations, he tried to ignore them. However, the American government of 1845 would not let him. He was arrested and put in the Concord jail for failing to pay his poll tax--a tax he believed unjust because it supported the government's war with Mexico as well as the immoral institution of slavery. Instead of protesting his arrest, he celebrated it and explained its meaning by writing "Civil Disobedience," one of the most famous English-language essays ever written. In it, he argues persuasively, "Under a government which imprisons any unjustly, the true place for a just man is also a prison" (230). Thus the doctrine of passive

Turner 2

resistance was formed, a doctrine that advocated protest

against the government by nonviolent means:

INDENTED 10 SPACES ←——————→

How does it become a man to behave toward this

American government today? I answer that he

QUOTATION OF MORE THAN 4 LINES IS PRESENTED IN BLOCK FORMAT.

cannot without disgrace be associated with it. I

cannot for an instant recognize that political **PAGE NUMBER IS OUTSIDE**

organization as my government which is the slave's **PERIOD FOR INDENTED**

government also. (224) **PASSAGES.**

SIGNAL PHRASE INTRODUCES According to Charles R. Anderson, Thoreau's other writings,

THE NAME OF THE such as "Slavery in Massachusetts" and "A Plea for Captain **PARTIAL QUOTATION**

SECONDARY **IS WORKED**

SOURCE John Brown," show his disdain of the "northerners for their **INTO**

AUTHOR. **SENTENCE**

cowardice on conniving with such an institution" (28). He **IN A GRAMMATICALLY**

wanted all free American citizens, north and south, to revolt **CORRECT WAY.**

and liberate the slaves.

In addition to inspiring his countrymen, Thoreau's view of

the sanctity of individual freedom affected the lives of later

generations who shared his beliefs (King). "Civil Disobedience"

had the greatest impact because of its "worldwide influence on

Mahatma Gandhi, the British Labour Party in its early years,

the underground in Nazi-occupied Europe, and Negro leaders in

the modern south" (Anderson 30). For nearly one hundred fifty

WRITER years, Thoreau's formulation of passive resistance has been a

SWITCHES TO part of the human struggle for freedom.

DISCUSSION

OF A Thoreau also wanted to be free from the everyday pressure

SECOND

WORK to conform to society's expectations. He believed in doing and

AFTER

DISCUS- possessing only the essential things in life. To demonstrate his

SION

OF FIRST

WORK IS case, in 1845 he moved to the outskirts of Concord,

COMPLETED.

Massachusetts, and lived by himself for two years on the shore **ABBREVIATED**

IDENTIFI- **POPULAR**

CATION of Walden Pond (Spiller et al. 396-97). Thoreau wrote Walden to **TITLE IS LISTED AFTER**

FOR **WORK'S FIRST**

WORK explain the value of living simply, apart from the unnecessary **REFERENCE.**

WITH

MORE

THAN complexity of society: "Simplicity, simplicity, simplicity! I say,

THREE

AUTHORS. let your affairs be as two or three, and not a hundred or a

thousand" (66). At Walden, he lived as much as possible by this

Turner 3

statement, building his own house and furniture, growing his own food, bartering for simple necessities, attending to his own business rather than seeking employment from others (Walden 16-17).

PAGE NUMBERS FOR PARAPHRASE ARE INCLUDED.

Living at Walden Pond gave Thoreau the chance to formulate many of his ideas about living the simple, economical life. At Walden, he lived simply in order to "front only the essential facts of life" (66) and to center his thoughts on living instead of unnecessary details of mere livelihood. He developed survival skills that freed him from the constraints of city dwellers whose lives depended upon a web of material things and services provided by others. He preferred to "take rank hold on life and spend my day more as animals do" (117).

PAGE NUMBERS ALONE ARE SUFFICIENT WHEN CONTEXT MAKES THE SOURCE CLEAR.

While living at Walden Pond, Thoreau was free to occupy his time in any way that pleased him, which for him meant writing, tending his bean patch, and chasing loons. He wasn't troubled by a boss hounding him with deadlines or a wife and children who needed support. In other words, "he wasn't expected to be anywhere at any time for anybody except himself (Franklin)." His neighbors accused him of being selfish and did not understand that he sought most of all "to live deliberately" (66), as he felt all people should learn to do.

Then as now, most people had more responsibilities than Thoreau had and could not just pack up their belongings and go live in the woods--if they could find free woods to live in. Today, people are intrigued to read about Thoreau's experiences and inspired by his thoughts, but few people can actually live or do as he suggests in Walden. In fact, most people, if faced with the prospect of spending two years removed from society, would probably think of it as a punishment or banishment, rather than as Thoreau thought of it, as the good life (Poger).

Practical or not, Thoreau's writings about freedom from

Turner 4

government and society have inspired countless people to
reassess how they live their lives. Though unable to live as he
advocated, readers everywhere remain inspired by his ideal,
that one must live as freely as possible.

WRITER'S CONCLUSION REPEATS THESIS ASSERTION.

Turner 5

HEADING CENTERED

Works Cited

Anderson, Charles Roberts, ed. <u>Thoreau's Vision: The Major</u>   **DOUBLE SPACE**

    <u>Essays</u>. Englewood Cliffs: Prentice, 1973.

Franklin, George. Professor of American Literature, Northfield

    College. Personal interview. 5 April 2000.

"Ghandi." <u>Britannica Online</u>. Vers. 97.1. Mar. 1997.

    Encyclopedia Britannica. 2 Mar. 1998 <http://www.eb.com:180>.

King, Jr., Martin Luther. "Letter from Birmingham Jail." 28 Aug. 1963.

    <u>Civil Disobedience in Focus</u>. Ed. Hugo Adam Bedau.

    New York: Routledge, 1991. 68-84.

Poger, Ralph. <u>A Postmodern Point of View</u>. 2 April 2000

    <http://www.acu.edu/~rpoger>.

WORK WITH MORE THAN THREE AUTHORS IS CITED WITH FIRST AUTHOR'S NAME AND "ET AL." Spiller, Robert E., et al. <u>Literary History of the United States:</u>

    <u>History</u>. 3rd ed. New York: Macmillan, 1963.

Thoreau, Henry David. "On the Duty of Civil Disobedience."   **FORMAT FOR WORKS WITHIN AN ANTHOLOGY**

    <u>Walden and Civil Disobedience</u>. New York: NAL, 1960.

---. "Walden, or, Life in the Woods." <u>Walden and Civil</u>

INDENTED 5 SPACES   <u>Disobedience</u>. New York: Harcourt, 1987. 6-187.

Documenting Sources: APA

This chapter describes the aims, style, forms, and documentation conventions associated with disciplines in the social sciences: psychology, sociology, anthropology, political science, economics, social work and education. The system of documentation described here is based on guidelines published by the *American Psychological Association (APA)*.

THE AIMS OF WRITING IN THE SOCIAL SCIENCES

The social sciences examine the fundamental structures and processes that make up the social world. Sociology examines social groups; political science examines the methods of governance and social organizations; anthropology examines social cultures; economics examines the allocation and distribution of resources among social groups; and psychology examines the mind as both a biological and social construction. The social sciences use methodical and systematic inquiry to examine and analyze human behavior, commonly asking questions such as the following:

- What is society? Can it be isolated and observed? How can it be described?
- How do social and psychological systems function? What forces hold them together or lead to their breakdown?
- Why do social organizations and individuals behave the way they do? Can governing laws be identified, explained, and understood?

Most writing in the social sciences explains findings based on factual research: either *empirical research*—based on firsthand observation and experimentation—or the wide reading that results in a *literature review*. Social scientists must also interpret their factual findings in a carefully reasoned manner and based on clear evidence objectively presented.

Writing in the social sciences must be clear, with connections among ideas explicitly stated. Language should be precise and informal diction discouraged. However, social science writing need not be dull or dry. Readers of the social sciences look for clarity, smoothness, and economy of expression. Writers should therefore avoid unnecessary jargon, wordiness, and redundancy.

COMMON FORMS OF WRITING IN THE SOCIAL SCIENCES

Two forms of social science writing that require extensive research and documentation include the following:

- *Research reports.*   Empirical studies, those based on surveys and experiments, are common in the social sciences. In political science, a study might be based on an opinion poll about an election; in psychology, on the effects of a particular stimulus on behavior. The conventional form for research reports varies somewhat from discipline to discipline, so check with your instructor.
- *Literature reviews* (sometimes called literature surveys).   Often written as independent documents. Preparing a literature review exposes you to knowledge generated by social science methodology and also acquaints you with the conventions of experimentation and documentation.

Reviews are generally written in the style of an essay, with one paragraph devoted to each article surveyed. The precise form, length, and name of these papers varies slightly from discipline to discipline, so check with your instructor.

DOCUMENTATION AND FORMAT CONVENTIONS: APA GUIDELINES

Disciplines in the social sciences—psychology, sociology, anthropology, political science, and economics, social work, and education—use the name-and-date system of documentation put forth by the American Psychological Association (APA). This citation style highlights dates of publication because the currency of published material is of primary importance in these disciplines. Also, listing *all* the authors is more strongly emphasized in the APA than in the MLA system as collaborative authoring is common in the social sciences so all authors are entitled to credit. For more about the foundations and purposes of the APA system, see the *Publication Manual of the American Psychological Association,* 5th edition (Washington DC: APA 2001) or the pocket edition, *Concise Rules* (2005). For "Frequently Asked Questions" about the Publication Manual and APA style, please consult http://www.apastyle.org/faqs.html.

Conventions for In-Text Citations

1. Single work by one or more authors

Whenever you paraphrase or summarize material in your text, you should give both the author's last name and the date of the source. For direct quotations, you should also provide specific page numbers. You may also provide page references, as a convenience to your readers, whenever you suspect they might want to consult a source you have cited. Page references in the APA system are always preceded, in text or in the reference list, by the abbreviation *p.,* in the case of a single page, or *pp.,* in the case of multiple pages.

According to the APA system, authors' names, publication dates, and page numbers (when listed) should be placed in parentheses following citable material. If any of these elements are identified in the text referred to in the parenthetical citation, they are not repeated in the citation.

Exotoxins make some bacteria dangerous to humans (Thomas, 1974).

According to Thomas (1974), "Some bacteria are only harmful to us if they make exotoxins" (p. 76).

We need fear some bacteria only "if they make exotoxins" (Thomas, 1974, p. 76).

For a work by *two authors,* cite both names each time the source is cited.

Smith and Hawkins (1990) agree that all bacteria producing exotoxins are harmful to humans.

All known exotoxin-producing bacteria are harmful to humans (Smith & Hawkins, 1990).

The authors' names are joined by *and* within your text, but APA convention requires an ampersand (&) to join authors' names in parentheses.

For a work by *three to five authors,* identify all the authors by last name the first time you cite a source. In subsequent references, identify only the first author followed by *et al.* ("and others").

The most recent study supports the belief that alcohol abuse is on the rise (Dinkins, Dominic, Smith, Rogers, & White, 1989). . . . When homeless people were excluded from the study, the results were the same (Dinkins et al., 1989).

If you are citing a source by *six or more authors,* identify only the first author in all the references, followed by *et al.*

2. Two or more works by the same author published in the same year

To distinguish between two or more works published in the same year by the same author or team of authors, place a lowercase letter (*a, b, c,* etc.) immediately after the date. This letter should correspond to that in the reference list, where the entries will be alphabetized by title. If two appear in one citation, repeat the year (Smith, 1992a, 1992b).

3. Unknown author

To cite the work of an unknown author, use the first two or three words of the entry as it appears in the reference list (usually by the title). If the words *are* from the title, enclose them in quotation marks or underline them, whichever is appropriate.

Statistical Abstracts (1991) reports the literacy rate for Mexico at 75% for 1990, up 4% from census figures 10 years earlier.

Many researchers now believe that treatment should not begin until other factors have been dealt with ("New Evidence Suggests," 1987).

4. Corporate or organizational author

If a citation refers to a work by a corporation, association, organization, or foundation, spell out the name of the authoring agency. If the name can be abbreviated and remain identifiable, you may spell out the name the first time only and put the abbreviation immediately after it, in brackets. For subsequent references to that source, you may use only the abbreviation:

(American Psychological Association [APA], 1993).

(APA, 1994).

5. Authors with the same last name

To avoid confusion in citing two or more authors with the same last name, include each author's initials in every citation:

(J. M. Clark, 1994).

(C. L. Clark, 1995).

6. Quotation from an indirect source

Use the words *as cited in* to indicate when a quotation or any information in your source is originally from another source.

Lester Brown of Worldwatch believes international agriculture production has reached its limit and that "we're going to be in trouble on the food front before this decade is out" (as cited in Mann, 1993, p. 51).

7. More than one work in a citation

As a general guideline, list two or more sources within a single parenthetical reference in the same order in which they appear in your reference list. List more than one work by the same author in chronological order with the author's name mentioned once and the dates separated by commas:

(Thomas, 1974, 1979).

Works by different authors in the same parentheses are listed in alphabetical order by the author's last name, separated by semicolons:

(Miller, 1990; Webster & Rose, 1988).

8. Long quotation set off from text

Introduce long quotations (40 or more words) with a signal phrase that names the author and ends in a colon. Indent this entire block quotation five spaces. If you quote more than one paragraph, indent the first sentence of each subsequent paragraph five spaces. At the end of the quotation, after the final punctuation mark, indicate in parentheses the location of the quotation in the source—page numbers for a print document, a section and part number for an online source.

According to Langlacker:

> Language is everywhere. It permeates our thoughts, mediates our relations with others, and even creeps into our dreams. The overwhelming bulk of human knowledge is stored and transmitted in language. Language is so ubiquitous that we take it for granted, but without it, society as we now know it would be impossible. Despite its prevalence in human affairs, language is poorly understood (1968, p. 3).

Conventions for Footnotes

Footnotes are used to provide additional information that cannot be worked into the main text, information highly likely to be of interest to some readers but also likely to slow down the pace of your text or obscure your point for other readers. Therefore, even the footnotes you do choose to provide should be as brief as possible; when the information you wish to add is extensive, it is better to present it in an appendix. Footnotes are indicated by an asterisk to avoid confusion with endnote notations. Endnotes should be numbered consecutively with superscript numbers, should follow the reference list on a page headed "Endnotes," should be double spaced, and should have their first line indented five to seven spaces.

Conventions for the Reference List

All works mentioned in a paper should be identified on a reference list according to the following general rules of the APA documentation system.

Format

After the final page of the paper, title a separate page "References," with no underline or quotation marks. Center the title an inch from the top of the page. Number the page in sequence with the last page of the paper.

Double-space between the title and the first entry. Set the first line flush with the left margin; the second and all subsequent lines of an entry should be indented five spaces from the left margin. This format is called a hanging indent.

Also double-space both between and within entries. If your reference list exceeds one page, continue listing your references in sequence on an additional page or pages, but do not repeat the title "References."

ORDER OF ENTRIES.   Alphabetize the list of references according to authors' last names, using the first author's last name for works with multiple authors. For entries by an unknown author, alphabetize by the first word of the title, excepting nonsignificant words (e.g., *A, An, The*).

AUTHORS.   List the author's last name first, followed by a comma and the author's initials (not first and middle names). When a work has more than one author, list all authors in this way, separating the names with a comma. When listing multiple authors for a single work, place an ampersand (&) before the last author's name. A period follows the author name(s).

TITLES. List the complete titles and subtitles of books and articles, but capitalize only the first word of the title and any subtitle, as well as all proper nouns. Italicize book titles and journal or publication titles, but do not underline article titles or place quotation marks around them. Place a period after the title.

PUBLISHERS. List publishers' names in shortened form, omitting words such as *Company*. Spell out the names of university presses and organizations in full. For books, use a colon to separate the city of publication from the publisher.

DATES. For magazines and newspapers, use commas to separate the year from the month and day, and enclose the publication dates in parentheses: (*1954, May 25*). If no date is given in the document, write (*n.d.*) in parentheses.

PAGE NUMBERS. Inclusive page numbers should be separated by a hyphen with no spaces: *361-375*. Full sequences should be given for pages and dates (not *361-75.*) If pages do not follow consecutively (as in newspapers), include subsequent page numbers after a comma: *pp. 1, 16*. Note that *pp.* precedes the page numbers for newspaper articles but not for journal articles.

ABBREVIATIONS. State and country names are abbreviated, but months are not. Use U.S. postal abbreviations for state abbreviations.

Following are examples of the reference list format for a variety of source types.

Documenting Books

1. **Book by one author**

Benjamin, J. (1988). *The bonds of love: Psychoanalysis, feminism, and the problem of domination*. New York: Prometheus Books.

2. **Book by two or more authors**

Zweigenhaft, R. L., & Domhoff, G. W. (1991). *Blacks in the white establishment?* New Haven, CT: Yale University Press.

Include all authors' names in the reference list, regardless of the number of authors associated with a particular work.

3. **More than one book by the same author**

List two or more works by the same author (or the same author team listed in the same order) chronologically by year in your reference list, with the earliest first. Arrange any such works published in the same year alphabetically by title, placing lowercase letters after the dates. In either case, give full identification of author(s) for each reference listing.

Bandura, A. (1969). *Principles of behavior modification*. New York: Holt, Rinehart, and Winston.

Bandura, A. (1977a). Self-efficacy: Toward a unifying theory of behavioral change. *Psychological Review, 84,* 191-215.

Bandura, A. (1977b). *Social learning theory*. Englewood Cliffs, NJ: Prentice Hall.

If the same author is named first but has different co-authors, subalphabetize by the last name of the second author. Works by the first author alone are listed before works with co-authors.

4. Book by a corporation, association, or organization

American Psychological Association. (1994). *Publication manual of the American Psychological Association* (4th ed.). Washington, DC: Author.

Alphabetize corporate authors by the corporate name, excluding the articles *A, An,* and *The.* When the corporate author is also the publisher, designate the publisher as *Author.*

5. Revised edition of a book

Peek, S. (1993). *The game inventor's handbook* (Rev. ed.). Cincinnati, OH: Betterway.

6. Edited book

Schaefer, Charles E., & Reid, S. E. (Eds.). (1986). *Game play: Therapeutic use of childhood games.* New York: Wiley.

Place (*Ed.*) or (*Eds.,*) capitalized, and in parentheses, after the singular or plural name of the editor(s) of an edited book.

7. Book in more than one volume

Waldrep, T. (Ed.). (1985–1988). *Writers on writing* (Vols. 1–2). New York: Random House.

For a work with volumes published in different years, indicate the range of dates of publication. In citing only one volume of a multivolume work, indicate only the volume cited.

Waldrep, T. (Ed.). (1988). *Writers on writing* (Vol. 2). New York: Random House.

8. Translated or reprinted book

Freud, S. (1950). *The interpretation of dreams* (A. A. Brill, Trans.). New York: Modern Library-Random House. (Original work published 1900)

The date of the translation or reprint is in parentheses after the author's name. Indicate the original publication date parenthetically at the end of the citation, with no period. In the text, parenthetically cite the information with both dates: (*Freud 1900/1950*).

9. Chapter or article in an edited book

Telander, R. (1996). Senseless crimes. In C. I. Schuster & W. V. Van Pelt (Eds.), *Speculations: Readings in culture, identity, and values* (2nd ed., pp. 264–272). Upper Saddle River, NJ: Prentice Hall.

The chapter or article title is not underlined or in quotation marks. Editors' names are listed in normal reading order (surname last). Inclusive page numbers, in parentheses, follow the title of the larger work.

10. Anonymous book

Stereotypes, distortions and omissions in U.S. history textbooks. (1977). New York: Council on Interracial Books for Children.

GENERAL FORMAT FOR BOOK, APA

Author/editor(s). (Year of publication). *Book title*. City of publication: Publisher.

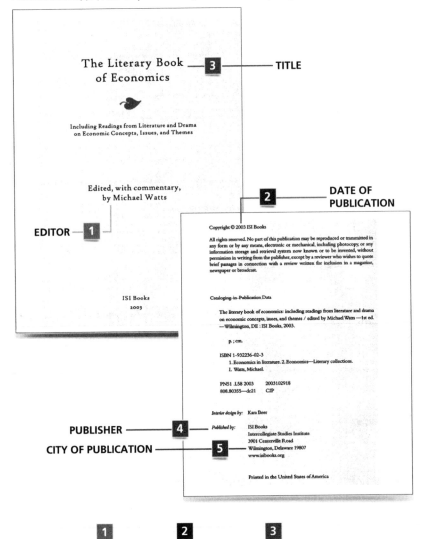

Watts, M. (Ed.). (2003). *The literary book of economics.*

Wilmington, DE: Intercollegiate Studies Institute.

Title and copyright pages in front of book to be referenced

1 AUTHOR.

List the author's last name first, followed by a comma and the author's initials (not first name). When a work has more than one author, list all authors in this way, separating the names with a comma, placing an ampersand (&) before the last author's name, and ending with a period (*Smith, A. C., Jones, B., & Watts, M.*). If more than one work by the same author, list the earliest first.

> Watts. M. (1987). Student gender and school district differences
>
> > affecting the stock and flow of economic knowledge. *Review of*
> >
> > *Economics and Statistics, 69*, 561–566.
>
> Watts. M. (Ed.). (2003). *The literary book of economics*. Wilmington, DE:
>
> > Intercollegiate Studies Institute.

2 DATE.

Following author's name, give year of publication in parentheses.

3 TITLE.

List the complete titles and subtitles of books, but capitalize only the first word of the title and subtitle, as well as all proper nouns (*The literary book of African economics*). Italicize book titles and place a period after the title.

4 PUBLISHER.

List publishers' names in shortened form, omitting words such as *Publishers, Inc.,* or *Company*. Spell out the names of university presses and organizations in full (*New England University Press*). Use a colon to separate the place of publication from the publisher (*Wilmington, DE: Intercollegiate Studies Institute*).

5 CITY OF PUBLICATION.

Use U.S. postal abbreviations for state and country (*VT for Vermont, etc.*).

11. Government document

U.S. House of Representatives, Committee on Energy and Commerce. (1986). *Ensuring access to programming for the backyard satellite dish owner* (Serial No. 99-127). Washington, DC: U.S. Government Printing Office.

For government documents, provide the higher department or governing agency only when the office or agency that created the document is not readily recognizable. If a document number is available, list it after the document title in parentheses. Write out the name of the printing agency in full, as the publisher, rather than using the abbreviation *GPO*.

GENERAL FORMAT FOR JOURNAL ARTICLES, APA

Author(s). (Year of publication). Article title. *Journal Title, volume number* (issue number), inclusive page numbers.

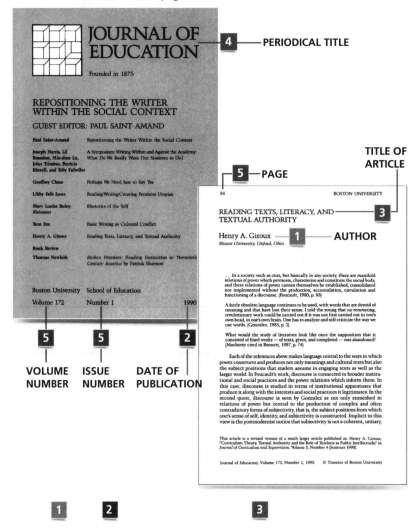

Giroux, H. A. (1990). Reading texts, literacy, and textual authority.

Journal of Education, 172(1), 84–103.

12. Religious and classical texts

References are not required for well-known classical or religious works. However, the first in-text citation should identify the edition used. For example, referencing *The Quran: The Final Testament (Authorized English Version)* would require, in parentheses, following the naming of the text (Authorized English Version).

> ### 1 AUTHOR.
> List the author's last name first, followed by a comma and the author's initials (*Giroux, H. A.*). When a work has more than one author, list all authors in this way, separating the names with a comma and place an ampersand (*&*) before the last author's name (*Giroux, H. A., Smith, D., & Jones, M.*).

> ### 2 DATE OF PUBLICATION.
> Following author's name, give year of publication in parentheses (*1990*). For magazines and newspapers, use a comma to separate the year from the month or month and day, and enclose in parentheses (*1954, May 25*). If no date is given in the document, write *n.d.* in parentheses followed by a period (*n.d.*).

> ### 3 TITLE OF ARTICLE.
> List the complete titles and subtitles of articles, but capitalize only the first word of the title and subtitle, as well as all proper nouns. Period. Do not underline article titles or place quotation marks around them (*Reading texts, literacy, and textual authority: A study of American culture*).

> ### 4 TITLE OF PERIODICAL.
> Italicize jounal or publication titles. Capitalize the first letter of all words in the title, except articles, prepositions, and conjunctions less than four letters long.

> ### 5 VOLUME, ISSUE, AND PAGE NUMBERS.
> In an article in a journal paginated by volume (continuous pagination), include only the volume number (*in italics*), not the issue. In an article in a journal paginated by issue, list the volume number (*in italics*) followed by the issue number in parentheses but not in italics: *172(1)*. Comma. Inclusive page numbers for pages and dates should be written out in full, separated by an en-dash with no spaces (*361–375 not 361–75; 204–205, not 204–05*). If pages do not follow consecutively (as in newspapers), include subsequent page numbers after a comma (*pp. 1, 16*). Note that *pp.* precedes the page numbers for newspaper articles but not for journal articles.

Documenting Periodicals

In citing periodical articles, use the same format for listing author names as for books.

13. **Article in a journal paginated by volume**

Hartley, J. (1991). Psychology, writing, and computers: A review of research. *Visible Language, 25,* 339–375.

If page numbers are continuous throughout volumes in a year, use only the volume number, underlined, following the title of the periodical.

14. Article in a journal paginated by issue

Lowther, M. A. (1977). Career change in mid-life: Its impact on education. *Innovator,* 8(7), 1, 9–11.

Include the issue number in parentheses if each issue of a journal is paginated separately.

15. Magazine article

Garreau, J. (1995, December). Edgier cities. *Wired,* 158–163, 232–234.

For nonprofessional periodicals, include the year and month (not abbreviated) after the author's name.

16. Newspaper article

Finn, P. (1995, September 27). Death of a U-Va. student raises scrutiny of off-campus drinking. *The Washington Post,* pp. D1, D4.

If an author is listed for the article, begin with the author's name, then list the date (spell out the month); follow with the title of the newspaper. If there is a section, combine it with the page or pages, including continued page numbers as well.

17. Review

Ross, A. (28 Mar. 2005). [Review of the play *Kafka's trial*]. *New Yorker:* 80.

Entries for reviews should begin with the reviewer's name, if known, followed by the complete date, then the words "Review of [genre, *title*]". If a review is unsigned, list it as *Rev. of* [genre, title] and alphabetize it by the name of the work reviewed.

18. Article by an unknown author

Conventionalwisdomwatch. (13 June 2005). *Newsweek,* 5.

Documenting Fixed Electronic Sources

APA conventions for documenting fixed electronic sources such as CD-ROMs, diskettes, and magnetic tapes list author, date, and title followed by the type of electronic source— for example, *[CD-ROM]*—in brackets and the complete information for the corresponding print source if available.

19. CD-ROM

Krauthammer, C. (1991). Why is America in a blue funk? [CD-ROM]. *Time, 138,* 83. Abstract from UMIACH file: Periodical Abstracts Item: 1126.00

20. Computer software

HyperCard (Version 2.2) [Computer software]. (1993). Cupertino, CA: Apple Computer. Provide the version number, if available, in parentheses following the software name. Add the descriptive term *[Computer software]* in brackets, followed with a period. Do not underline the names of computer programs.

Documenting Online Sources

An APA Internet citation should provide essentially the same information as any textual source: author (when identified), date of site creation, title (or description of document), date of retrieval, and a working address (URL).

Try to reference specific documents or links, whenever possible, rather than general home or menu pages, since such pages commonly contain many links, only one of which you are citing.

To transcribe a URL correctly, keep your word processing file open and copy the URL directly from the Internet site to your paper. (Make sure your word processor's automatic hyphenation feature is turned off since an automatically inserted hyphen will change the URL; if you need to break a URL, do so after a slash or before a period.) APA does not recommend using angle brackets to indicate an Internet address.

If electronic sources don't provide page numbers, use paragraph numbers only if numbered in the document: (*para 4*). If the source is divided into chapters, use chapter and paragraph numbers: (*chap 2.12*). If the source is divided into sections, use section and paragraph numbers to identify the source location: (*section 6, 8*).

For more details than the following examples can provide, consult the APA's Web page at http://www.apa.org/journals/webref.html.

21. Online periodical article

Kapadia, S. (1995, November). A tribute to Mahatma Gandhi: His views on women and social exchange. *Journal of South Asia Women's Studies,* 1(1). Retrieved December 2, 1995, from http://www.shore.net/~india/jsaws

Indicate the number of paragraphs in brackets after the title, and add the term [*Online serial*] in brackets between the journal name and the volume number.

If you have viewed the article only in its electronic form, you should add *Electronic version* in brackets after the article title as in the following example:

Smithsonian Institution's Ocean Planet: A special report. (1995). [Electronic version]. *Outdoor Life 3,* 13-22. Retrieved November 1, 1999, from http://www.epinions.com/mags-Outdoor Life

22. World Wide Web site

To document a specific file, list the author, the date of publication, the titles of the document and the complete work (if any). Add relevant information such as volume or page numbers of a print source. Conclude with a retrieval statement.

Williams, Scott. (1996, June 14). Back to school with the quilt. *AIDS Memorial Quilt Website.* Retrieved June 14, 1996, from http://www.aidsquilt.org/newsletter/stories/backto.html

Start with the title if no author is identified.

Motorcycle Safety Foundation (n.d.). Retrieved March 30, 2006, from http://www.msf-usa.org/

GENERAL FORMAT FOR ONLINE SOURCES, APA

Author(s). (Date of electronic publication). Title of site. Date of access, electronic
  address

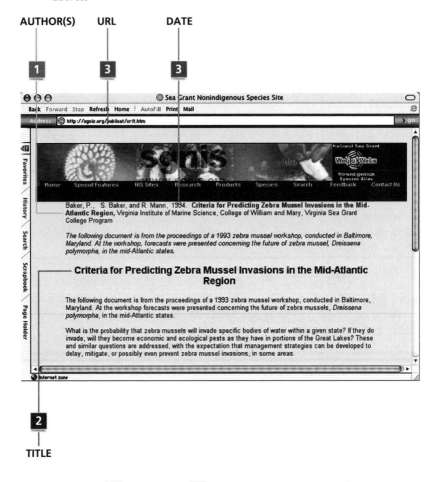

AUTHOR(S)   URL   DATE

TITLE

1   **3**   **2**

Baker, P., Baker, S., & Mann, R. (1994). Criteria for predicting zebra mussel
  invasions in the mid-Atlantic region. Retrieved June 8, 2005, from
  http://sgnis.org/publicat/crit.htm

3

Condensed proceeding published on Internet from zebra mussel workshop,
Baltimore, MD, 1993

> **1** **AUTHOR OF MATERIAL ON WEB SITE.**
> Follow rules for citing books and periodicals. Last name, followed by initials for first and middle names (*Baker, P., Baker, S., & Mann, R.*). If no author is listed, begin with page title.

> **2** **TITLE OF MATERIAL ON WEB SITE.**
> Capitalize first word in site title and subtitle and any proper names only. Period. Do not enclose in quotation marks (*Criteria for predicting zebra mussel invasions in the Mid-Atlantic region*). If no title is obvious, use home page name as title (found in URL).

> **3** **PUBLICATION INFORMATION.**
> List two dates for each Internet site: first, the date the site was created or last revised (*1994*). Second, list the date you accessed the site with the words *Retrieved from* followed by the date and electronic address, no concluding period (*Retrieved June 8, 2005, from http://sgnis.org/publicat/papers/crit.htm*).

23. Work from an online database

Conniff, R. (May 1993). Approaching *Walden. Yankee. 57*(5), 84. Retrieved 2 Jun. 2005 from ArticleFirst database.

Give the print publication information and when it was retrieved from which database. No URL is required.

24. Weblog entry

Rickey, A. (8 June 2005). Three years of hell to become the devil. Retrieved 10 June 2005 from http://www.threeyearsofhell.com/

25. File transfer protocol (FTP), telnet, or gopher site

After the retrieval date, supply the FTP, telnet, or gopher search path.

Altar, T. W. (1993). *Vitamin B12 and vegans.* Retrieved May 28, 1996, from ftp://ftp.cs.yale.edu.Clinton, W. (1994, July 17). Remarks by the President at the tribute dinner for Senator Byrd. Washington, DC: Office of the White House Press Secretary. Retrieved February 12, 1996, from gopher://info.tamu.edu.70/00/.data/politics/1994/byrd.0717

King, Jr., M. L. (1963 August 28). I have a dream [speech]. Retrieved January 2, 1996, from telnet://ukanaix.cc.ukans.edu

26. Synchronous communications (MOO, MUD, IRC)

To document a *real-time communication,* such as those posted in MOOs, MUDs, and IRCs, describe the type of communication (e.g., *Group discussion, Personal interview*) if it is not indicated elsewhere in the entry.

Harnack, A. (1996, April 4). Words [Group discussion]. Retrieved April 5, 1996, from telnet://moo.du.org/port=8888

27. Web discussion forum

Holden, J. B. (2001, January 2). The failure of higher education. [Formal discussion initiation]. Message posted to http://ifets.mtu.edu/archives

28. Listserv (electronic mailing list)

Weston, Heather (2002, June 12). Re: Registration schedule now available. Message posted to the Chamberlain Kronsage dormitory electronic mailing list, archived at http://listserv.registrar.uwsp.edu/archives/62.html

Note that APA prefers the term *electronic mailing list* to *listserv.*

29. Newsgroup

Hotgirl (2002, January 12). Dowsing effort fails. Message posted to news://alt .science.esp3/html

30. Electronic newspaper article

Kolata, G. (2002, February 12). Why some people won't be fit despite exercise. *New York Times.* Retrieved February 12, 2002, from http://www.nytimes.com

31. Document available on university program or department Web site

McClintock, R. & Taipale, K.A. (1994). *Educating America for the 21st century: A strategic plan for educational leadership 1993–2001.* Retrieved February 12, 2002, from Columbia University, Institute for Learning Technologies Web site: http://www.ilt.columbia.edu/ilt/docs/ILTplan.html

32. E-mail messages

Under current APA guidelines, electronic conversations are not listed on the References page. Cite e-mail messages in the text as you would personal letters or interviews.

R. W. Williams, personal communication, January 4, 1999.

Following is an in-text parenthetical reference to a personal e-mail message:

James Tolley (personal communication, November 2, 2002) told me that the practice of dowsing has a scientific basis.

Documenting Other Sources

33. Film, recording, and other nonprint media

Curtiz, M. (Director). (1942). *Casablanca* [Film]. Hollywood, CA: Warner Bros.

Alphabetize a film listing by the name of the person or persons with primary responsibility for the product. Identify the medium in brackets following the title, and indicate both location and name of the distributor (as publisher). Other identifying information should appear in parentheses.

34. Audio recording

Springsteen, B. (2005). Devils & dust. On *Devils and dust* [CD]. New York: Sony BMG Music Entertainment.

Depending on the focus of your essay, begin with the artist, composer, or conductor. Continue with date and title of whole work. Specify medium. End with the company label.

35. Television or radio broadcast, single episode

Carson, D. (Director). (1993). Emissary. [Television series episode]. In *Star trek: deep space nine.* West Palm Beach: Fox.

For a single episode, begin with director's name. If the broadcast is not an episode of a series or the episode is untitled, begin with the program title. Include date of broadcast, series title, city and network. Leading off with other information—such as narrator, writer, or performers—depends on the purpose of your citation.

INFORMATIONAL RESEARCH PAPER: APA STYLE

The research essay "Green Is Only Skin Deep: False Environmental Marketing," by Elizabeth Bone, was written to identify and explain one problem in contemporary American culture. Elizabeth's essay is documented according to the conventions of the American Psychological Association (APA). This sample includes title page and abstract; check with your instructor to find out whether these are required for course papers. The References page shows hanging indent style, with each first line full measure and subsequent lines in an entry indented 5 to 7 spaces. In APA style, student papers may use a first-line indent instead. Check to see which style your instructor prefers.

Green

1

Green Is Only Skin Deep: **TITLE**

False Environmental Marketing

Elizabeth Bone   **AUTHOR**

Professor John Clark   **INSTRUCTOR**

English 1   **COURSE**

December 6, 2000   **DATE**

ABSTRACT SHOULD BE PRINTED ON A SEPARATE PAGE
FOLLOWING THE TITLE PAGE.

Green

2

HEADING
Abstract ∕ **CENTERED**

NO PARAGRAPH INDENT   Most Americans consider themselves environmentalists and   **DOUBLE SPACE**

favor supporting environmentally friendly or "green"

THE ABSTRACT SUMMARIZES THE MAIN POINT OF THE PAPER.   companies. However, companies use a number of false

advertising practices to mislead the public about their green

practices and products by (1) exaggerating claims, (2)

masking false practices behind technical terminology, (3)

missponsoring green events, (4) not admitting responsibility

for real problems, (5) advertising green by association, and (6)

solving one problem while creating others. Consumers must

be skeptical of all commercial ads and take the time to find

out the truth behind advertising.

1/2"

Green

4

TITLE IS REPEATED FROM
TITLE PAGE.

Green Is Only Skin Deep:

False Environmental Marketing

A recent Gallup poll reported that 75% of Americans
consider themselves to be environmentalists (Smith & Quelch,
1993). In the same study, nearly half of the respondents said
they would be more likely to purchase a product if they
perceived it to be environmentally friendly or "green."
According to Smith and Quelch (1993), since green sells, many
companies have begun to promote themselves as marketing
products that are either environmentally friendly or
manufactured from recycled material. Unfortunately, many of
these companies care more about appearance than reality.

AUTHOR'S
NAME, DATE,
AND PAGE
NUMBERS
ARE IN
PARENTHESES.

DOUBLE
SPACE

INFORMATIONAL
THESIS IS AT
END OF FIRST
PARAGRAPH.

The most common way for a company to market itself as pro
environment is to stretch the definitions of terms such as
"biodegradable" so that consumers believe one thing but the
product delivers something else. For example, so-called
biodegradable plastic, made with cornstarch, was introduced
to ease consumers' fears that plastic lasts forever in the
environment. However, the cornstarch plastic broke down only
in specific controlled laboratory conditions, not outdoors and
not in compost bins. The Federal Trade Commission has
updated its regulations to prevent such misrepresentations, so
that now Glad and Hefty trash bags are no longer advertised as
biodegradable (Carlson, Grove, & Kangun, 1993).

FIRST
EXAMPLE OF
FALSE
ADVERTISING
IS
INTRODUCED.

The use of technical terms can also mislead average
consumers. For example, carbon fluoride compounds, called
CFC's, are known to be hazardous to the protective layer of
ozone that surrounds the earth, so that their widespread use in
air conditioners is considered an environmental hazard (Decker
& Stammer, 1989). Chrysler Corporation advertises that it uses
CFC-free refrigerant in its automobile air conditioners to appeal
to environmentally concerned consumers ("Ozone layer," 1994).

SECOND EXAMPLE
IS GIVEN.

PAGE NUMBER IS NOT
LISTED WHEN IT IS
LISTED ON REFERENCE
PAGE.

AUTHOR QUOTED BY NAME IN THE TEXT IS FOLLOWED BY PUBLICATION YEAR IN PARENTHESES.

However, Weisskopf (1992) points out that the chemical compounds that replace CFC's in their air conditioners pose other environmental hazards that are not mentioned.

TRANSITIONS KEEP THE READER ON TRACK. Another deceptive greening tactic is the sponsoring of highly publicized environmental events such as animal shows, concerts, cleanup programs, and educational exhibits. For example, Ocean Planet was a well-publicized exhibit put together by the Smithsonian Institution to educate people about ocean conservation. Ford Motor Company helped sponsor the event, which it then used in its car advertisements: "At Ford, we feel strongly that understanding, preserving, and properly managing natural resources like our oceans should be an essential commitment of individuals and corporate citizens alike" ("Smithsonian Institution's Ocean Planet," 1995, p. 14).

While sponsoring the exhibit may be a worthwhile public service, such sponsorship has nothing to do with how the manufacture and operation of Ford automobiles affect the environment. In fact, Ford was ranked as among the worst polluters in the state of Michigan in 1995 (Parker, 1995).

Some companies court the public by mentioning environmental problems and pointing out that they do not contribute to those problems. For example, the natural gas industry describes natural gas as an alternative to the use of ozone-depleting CFC's ("Don't you wish," 1994). However, according to Fogel (1985), the manufacture of natural gas creates a host of other environmental problems from land reclamation to the carbon-dioxide pollution, a major cause of global warming. By mentioning problems they don't cause, while ignoring ones they do, companies present a favorable environmental image that is at best a half truth, at worst an outright lie.

SHORTENED TITLE IS USED WHEN NO AUTHOR IS CREDITED ON REFERENCE PAGE.

Green

6

Other companies use a more subtle approach to misleading green advertising. Rather than make statements about environmental compatibility, these companies depict the product in unspoiled natural settings or use green quotations that have nothing to do with the product itself. For example, one Chevrolet advertisement shows a lake shrouded in mist and quotes an environmentalist: "From this day onward, I will restore the earth where I am and listen to what it is telling me" ("From this day," 1994). Below the quotation is the Chevy logo with the words "Genuine Chevrolet." Despite this touching appeal to its love of nature, Chevrolet has a history of dumping toxic waste into the Great Lakes (Allen, 1991). Has this company seriously been listening to what the earth has been telling it?

QUOTATION OF FEWER THAN 40 WORDS IS INTEGRATED INTO THE TEXT.

The most common manner in which companies attempt to prove they have a strong environmental commitment is to give a single example of a policy or action that is considered environmentally sound. Chevron has had an environmental advertising campaign since the mid-1970's. More recent ads feature Chevron employees doing environmental good deeds (Smith & Quelch, 1993). For example, one ad features "a saltwater wetland in Mississippi at the edge of a pine forest . . . the kind of place nature might have made" and goes on to explain that this wetland was built by Chevron employees ("The shorebirds who found," 1990). However, during the time this advertisement was running in magazines such as *Audubon*, LaGanga (1993) points out that Chevron was dumping millions of gallons of nasty chemicals (carcinogens and heavy metals) into California's Santa Monica Bay, posing a health risk to swimmers. The building of the wetland in one part of the country does not absolve the company of polluting water somewhere else.

ELLIPSIS POINTS INDICATE MISSING WORDS IN QUOTATION.

It should be clear that the environmental image a company

Green

7

projects does not necessarily match the realities of the company's practice. The products produced by companies such as Chrysler, Ford, General Motors, and Chevron are among the major causes of air and water pollution: automobiles and gasoline. No amount of advertising can conceal the ultimately negative effect these products have on the environment (Kennedy & Grumbly, 1988). According to Shirley Lefevre, president of the New York Truth in Advertising League:

COLON IS USED TO INTRODUCE A LONG QUOTATION.

DOUBLE SPACE

It probably doesn't help to single out one automobile manufacturer or oil company as significantly worse than the others. Despite small efforts here and there, all of these giant corporations, as well as other large manufacturers of metal and plastic material goods, put profit before environment and cause more harm than good to the environment (personal communication, May 1995).

QUOTATION OF 40 WORDS OR MORE IS INDENTED 5 SPACES

Consumers who are genuinely interested in buying environmentally safe products and supporting environmentally responsible companies need to look beyond the images projected by commercial advertising in magazines, on billboards, and on television. Organizations such as Earth First! attempt to educate consumers to the realities by writing about false advertising and exposing the hypocrisy of such ads ("Do people allow," 1994), while the Ecology Channel is committed to sharing "impartial, unbiased, multiperspective environmental information" with consumers on the Internet (Ecology, 1996). Meanwhile the Federal Trade Commission is in the process of continually upgrading truth-in-advertising regulations (Carlson et al., 1993). Americans who are truly environmentally conscious must remain skeptical of simplistic and misleading commercial advertisements while continuing to educate themselves about the genuine needs of the environment.

INTERVIEW CONDUCTED BY AUTHOR IS NOT LISTED ON THE REFERENCE PAGE.

SECOND CITATION OF MORE THAN THREE AUTHORS IS SHORTENED TO FIRST AUTHOR'S NAME AND "ET AL."

THESIS IS REPEATED IN MORE DETAIL AT END.

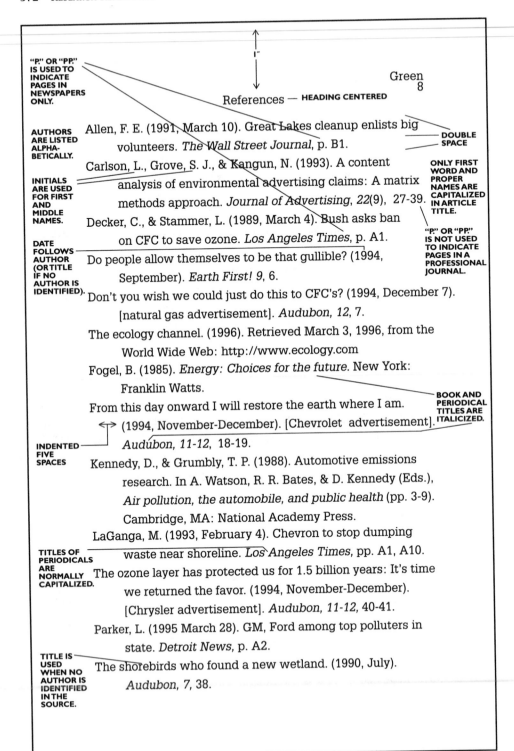

Green
8

References — **HEADING CENTERED**

**"P." OR "PP."
IS USED TO
INDICATE
PAGES IN
NEWSPAPERS
ONLY.**

**AUTHORS
ARE LISTED
ALPHA-
BETICALLY.**

Allen, F. E. (1991, March 10). Great Lakes cleanup enlists big
volunteers. *The Wall Street Journal*, p. B1.

**DOUBLE
SPACE**

Carlson, L., Grove, S. J., & Kangun, N. (1993). A content
analysis of environmental advertising claims: A matrix
methods approach. *Journal of Advertising, 22*(9), 27-39.

**INITIALS
ARE USED
FOR FIRST
AND
MIDDLE
NAMES.**

**ONLY FIRST
WORD AND
PROPER
NAMES ARE
CAPITALIZED
IN ARTICLE
TITLE.**

Decker, C., & Stammer, L. (1989, March 4). Bush asks ban
on CFC to save ozone. *Los Angeles Times*, p. A1.

**DATE
FOLLOWS
AUTHOR
(OR TITLE
IF NO
AUTHOR IS
IDENTIFIED).**

**"P." OR "PP."
IS NOT USED
TO INDICATE
PAGES IN A
PROFESSIONAL
JOURNAL.**

Do people allow themselves to be that gullible? (1994,
September). *Earth First! 9*, 6.

Don't you wish we could just do this to CFC's? (1994, December 7).
[natural gas advertisement]. *Audubon, 12*, 7.

The ecology channel. (1996). Retrieved March 3, 1996, from the
World Wide Web: http://www.ecology.com

Fogel, B. (1985). *Energy: Choices for the future*. New York:
Franklin Watts.

**BOOK AND
PERIODICAL
TITLES ARE
ITALICIZED.**

From this day onward I will restore the earth where I am.
(1994, November-December). [Chevrolet advertisement].
Audubon, 11-12, 18-19.

**INDENTED
FIVE
SPACES**

Kennedy, D., & Grumbly, T. P. (1988). Automotive emissions
research. In A. Watson, R. R. Bates, & D. Kennedy (Eds.),
Air pollution, the automobile, and public health (pp. 3-9).
Cambridge, MA: National Academy Press.

LaGanga, M. (1993, February 4). Chevron to stop dumping
waste near shoreline. *Los Angeles Times*, pp. A1, A10.

**TITLES OF
PERIODICALS
ARE
NORMALLY
CAPITALIZED.**

The ozone layer has protected us for 1.5 billion years: It's time
we returned the favor. (1994, November-December).
[Chrysler advertisement]. *Audubon, 11-12*, 40-41.

Parker, L. (1995 March 28). GM, Ford among top polluters in
state. *Detroit News*, p. A2.

**TITLE IS
USED
WHEN NO
AUTHOR IS
IDENTIFIED
IN THE
SOURCE.**

The shorebirds who found a new wetland. (1990, July).
Audubon, 7, 38.

Smith, N. C., & Quelch, J. A. (1993). *Ethics in marketing.*
Boston, MA: Richard D. Irwin.

Smithsonian Institution's Ocean Planet: A special report. (1995,
March). *Outdoor Life, 3,* 13-22.

Weisskopf, M. (1992, February 23). Study finds CFC alternatives
more damaging than believed. *The Washington Post,*
p. A3.

Acknowledgments

Chapter One

Page 4: Calvin and Hobbes (c) 1993 Watterson. Distributed by Universal Press Syndicate. Reprinted with permission. All rights reserved.

Chapter Three

Page 22 (top): Walker Evans/Courtesy of the Library of Congress; page 22 (bottom): (c) Minnesota Historical Society/Corbis; page 24 (top): Dorothea Lange/Getty Images Inc.—Hulton Archive Photos; page 24 (bottom): Walker Evans/Library of Congress/Corbis; page 25: Dorthea Lange/Courtesy of the Library of Congress; page 26: Jack Delano/Courtesy of the Library of Congress; page 27: Marion Post Wolcott/Courtesy of the Library of Congress; page 28 (top): Dorthea Lange/Courtesy of the Library of Congress; page 28 (bottom): Dorthea Lange/Courtesy of the Library of Congress; page 29: Estate of Martin Luther King Jr.; page 30 (top): Corbis RF; page 30 (bottom) and page 31: (c) The New Yorker Collection 2005/Mike Twohy from cartoonbank.com. All Rights Reserved; page 32: National Center for Family Literacy; page 33: National Crime Prevention Council; page 34 (top): National Trust for Historic Preservation; page 34 (bottom): Reprinted with permission (c) 2005 American Lung Association; page 35 (bottom): (c) Peyo—2006—licensed through Lafig Belgium—www.smurf.com.

Chapter Five

Page 50: Toby Fulwiler.

Chapter Six

Page 62: Jess Shirley/Michael Burns.

Chapter Nine

Page 90: Corbis/Sygma; page 92 (top and bottom), page 93: Toby Fulwiler.

Chapter Ten

Pages 115 and 116: (c) Peyo—2006—licensed through Lafig Belgium—www.smurf.com.

Chapter Eleven

Page 133: Peter DeSantis/New England Mountain Bike Association; page 135: Duncan McNicol/Stone/Getty Images; page 136: Reprinted by permission of Western New York Mountain Biking Association and Todd Scott, Executive Director of the Michigan Mountain Biking Association.

Chapter Twelve

Page 139: "We Real Cool" from *Blacks* by Gwendolyn Brooks. The Third World Press, 1987. Reprinted by consent of Brooks Permissions.

Chapter Thirteen

Page 150: National Archives and Records Administration; pages 153 and 154: "Alien Territory," from *Good Bones and Simple Murders* by Margaret Atwood, copyright © 1983, 1992, 1994, by O.W. Toad Ltd. A Nan A. Talese Book. Used by permission of Doubleday, a division of Random House, Inc. and McClelland & Stewart, Ltd.

Chapter Fourteen

Page 162: (c) Tom Stewart/Corbis.

Chapter Fifteen

Page 170: Toby Fulwiler.

Chapter Sixteen

Page 175: Toby Fulwiler.

Chapter Twenty-One

Pages 216, 219, 224, and 225: Toby Fulwiler. Pages 217 and 228: Courtesy of The University of Wisconsin—Milwaukee.

Chapter Twenty-Two

Page 232: US National Oceanic and Atmospheric Administration; page 233: L. Lefkowitz/Getty Images, Inc.—Taxi; page 235: Family of Vice Admiral H. Arnold Karo, C&GS/US National Oceanic and Atmospheric Administration; page 236: US National Oceanic and Atmospheric Administration/Commander Marcella Bradley.

Chapter Twenty-Three

Pages 239 and 244: Toby Fulwiler.

Chapter Twenty-Four

Page 249: Reprinted by permission of the University of Wisconsin—Madison.

Chapter Twenty-Five

Page 272: Reprinted by permission of the National Renewal Energy Laboratory; page 273: Reprinted by permission of Public Broadcasting Services; page 274: Reprinted by permission of The Auto Channel.com.

Chapter Twenty-Six

Pages 277 and 282: Toby Fulwiler.

Chapter Twenty-Seven

Page 290: Reprinted with permission from Universal Syndicate

Chapter Twenty-Eight

Page 313 (top): Reprinted by permission of the Oklahoma Council of Public Affairs, Inc.; page 313 (bottom): Reprinted by permission of Wayne State University.

Research Reference 1

Page 319: Reprinted by permission of the Modern Language Association; page 334: University of Mississippi English Department. Reprinted by permission of John Padgett.

Research Reference 2

Page 362: National Sea Grant College Assoc. Matthew Tift—Publ. Asst. mctift@seagrant.wisc.edu. Reprinted by permission of SGNIS, a Sea Grant Site.

Index